DISTANT INTIMACY

FREDERIC RAPHAEL

Distant Intimacy

JOSEPH EPSTEIN

A Friendship in the Age of the Internet

YALE UNIVERSITY PRESS
NEW HAVEN AND LONDON

For information about this and other Yale University Press publications, please contact:

U.S. Office: sales.press@yale.edu www.yalebooks.com
Europe Office: sales@yaleup.co.uk www.yalebooks.co.uk

Set in Minion Pro by IDSUK (DataConnection) Ltd
Printed in Great Britain by TJ International Ltd, Padstow, Cornwall

Library of Congress Cataloging-in-Publication Data

Raphael, Frederic, 1931-
    Distant intimacy : a friendship in the age of the internet / Frederic
    Raphael and Joseph Epstein.
      p. cm.
    Includes bibliographical references and index.
    ISBN 978-0-300-18694-9 (hardback)
1. Raphael, Frederic, 1931–Correspondence. 2. Epstein, Joseph,
1937–Correspondence. 3. Electronic mail messages. I. Epstein, Joseph,
1937–II. Title.
    PR6068.A6Z48 2013
    823.914—dc23
                                                                    2012040253

A catalogue record for this book is available from the British Library

10 9 8 7 6 5 4 3 2 1

The reciprocal civility of authors is one of the most risible scenes in the farce of life.
—Samuel Johnson

Contents

Introduction

Joseph Epstein

Twenty-five, it may have been thirty years ago I wrote to my friend John Gross suggesting that we write a book together that would comprise letters on the literary and cultural life of our respective countries, England and the United States, which we would send to each other over the course of a year. John was then editor of the *Times Literary Supplement* and I the editor of the *American Scholar*. Our jobs, I felt at the time, may have given our observations and insights and animadversions additional cachet. I thought it a good idea – a better one, apparently, than did John, who also may not have had time to write such letters. Editing a crowded weekly such as the *TLS*, after all, makes immensely greater demands on a man than running a leisurely quarterly. The notion was let drop.

Then, a little more than a year ago, Frederic Raphael, the English novelist and screenwriter, proposed the same idea to me. I was delighted to take him up on it. I was especially pleased at the invitation because he was Frederic Raphael and I was I, to paraphrase Montaigne's simple yet profound explanation of his friendship with Étienne de La Boétie. Apart from the fact that Freddie, as he has since become to me, is not La Boetié and I am even further from being Montaigne, Frederic Raphael and I have never met or even spoken over the telephone. We know each other only from our discrete – if far from discreet – scribblings and occasional e-mails.

The name Frederic Raphael first came across my screen, as we say in the digital age, when I saw, on PBS, *The Glittering Prizes*, the dramatization of his *roman à clef* of the bright young things with an interest in theater at Cambridge in the early 1950s. The part of Adam Morris, Freddie's protagonist, was played by Tom Conti, and played so well that even today when people meet Frederic Raphael for the first time – something I have yet to do – they are slightly surprised to discover that he doesn't look at all like the actor.

The television version of *The Glittering Prizes* offered a glittering prize of its own: dialogue so smart that one hunched forward while watching it lest one miss one of the author's throwaway *mots*, of which there seemed to be an inexhaustible supply. I soon learned that Freddie's dialogue could float and then set aloft an entire novel. A reviewer of one of his novels said its author goes "for the jocular and jugular with equal relish," something that I think can be said of the dialogue in all his writing. I made a note of the name Frederic Raphael.

I soon discovered that he was the author of the screenplay for the movie *Darling*, which was, as *The Glittering Prizes* was for Tom Conti, the making of Julie Christie (and by the way won Freddie an Oscar). Many are the rewards of screenwriting, but recognition, let alone fame, outside the movie business itself, is not one of them. (Most people, including inveterate moviegoers, cannot, I'd wager, name five living screenwriters.) I subsequently learned that Frederic Raphael wrote the screenplays for *Two for the Road* (with Audrey Hepburn and Albert Finney), *Far From the Madding Crowd*, and many other excellent movies, including Stanley Kubrick's final film, *Eyes Wide Shut*.

While working away at a successful screenwriting career, Frederic Raphael also quietly assembled an impressive body of fiction, novels and short stories, made translations (from Greek and Latin), wrote biographies (of Lord Byron and Somerset Maugham), kept and published journals as well as a large book on the culture of the ancient Greeks: in short, he was a literary man of all work and to a very high power. He also from time to time published in the *TLS* and elsewhere dazzling reviews of philosophy books – he studied Moral Sciences at Cambridge during the age of British analytic philosophy – which he seemed to knock off with his left hand. Frederic Raphael qualifies as a Man of Letters, but the tag smells too strongly of the library and the study, and is altogether too musty for a man as engaged with contemporary life as Freddie, his whole career long, has been.

I sent away to England for his fiction when it appeared and I acquired his other books from the university library in my neighborhood. I much admired his energy and his wit, his worldliness and intellectual courage. Alas, not many people in America knew about Frederic Raphael, though whenever I brought his name up in conversation, the mention of the screenplays he had written got, as we now say, their attention. (Movies can excite interest like few other cultural subjects; I never found greater 'dinner-party interest' in my own writing than the one time I was working on a screenplay for Warner Brothers for a movie that never got made.) Although born to an American mother and an English father and himself a man of cosmopolitan spirit who lives half the year in France, might Frederic Raphael, who was born in Chicago in 1931, be too British, too irony-laden and subtle, for a wide American audience? I prefer to think not. Certainly his movies haven't been.

A few years ago, a young American editor called me "the American Frederic Raphael." As the above paragraphs will make plain, I was much pleased by the remark. What I hope he meant by it was that I didn't think being serious in my writing altogether precluded being entertaining. But even when Freddie is dead serious I find him entertaining. One of the roles he has taken up latish in life is that of a one-man literary equivalent of the Simon Wiesenthal Foundation. He is death on anti-Semitism in literature and on memoirs and historical books that neglect to mention, for example, the rounding up of Jews under the Vichy government, or which otherwise soft-pedal the immense slaughter that was the Holocaust – and he does so with a wit that is withering in its controlled contempt.

I am one of those readers who write notes of appreciation to writers whose books or essays or stories give me deep pleasure. For some reason I held back writing to Frederic Raphael until a copy of his 1989 lecture at the University of Southampton called "The Necessity of Anti-Semitism," a title with a triple-barreled irony, came into my hands. Freddie wrote back to me cordially. We exchanged further e-mails, though without regular rhythm. And then, when I came to put together an anthology called *Literary Genius*, which included twenty-five essays on figures in Anglophone literature who I thought qualified for the 'genius' label, I invited Frederic Raphael – not yet Freddie – to write the essay on William Hazlitt. I was a bit chary about inviting him to do so, for I could only offer each of the volume's contributors the same fee of $1,350 – not a disgraceful sum, to be sure, but for a man who had been cashing movie checks, perhaps a trivial one. He wrote back saying that he would be pleased to write the essay, and as for the sum, that he would accept it; but if he were ever to learn that any other contributor had been paid more he would see that I would be put instantly to death.

The Hazlitt essay was splendid, and Freddie and I began exchanging e-mails more frequently. We found that we had much in common in the way of literary tastes and general outlook, not to mention a common birthplace in Chicago. Neither of us wished the other public disgrace and humiliation – already an astonishing bit of *politesse* among writers – nor were we bashful about praising the other's work when we genuinely admired it. Not long afterward Freddie suggested to me, without knowing that decades before

I had suggested something very similar to John Gross, the book now in your hands.

Although there is no shortage of collections of correspondence between literary men – I have on my desk at the moment a slender volume of the letters exchanged between Flaubert and Turgenev – I don't know if any yet has been done under aegis of the great god E-mail. As with writing using computers generally, e-mail encourages a certain literary fluency, let us not say garrulity (also candor); I'm not sure that anyone in the past century could have written with the same regularity and volume – roughly 3,500 words a week over the course of a little over a year – as did Freddie and I through the quasi-magical dispensation of e-mail. I can speak only for myself here, but I never found my weekly 1,500–1,800-word share of our confabulation in the least burdensome; now that it is over, truth is, I find I miss it.

Unlike the book I proposed to John Gross, which would have been more journalistic, featuring comments on happenings of the day, Freddie's and my book is more autobiographical and hence personal. In these pages we write of our schooling, our parents, our wives, our children, our literary tastes, our enmities, our delights, our beliefs; we also write a fair amount about our professional lives as writers, about our skills and want of skills, our reputations, and our experiences with editors, with (in Freddie's case) producers and actors, with fellow scribblers. The general tone and feeling of our communications, I think it fair to say, is intimate.

What makes this intimacy a touch magical is the fact that, as mentioned earlier, Frederic Raphael and Joseph Epstein have never met nor have they ever even spoken on the telephone. They are two men of the same generation, with six years difference in their ages, who work at the same trade and who happen to have a remarkable rapport – or as I like to think of the word, giving it a Jewish spin, *rappaport*.

Freddie and I have ceased our regular weekly round of e-mail, though we continue to send irregular yet frequent shorter e-mails to each other. We also send each other copies of things we have recently written. Reading over what we wrote to each other over the past year, I discovered a fine exuberance in it; I hope readers of our book, my dear friend Freddie's and mine, will also find that and a lot more.

Dear Joe,

Well, we did the common festival, and the common turkey, and all was well; and that's fine for a year, if we live so long. New Year's Eve is going to be an oldsters' dinner party, which is about the pace we can trot at. And so it goes. I am deep in the heart of Flavius Josephus, with notes as fat as the national debt (choose your country, it's still fat), and beginning to see him in manageable form, that of the First Journalist, which takes us all the way to Karl Kraus, Robert Fisk and who knows who. I have two questions. The first: did my quaint lil ole publishers Carcanet send you a copy yet, or indeed so soon, of *Ticks and Crosses*? If (as I suspect) they did not, I will hie me to the PO with a copy for you this week. The second is tricky (time bomb within) and concerns a book I recommended in the *TLS* international show-off selection, the correspondence between B.-H. Lévy and Michel Houellebecq, or letters to that effect. Primo, have you seen it by any chance? If not, you might enjoy it, but it ain't over yet, because here's what puts the ouch in the kicker: might there be some fun, not to mention $$$ etc., in a year's (say) correspondence between . . . you *cannot* have guessed. Well, might there? *Chicago, Chicago* and how cookies do crumble and what if and what about books and writing and coincidences and divergences; something piquant, is there not, in two friends who have never met, who do not need (and seem to have no inclination) to put each other down, compete, or anything, and yet . . . Unparallel lines that don't meet and can't wait for infinity. So there you have it: the embarrassment of the year that ain't even begun yet. I think that the correspondence might be something of an *autobiographie involontaire* and might discover us to ourselves as well as to each other, if that's something either (no, both) of us want. Say, well, er, um and no damage or offence will be done or taken. It's cold here and I am perhaps warming myself up with rubbing hands that should never meet. *Basta così.* Don't say yes and don't say no and I shall know I have the man I think I have. Busy? Sure I am and sure you are, but isn't there a lot of slack to be cut in this: really we do and really do not know each other. Well, once I press that button this thing will go and nuttin' I can do to stop it. But, seriously, treat this as a joke, unless it makes you laugh. *Tout à toi, bonne année,*

Freddie

So, dear Freddie, let us begin.

I, too, have nothing to declare – the title of a memoir, I believe, by a Jew-hating Greek named Taki Somethingorotheropopoulos – and even less to confess. As for wives, we seem to have in common – what a weird kink, especially for writers! – loving our wives and not wishing to disgrace or otherwise degrade them, unlike old Edmund Wilson, whose idea of a swell time was describing bonking his various wives in his published journals. I feel as you do about your wife in not wanting to drag my wife Barbara into my scribblings; she has a refinement that naturally turns her away from all publicity. Besides, we both seem to have more Jews than sex in our heads.

On the subject of Jews, though we each have Jewish mothers (also fathers), both born in Chicago – I like to think that, had they met, they would have been friends – your upbringing as a Jew in England strikes me, from published writings of yours and from our past correspondence, as more difficult than mine. My father, born a Canadian, a Montrealer, had memories of Canuck kids tormenting old Jewish men – pulling beards, crying out "sheeny," that sort of delightful stuff – and was himself for always ever after on the *qui vive* for anti-Semitism. His son, though, had very little of it to deal with in Chicago, probably because the neighborhoods he grew up in and the public schools he went to were at least half populated by Jews. I remember driving through other neighborhoods which my mother instructed me were "restricted"; I'll let you guess from whom. And certain Chicago high schools, attended by German and Swedish working-class kids, had the reputation of having it in for Jews. I was never free of the consciousness of being Jewish, but, for the most part, didn't find this much of a burden. I was myself very little affected, at least directly, from blatant, or even subtle, anti-Semitism.

My sense is that in your much better English schools you stood out as a Jew and were made to feel your Jewishness in a way I never was. As a Jew, you, I suspect, never felt entirely at home in the milieu (the writer Josephine Herbst always pronounced this word "maloo," and so I now always hear it: *maloo*, as in the American folk-dance song that has the line "skip to maloo, my darling") of Charterhouse and Cambridge. English upper-middle and upper-class anti-Semitism is not only subtler but more insidious than the American brand. In America, most – not all, to be sure – anti-Semitism is practiced at the blatant level, and so it allows one to feel easily superior to one's detractors.

I don't mean to strike an invidious note here, but I think between us I am the more Jewish writer. Without Jews to write about, without my deeply Jewish (I do not say Judaic) outlook, I would be out of business. I don't think the same is anything like as true of you, certainly not in your job as a screen-writer or, for the most part, as a novelist. Yet in another sense, you have in recent years turned yourself into a defender if not quite of the faith than of the justice due to the Jews, firing off letters to various editors reminding their writers and reviewers that they have neglected if not overlooked the vicious anti-Semitism lurking in their subjects. I like you in this mode – much admire you in it, in fact.

Jews, Jews, might it be they and not literature (contra Old Ez, another unfriend of our co-religionists) who stay news. I shall try to sound the Jew-note (Chicago had a once-famous jazz club called The Blue Note) less insistently in future. But I did think it made sense to clear the deck – clear the dreck – of this early in the proceedings.

How does the following strike you as a title for our little book: "Dear Freddie, Dear Joe: Chronicle of a Distant Intimacy"?

Jewily yours, Joe

Dear Joe,
How pleased Freud must have been when he heard Charcot's phrase '*c'est toujours la chose génitale*', because, of course, as your unashamed – that's a true British term for a Jew who actually says he's a Jew – confession (there's another) revealed, what's really *toujours* is *la chose juive*. Which leads to: Did Eliot use a small j for 'the jew is underneath the lot', until he agreed to change it to a capital J, because he was imitating the French use of a minuscule when it came to national denominations? Shall we ever know? Shall we ever care? Christopher Ricks promises that Eliot wasn't an anti-Semite (he didn't have the nerve even to be a bully, one guesses, so Cricks may be right) and Anthony Julius, one of that legion of 'our people' I should just as soon see in the ranks of Tuscany, will tell us that of course Old Tom was a bad, bad man, although a good, good poet. Everything is true of everything, some say, following Paul de Man, which is not a scent that appeals to me. Everyone can be what they like, or should be, old/young man Sartre told the waiting world in 1947 – when he had to say something existential about anti-Semitism – except for the Jews, who had to accept being what other people said they were, if only (we have to believe) up to a point: *juif, oui; youpin*, punch in the *nez*, seems the recommended formula. My father, being British, was a great believer in the straight left, a tactic employed by a succession of horizontal British heavy-weights (Bruce Woodcock the most fairly famous) in the 1940s, when they confronted men such as (NOT 'like') Joe Baksi and Jersey Joe Walcott, who

did hooking and bolo-punching and all those rather uncomely things and so flattened our (as they had then become for your Chicago-born Semite correspondent) boys who had been deprived of steak and so not only failed to punch their weight but didn't have the weight to punch.

What was I saying, as an academic said to my wife one evening at a dinner party, in the tone of a beak who suspects that one of the class was dozing off while he spills the pearls before the swine. Beetle, as you will, I hope, become accustomed to my calling her, even though she has a perfectly beautiful name, Sylvia/Sylvie, which we use when in France because Les Beatles they can do, but a singular Beetle defeats them (racial defects, see under) – Beetle saw him off with something of the order of 'Do you really want to know?' She takes no prisoners, but she treats them well. Oh yes, *la chose juive*. We shall need to find another topic, and will, not least because our attitudes are so much in accord that, as Noël Coward said of some luckless girl's eyes, you can't get a pin between them. Yet it will recur.

I think (you're right: I know) that it was Albert Camus – whom Sartre envied not for his literary ability but for his good-looking successes chez les femmes and his prowess (what else?) as a goalkeeper – who said that the only/ great philosophical question was why not to commit suicide, or Gallic words to that effect. When you consider that le bon Albert, unlike Poulou, had actually done some resisting and had come through, we like to imagine, with honour and skin intact, it seems very odd, looking back (and by God I fear I am likely to do some of that), that, having survived the war, suicide should seem a pressing crux. I read recently (and probably a long time ago too, only I didn't remember) that Émile Durkheim, in the course of his sociological researches (another way of flying from his Jewish specificity, according to Pierre Birnbaum in a recent fat study of the order my local Dordogne bookseller calls 'un pavé'), discovered that Jews have/had the lowest suicide rates among all his sample of religiously-designated frogs. Perhaps it smacks of undue assimilation for Jews to kill themselves when so many people down the years have been willing to take care of that side of things for them. Of course, I know, I know, things got worse in the post-Anschluss days when the Austrian gas company disconnected Jewish subscribers on the grounds that they overused their supply and then were too dead to pay for it. I wish that was a joke. The Austrians think it was.

You're very good at culling/embellishing/delivering Jewish jokes. Thanks to them, I can have great social success passing myself off as the J. Epstein/Leo Rosten of my set. How I laughed at Hyman Kaplan, and how right, I suspect, never to read him again! One of the first 'adult' jokes I ever heard was about the man who was always being asked by his friend to come to the ball game, and every time he agreed, he cancelled because 'Levinsky's playing'. I suspect that this is one of the oldest hats on the rack – do you know it? It comes in the little bundle of emigrant's baggage that travelled with me from NYC to London. What's a schmuck again? An emigrant from NYC to London in 1938. *That's* what a schmuck is. No wonder my whole life has been an exercise in cover-up. My mother gave me Franz Kafka's 'Letter to My Father' for Christmas. Imagine if I had the time to write one to mine: it would not be to complain about how his huge personality crushed mine, but to ask how he could do me the cruel service of giving me that British education you, my dear professor in green retreat, think was such a boon.

I wanted to talk about Gore Vidal (toadied at in the *NYRB*) and Susan Sontag (*Never On Susan* is the planned movie title) and how she loved André Gide when she was a teenager. In French *déjà*? It doesn't say in the long, long spread accorded her. The truth is, if you want to be pretentious, start early. More soon.

Happy 2009. Remember our cracker motto for the year: However well things are going, they could be worse.

Amities, F.

Dear Freddie,

Allow me to take up where you ended, with Gore Vidal and Susan Sontag, though in doing so I feel that you have set me up by floating two gentle lobs that barely made it over the net for easy overhead smashes.

Gore Vidal is now in his early eighties, and is perhaps best likened to a car with a dead engine whose horn nonetheless keeps sounding off. His act has been that of the crusty American aristocrat – Henry Adams with a bit of Edmund Wilson thrown in, the Wilson who claimed to look at *Life* magazine and not recognize the America in which he grew up – who finds his country vulgar, make that greedy, vile and vastly ignorant. The twist Vidal rang on this great American crank act was to hate America from the left instead of, more traditionally for this role, from the right. Nothing in the country he couldn't look down his nose upon: its politics, its literature, its entertainment, above all its people. All this was admixed with a strong homosexual strain; Vidal used to call himself a "homosexualist," a term that always reminded me of an "aerialist." His gaiety, I always felt, was part of his general complaint – it left him more than a touch vulnerable, caused him to loathe from a position of weakness – though his complaints have been many. Chief among them is that he has been insufficiently appreciated as a novelist. My own sense is that he has been properly unappreciated. I've read the less than amusing *Myra Breckenridge* and *Julian* (about our good friend The Apostate), and one or two other of his novels, and remember from it all only that Julian gets blown a fair amount by young men. Vidal's reputation now stands on his being a putatively great essayist, but I don't think this holds up either. So much of his writing is marred by his nastiness. He has been accused of being an anti-Semite, and I think there is something to it, probably because he resented the novels of Bellow, Roth & co. getting so much more attention than his own. But Vidal is no Jew-hater merely; he is a hater generally, of anyone who doesn't feel about the world as he does. As for how he feels about the world, I should say that he doesn't like it very much, that he finds it stupid and ugly and, greatest crime of all, insensitive to his own glorious talents. As for his talents, I think he is best at homosexual gossip, telling mean stories about Truman Capote and amusing ones about Tennessee Williams. A friend of mine named Eve Auchincloss once told me that Vidal and Jason and Barbara Epstein and friends used to play a little game in which they guessed which figures in recent history – John F. Kennedy, Adlai Stevenson – were circumcised and which not. Such is decadence, *New York Review* variety! What fun! Gore Vidal was handsome as a young man, but now in his old age has grown fat and pinch-faced, having come into the body and face he deserves.

If Susan Sontag only looked like Cynthia Ozick (plain, matronly, white hair, large round spectacles), American intellectual life would be a good bit healthier today. We have this new baggy-pants term in America, "public intellectual" – I don't know if it has hit France and England yet – but our Susan has always been mainly a publicity intellectual. She was able to garner so much publicity, I believe, not on her foolish ideas alone but because of her (when young) good looks. She had the look of the wild bohemian girl that every half-educated man wished he had bonked through college or graduate school. (Surprise, surprise, but sorry boys: she was, we now know, a lesbian all along, despite time-out for a quick marriage to a wildly anglophile sociologist named Philip Rieff and the birth of a son.) When our Susan died, the *NY Times* ran no fewer than seven photographs with her obituary – she was pure intellectual cheesecake. Her last lover, appropriately, was the photographer Annie Leibowitz, who photographed her on her deathbed. She was made to be photographed, just as certain of the authors she wrote about with such elevated enthusiasm – Walter Benjamin, Roland Barthes, etc. – aren't really meant to be read but to be written about by our very own Susy in prefaces and introductions. She was four years older than I, but I remember when she crashed the publicity barrier with her not very impressive essay on the extremely unimportant subject of Camp. She then came out with essays "Against Interpretation," holding that aesthetics were all that mattered (a notion she later retracted), the meaning or moral import of a work being negligible. Her intellectual prose gave no pleasure, her fiction even less. I would as lief cut off both thumbs than see the movie(s) she made. She was a wholly derivative person, basing her writing, her life, everything on her impression of the idea of a French intellectual. Her political ideas were all wrong, though gaudily so: the white race is the cancer on the world, the North Vietnamese were a gentle peace-loving people, the United States deserved what it got on September 11. One of her specialties was to say extraordinarily stupid things and then, much later, recant them: sometime in the 1980s, for example, she had a Eureka moment and came round to believe that maybe Communism wasn't such a hot idea after all. She was an exemplar of Orwell's remark that "only an intellectual could be so stupid." The reason she was so stupid, I suspect, is that all her knowledge was acquired in books, very little from the world the rest of us live in. For the past twenty-five or so years, she was easily America's primary celebrity among intellectuals; and behind her celebrity was chiefly snobbery. She was herself a very great snob, though not of the amusing variety. Every story I have ever heard about dear Suzy-Q has her on display acting cruelly to young academics showing her around while visiting one university or another to talk for what I am confident were impressive fees. But then, as we know, a woman who so much loved The People figures not to have too much affection left for actual people. I thought her death would put an end to Susan, for who would want to reread her scribblings, but now the first of what are to be three volumes of dreary journals have appeared. I had hoped to spend these, my hazy sunset years, hearing no more about Susan Sontag, but it apparently is not to be. Sometimes an older gentleman just can't get a break.

Keep the faith.

Best, Joe

Dear Joe,

Hey, you know what? We just might do a version of Ravel's bolero on the subjects of Gore and Sontag: Unpatriotic Gore and Never-on-Sontag could be the double-bill that ran and ran. This one will limp and limp, did someone say?

We'll write an essay about the bastard. I suppose that the pair of them are terribly modern, and terribly ancient too. Odd that each was more or less exclusively homo-sexualist and homosexu-A-List as well, of course. Gore put affectations of pedantry between himself and the profane crowd, not least when he disapproved of the adjective homosexual being used as a noun; I recall asking him if, on the same principle, he described himself as an Americanist.

What's odd is not Sontag and Gore's orientation (what would Edward Said have sigh-eed if he could have been with us today? Occidentation, maybe?), and it is not what they do in bed or – favoured spot for today's cinematic heterosexualists – on the kitchen work-surface (an extension, for all I know, of the principle of product placement), but – here it comes – the fact, as I see it, that one of the plusses of homo-pleasuring is that you/they don't have to spend a lot of time on preliminaries. Except in those few uxorious cases that need not detain the jury, there is no rush to get home in the evening and spend time with The One (or Two) You Love. I have never wanted to work – still less have 'meetings' – which involves getting home later than 6.30 p.m., whereas the single-minded ambitious same-sexy talents have no appetite for domesticity and when it comes to Robert Graves's meum-tuum sense, they substitute the meum-meum sense, which means that they are, as the frogs say, 'disponibles' for careerism, upwardly-mobile bonking and night'n'day career moves like that.

As for La Sontag with Annie Leibowitz, well, who whom is the question that Lenin would be asking, but I don't give a damn; I'd sooner put my eye to a dime-in-the-slot peepshow of the 1960s than be privy to that performance. How sweetly apt that S.S. (God really can do the irony, can't She?) should end up (sic) with a photographer, after writing that seminal (has to be) essay on the subject. I can't remember whether she was for or against, and I don't care, although I do think she had a brief winning streak with 'Against Interpretation', the densest two-word essay of all time. How wonderfully apt that Sontag's last sexual trick could be billed/entitled exactly like a piece in the *NYRB*, 'Sontag on Leibowitz'.

But let me bitch the living, for a small change, because our daughter Sarah, who was as beautiful as a genius should ever be, and her handsome brother Paul were photographed for a big, big department store publicity campaign for which La Leib took the snaps. They were not going to be paid, because they were young and beautiful, but they *were* promised a signed print, a print signed even, by La L. Did they get it? Would I be telling you if they had? They *did* appear on the sides of many London buses and I was more than slightly thrilled to see them up there (of whose but one's own children's publicity – does the grammar work there? – can one say that?), but it might have been nice if The Greatest Living Female Photographer had actually delivered. I will now tell you what La L.'s 'people' will be saying: Annie never heard about this/ Annie is talking to her lawyer/Annie sent those prints and she remembers doing so because your son and daughter (in particular) were the most beautiful people she ever clicked a shutter at.

On Gore, as a post-postscriptum (he does love the Latin, does he not, even if he thinks, and prints, respublicus, among a number of gross errors which, since they passed unremarked, except by the guy who risks being written out of lit/crit history for doing it, your 'umble correspondent), we can say that he must stand, or slouch, as evidence that the intellectual decline which he thinks to chart from the far shore is indeed a steep one. Uncle Edmund, with all his faults, did learn the essential grammar of the languages he affected to use, even if it is one of the greatest of all acts of literary hubris to have crossed dictionaries with Volodya on the Onegin translation; E.W. had only himself to blame when Pushkin came to Shovekin. Gore has not only passed himself off as Mr Cosmo, he has even had delusions of Capet monarchy and, as you will know, designated his 'Dauphin'; and it had to be Christopher Hitchens, who makes the same kind of falsely sophisticated mistakes that all those fancy editor friends of his/theirs either don't know are solecisms or lack the nerve to say so. Those who live by publicity live by publicity. As tautologies go, it stays.

I met La Sontag just once, in Soho Square. She must have been in her earlyish thirties. She condescended even then. I recall she had a white flash in her black hair. So did Aldo Moro, the Italian politician (you remember, but they don't) who wound up dead in the trunk of some idealist shit's car, after his close friends in the Democrazia Cristiana didn't work any too hard to save him. The excerpts from her Diaries so lavishly spread through the NYRB which I happened to scan at the library confirm that she was onto André Gide when she was fifteen. This puts her up there (the same as down there) with Harold Pinter who once told us, in an essay that I had solicited for A Good Cause, that 'In my teens, I read Jules Laforgue'. All the kids in the East End were swapping imagist texts between fending off Oswald Mosley with their straight bats.

À toi, mon vieux.
Freddie

Dear Freddie,

Today, January 9, is my birthday. I am 72, a stately fucking age, entailing, I fear, more stateliness than actual fucking. I do not come from a family that made much fuss about birthdays, and no fuss will be made about mine today. My wife will take me to dinner tonight at a neighborhood restaurant we like called Chef's Station, where I shall eat a chop (veal or pork) and drink a glass of champagne, and that will be that. My dear and very smart mother used to claim that she wasn't quite sure whether her birthday was October 30 or 31. My parents, who were very good to me and my five-years-younger brother – allowing us lots of freedom and imbuing us with few neuroses – were highly unsentimental people. They simply didn't see the significance in a day being a person's birthday; after all, I can hear one or the other of them saying, a person had to be born on some day or other, so what's the big deal, and not merely on Madonna Street (wasn't there a movie called *Big Deal on Madonna Street*?). My mother's mother, who came to Chicago by way of Leeds, had a Cockney maid named Minnie Tumbletee, who used to send me a birthday card with a single dollar in it every year on my birthday until I reached the age of thirty, at which time she must have assumed that I could make it on my own. When I asked my mother how it was that her mother, who was a far from well-to-do woman, had a maid, she told me that her mother's sister caught her husband, a wealthy cap manufacturer in Leeds, with a lady friend. As part of the agreement for her mother's sister remaining with him – or perhaps the agreement was that he could keep his lady friend – the husband sent his sister-in-law in Chicago, my grandmother, $100 a month, which she used for the services of Minnie Tumbletee. Such is family history among us La Rochefoucaulds.

At 72, I'm still pleased to be in the game. I believe I am to insert a sentence here about cherishing every day, and so on. The fact is that I waste as much time as ever, and have not grown wiser. I continue to let small things upset me, itch at the scabs of old resentments, collect injustices, and where possible give lyrical expression to my grievances. Yet I also know how, historically, fortunate I have been. My generation missed out on all the wars: we were children in WWII, still too young for Korea, too old for Vietnam. We've also lived through a stretch of unrelieved (until perhaps just now) prosperity. Had I been born fifty years earlier, I should probably be dead for want of sophisticated medical practice: I've had bypass surgery and not long ago had something called auto-immune hepatitis, from both of which health problems I should probably have pegged out long before the age of 72. Meanwhile, I'm still asked by publishers and magazines to scribble away at subjects that amuse me and, though less gorgeous and lithe than formerly, am feeling no physical pain. (Touch wood – not unmindful of the possibility of acquiring cancer of the knuckles from doing so too often.) In short, Señor Freddie, much as it goes against my natural penchant for complaint, I have to consider myself one lucky mother-humper, which I secretly do.

Best, Joe

Dear Joe,

Many Happy Returns, as the English say, in their modification, I suppose, of 'I wish you long life'. As a veteran of more years but of no more wars than you, I share your sense of having sidestepped the crueller tests of manhood, if that is what steadiness under fire demonstrates (as Dr Johnson, who shared our luck, certainly thought). I have fought only a number of pop-gun wars, in which I have been accused sometimes of 'moral courage', which seems to me to be a negligible quality, though often deficient in those of whom, till a moment or two ago, one thought well. I quail even so when I have fired my verbal volley and wait, like Ryan O'Neal in that barn in *Barry Lyndon*, for my opponent's fire. I can dish it out, but who likes taking it?

As time's callous calendar would have it, your birthday date precedes that of the death of our daughter Sarah, eight years ago. Each year, as it turns to the next, I dread the approach of January 10th; as much, even this confessed egotist can say honestly, because of what Beetle will be feeling but will never allow quite to express itself, as on account of anything I feel myself (loss to me of her, loss to the world of all the beauty she might have created, even when on the telephone). I take it that this correspondence is not being blemished or blighted by reference to unamusing things. Sarah was very amusing, and very amused, and very accurate in her scorn and very brave in her resolution. When she had a show at Agnew's, a very fancy Bond Street gallery in London, they hung her pictures in an upstairs gallery with walls upholstered in red plush, of a kind that John Singer Sargent might have regarded as his due, but which did not at all suit Sarah's colours. She came on the eve of the show to see how they were, as the marines say, hanging and was not AT ALL pleased. Either the walls would have to be re-covered with a suitably pallid, neutral material or she was pulling the show. Such things are not said, often, by young persons in august galleries, but Sarah was as courageous as she was brilliant, and she prevailed. She was valiant but not strong; brilliant, witty, beautiful, but not wise, not self-preserving. Something Byronic there, but entirely in the feminine register, all the panache and daring, but without a shred of Byronic bluff and facetiousness; humour, yes; wit, often; accuracy, always, in mimicry as in observation. People live, people die. Birthdays and deathdays carry the same message: brackets open, brackets close.

I should, I know, be thinking, like a philosopher, that Sarah's death is no different, no more 'tragic', perhaps less so, than the innocent (children's) deaths in the Gaza Strip which put us, put me at least, in the situation of feeling I must say something and of having nothing to say that is not somehow taking a kind of responsibility that I do not feel, or else will seem callous and unfeeling. Unfeelingness is, it is tempting to say, the response of a Jew with no, as they say, affiliations with Israel and, as you were saying, nothing much in the way of 'faith', confronted for too many years with promises from the Other Side that they would like to kill us all, even if we are not doing anything except, dear God it must be said, feeling some involuntary solidarity with, yes, Our People.

I gave up trying to stand on any moral ground (how slippery it gets with blood!) back in 1967, when I was shocked (I confess or I boast) when Israel didn't give back the land it had captured, not because – as Ben-Gurion said – it was untenable but because, so I thought, with my British education (and without), the Arabs might be touched and there would be common dancing. Life is not a musical; there is no common dancing with those who seek power or attach their waggon to some implacable doctrine. Not even Groucho Marx could have converted Hitler, although Mel Brooks has probably done more to make sure he doesn't come back than any earnest philosopher. Yes, I had to talk about Sarah and, yes, I am trying to change the subject, which leads me to blunder into the Middle East, which I have been researching, between rocks and hard places, in which it abounds, for months now, in preparation for that book about Flavius Josephus that Pantheon have commissioned and I must do, God help me, like the scholar I am not quite. You must know, jeune homme – as the fishmonger lady calls me in the market in Saint-Cyprien, with the insolence which, for some reason, seems to be a common feature of fishwives – that there is nothing quite so naïve as the credulity of those who live adjacent to Academe and wish, slightly, that they had earned the title Professor. There, I have wrapped you a smile to add to your birthday smiles.

Sarah lived and loved, and did her work. What more should anyone want to have said of them? But would that I had not to use that past tense. Do not pity me as I write; the writer's brain is a frigid article, I have found (have you?), with small capacity for being, as the English say, choked. So, smile and sigh to yourself and do not feel that you must clear your throat and say something . . . appropriate. No, no, 'fuck it all' will do; but then again, there are the living. Jesus was a hard-hearted Jewboy, but he was sometimes right, wasn't he? I damned well DO wish you long life as I think of Sarah's shortened one. No-one owns the years.

Tout à toi,
Freddie

Dear Freddie,

Another thing we have in common is our membership in the sad fraternity of parents who have buried a child. All I know of your daughter Sarah is the striking paintings on some of your books; these paintings suggest, along with obvious skill, wit and intellectual penetration. I also have some inkling, from your occasional mention of her to me in our correspondence, what a large hole her death has left in yours and your wife's lives. My son Burt died at the age of twenty-eight, before he really got going. He was charming, risk-taking, physically fearless, and wild in lots of ways. I miss him, of course, but days, even weeks go by when I do not think of him. Then he will show up, usually as a sweet child, in one of my (standard) bizarre dreams. My only, quite unoriginal thought about his death in his late twenties is that of waste – he enjoyed life and missed out on so much of it. He left a daughter – he died when she was ten months old – named Annabelle, in whose upbringing my wife and I have taken a more than usually strong interest. She is now nineteen, in art school, and has lived with us for the past five years. The true loss incurred by my son's death is that of his daughter, left a fatherless child, and it is a loss I can't bear to think of for long.

I am extraordinarily lucky, though, in my other son, Burt's older brother Mark. He is now forty-eight, and has become my dearest male friend. "When your son becomes a man, make him your brother," runs an Arab proverb (too bad it couldn't be a Jewish proverb, but you can't have every-thing), and this is what seems to have happened with Mark and me. Our sense of humor is fairly congruent; my son is, I think, smarter than I, able to concentrate more intensely on what he does; is better at handling many things at once; and is a more powerful money-maker than his old man. (He lives in northern California and is in the business of arranging the financing for small municipalities that are undergoing improvements. He also runs a small vine-yard, growing Cabernet Sauvignon grapes.) I am able to talk to him with nearly complete candor (I don't even talk to myself with complete candor, you understand) about all subjects. He is a great pleasure in my life, and knowing he is going to be around after I'm dead, to help look after my wife and my dead son's daughter, is a genuine comfort to me.

Enough on the gloom front. Colder here in Chicago than a long-since-divorced spouse. (I devised this little simile hoping it is an improvement on "colder than a well-digger's bottom" or "a witch's tit.") Apartment-bound by the stark weather, I have been reading and scribbling away. *Newsweek* magazine asked me for two different pieces, one on the Sasha Stavisky of our day, Bernie Madoff and his swindling of the Jews, and another, for its international edition, on the relation of the American tradition of thrift to the current economic meltdown. *Newsweek* pays me $2 a word, and I take some small pride – pride in craft – at being able to turn out such journalism fairly quickly. Earlier this week I read a quite decent novel called *Apology for the Woman Writing* by the English writer Jenny Diski on the interesting subject of the crazed Marie de Gournay, who convinced Montaigne to allow her to become the editor of the *Essais*. (Talk about a small audience subject!) The novel is well made, and since I have an unending interest in Montaigne, it held me all the way. I have, you should know, more than once been called the American Montaigne, which comes under the category of unbelievable, because too extravagant, praise. Whenever it occurs, I always try to imagine Montaigne saying, "You know, I do believe that I am the French Joseph Epstein," and, poof, the praise all blows away. I have been reading, as my early morning (with tea and toast) book, Alexander Waugh's *The House of Wittgenstein*, which is not a great book but one filled with interesting information, lots of it new to me. In some ways Paul Wittgenstein, poor one-armed pianist Paul, was a more interesting human being than Ludwig. Karl Wittgenstein, the father, makes Kafka's father seem as benign as Dagwood Bumstead. The family itself, as you will have gathered from Ray Monk's excellent book on Ludwig W., is quite mad. "A tense and peculiar family, the Wittgensteins," to adapt what Max Beerbohm said about the Oedipuses. I recently reread I.J. Singer's *The Brothers Ashkenazi*; I.J., older brother to I.B., may not have been the greater writer but I think he was the better novelist; I'm currently reading his memoir *Of a World That Is No More*, about the awfulness of shtetl life in early-twentieth-century Poland – I know of no better antidote to the sentimentality of the subject presented in *Fiddler on the Roof*. So don't worry, Ma, I'm reading good.

Best, Joe

Dear Joe,

I had no idea about your son Burt having died. Might I have divined something from the measuredness of your response to all kinds of things, a sense
of proportion that I wish I shared? When Sarah died, I felt too many confused
emotions ever to have faith in the specificity of all those emotional states
supposedly so sharply defined from each other: rage, pity, shame, disillusion-
ment. Grief is edged by other ingredients, some as disreputable as resentment,
some frankly disloyal: I recall wanting to be among people who didn't know
what had happened so that I could smile and, God help me, amuse or charm.
The self intrudes, pained and, yes, indignant: how could this happen to her
edged with how could it happen to me, and hoping, with whatever emotion it
may be, that others (in other words, Beetle) will not be as . . . whatever it is
that one is oneself: tearful, helpless, broken. I cannot fill in the details of the
following days and weeks. I recall that *The Sunday Times*, to which I have
contributed for more than forty years, rang to say that they wanted to run a
piece about Sarah and that they didn't expect me to do it, but had to ask me
first. I realise now, and I fear I did then, that this was an opportunity to shut
myself away, as I have so often in life, and have an excuse to be too busy to
face the world. So I did a long piece: work as anaesthetic. The brain, I then
found, is a cold faculty and, if you have the words in the tank, always disposed
to get busy.

   Montaigne (and you) knew/know a lot about the first person. Le bon
Micheau was one of the first people to do so; he recognised the element of –
what? – detachment in desire and even in parenthood. But then he lived in a
time when bereavement was a function of growing up. We lucky ones have
been insulated from pain and death except as elements in entertainment. The
news is all about the deaths of others and our easy endurance of them, our
boredom even (enough of Rwanda, for instance), and shows how cleverly
(because without intention) the media batten on our dreads and serve them
back to us so prettily, so painlessly garnished, that we are schooled and
schmoozed into immunity to, hence pleasure in, the very things that once
were part of every man's cruel expectation: war, pain, loss.

   Dr Johnson's mot, re one Dr Dodd (wasn't it?), that knowing you're going
to be hanged in a fortnight 'concentrates a man's mind wonderfully' is one of
those straight-camp, slick pseudo-aristocratico-dandyesque remarks that
have no observed content at all. I have no idea of what it would be like to be
in the condemned cell, but then, in some sense (ah there's the key that unlocks
it!), that's where we are, and I don't think it leads to concentration at all;

anything but. At the time I remember thinking of Byron's remark, when he heard of the death of Allegra, his five-year-old daughter by Claire Clairmont: 'I shall go to her but she shall not return to me.' It sounds real Byron, i.e. slightly phony, and markedly egotistic: her loss is of his company, but he'll join her later; now go to sleep. 'It's God's will', he even had the nerve to say. In fact, as you know, Byron had shipped Allegra off to the nuns and saw virtually nothing of her during her brief, hushed life.

I thought, after Sarah died, that I would lose interest in petty things and even that I should cease to care if I lost at Scrabble or tennis or when critics spoke scathingly of me (or even if they spoke well). Montaigne might smile; and so should you who probably have whiter teeth. Have you ever been to his ancestral place? I think you told me you had. You understand why that part of the world (he was in the Gironde, adjacent to our department, the Dordogne) is good for writing. *Nihil humanum* is wholly alien maybe, but most of humanity is fortunately distant.

I am not conscious of having known many people who killed people, though I suppose we sit in the subway with them and in restaurants and where all else, all the time. Last week I was asked to appear, or rather be heard, on a cultural radio programme on the BBC, which still does that kind of thing, albeit with an unfunded (and unpaying) sigh. There used to be a station called The Third Programme, which was once unabashedly – and bashedly sometimes, with the satires of Hilda Tablet and all that forties/fifties stuff – high falutin'. It now chooses to falute only in the middle register, under the rubric of Radio Three, which is allegedly less off-putting. I did a translation of Petronius's *Satyrica* about nine years ago; the cover drawing is the last thing Sarah did, the night before she died, and is as carefully, as cleverly done as anything, everything she did. Now it's out in paperback and my small, brave, penniless publishers, run by an excellent, irreplaceable man you may have heard of, Michael Schmidt, a Mexican already, poet and prof, fixed for me to publicise it on this arcane programme. Of course in the nature of modern media, they had to convene a cross-sectional covey of folk, some old (F.R.), some young (a poet called Kerr, I think, pronounced cur), a critic (movie critic/expert on E.A. Poe) and a middle-aged, close-shaved youngishster called Ronan Bennett, who is probably more famous than I am, because he writes about violence and Irish things like that, but of whom I had not heard.

His primacy was established by his taking pole position while the first chapter of his work-in-progress was read by an actor called Corin Redgrave, one of those quasi-blue-blooded Redgraves. I sat next to the author, my head lowered as if in respect, as the famous man read the text in that over-emphatic way that actors have when the prose cannot be suffered to speak for itself. Stories should not, I have found, be read by actors, since they always intrude syncopated rhythms into their reading and too-heavy emphasis into the dialogue. The subject was a meeting between a man and a woman of a certain age, whose character, such as it was, I realised to be based on Julie Christie. He called her Miriam Gaynor. I remembered Mitzi, but who else did? On and on and then on and on it went, with never an amusing line or witty phrase for twenty minutes (a synonym, in this case, for forever) after which there was a non-denominational silence. The author did not sigh, and he did not smile. I smiled sideways, but did not sigh and – trying to say something amiable – came out with 'What did you think?' Not all that amiable, but not ill-intentioned; I swear. He seemed very happy with the performance, his and the over-actor's.

Of course there was almost no time for Petronius: the extract that I read, not badly – a somewhat standard ancient anecdote about a paedophile tutor and how he bribes his charge to let him have his way – was not in the final cut, whereas the whole of Mr Bennett's verbosity was delivered intact. Serves me right for playing fair, or playing at all. Never again, said I to myself, again (better *The Kupcinet Show*, of which I have a memorial mug on my desk, charged with pencils). That was almost that and who cares? But I mentioned to a culturally-savvy friend of mine, with Intelligence connections, as well as high intelligence, that I had been on the show with Ronan Bennett; had he ever read him? 'Isn't he a murderer?' he said. I thought not; he had seemed a working pro with a penchant for drama/doc on terroristic topoi, and a muted Belfast accent but . . . murderer? I Googled the guy and there it was, as if some kind of academic distinction: he had been convicted of murdering a police inspector, while still a schoolboy. The conviction was, however, overturned on appeal. He then came to live in London, was accused of conspiracy to cause explosions, spent 16 months in jail on remand, defended himself, and others, in court and was acquitted, went to UCL, got a first-class degree in history and then a PhD (I think) and then became the award-winning author. What a thriller-style life some people have, and, dear God, what boring first chapters they can still write!

Tout à toi,
Freddie

Dear Freddie,

Your recent radio adventure with boring and impossible co-panelists reminds me that, some years ago, I appeared on a television panel in San Diego, on the subject of government and the arts, with, among others, Edward Albee, one of the great (sigh) figures of the American stage. Albee is a man who begins with deep agitation and shifts quickly into full rage from there; he is quite as dark and disagreeable in temperament and manner as his plays (yet another case of imperfection of the life and work both). As I recall, Albee began the discussion by saying that, until such time as every American congressman had a thorough education in aesthetics, the country was in danger of lapsing into fascism. Since there has never been a congressman – or a professor of philosophy, for that matter – with a thorough aesthetic education, this seemed a shaky point on which to begin the proceedings. Panels have ever since not been my notion of a good time, and I have done my best to avoid them.

I do, though, regularly flog – I love that word, "flog," suggesting as it does beating a dead horse – new books of mine on radio and television shows and in bookstores. Not that I get all that much pleasure from it, but it is now in America considered de rigueur to do so. My old view was Edmund Wilson's: I write the books, you, dear publisher, sell the poor things. (Wilson wouldn't sign books for strangers, do interviews, or anything else by way of promotion.) But this is no longer good form. Or even quite possible. When in the early 1970s I reported to Georges Borchardt, my agent, that I didn't want to promote my first book, which was on the tender subject of divorce in America, he instructed me – correctly, I fear – that I really had no choice: "The publisher will say [imagine please a slight French accent here] recalcitrant author – screw him!" I suppose I ought to consider myself lucky that I am considered mildly promotable; a great many fellow American scribblers, I'm told, are mad about the idea of going on radio and television shows but, like unattractive nymphomaniacs on Saturday night, they sit at home with no askers.

I have a number of literary projects on my desk at the moment, but have decided to take time out to do a take-down of a youngish journalist, a *New Yorker* writer, named Malcolm Gladwell, whose books on semi-social-scientific subjects (their titles are *Blink*, *Tipping Point* and *Outliers*) rest for long periods atop the *New York Times* bestseller lists. Gladwell is a Village Explainer: with the aid of second-line academic psychologists he'll tell you why certain shoes come back into style or how people decide to hire tall CEOs or why Korean airline pilots had a strong propensity for crashing their planes.

None of it is quite convincing; all of it flattens out the world, robbing it of its rich complexity. Gladwell himself is a terrific self-starter; he is said to give talks to corporations for as much as $40,000 a whack (that's a pretty good whack, I'd say). He is youngish, wiry, bi-racial with an Afro hairdo in such dishabille that he looks as if, instead of combing his hair, he chose to put his thumb into a live electric socket. He looks like the old figure who emerges from the Jack-in-the-Box. Given his penchant for setting himself up as an original thinker, someone who claims to see through received opinions, I think of him as Jack-out-of-the-Box. (That "out of the box" cliché really must go, and perhaps my giving this little piece the title Jack-out-of-the-Box will give it a small shove on its way out the door.)

I shall have to read Gladwell's three books (which, taken together, run to some 900 stylistically un-interesting pages) and take perhaps four or five days to set up my howitzers and sharpen my epees and other foils. For this I shall get a fee of (perhaps) $3,500 and a bit of attention from the small though feckless world of people who care about such things. Why, perhaps not you but I certainly ask, bother? Because I feel this fellow's success is, if explicable, unjustified; that he needs to be apprehended. But why me? (I asked a younger friend, a former student, to take on the job, but he chose not to do so.) Who appointed me sheriff, that old unmasked rider, astride his broken-down white horse – Rocinante, to the road again – who brings literary justice wherever he goes? I have no clear or firm answer, but pose the question to you, who, I do believe, suffers from the same illness, the Literary Sheriff Syndrome, let's call it.

Best, Joe

Dear Joe,

I call publications such as *Outliers* skipping-rope books: they're meant to give you a little gentle mental exercise, or the illusion of having had a mental work-out, but raise no kind of a sweat. You skip all right, because every other word is quite sufficient. You think you're learning something because that kind of text almost always has diagrams to make it look academic. The marketing persons always bulk them up fatter than they need to be, rendering their prosthetic prose as void of meaning or flavour as those jelly-fishy mammary inserts which raise a girl's alimony prospects along with men's amorous propensities (Dr Johnson again, re Garrick's chorenes, I think).

Why you and I are so easily lured into saddling up and riding out against this kind of confectionery, who knows? I suppose part of one's sense of outrage has to be envy that such books sell so copiously and are so urgently enjoined upon the public, but there has to be (say it IS so, Joe) some sense of outrage at the speed with which the bogus is allowed to pass as the kind of thing we should be writing, or wish we could, an we had the wit. Why else rail against the triumph of the specious pretty well everywhere? The false readings of merit are even more infuriating when they are certified by Famous Name acclaim (in so-called reviews) as well as by the irrefutable votes, and cash, of the buying public. What sells sells and there abides a tautology that brooks no denial, however maddening; but when it comes to, oh, David Hockney being a great artist, when I think he is a lousy, perfunctory draughtsman whose subjects all get to belong to the same skimpy club, or Schlink's *The Reader* being an important or even 'brave' book or a movie that is anything but framed-up witlessness, or even the idea that Clint Eastwood is a director of the smallest interest, well, either one tries to tell SOMEONE why the whole Gadarene fraternity is wrong, wrong, wrong or one might as well go galloping over the precipice into the sandpit with them.

I heard Ron Howard – just the kind of name which it would be impossible to allocate to a fictional character in whom one was going to invest weeks of inventive attention – being pseudo-modest about his 'movie' about Nixon and Frost, of which, of course, Frost is the hero and Dick the nailed villain, who finally gets sincerely tricked into coughing up a ratings-rated confession. Frost is thus able to retrieve his career as the syndicated conscience of the TV world, quizzing people who have actually done something, perhaps even something worth doing, from the stance of a man with perfect moral pitch, even though he has never done anything except cultivate his own fame and, God knows, fortune. I have never heard him saying anything spontaneously clever or witty and when, very infrequently and long ago, he did say something – a little 'satirical' number – which was mildly (and, once, VERY) funny, well, I assumed, rightly or wrongly, that he had rented or cadged or plagiarised it from some sad little scribe. The v. funny occasion was a parody of an ancient Egyptian weather forecast in which, of course, frogs coming in from the south were only one of the plagues that were blowing in. Funnier in his nasally-enhanced performance.

I must be the only person with the smallest claim to fame who has never met him, who is now high in the ivy above my head in the social register (Sir, even). I do know a good story about him though, and if not now, then when? Viz: In the early 60s, when *Beyond the Fringe* raised Jonathan Miller and Dudley Moore and Peter Cook and Alan Bennett (a typical English national treasure, an extremely competent deviser of his own advancement, social and otherwise, who carefully preserves the lineaments of the local lower-middle-class provinciality which he seems to have done everything possible to leave behind, except that his Yorkshire-flavoured accent never fails to remind you of what kind of pudding he originally was) to the forefront of the smart set, they were all in New York doing the show. On the weekend they had a place somewhere, I think, on Long Island where my quondam agent, Judy Scott-Fox, a lady of upper-classy vowels and provenance, was employed as den-matron. One such weekend, Frost self-invited himself to drop in on the quartet. He too was a ranking satirist on London TV and hence felt he had passe-partout status. They spent the morning by the pool, in which Frosty (suitably named for a sugary Kellogg flake) did not choose to immerse himself. Finally Judy announced lunch indoors, to which they all repaired except for David who took the opportunity to immerse himself, *en solitaire*, in the empty pool for a reason which was understandable if embarrassing (for him): he had been so busy on the ladder to fame that he had never learnt to swim. He made a few tentative passes in the shallow end and, perhaps managing, just, to achieve lift-off, proceeded to the place where shallow tilted at an abrupt angle into depth . . .

One of the famous quartet called to him to come to lunch, but he did not respond. Inside the open-windowed room, Judy told me, they heard gurgling and choking noises and incoherent cries from poolside. Peter Cook, not a known Samaritan, wandered out and saw Frost in the deep end, spluttering and splashing and reaching with helpless feet for the bottom that wasn't there. Cook stood poolside, with a facsimile of a concerned frown on his unconcerned face, as Frost flailed and wallowed and eventually reached somewhere near the edge. His water-clogged voice box managed to utter something like 'Help', or even, the very British, 'Give us a hand' and, one can safely assume, Cook did the least he could to assist his gasping fellow satirist from the deep. At the lunch table, when Frost had disposed of the water in his lungs and regained his customary vocal fluency, he said, with cheerful reproach, 'Why didn't you help me, Peter, when you saw me going down for the third bloody time?' Cook said, 'I thought you were taking a satirical swipe at drowning'. Genius and bastard: common combo.

Howard's so-called movie not only makes a hero of Frost (whereas, of course, it would be more 'creative' to reappraise Nixon, not all of whose policies were as contemptible or pointless as certain others' enterprises), but also of Frost's chum, one John Birt, whose 1990s hegemony of the BBC brought that once great, if stuffy, corporation to the state in which it has languished ever since, a vast bureaucratised enterprise, more chiefs than Indians. Birt became its gawdfather and centralised the enterprise in such a way that all editorial decisions were made either by him and his apparatchicks (many of the top und middle decision-makers are now women). Birt dismantled the petty fiefdoms that procured programme variety and instituted a centralised, committee-ridden regime that still persists. Birt himself became an adviser to Tony Blair and a Lord already, although a man who makes Frost seem like an intellectual. Oil and water blend superbly in their instance.

Boats against the current are the only kind I should choose to embark on; the going's tough, but your fellow passengers are better company than you will ever find going with the flow. One more thing? Why not? The Roman Catholic magazine, the *Tablet*, featured on its front cover this week/month the news that Harold Pinter was fellow-travelling towards Rome before he was assumed to preside over the great theatre in the sky. I recall Dorothy Parker's review of *Winnie the Pooh* (a classic *quand même*): 'Common Reader frowed up.'

Tout à toi,
Freddie

Dear Freddie,

All of what you say calls to mind a phrase I came upon in rereading Santayana's *The Last Puritan* a few weeks ago. In the novel, Santayana writes of certain Bostonians having "a second-class standard of firstness." The novel was published in 1935; today we operate under a third-, or maybe fourth-class standard of firstness. So much that is crappy is considered astonishing stuff, so many new geniuses proudly and regularly declared by idiots, so many rainy days in the old Republic of Letters.

In movie-making you mention Ron Howard and Clint Eastwood, who are able to turn out a few watchable flicks, but the merely watchable, next to all the utterly unwatchable that is also, as they say, grossing nicely, suddenly comes to seem subtle, elegant, magnifico. In literature, ask any happy reviewer to name the three greatest living American writers and he is very likely to say John Updike, Toni Morrison and Philip Roth. Updike gives a lyrical spin to fancy fornication, Morrison vastly and repetitively over-dramatizes the sad race question in America, Roth is the solipsist par excellence, who, now in his mid-seventies, isn't too crazy about the idea that he just might die and that, even worse news, his sexual powers (not to speak of his attractiveness) seem on the wane (and not John, either, Pilgrim). They are nonetheless great, classical, all of them if not now then surely soon to be in the hallowed Library of America. Ah, if this be the music of literature, Pléiade.

How did standards slip so? I suspect that the slippage is in good part owing to the end of High Culture, or at least the end of reverence for it, which carried with it a heavy freight of seriousness. You remember High Culture, I'm sure: Joyce and Proust, Kafka and Valéry, Matisse and Cézanne, Schoenberg and Ravel, and all that gang. A very exclusive club, the High Culture, membership limited, exceedingly difficult to get into. No guests allowed. Middlebrows and other tradesmen enter at rear. People, I gather, couldn't stand the exclusivity of it – it went too abrasively against the spirit of the age. So they opened up lots of culture clubs of their own, admitting the David Hockneys and Andy Warhols and John Ashberys, the Seamus Heaneys and Don DeLillos and John Williamses. Pop, Op, Bop, Hippity-Hop, it's all one swell cassoulet – make that kugel – all given equal time and treatment in the Arts and Leisure Section of the *New York Times*. Hey, there's room for everybody, and let's not hear any of that high standards bullshit, either.

As I tap this out, I hear the squish of sour grapes. Not that I would myself have ever qualified for the High Culture Club. I never aspired to it, nor was ever likely to be in even distant contention for membership. But I nonetheless much liked the idea of the Club being there. It gave one something to shoot for; better still, it put lots of fifth-rate artists in their proper place.

But it's done for. Nobody wants to hear about it. A few older duffers – present company included – remember the grandeur of it all. I prefer to think that this isn't the plaint of an old duffer merely. To return to the even older duffer, that now-dead duffer Santayana, he also says, in one of his letters, that older people decry the current state of the world, see it rapidly going to hell, for the sad but simple reason that they cannot imagine how it can be any good when they soon shall not be a part of it. Not infrequently these days, when more junk culture is treated as great art, leaving a residue of depression, after the initial disgust fades away, I find myself saying to my wife, "You know, kiddo, I think we may be departing the planet just in time."

Not that I'm ready to leave just yet. I'm still curious to see how it all plays out, even if my seat is well on the sidelines, a glass of wine in my hand, an unsphinxish grin on my increasingly mottled face.

Best, Joe

Dear Joe,

Oh sure, sour grapes are on every writer's sideboard, even those whose cups are running over. In the 1960s, Nabokov composed the Enoch Soamesish anecdote about time-travelling to the 23rd century and going into a library (never mind the improbability of such an edifice being anything but virtual) and asking the librarian which novelists of the 20th century were still being read. You know the story? Then, like everyone over a certain age, I'll go on with it: the librarian replies that only two from that distant epoch still count for anything: Vladimir Nabokov and – I forget what name V.N. chose – Philip Robinson, say. V.N. is both gratified and consumed with jealous curiosity: who is this Robinson and how come he can be mentioned in the same breath as *ipsissimus* Volodya?

When I was young, it seemed enough to be any kind of a recognised, ranking cock. The dream of joining the pantheon, the Pléiade, the Parnassians, supplied a common, almost unreachable goal to those growing up in lonely, ill-favoured, suburban locations. Imagine membership in an exclusive club where the Secretary-General of Literature welcomed Jew and Gentile alike as long as they had manifest genius! All the paradigmatic guys (no dolls, note) that you mention were Europeans who transcended class and racial barriers and were elevated into exile-heaven (Kafka, Schoenberg, Heine, even Joyce were more or less *apatrides*). Neither sales nor sexy reputation got you past the gate. Virginia Woolf wondered with cruel pity what it could be like to be obliged to write, as Willie Maugham did, for money. Literature, like academic life, was a vocation, not a trade. Hence British critics dismissed Anthony Trollope from the regiment of artists after he had made the unwisely frank confession, in his autobiography, that he always wrote so many words a day, and stopped when he had done his, yes, stint. Stint has a root meaning – my etymological dictionary has just reminded me – of 'cease or cause to cease', although it's come to mean a routine quota of work, hasn't it? That's why real artists have to write without it, even if it means that they turn into Thomas Wolfe and can never go home again; in his case, one suspects, because he couldn't get through the door.

Wolfe supplies a segue into the company of a revered figure to whom too many aspiring genii bent the knee, while others, *encore pires*, seek to emulate him: I refer (you guessed) to Maxwell Perkins and his epigoni in the publishing trade. It may be that Perkins provided a fertilising influence but he was a combination of Maecenas – no necessarily untainted predecessor – and today's marketing director, the latter a being divested of all affectations of literary perfect pitch, but decisive when it comes to even the fanciest publishing house accepting a new book from neophyte or gerousiac. The Great Editor has degenerated into the pusher's lab-hop (English Public School jargon for laboratory assistant) in the dispensary of literary narcotics, pumping and palping prose into a form that can masquerade as Important, Prize-Winning, Indispensable, boneless. The bestseller list has melted the snows of Aunt Anne and turned the summit of Parnassus to slush. Where Trillings trilled, the sound of the Oprah is heard loud and high.

Listening to that American Poet declaiming her schoolgirl verses at Obama's inauguration, you realised that only High Platitude can now be served to the mass audience whose (embarrassed, I hope) applause greeted the coronation of the cliché. To think that that cracker motto Occasional Poem was the last sorry descendant of paid-by-the-line Pindar, whose complicated allusiveness may have amused those smart-aleko Greeks in the Olympic executive seats but would have left modern America, never mind England (who does?), from top (wherever that is) to bottom wondering what the HELL that was all about.

So that is what happened to all yesterday's ambitions, which were vulgarly spelt out, for Nobel motives, in hormone-fattened *Humboldt's Gift*, where the Delmore Schwartz figure stands for old-style highbrowism (he wasn't THAT hot, if 'In Dreams Begin Responsibilities' is a fair instance of his genius) and the narrator – forget his name – is the coming man, Mr Love Life with his Big Biggie, even if you don't believe a word of it, even when a brand new Merc gets the baseball-bat treatment. What Updike, Roth, Bellow, Mailer and who all else of Our Betters have in common, apart from being Great Writers at the Peak of their Powers, is that not one has created a female character whose name (as against their tits, against which I have nothing) can be remembered. Anna Karenina? Forget her. The blokeishness (as the Brits say) of modern fiction is evidence of its relentless male-orderliness. The want of the female spirit, the wit, the nerve, the anti-ness of the right kind of woman, the lure and the elusiveness of the sexual Other, that's all been lost in an amalgamation of motives and appetites, the commodification, comrades, of what we want and who we are.

D.H. Lawrence had a great phrase (quite a few actually) about a certain kind of work 'wetting on the flame'. I daresay I've done some pissy work; maybe you have; but some people don't even know what could possibly be wrong with doing it; failure to know that clichés also kill is only the most common symptom of the aesthetic of give-'em-what-they-want. Roth did a clutch of good recentish novels, starting with *American Pastoral*, but nowa-days he doesn't seem to know, or care, when he is turning out product. Oddly enough, the movies they have made of his stuff make manifest what's wrong with his genius, the confected, monotonous heartlessness of its invention; it may be perverse, but polymorphous? Nah.

Tout à toi,
Freddie

Dear Freddie,
To add to one point in your previous e-mail, for Mailer, Updike, Roth & co., sex is often the central point in their fiction: bonking is what gives their scrib-bling its drama, what the old-style English department boys and girls would call its "tension" and, let us not forget, its "resonance." This same concern with the great bonk is also what makes them so boring and – yes, even Roth – humorless. I happen to believe that it will eventually manage to sink any further interest in their scribblings. My own view of sex, one Dr. Freud would consider pure subterfuge, is that it can be a superior indoor sport, made all the more superior when the element of love is admixed. (Shake gently and serve at room temperature.) Now that, for better and for worse, sex has been made more easily obtainable than when these novelists were coming of age, their obsession with it is likely to seem dopey at best, though more likely over-heated in an idiotic way. At least I hope it will soon so seem. I would also agree with you that Mailer, Roth, Updike and Bellow have not among them created a single memorable female character. Women, for them, are for bonking, not for being memorable.

Saul Bellow, being older than Mailer, Updike, Roth & co., did not, at least in his fiction, allow sex to occupy center-stage. He was of the generation that thought it distasteful, to have, as in the swell Henry Reed poem, 'Naming of Parts'. He preferred sententiousness over sex: lots of talk about the soul and higher things, none of which he came close to realizing in his own complexly ragged life. In that life he was immensely flirtatious. When I was in his company, if an even mildly attractive woman was nearby, he was gone: the pure type of the notorious heterosexual. I'm not sure that sex itself interested him all that much; as a narcissist, what seemed to be of interest was whether his charm worked on women, whether they found him attractive. In James Atlas's biography of Bellow, which you reviewed with witty severity in the *Los Angeles Times Book Review* of sainted memory, a woman who slept with Bellow, a poet named (as I recall) Sandra Hochman, told Señor Atlas that he,

S. Bellow, didn't seem to know "a clitoris from a kneecap." Put that fairly high on the little list of things one would prefer not to have said about one.

Barbara and I have been in northern California since Friday afternoon. We spent the weekend at our son Mark's recently acquired and vastly refurbished house in a town called Forestville; the house is an old fishing lodge over-looking the Russian River, and has animal heads on some of its walls and bear-skin and antelope-hide rugs in its bar room. What my son's great-grandfather, Raphael Epstein, formerly of Bialystok, a man who took a serious interest in Hebrew education in the city of Montreal where he lived out his years, would have made of it all is not easily fathomed, though blank bloody fucking astonishment is my first guess. Yesterday, Sunday afternoon, Mark drove us to Stanford, presenting us first with two bottles of (as near as I, with my leather palate, can judge) excellent Cabernet Sauvignon from his one-acre vineyard. I, usually from the school of non-huggers, hugged him and reminded him that he is the best of all sons.

We have been put up, quite comfortably, at the Stanford Faculty Club, where we have a decent-size bedroom and sitting room, with a kitchenette, and nothing academic-shabby about the premises generally. (You must know the old Sydney Smith story about his noting two women in Glasgow, yelling at each other from the windows of their respective apartments across a narrow mews. "They'll never reach agreement," Sydney S. said, "for they are arguing from different premises.") We brought in food from a nearby student restaurant and ate it while watching the Australian Open on a large television set.

I don't know if you have ever visited the Stanford campus, but it is very beautiful, with lots of new world Spanish architecture. I should be prepared to say of it, as Bishop Heber said of Ceylon, that here "only man is vile." In fact, with apologies to the good bishop, the students we have encountered all seem well mannered and winningly cheerful – glad, perhaps, to be in such a setting. Half of them are Asians, mostly Chinese. On the snob scale, Stanford stands proudly with Harvard, Yale and Princeton. So all these kids are pleased to be in this handsome setting, knowing that in future years they can begin lots of sentences, "When I was at Stanford . . ." Mark went there, but is too accomplished to mention it in public.

The professors, like American professors everywhere, look much the same. I have a little problem here. Having worked around academics for thirty years, I consider them all – at least in the humanities and social sciences – guilty until proven innocent. You may recall my writing to you earlier about

Umberto Eco's theory of death: according to this theory, the older one gets the more groups one writes off as idiots (in my case the list now includes: the ignorant rich, academics, psychotherapists, poets, actors, politicians) until in the end there is no-one whom one respects except oneself, and then one dies. I am, not all that slowly, getting there, I fear.

Keep the faith.

Best, Joe

Dear Joe,

Before you become anything so dry as a source, may I take time out to correct your having once assumed, in a non-canonical communication, that my father was an 'engineer'? *Tout au contraire*, he was mechanically a gentleman to his clean fingertips. He actually read Greats at Oxford, though I am not sure how much reading he really did: his 'major', as you might say, was the tango. He did, however, give his Oxford texts to me, with the difficult words written in over the top (do not imagine your correspondent incapable of such things). These texts are, in today's editions, clothed all in blue, of the Oxford hue, but were then orange, and not too stiffly boarded; oddly enough they were much the same shade as the early editions of Victor Gollancz's Left Book Club. Victor – for whom Beetle worked for what seemed in those days quite a long time (nine months) – was an Oxonian Christian Jew Communist Property Owner publisher of genius; a pacifist who shouted at his employees (except Beetle) and stamped his feet, while sitting down, in fury. Although capable of wishing a host of pro-Communist tracts and pseudo-documentary stuff on the *bien-pensant* world, he did bring out George Orwell's *Road to Wigan Pier* and other work, including (I think) his far from clever novels, but he (V.G.) then turned down *Animal Farm*, on the v. British grounds that 1944 was not quite the time to dish it to the Stalinists, pigs as they might be, because they were doing God's work over there on the Eastern Front. He lost Orwell and a fortune, what with *1984* and the promotion of the man who used to be known, at the BBC, as 'Gloomy George' (my source being my friend Michael Ayrton, the sculptor and polymath who died of undiagnosed diabetes in 1975), to the Secular Sainthood by Christopher Hitchens, whose itchens include a play for the title of G.O. II as well as Gore's dolphin.

Victor also published Koestler and who all else and was A Good Thing, although not right through maybe. He called Beetle 'Sheba', as in the Queen thereof, which marks him as a man who could spot beauty when it hit him in the eye and intelligence when deployed for his benefit. He and his long-suffering wife Ruth took us out to dinner when I was doing the Cambridge University Footlights show in London in the summer of 1954. He was impelled to the Phoenix Theatre, where I was performing the pseudo-sophisticated skits and songs which, in those days, were parcelled under the theatrical rubric 'Intimate Revue' (implying a certain raciness). I wrote and performed quite a bit, my greatest applause coming for a number I wrote about Evelyn Waugh and Graham Greene. 'Religion is our pigeon' and similar bold brassinesses decorated the text, which included a dialogue about publishers . . . 'We were nearly subjected to rape/ By the man from Jonathan Cape . . ./ Even Routledge and Kegan pall' (Paul being the last name so wittily punned upon), etc., culminating in: G.G.: 'Victor Gollancz?' E.W.: 'No thanks.' Hence V.G.'s presence: some people, I am told, will do anything to be pilloried.

On the way to dinner, V.G. asked what I was going to do, as they say. I replied that I was going to be a writer. He thought this a very poor idea and did NOT ask to see a sample of my work either soonest or at any other time. At dinner, we learned, with small embarrassment, which has grown over the years, that that evening was the Gollanczes' wedding anniversary. How pleased his wife was to be at table with a garrulously precocious young man and a beautiful woman off from whom V.G. kept his hands only because he was talking with them! (See under Anti-Semitism, its persistence even among those who should know better.) When I did finish my first novel, I sent it to V.G.'s nephew who was then being groomed as his heir. Hilary Rubinstein, who later became my agent, and a friend of a kind, was in pole position because he had brought his friend Kingsley Amis's first novel to his uncle's house, but did no such service to me. The bum's rush wasn't fast enough for him (fortunately, *Obbligato* was very soon acquired by Macmillan, the Right people's publisher). Far be it from me to allege that Hilary was somewhat jealous of the way that Beetle used to rush up to Cambridge to see me at the weekend, but not all that far, to tell the truth. In the end, *quand même*, V.G. neglected to imitate Julius Caesar and bequeath his empire to his nephew, who then went sideways into repping.

My father was no keener that I become a writer than V.G. had been. Years later, I met a semi-namesake Chaim Raphael, a civil servant of quality, whom my father took to lunch with me, probably during my last Cambridge year, in the hope that Chaim would talk me out of a lit. career. In the event, Chaim talked so much about himself and his books (he wrote detective stories under the muy goyische name of Jocelyn Davey) that he omitted to deter me. In any case, as you know, all deterrence from unwise courses is a waste of time: 'Eve, put that apple down, NOW' – but did she? Curious that fathers are so wise about sons, if they are, and not all that smart for themselves! Not curious at all, you're right: anyone who gives his fortune for care and growth to a guy called Madoff, who Ben Jonson could have told them was destined to make off with it, well, call those people smart? I hear that Steven Spielberg was among his victims as were a number of other prime accumulators in the show business. I have a horrible feeling that only David Geffen (tell me you've never heard of him) was too smart not to read the writing on the Wall St. (It doesn't quite work, does it, but I cued it with 'the show business' and, as the suckers will tell you, you can't win 'em all.) My father never won ANY of them. He got some good tips in the days when insider trading was what trading was but never bought enough and always sold too soon. The best tip he ever had was for an Australian share called Hampton Gold Mines (the joke gets better if you recall that Hampton, in old English slang, was a *nom de gare* for *membrum virile*). He bought not many at pennies and sold at as many pounds, but 'forgot' to tell me about the share at all and then watched it go thrice as high as when he bailed out. I suppose fathers too can suffer from sibling rivalry.

Cedric would have been the happiest, and probably the most generous, playboy alive if his rich uncle, Jessel, had dumped a few million on him. As it was, he worked all his life for Shell, many of the years being made miserable by petty office politics (and anti-Semitism in New York in the 1930s, when his boss, called Kittinger, was said to be a member of the German-American Bund). I never knew him, my father I mean, although he did play patient bridge and golf with me. He never shouted in his life and never used a fouler word than 'bugger', quietly. He and I had icy 'discussions' which left my mother in tears of frustration at the degree of scorn and rage that we exchanged. He wasn't as clever as I was, I think, and it made him proud in public (Cambridge scholar) and threatened in himself. People say I am beginning to look like him, but I don't see it. At least I don't look like V.G.

Tout à toi,
Freddie

Dear Freddie,

Please to forgive my mistake about your father's profession. Somehow I (wrongly) assumed that a man who worked for Shell would naturally be a petroleum engineer. I assumed an engineering career even more in your father's case for in those good/bad old days not many Jews worked for large corporations in other than scientific jobs. Your father's unhappiness at Shell is perhaps owing to his ignoring the first tenet of Jewish wisdom, often expressed by my father: to wit (if not too wittily), "Only a schmuck works for somebody else." Something – a lot, actually – to it. The point is, of course, that it is a very great torture to have your destiny in the hands of idiots, bullies, anti-Semites and peckerheads. My father worked for others until 1946 – he often referred to himself in these jobs as "a flunky" – when he was thirty-eight and went into business for himself with a partner, whom he later bought out. He was able to say, as neither of us ever shall, "Either you buy me out or I shall buy you out, but by next Tuesday one of us isn't going to be here." This is usually said, not at all by the way, by the man who, having more money, also has the whip hand.

I was much interested in your saying, "I never knew him, my father . . ." I think our parents' generation did not go in for intimacy, perhaps especially with their children. During my adolescence I worked with my father in the summer months (I was his flunky), and driving him across the Midwest and sleeping in the same room in less than first-class hotels in Des Moines, Minneapolis and Columbus, he did most of the talking, and it was almost exclusively about business, a subject on which he homilized to me with great enthusiastic repetitiousness: "You want to keep a low overhead," he would say. "You always want to put something away for a rainy day," he would say. "You make your money not by selling but by buying right," he would say. Sometimes he would analyze, not very penetratingly, his customers, some of whom had such exotic names as Jockey Fisher or Sammy Tepper (isn't he a character in Dickens?). He never suggested any line of work I might go into. I knew I could not be happy working with him at his business, for he used up all the available oxygen there. He did say, also time and again, that, in the realm of work, I must find something that I truly loved doing, for if I didn't life would be hell. (Damn sound advice, this, no?) But we never talked about either of our dreams or aspirations, or about my mother or younger brother or members of our extended family. And, somehow, I didn't mind – I never felt he was letting me down by not telling me how he thought the world worked outside of business. And he thereby left me a great deal of time for my own preposterous daydreams.

Our parents were, I think, the last generation to live outside the modern spirit of psychology. People to them were good or bad, decent or not, without much time spent investigating motives or rocky childhoods. The idea of therapy, and all the assumptions behind it, was alien to them. When my mother was discovered to have cancer, which she read, correctly, as likely to be terminal, it sent her into hitherto unfamiliar depression. Death by cancer – not a bad reason for depression, I'd say. I recall mentioning my mother's depression to an acquaintance, who told me that there are excellent "support groups" for people with terminal diseases. I thought that, were I to suggest her attending such a group, my mother would say to me, "Let me get this straight. You think that my going into a room and telling all my problems to strangers will make me feel better. I see I seem to have raised an idiot for a son."

Blasphemous though it may seem in the spirit of the times, I rather admire this holding back on intimacy and distrusting the psychological on the part our parents, or at least my own parents. The result of it was to make them independent, unsniveling, you should pardon the expression, "adult."

I much like your account of Victor Gollancz. Publishers have been some of the great comic figures of the past century. I met George Weidenfeld only once, but he seemed to me born to be a minor grotesque comic figure in several English novels. In America we had Alfred Knopf, a great wine snob (he once told his brother that he couldn't be expected to judge an expensive wine the latter had bought because of the poor quality of the glasses his brother served it in); Roger Straus, of Farrar Straus, a scion of the Guggenheim family, who dressed like a gangster in thickly striped bespoke suits and single-handedly made the reputation of Susan Sontag by promoting her around the world and writing angry letters to people who did not review her admiringly; and many more. I didn't know that Gollancz had turned down *Animal Farm*. Someone ought to write an essay on famous bumbling decisions in publishing, beginning perhaps with Gide rejecting Proust at Gallimard. The other day I read, in an obituary of the American editor Robert Giroux, of an editor at Doubleday who turned down *The Catcher in the Rye*, a novel that American children are now required to read at the baptismal fount or while under the cirumcisional blade. Victor Gollancz's rejection of *Animal Farm* deserves a prominent place in such an essay.

Your line about Routledge Kegan palling reminded me that Lord Berners, who liked to create frivolous riddles, devised the following: If clocks complained that they had no-one to talk to or keep them going, what publisher would they be most comfortable with? Answer: Chatto and Windus. On which forced note, Monsieur Freddie, I leave off, for I have lunch presently with a divorce lawyer who regales me with tales of amusingly rapacious behavior on the part of people who once claimed to love each other.

Best, Joe

Dear Joe,

I had better check whether it was indeed *Animal Farm* that led Orwell to leave
V.G. or whether (my apprehension revealed) *1984* provoked the rupture. It
don't matter much, though it would make a better story if it were *Animal
Farm* which is, arguably as they will say, his only work of art. No surprise that
it is, in general form and simplicity of text, a children's book, which offers the
spoonfuls in which the British like their medicine served. *Gulliver's Travels*
doesn't embarrass as *A Modest Proposal* does. It's an odd aspect of some of the
slang I use ('Nil Return' is another) that it is leaked from the servicemen I
overheard during the war or those who came to Cambridge after having done
what the British call 'National Service'. I was never at the rough end of those
sticky activities and have always been slightly, but only slightly, ashamed of
my good fortune.

'You've got two chances: a dog's chance and fuck-all chance' was another
phrase that Wordsworth never heard, I suspect, in the college we both went
to, though T.E. Hulme certainly may have used it after he had been sent down.
I have always liked his 'collected poems', which (all seven or eight of them) are
printed at the end of my aged (Routledge?) edition of his *Speculations*. He is
often depicted as a proto-fascist: as brave as he was right-wing, he died early,
in the trenches, or fresh out of them, as a result. 'In finesse of fiddles found
I ecstasy' is a line that sits tight in my balloon when fancier phrases are jetti-
soned. I can imagine that Bernard Madoff might care to make use of it on his
tombstone or cinder-vessel, but I doubt whether he has ever heard of T.E.H.
My favourite prosaic story about the latter is of his being 'caught short', as the
English say, on his way home from some binge. He stood in some square
pissing through the railings into the shrubbery when a policeman approached
and announced that he was going to take him in for 'committing a nuisance'
(*ah les bons Anglais!*). As Hulme finished streaming, he said, in his appropriate accent, 'I would have you know, officer, that I am a member of the
middle class'. The policeman touched the peak of his odd headgear and said,
'Beg your pardon, sir'.

I think (know?) Max Beerbohm called his first book *The Collected Works
of Max Beerbohm*, but he was comparable Max on this occasion. He went to
the same school I did but did not share the endemic Carthusian anti-
Semitism; when accused of the deicidic taint, he regretted he did not deserve
the honour. What a parodist, by the way! Which does hint at the mutability of
all our race, some of it; you can write dialogue, so can I, but – oh – George
Steiner . . .? The monologue is his only art form.

Fathers; yes. I mentioned that my mother gave me Kafka's letter to his pop for Christmas last time around. She has these moments of surprising (belated?) aptness. Poor Franz uses pretty well the same phrase you did about your father (I expect I was meant to spot the allusion, now I think about it) using up 'all the available oxygen'. Kafka's accusations are a lot less amiable than yours, but the more he beats on his robust papi the more sympathy you feel for the hard case and the more you wish that Franzi would pause a moment and imagine what kind of a figure he is cutting. Being a phthisicky kid, he was also sly enough to accuse pop of stifling his wife, F's long-suffering mama, and so became a sort of unmuscled defender of the mother he lacked the nerve to jump in the fantastic Freudian sense. I never had that feeling about my father, although I did more than somewhat envy his chassis-reverse when reaching the corner of the ballroom and I did wish that I could strike a golf ball with his regular accuracy.

I feared the days when he would, often while shaving in white silk (?) drawers, ask me if I had time for 'a word'; the last one would be his, but my dread was never of anything physical nor even of any harsh justice, it was rather of that tone of patient chiding, often over how I treated my mother (whose capacity for absorbing flattery and devotion has never been quantified). In fact, Irene was a source of pride to me, since she was young and beautiful and amusing and smart, but in my adolescence she was so jealous of my very chaste romances that it made her a moralist. Cedric echoed this zeal for propriety although (more probably because) when I was in my forties, I discovered that he was, in fact, the father of an illegitimate girl, born before he met my mother. Did he ever think that the urethral stricture from which he suffered tortures all his life was somehow the punishment for his youthful wantonness? I doubt it, but then again . . .

Perhaps his not-very-dirty secret was what made him tight-lipped and reticent. I once said that I envied him his courage (he endured pain with what the Brits used to call phlegm). He said, 'If you only knew . . .' What? WHAT? Time's up: I shall never quite know, but then guessing is my game. Do you know that cartoon of Max Beerbohm, showing Henry James in a hotel corridor, sniffing the shoes that have been put out for polishing overnight, and captioned (roughly speaking from memory), 'Mr Henry James seeking from what is outside the bedroom door to divine what is taking place within'. It must have been better said than that, but that was the (overlong) gist. H.J. is an odd addiction, which Graham Greene had to excess. I gagged on *The Princess Casamassima*, but H.J. did have the chess-player's capacity to take forever and then, damn him, make a masterly move. He called sex 'the great connection'. And never found out, despite Hugh Walpole offering him a helping hand, or whatever, what it felt like, at least with another.

I never knew Knopf, though I knew about the wine snobbery. There's a story about him asking some 'hooligans' to leave a restaurant because one of them was smoking a cigar and ruining Knopf's claret, isn't there? He offered to pay their bill if they'd go LIKE NOW! They did. Cowards. As for glasses, I like the story about Mr Gladstone who, after dinner in a country house, was heard to say, 'Very good port this; but why serve it in a sherry glass?' I met Weidenfeld (still active) only a couple of times, one of which you'll find described in *Ticks and Crosses*. The first time, when I was a v. young novelist, he invited me to dinner to meet Saul Bellow. Oddly enough, we lived in a basement flat (sans daylight) directly below George W. Since I was invited alone, I declined. Doubtless Beetle would have been welcome, had W. known of her, but I just refused; and was never asked again. I think that was before even *Henderson the Rain King* (what a shower that was!), at the time when I admired *The Victim*, though it was not as good as a book by that Jewish writer with three names (NOT Erle Stanley Gardner) in which his wife 'exposes herself', after a fall, to a villain who then pursues her and persecutes whatever-his-name-is. This writer also wrote movies, or some of some of them, and was not prolific, although to my taste. Can you do his name for me? It wasn't Stanley Edgar Hyman either, whose ill-regarded synthesis of the New Crits I found very informative when lagging behind the smart set. Maud Bodkin – the Lady with the Archetypes – and Kenneth Blackmur and Kenneth Burke (a lasting taste of mine) were among the specimens S.E.H. chose to fillet.

'What is good/ for Spottiswood/ is not/ so hot for us' was another of the lines that laid them in the aisles when I was a Catholic novelist. Self-quotation is the stepmother of the muses.

Tout à toi,
Freddie

Dear Freddie,

Unlike you, I did serve two years in the Army, while the draft, or conscription, was still in force, between the Korean War and the close of the Vietnam War. This makes me, I do believe, an actual cold warrior. I was an enlisted man; I would have had to serve an extra year if I went in as an officer. The army is well known to be one of those experiences that look better the further away in time one is from it. All that I can say for it is that it does take one outside one's social class – mine would have been squishy-middle, with pretensions toward culture – and drop you dab in the middle of the democratic slush pile. Which meant that I slept in large rooms with American Indians, black guys from Detroit, Appalachians who had had all their rotted-out teeth removed, and various rednecks. As you will have noticed, I survived. The good thing about those years is that they pulled me out of the marketplace. Had I not gone into the army, I might have lost my nerve and done something foolish, like go to law school, grow prosperous, and today would never have heard the name Frederic Raphael.

As for army slang, one of my favorites is "fuckin' the dog," meaning "to engage in a perfectly useless activity" (unless one is another dog), as in, "What're you young troopers doing here besides fuckin' the dog?" The army was impossible without profanity and tobacco. Many moons ago, I was asked by the *TLS* to review volume one of the *American Dictionary of Slang*, which, as I recall, went up to the letter G. No fewer than twelve pages were devoted to the great F-word. In the course of my review of this indelicate vol., I believe I set the *TLS* record for the frequent use of this word in a single piece. I quoted, for example, and the *TLS* printed, a sentence recalled from my army days that rhythmically ran: "The mother-fucking motherfucker mother-fucked me."

When I turned seventy I resolved to cease using profanity, so heavily was I availing myself of it, splitting infinitives and even single words (unfucking-believable) with it. I decided that it was unseemly in a man of my stately age to be cursing away so flagrantly. I've had a reasonable success in this resolution, slipping back only rarely, though in unmixed company (when alone, that is, in my own fiendish mind) I still let fly.

I thought the Max Beerbohm caption was simply, "Mr. Henry James learns about sex." But I have now looked up the drawing in S.N. Behrman's fine book *Max*, and there discover a drawing of James, in profile, down on one knee, staring with ferocious scrutiny at a pair of man's and a pair of woman's shoes outside a hotel-room door, with only the words "Henry James" below. Beerbohm, a writer with perfect tact, was right yet again: no caption is required. As for Beerbohm's Jewishness, he, though not Jewish, did something that neither you nor I have done: he married a Jewish woman, the actress Florence Kahn. Somebody, after all, has to keep the race going, even if Max B. produced no children.

Mischievous old Malcolm Muggeridge used to put it about – in the *New York Review* no less – that Max Beerbohm was Jewish and also homosexual. I suspect that Muggeridge claimed the latter because for a bit Max hung out with that *Yellow Book* crew. He was also great friends with Reggie Turner, who was counted among the *gayim*. (That term, invented by my friend Edward Shils, could so easily have been a Raphaelian coinage; not, you understand, that I wish to get you in trouble with the PCP, or political correctness police.) My own view is that the true dandy is too narcissistic to be much interested in sex; and Max was a dandy, the charmingest of all dandies, for my few shekels. He wasn't, I think, without interest in women, but neither was he a notorious heterosexual, feeling, like the rest of us brutes, at least in more brutish days, he had to bonk every passing skirt.

The same – though non-Muggeridgean – forces are at work at turning Henry James into a certified homosexual. The academics won't rest until the old boy is rendered fully queer. Fellow named Colm Tóibín has been very active in this line. Tóibín is an Irishman, a not very good novelist, and something of a professional homosexual himself. (You must know the definition of an Irish homosexual: an Irishman who prefers women over whiskey.) Tóibín's novel *The Master* has old James ogling guardsmen and servants, though at least he doesn't tumble him into the sack with any of them (although earlier he has him cuddling with, of all people, Oliver Wendell Holmes, Jr., later Justice Holmes, who gets no justice from Tóibín). I don't buy it. I don't believe Henry James, in the politicians' phrase, ever pressed the flesh, nor was he, with an imagination of the intensity of his, ever meant to do so. People somehow don't want to believe that anyone can live without sex, or without its being nearly full-time in the forefront of everyone's mind. But then James wasn't everyone. He wasn't like anyone else, really. As my army buddies might have it, he was Henry fucking James, who better enjoyed imagining the "great connection" than actually getting down to doing the messy thing.

Lots of dirty talk here. I'll try to clean up my act in future communications.

Best, Joe

Dear Joe,
Why do I feel that I need to say – before I say anything else – that in fact, although it doesn't matter, or even show, our congruences and convergences (all it needs is a colon and another phrase and we have an academic tritle (sic) in embryo) also have their distinctions and divergences (yep, another colon could put another unreadable title on our list). So, listen, much it matters: my wife is Jewish, by Hitler's definition at least. That doesn't entail anything much, except a lot. We have never been to synagogue together or severally

except when we were married. In pious deference to, in particular, Sylvia's parents, we stood together under that *huppa* (sp?) canopy and were sanctioned by an Orthodox rabbi in a language I am willing to honour, from right to left and back to front, but cannot understand; and then when in Cordoba, we walked under the orange trees to the little whitewashed, white-walled, faintly embellished meeting place where Maimonides led the congregation in, I suspect, classier disputation than you could get down the street *chez les Chrétiens*, until the usual fractiousness sent even the great Aristotelian heading east and then, of course, we did Vaporetto down the Grand Canal in Venice to the ghetto, where a choice of synagogues – his and his, yours and mine – Sephardic or Ashkenazi stand in close fraternal contention.

Thanks (if thanks be due) to Shakespeare, we have the idea (some of us) that Venice was a spiteful, anti-Semitic place in which Shylock and his kind were unkindly used. But a much crueller place was, of course – not least in William's day – England, which furnished his imagination no end with a menu of objective correlatives. He may well have seen – and maybe laughed along with – the mass audience as Ruy Lopez, Elizabeth I's doctor, was conspired against and tortured to death in public despite his comic proclamation that he was a Christian. The danger of being a favoured Jew has often been that you get hung drawn and quartered because the mob, the toffs, the whoever, dare not attack the man/woman at the top who is their real target. You knew this?

I have discovered recently, while honouring my commitment to Nothing But Serious Books during the last fifty years of my life, a man called Isaac Cardoso, a Marrano who lived a Christian life in Inquisitional seventeenth-century España, then got out and went to Italy, Venice then Verona and converted back again to full-time Jewish apologetics and medicine. The tale has been earnestly and in scholarly fashion retrieved by Yosef Yerushalmi, whose psychoanalysis of Freud's *Moses and Monotheism* is a masterpiece of deferential knocking. In both Venice and Verona Cardoso was respected by the local Christians (the term which my father always applied to what you people, I believe, call the *goyim*) and neither municipality had any time for the Inquisition and its inquiries. In the same period, the British continued formally to ban Jewish immigration, though Cromwell was an early version of the guy in that Cruise movie who said, 'Show me the money!' When they did, the side-gate was unlatched. This is known as tolerance.

I have a particularly affectionate memory of the Cordoba synagogue because of the toothless old custodian who used to unlock it, back in good King Franco's ugly old days, and announce, in a voice that seemed to come from some tobacco pouch deep in his scrawny throat, 'antigua sinagoga ebraica'. The contrast with Cordoba's combined Moorish'n'Christian cathedral, the latter inserted in the midst of the former, was all to the credit of the discredited: while the Christian insertion was a vulgarity (which even Carlos V regretted, though he did much the same vandalising thing to the Alhambra in Granada), the Mezquita was superb and archly grandiose, and the little meeting place of the Jews made modesty memorable (cf. the poems of Cavafy as against Seferis or almost anyone you'd care to anthologise).

You are, of course, not the first to think that Beetle cannot be Jewish, perhaps because in an effort not to be too à clef I gave Adam Morris a non-J wife in *The Glittering Prizes*, which doubles as the laurel wreath and the millstone around my reputation's neck. I'm going to make the best of it by adding a third volume to the series and so getting my trilogy badge (perhaps I should add a senile satyr play, just to show how difficult comedy is, but would that be WISE?). The question of being remembered for something does, I suppose, pose itself when you get to be my age, not that I ever shall, of course. As a result of some antique spat not worth bleating about, I had a letter a couple of years ago from the champion of a woman whom I had, he thought, Treated Badly; not in the usual let-me-get-my-shotgun way, not at ALL, but she was aggrieved about what I had said about or done to her ex-husband (including lending him money out of the goodness of my vanity), after which she became convinced that I hated him. Enough backstory, am I right?

So this journalist, whose name was Bor, and probably still is, wrote me a letter out of the beige in which he stuck it to me to the extent of wondering how it must feel to be someone like me who in all his writing career 'had only ever done TWO THINGS that anyone would ever remember'. I felt duly felled of course, for a while, and then I resurrected at a touch of the replay button and decided that it was not that bad to have done that much, and then again, what precisely can the Bor have had in mind?

So (not really: anacoluthia is not my style but a figure worth mentioning to vex the annoyim) I retained the nerve to go to Glasgow this week, for one night only, folks, in order to electrify the Suliots – a reference to Byron which you professorial persons will latch onto and hurl back with all the disdain I deserve for trying to outsmart the doctors – in my friend and publisher Michael Schmidt's Creative Writing postgraduate course, screenwriting being one of their preferred art forms. Why do it? Michael is very good to me and a decent man; professor, publisher, editor (of a mag called *PNR*, *Poetry Nation Review*, which used to be rightissimo-whinge when under the influence of

Donald Davie and C.H. Sisson, but where I can denounce Ian McEwan and other of fortune's darlings without being advised for my own good to clap along with the award-bestowing company). Have you ever been to Scotland? Glasgow is a craggy, high-shouldered place, with a lot of air in its granitic grandeur and no affectations of trendiness; a good spot to visit in a time of moral and economic collapse, since it has a rugged refusal (to be English, or trendy) implicit in its once-greatness: all the warships that the British didn't build on the Tyne they built on the Clyde, and the cross-Channel steamers too, one of which we used to take across the Aegean, long after its licence had expired. I did three almost-two-hour one-man shows in which I tried to come across as the genius with a human face (a few louche jokes confirm one's standing as a man who doesn't spend all his time high on Parnassus), pausing only to ask them, repeatedly, whether they had read this or seen that. I don't know what they do read or see, but it was never Thomas Mann or Alberto Moravia or Michelangelo Antonioni or... Never mind, and why should I when they laughed and applauded and bought copies of my novels? Some of the women even vied (vy not?) to walk me home, perhaps thinking that they could never forgive themselves if I was discovered slumped in a tenement doorway slurring the verses of 'Glasgy Belongs to Me'. These are the culminating, slurred words of a music hall song of one Will Fyffe, a man with a knobbly stick and a Tam O'Shanter who, before the wars, was England's professional Scot, just as that *salaud* Maurice Chevalier was America's favourite frog. The latter (*celui-ci* even) did sing 'I Remember It Well' well, but 'Sank Evan for Leedle Girls' has an unsavoury Lolitan ring to it, and so does *Lolita*; I yield to few in my admiration for V.N., not least *Pale Fire*, but Girodias was right to print *Lolita* along with *Thongs* and *White Thighs* and other Saint-Germain-des-Prés favourite reading of the 1960s, because Volodya's novel, for all the elegances, is a paedofile. Kingsley Amis, who will not be hugely vaunted in my pages, reviewed the chronicles of Humbert Humbert under the rubric 'What DOES he think he's up to?' or plain-stitch Anglo-Saxonry to that effect. One could have said the same of the 110%-proof Kingsley in his later years, but he had become a national treasure and hence deserves his plinth, whatever pigeons like me may try to do to it. I had nothing against him, and nothing for him either, which got me a petty place in Zachary Leader's index.

Hey, was that the bell? Gene Tunney's Long Round has nothing on me, it seems. Tag time, Epstein.

As ever,
Freddie

Dear Freddie,

I am a touch ticked-off with myself for getting Mme Beetle's irrelevant religion wrong. You are quite right, bye the bye, that the source of my misinformation is *The Glittering Prizes*, which Barbara and I watched (re-watched, after a lacuna of a mere thirty-three years) on three consecutive nights two weeks ago. (It is still immensely enjoyable, not at all bye the bye. I gather from an entry in your recently published journal that Tom Conti was reasonably accurate in doing Adam/Freddie.) What ticks me, as the mattress people like to say, is that I read straight autobiography in your story, which is, true enough, loaded with autobiographical references. I much dislike, though, the notion that writers cannot really invent anything, and that everything has to have an autobiographical referent, the more direct the more comforting. I am always myself slightly put off when someone tells me that he has recognized a character in one of my stories – a character usually that is wholly my invention – and informs me that he is of course meant to be Sheldon Berman or Jacqueline Pollack or someone with whom he went to high school.

I, who have twice foregone marrying Jewish women – Barbara is my second wife, soon to be a wife of thirty-three years, which qualifies her, I do believe, for the mantle of "long-suffering" – am much more sentimental about Jews and Jewishness than you. I know no-one more on the *qui vive* for anti-Semitism than you, who also bravely goes to war against it where he finds it. But I'm not sure that you are as keen on Jewish differences (from everyone else) and preserving those differences as I. By differences I mean vulgarities and refinements both; Jews are after all like everyone else, only more so. And *vive la* more so. Three weeks ago an old and dear friend of mine told me, with some chagrin, that his new (and first) grandson was being baptized, bringing to pass the riddle that asks: What do three generations of intermarriage yield? Answer: A Christian. My friend's grandfather was, in his day, a locally famous rabbi, Orthodox, bearded, kosher-keeping, the works; and now his little great-great-grandson is a Catholic. Hearing this made me sad. Have I any right to my sadness? I'm not sure that I do, but deep sadness is what I felt nonetheless.

What I fear is the elimination of the Jews by assimilation and the lessening of anti-Semitism, both goals once devoutly to be wished. (There's that heavy-handed celestial ironist of yours at work yet again.) I shouldn't like it if the Jews were like everyone else. This has happened to Catholic culture in the United States in my time, so that, unlike in my boyhood or even as recently as thirty years ago, one could tell a Catholic, for better *and* worse, by the way he carried himself, talked, argued, today Catholics may as well be Unitarians. You know of course the joke that asks what do you get when you join a Unitarian with a Jehovah's Witness? Answer: Someone who knocks upon your door with absolutely nothing to say. Preserve the Jews, I say, in all our brilliant, maddening, infuriating, vulgar, sweet glory.

This past Thursday, *Newsweek* asked me to write another piece for them, this time on the subject of the early days of Barack Obama's presidency. (It runs in the current week's issue; I shall send you the piece under that separate and doubtless by now soiled cover.) I had a day to write it, and did so with some pleasure in the composition. ("You never want to run away from business," is another of my father's business maxims, which seems to have stuck to the impressionable psyche of his frivolous son.) I've found I am able to write much more quickly now than twenty or so years ago. I tell myself that it shows an advance in my craft. (Another possibility, of course, is that my standard is lower.) Doing so I feel less the false artiste, and more like, you should pardon the expression, Working Press.

I did get off one solid line in the aforementioned piece. I referred to the Democratic Party's leaders in the Senate and House of Representatives – characters named in so-called real life Harry Reid and Nancy Pelosi – "the Frick and Frack of heavy federal spending," and then I wrote (await the majesty of the line) that they were "as interested in bipartisanship [working with the Republican Party] as Lord Byron was in marriage counseling."

Which reminds me to report that I took your *Byron* from the university library and am reading it with much pleasure. I think the tone is just right. Byron was Byron, no doubt about that, but he was also a bit of a booming international joke, limping and scribbling and fucking his way across the Continent. And treating him, as you do in the early pages of your book, in a jokey way works splendidly. I've also finished *Ticks and Crosses*, which has been my bedtime book, read at roughly ten-page draughts. I like it all, but the bits about Hollywood and your self-analysis and the isolated aphorisms I like best of all. I, too, am a journal-keeper – another of our congruences – but my journals are nowhere near so well composed as yours. I tend rarely to write more than a paragraph a day in mine – usually in the morning – and my subject matter is what I have done the day before, with (increasingly, alas) a paragraph on the death of friends or artists I care about. They are, my journals, equally distanced from the soulful journals of Amiel and the social-climbing ones of Chips Channon. I seem to recall that the highlight of Chips C.'s life was the night he had two queens (not homosexuals, please mind you, but flamin' royals) over to dinner, and was so exhilarated about it that he became completely drunk and, though his corpse was present, seems to have missed the entire evening.

A note on Señor Bor saying that you would be remembered for only Two Things. I gather the second thing he had in mind, after *The Glittering Prizes*, is the screenplay for *Darling*, which I have recorded on my television DVR and plan to watch later in the week. (As you can see, we're having, *chez* Epstein, a regular Freddie-*fest*.) First, I agree with you that Two Things are rather a lot. And second, who can know what anyone will be remembered for? If I had to bet, I'd say that your journals figure to be of great interest somewhere down the road. Yet on our current downhill course – Decline and Blumenthal, friend – remembering itself may be out. What will last? I suppose this is an inevitable and yet bad question for a writer to ask about his own scribblings. The whole thing is reminiscent of old baggy-pants Connolly saying that all that mattered in literature was the writing of masterpieces, which he, Cyril C., never came close to doing. I should myself like to write my own masterpiece, so that I could knock off for a day or two. Since it doesn't seem to be in the works, I write for my own amusement, a few shekels, and a bit of very inconstant attention, the best of which comes from the rare sweet smart small band of readers who tell me that my scribbles have brought them pleasure.

But I do go on – more than 1,500 words, I see by my gas meter – and so had better stop here.

Best, Joe

Dear Joe,

Back last night from Dublin, which I have never visited before. I was asked to go because they have a film festival to which I was invited. When the stately Buck at immigration asked me in what capacity I was attending, I said 'As an antiquity'. He did not affect surprise. They were showing *Two for the Road*, subtitled in the only print that was available as *Dos por la carretera*, which doesn't have quite the same charm. It came out in 1967 and I went to NY for the opening without Beetle, who was heavily pregnant. The movie was showing at Radio City Musical Hall, because everything Audrey was ever in opened there. It was as unsuitable a venue as vanity could contrive: the screen was two-houses wide and the dialogue seemed to be hawked through loud-hailers. The picture should have opened in a small house and gathered its audience that way, but Audrey was Audrey. *Two for the Road* has since become a quite famous, much 'taught' movie (Richard Gere selected it a couple of months ago as his favourite romantic comedy), but – in the year that the kids were cheering *Bonnie and Clyde* – it was reviewed without great enthusiasm by Bosley Crowther, who was then the *NYT* maker-and-breaker, quite as if there was nothing unusual about making a movie with no plot apart from the ups and downs of a marriage, and unique only in taking place in six or seven intercut time periods. Stanley Donen met Bosley Crowther by chance in a 42nd St bar some shortish time later. In the way of his kind (critics), Bosley waved cheerfully and called out 'Hullo' to Stanley who replied very coldly, 'Hullo, Bosley'. Crowther came over and asked whether something was wrong. Stanley said, 'No'. 'You seem . . . distant,' Bosley said. Stanley said, 'Did you ever read the things you said about my last four movies?' 'Stanley, I'm your friend', Crowther said. 'And one of the things about being a friend is, well, when you're disappointed, you have to say so. I only say what I really feel about people I truly admire. That's why I said what I did.' Stanley said, 'Bosley, don't be my friend. Just say nice things about my movies in the newspaper'.

Stanley will never be forgotten for some of his work and will be fortunate if for some of it he is not remembered (*Deep In My Heart* comes to mind, but gets no big welcome). A week or so ago I happened to be looking at *Commentary* and saw the latest list of *Cahiers du Cinéma*'s Ten Greatest. I can't name them all, but *Citizen Kane* was still there and so, of course, was *La Règle du jeu* (subtitled in a low French joke as *The Jew with the Curse*) although I have never thought it anything but a show-off mess and so was *Les Enfants du paradis*, a pretentious costume piece made by a bunch of French quasi-collabos in the last years of the war. They spun out the shoot so as to have location catering until the Americans and the British came and called it a wrap. Hitchcock was there for something, probably *N By NW*, which grows sillier with every *hommage*, and what all else. One of the ten was *Singin' In The Rain*, and it was the only choice to which no directorial auteur was assigned. I haven't spoken to Stanley for some years, as the consequence of a *brouille* too trivial to describe at length and too toxic to be repaired with ease. But I do love the guy and the movie he got made, against all the odds, so I sent an e-mail to *Commentary*, protesting at the omission of Donen's name (and, not that I cared, at that of Gene Kelly). It was the least I could do, so I did that. Gene (whom Stanley came to dislike, not to say despise) spent most of the movie in front of the camera, hence it's likely that its vitality – remember Donald O'Connor, all in one take? – was due to S.D. The *Commentary* letters editor wrote back 'Wow', quite as if he had heard unexpectedly from the Delphic Oracle, so I guess they will print my petty gesture of abiding friendship for Stanley. Hope so. Then newly enchaired young Podhoretz wrote and asked me to do a piece for him. I thought of asking for the same rates as that Epstein guy, but then I remembered my place; so I'll do something for him about the movies. Right now I am hoping that Kate Winslet will be Kate Losesit, though I fear that Harvey Weinstein can twist enough arms to have the unlikeable Stephen Daldry's detestable version of Stinky-Schlinky's *The Reader* turn to Oscar gold.

What was Dublin like? Well, we did a certain amount of hithering and thithering, not to mention the fluent dithering I did in front of an audience of film students, MA screenwriting coursers and so on. I gave them hell and they never noticed; they really wanted to be told stories about Stanley Kubrick. I said that he was one of the immortals and hence not dead and hence I could speak ill of him. But – wouldn't you know it? – I didn't really. My misfortune was to work with him when he was manifestly sclerotic and in the typical last phase of an emperor, the one in which he believes that he is still at the peak of his powers and has so intimidated those around him that there is no saving him from himself. If you need evidence that showbiz and politics have a lot in common it is that the great practitioners in both departments tend to go out at the nadir of their powers and after doing something very foolish. The great exception in this little island is Tony Blair, whose second-in-command was, for a full decade of economic ballooning, the envious, resentful Gordon Brown, who believed that every cheer that greeted Tony had been stolen from him. Blair went, to no great cheers (mainly because he'd backed the beastly Yanks), but still at the top of the market, literally. Within no time, Brown had the kingpin rôle of which he had always thought he had been robbed, upon which, none of your *après moi*: the deluge was instant and continues to fall *comme des cordes*, as they say in the Perigord. Of course we've all had our savings washed away, and only those who lied and cheated have any reason for satisfaction (at least they lied and cheated) and here we are, in the Brown stuff. But you have to imagine laughing as much as Blair surely does every morning. When your prayers get answered that fast, it's understandable to go Roman.

Ireland, where eating and DRINKING seem the main activities, languishes in Britain's slumping shadow, but is full of charming people and a posse of competent girls whose men, one suspects, never came home from the pub and are now superfluous. Despite the generosity of our hosts and the Georgian elegance of the city, I do not imagine that Jim Joyce had a daily wish that he was back on the iffy Liffey with stately Buck Mulligan. I asked a few people if they had read *Finnegans Wake*. They're all planning to start when they retire. I have a somewhat blank spot for Irish writing, though I admire it, I do. My Cambridge friend John Patrick Sullivan was Liverpool Irish and had me read a lot of the stuff, he did, and oy did, but it never TOOK with me, although I do remember some of the stories in *Dubliners*, they fade away compared with, oh, Hawthorne; but then most people's do. Yours don't. I swear to God, and will it be a drop of Jameson's you'll be having? You write good stories and you know it. And so do I. And to hell with Bosley Crowther.

Tout à toi,
Freddie

Dear Freddie,

I envy you (in a non-malignant way) your friendship with Audrey Hepburn. I was myself in love with her for many years, as I should think most men who are not straightaway brutes must also have been. She is one of the few movie actresses in the modern era who gave off fumes of genuine refinement; Deborah Kerr is the only other I can think of, though Kristin Scott Thomas, who I gather has now frogified herself, may someday qualify. All, please note, are English-accented women; I cannot think of an American actress whose specialty is refinement or stately elegance. Audrey Hepburn, with her splendid cheekbones, good accent and fine taste in clothes, is also to be commended for giving small-breasted women a new lease on life.

The only greatly famous actress I've ever met was Myrna Loy. At the time she was in a play in Chicago, and I met her at the home of a lion-collecting, lubricious attorney by the name of Samuel D. Freifeld; he collected me, a mere cub at the time, but only for a short while (strains of "Born Free" here playing in the background). Myrna Loy must then have been in her middle-seventies and, that evening at least, not at all glamorous but appealingly *haimish*, as our people say, foregoing the phrase "old shoe." I remember talking to her with Barbara and me sitting with her on the floor. I don't recall a thing we said, but do recall thinking here I am chatting with Myrna Loy and life is good.

Belatedly, it occurs to me that I also knew, and rather liked, Celeste Holm, with whom I sat for a number of years on something called the National Council of the National Endowment for the Arts. She was a sweet character, with few pretensions, who, during excruciatingly boring day-long meetings, got lots of crocheting done.

On the subject of the movies, Barbara and I spent last night *not* watching the Oscars. I even thought that, were we more sociable, next year we might have a Let's Not Watch the Oscars party. For one thing, such people as Steven Spielberg, George Clooney, Susan Sarandon, Robert Redford hold no interest for me. I do not, *mirabile dictu*, consider Woody Allen a genius. The self-congratulatory spirit of the event is off-putting, not to say nauseating. In the instance of this year's Oscars, I have not seen a single contending movie. Barbara and I go to the movies scarcely at all. I feel under no compunction to be au courant on the subject of the movies. (I recall a time in the 1970s where, if one went to dinner parties, one was expected not merely to have opinions on the most recent movies, but also to know the opinions of Pauline Kael, John Simon, Andrew Sarris, & co.) Ninety percent of movies are disappointing; the more serious they are in intent – and this year's Oscar contenders seem particularly heavy-handed in the line of pseudo-seriousness – the greater the likelihood of the let-down. I find I can wait to be disappointed, and so do not need to see any of these movies hot out of the can. (Does "can" in England, as here, also carry the meaning of toilet?) I am content to wait to see some of them months later on DVD. Chez Epstein we live chiefly on DVD movies and recorded (on our DVR) Turner Classics Movies. Saturday nights, if not otherwise engaged, we eat popcorn and apples and have a beer while watching a movie; it is family ritual.

The only good thing about the Oscars is, I suppose, winning one, which you, friend, have handily done. I should myself have liked to have won an Oscar and not show up to collect it. (Which I believe you also did.) Where do you keep your Oscar: on the mantel or in the drawer with your socks and underwear? A few years ago, in Brookline, Massachusetts, I visited a friend, Leslie Epstein (no relation), a novelist whose father and uncle (Philip and Julius) won Oscars for writing *Casablanca*. After dinner, we returned to Leslie's apartment, where I noted he had three or four locks on the front door. He explained that he had to have all these locks installed because he had his father's and uncle's Oscars, which he had been using as paperweights. Then someone sold an Oscar for a quarter of a million dollars, and so Leslie had to insure his two Oscars, and the insurance company instructed him that, to be insurable, he needed to have all those locks installed. Leslie's father Philip died young, but his uncle lived on to the age of ninety-one. In an interview, someone complimented Julius on the greatness of *Casablanca,* to which he replied, "Yeah, it's a pretty slick piece of shit." If Uncle Julius were in the audience, I would still watch the Oscars.

Yesterday, a Sunday, Barbara and I went to the Joffrey Ballet, a company that roughly fourteen years ago moved to Chicago. The program, which included a nice mix of classical and contemporary ballets, ended with a reconstructed (constructed, that is, as much as possible on its original Ballet Russes presentation) performance of *The Rites of Spring*. Powerful, good stuff. I have not seen this ballet before, and only now that I have seen it do I begin to understand Stravinsky's music for it; the music without the dancing is almost incomprehensible, at least to a musical illiterate (that would be me).

I mention going to the ballet not merely to establish my highbrow bona fides with you, but to underscore that I don't attend a lot of so-called performance art. I don't go to the theatre much, for the reason that I think most contemporary playwrights are a lot more stupid about the world than I; and this being so why should I pay to learn precisely how stupid they are? Barbara and I used to go to lots of concerts – Barbara still goes to some – but I have found myself more and more bored by them, unable to keep my mind in the room while the music is playing. I also didn't much care for the reverential feeling accompanying concert-going, which began more and more to feel like attending a church service: Our Lady of the First Mozart. I was pleased to read recently that Santayana began to feel the same way, and decided that he preferred to listen to serious music while standing up, which he was able to do at outdoor concerts in Rome. Ballet, though, for me has a double payoff: listening to the music and watching beautiful bodies flying around.

To re-establish my lowbrow bona fides, I recently subscribed to something called the Tennis Channel, which brings in lots of smaller tournaments and Davis Cup challenge rounds. I love turning it on late on weekend afternoons, setting myself on the couch facing our largish (42") television set, and to the sound of long rallies – pock, pock, pock – soon the old Jewish gentleman (that would be me, again) is gone.

A final point: I feel much as you do about Irish writing and about James Joyce, whom I admire without being particularly nuts about. I feel even less about Scottish writing (though I like Lord Jeffrey for his unfailing kindness to William Hazlitt), and when the annual *TLS* issue on Scotland arrives, I feel as if I have a week off. A Scottish editor at the *TLS*, fellow named James Campbell, once asked me if I thought he had edited me "too Calvinistically." When I asked him to clarify, he said: "You know, taken too many amusing things out of my piece," which in fact he had done, at least by my stony old Hebraic lights.

Best, Joe

Dear Joe,

I wouldn't claim to have been a friend of Audrey Hepburn's, although she was certainly very nice to me and did me the unrepayable good turn of making a script of mine without criticising a single word of the first draft she read. I wasn't on the set all that much, though Beetle and I did drive down the deserted Autoroute in the days when there was no limit on your vitesse. Vanity had impelled me to buy an Alfa Romeo 2800 Spider, a grey beauty that had three carburetors that snarled at each other at low speeds (disposing the car to boil in traffic) but were sweetly harmonious at 130mph on a spring morning when we were two-for-the-roading to the location. Audrey was on $750,000 a movie, quite a fee in those simple, soulful days; she behaved like a quasi-royal star but never a pampered or pretentious one. She had, as you probably know, thanks to the Biog Channel, quite a dangerous war in which, if I am to believe what I do, she used her durable innocence to carry messages to the Dutch resistance. Her father, who had deserted wife and daughter, was some kind of a Nazi; perhaps the lack of him, or his memory, disposed her to marry Mel Ferrer, a man of mature conceit and insistent tedium.

Stanley Donen and I went to visit them in their chalet house in Bürgenstock. Audrey had (I think I have this right) just had her second child with him. When Mel came downstairs from his den, where he was preparing a movie about El Greco, unless it was Goya, he was armed with a box of stills from his recce in España and showed them to us, with commentary and at length. As he came in, Audrey said, 'Here comes Melchior!' and I thought that sounded as though the marriage was terminal, which it was. Audrey was manifestly a tender toughie and her lack of criticism is probably the nicest notice, in showbiz, that I ever received.

After Beetle and I had arrived in our Alfa, I read the script that they were to shoot the next day and decided that it was not quite logical. I wrote a new version and slipped it to Audrey during the long-tabled open-air lunch which, in France, was laid at noon, after which the unit worked an uninterrupted slew of hours. A little later, she came to me and said, 'Frederico, I read the new scene and I prefer the old one'. I had the nerve, not to say the foolishness, to play the maestro. 'The old scene really doesn't make any sense, Audrey. Believe me, this one says what needs to be said, clearly.' She said, 'Would you come and read them with me?' Who wouldn't? So we went into her caravan and there I was, alone with Miss H., in the chastest possible intimate circumstances. She said, 'Which one shall we read first?' 'You choose.' She chose the old version. My big moment: I was about to do some acting with Miss H. But not a lot. Because she said the first line of the old scene, and I may have said the second, and she came back with the third (the one that wasn't 'logical') and I said, 'You're quite right; we'll do the first scene'. She kissed me as if there were quite a few people there with us, very nicely, and out we went into the Riviera light. That night Stanley, Audrey and Albert dined with me and Beetle. They looked at us (and the 2800 Spider) and said, almost together, 'Oh my God, we're doing their story'. They weren't, but they also somewhat were. I never guessed that Audrey and Albert were, as the handouts now insist, an item, but I gather that Audrey was sexually more voracious than her chaste, dancing rectitude suggested.

I still think she gave an Oscar-winning performance, but she wasn't even nominated, not for our movie: she was for *Wait Until Dark*, in which she played a blind girl. I never saw it, but I do remember a movie with a blind girl and a bad, bad doctor who seemed to be the goody until . . . she locked the good guy out and . . . Who was it? I think Brian Donleavy was the bad doc. (*Spiral Staircase*, was that the title?) Even back in the 1960s, long before Harvey Weinstein was Mr Hustle, there was a lot of studio politics in getting nominations. Fox put their padded shoulders behind *Doctor Doolittle* on which they had spent irrecoverable amounts of moolah. Stanley Donen was pretty sore when I was the only nominated element. I didn't win because *Guess Who's Slumming To Dinner* won all the awards: Spence and Katie (an odd couple indeed, one alcoholic, the other crypto-lesbian) pulled their writer to the podium, his name was Rose, I think; my mother's mother's maiden name and the nickname that anti-Semites called me at Charterhouse because I had red cheeks. It also rhymes with nose, you know.

I saw Audrey a couple of times thereafter, and she always ran prettily into my arms. Once I heard myself say, 'Slimmer than ever!' Not, perhaps, a speech we should leave in the script. I wrote a script of my novel *Richard's Things* some time in the 1970s, a story about a wife whose husband dies on a business trip and she goes to the place and finds that he was checked into the hotel with a woman who the wife then tracks down and – hey, you didn't guess, did you? – finally has an affair with. Audrey wrote me a very nice, many-paged handwritten letter, on blue paper, from Rome, where she then was with her second husband, a Dr Dotti who wasn't all that nice to her, I think, and said that she liked the script and loved me but her public would never understand if she did the things that my wife-character did. She had, of course, played a girl accused of being a lesbian in *The Loudest Whisper* but that was about being wrongly suspected not double-parked with another female. She was probably right not to break with her public's expectations (having a lover when married, in *Two for the Road*, was already breach enough), but I wish she, and not the less than lovable Liv Ullman, had made the pic, and also that Anthony Harvey had not directed it (poor little guy). Katie Hepburn, whose buddy Harvey was, read the script and said that she wished she wasn't too old to play it. She probably wouldn't have anyway, but . . .

The last time I spoke to Audrey I didn't actually see her. We were both staying in the Ritz-Carlton in Sydney, Oz, and I called her room from the lobby. She was very friendly and sweet, but it must have been 1989, I think, and she was on a tour for Save The Children, at a time when, it turned out, someone should have been trying to save her. We talked about working together, but she never worked again and died not long after. Odd, when I look back, how timid I was, and am, when it comes to stars of almost any kind. Is it vanity or modesty that makes me hang back? Don't tick the box, OK?

Tout à toi,
Freddie

Dear Freddie,

I was struck in your account of Audrey Hepburn by her two less than glorious marriages. Why is it that some – often highly intelligent – women seem to be stimulated by worthlessness in men? Neither of Audrey Hepburn's husbands seems quite worthless, but both seem far from good enough. Stimulated by worthlessness – there's the theme for a novel here, surely. Not long ago I wrote a less than successful short story about a woman who never found a man equal in attractiveness to her dead brother; I've known a few women in this condition. Their hearts belonged not to Daddy but to Brother. So much of fiction is about how men go about choosing women; perhaps not enough about how women choose men.

I also note your ownership of an Alfa Romeo Spider 2800. One of the regrets of my generally fortunate life is that I have never owned a sporty convertible. I vowed that I would never own a station wagon, and at least kept to that less than arduous vow. But not to have had at least one truly flashy set of wheels was, I now see, a mistake. I blame this on the University of Chicago, a school without any social but lots of intellectual snobbery. The not-so-hidden agenda there held, for example, that there are only four things worth doing or being in life: 1. An artist; 2. A scientist; 3. A statesman, of which there hasn't been any since Winston Churchill; and, 4. (the loophole) A teacher of artists, scientists, or statesmen. This is a dopey, not to say pernicious, idea, but there it is, and when young I subscribed to it.

The ethos of the University of Chicago also taught that there was something called materialism – not philosophical materialism but the coarse doctrine that held things, especially luxurious things, were to be eschewed. (Whenever I hear or see that word, I want to reply, "Gesundheit.") As a young man, I eschewed off much more than I could easily have swallowed. Among the things I eschewed were grand automobiles. I wanted to seem above such vulgarities, such obvious status symbols, as elegant and therefore expensive cars. Instead, by deliberation, I chose to drive relentlessly dull ones: Chevrolets, a mid-line Oldsmobile called the Cutlass (which was nothing like so dashing as its sobriquet). Only an intellectual, as Orwell said, could have been so stupid. Then one year, about to buy yet another dull-bladed Cutlass, I discovered that they had jacked the price up four or five thousand dollars, putting it above $20,000, and so I said, in what are reputed to be the deathbed words of W.C. Fields, "On second thought, screw 'em," and bought a small BMW instead. This fine little Krautmobile reminded me that driving could be amusing. I bought a few more BMWs over the years, and then switched to a mid-line Jaguar, called an S-Type, a 2007 black version of which I now drive. You will of course be shocked to learn that I know diddly about the inner workings of any car, and I buy such cars as I believe I can afford strictly on looks (the cars', not mine). I look upon the handsomely designed grill of my mid-priced (roughly $43,000) Jaguar, and I am becalmed. If this paragraph doesn't convince you of the shallowness of your correspondent, nothing will. As for the flashy convertible, I assume that this awaits me in the next life, a smashing young Chinese woman with an abiding penchant for grey-haired scribblers seated in the passenger seat.

Which reminds me that we have been corresponding for the past two months without either of us inquiring into the other's health. What kind of older Jewish men are we, anyway? By now we should know each other's cholesterol and PSA numbers. We should have traded hospital stories and the phone numbers of medical specialists in our respective countries, just in case one or the other of us is abroad. I have a good friend, a man a year younger than I, who yesterday reported to me that after a physical and follow-up examinations his new, young and very thorough physician revealed to him that he is on the brink of having diabetes, which runs in his family; some atrophy of his brain, which is normal, but atrophy remains atrophy; and problems with a heart valve, which may require invasive surgery. My first reaction on hearing this, after feeling sorry for my friend's medical travail, is that I don't want to submit myself to his physician. What might this inquisitive fellow discover in my own still slowly yet inexorably rotting carcass? No, no, don't, in the cant phrase, go there. I at least ain't going there.

Hospitals are perhaps the most dangerous places in the country – every country. People die under anesthesia, they die under the knife, and if the first two don't get you, infection (increasingly, it seems) will. My friend Edward Shils once asked the leading historian of medicine at what point in history physicians saved more patients than they killed. "Haven't," the historian replied calmly, "reached it yet." Although philosophically a Jewish Scientist (a Christian Scientist without the Christ or cheery parts), I do go to physicians; I have, in fact, an impressive staff of them: an internist, a cardiologist, a gastroenterologist, and, most recently, a dermatologist, who found and excised something delightful called a pre-cancerous lesion – are you now saying to yourself, I wonder, "I salute you, mon lesionnaire" – from my upper forehead. I go to physicians without glee; with, in fact, the fear and trembling that that old sit-down comedian Kierkegaard so famously referred to. Once one reaches 70 or so it seems to me, one is simply awaiting bad news. More than the old *condition humaine* is entailed; what is, is the "condition older mother-humper whose number can only soon be up." I think I can bear to die. Getting the damn notice of it, and then having to suffer through it, is what worries me.

Speaking of getting older, the other night something called *American Ballroom Challenge* was on television. Barbara and I chose not to watch it, but I asked her if she remembered the name of the actress who used (in the showbiz word) to "host" this show. Neither of us could recall it. (Barbara is eighteen months older than I; today is our thirty-third wedding anniversary. I joked with her that "they said the marriage would never last"; nobody of course was sufficiently interested to say any such thing. "Yes," she replied, "I remember the headline in the press well: 'Spinster Robs Cradle.'" She was 39, I, 37.) We did our ablutions and went off to bed still struggling to recall the woman's name. I thought she might be French, or at least had a French name. I recall that she had wonderful legs and had some sexual entanglements with the odious Frank Sinatra. At my second wake-up – "piss-call," as they delicately put in the US Army – I went over to my computer and Googled Sinatra's discography, where I discovered that the name that had evaded us all this while was Juliet Prowse, who was South African not French, whereupon I returned to bed and slept through the remainder of the night. To cite once again Orwell, who pegged out at 44, he didn't know the half of it when he said such, such were the joys.

Best, Joe

Dear Joe,

I've had a good experience with the (some) Jews this week. I committed myself weeks, *sinon* months, ahead to do a Jewish Book Week gig (a term I was always sure, as of so many things, that I would never appropriate, but is appropriate) at a venue called the Royal National Hotel, which sounds like the kind of place where some sad shit would go to commit joyless adultery in an early Graham Greene novel (they got earlier and earlier as time went by, but who needs a smartass paradox in the midst of narrative?), being situated near Russell Square, adjacent to the hindquarters of the British Museum and not far – aha, I can include another topic – from the Royal Neurological Hospital where, some three years ago, I had a tumour removed from my pituitary gland. It was benign and my surgeon, Mick (to his fellow sawbones) Powell was top of the range and fished out the excess matter with what, I think, they call a 'hockey stick', but not before the patient is anaesthetised, supine even, as Mr Eliot would recommend. The tumour was bulgy and soggy (are you sure we should pursue these medical things?) but pressed down on the optic nerve with enough insistence to have made me almost unable to read, let alone drive (which I was not eager to do). In addition (this is not a sad story, now) I had become listless, slow-witted and other sorry things I need not detail. The process of decline was quite long and no-one, until it was pretty critical, made a diagnosis that took account of all the phenomena/clues. Sherlock Holmes, where was he when I needed him? So now I am into a somewhat artificially stimulated late(r) seventies and quite invigorated enough to do stand-up in front of an assembled 350 or so people. I was supposed to talk about *Ticks and Crosses*, and had Tom Conti there to do some readings, but we scrapped all that and busked like crazy for an hour and a half, Tom tactfully deferring to my verbosity. It was all shamefully enjoyable, perhaps because I was run-in (in the old automotive sense) by having done stand-up in Glasgow two weeks earlier and Dublin last week; it's not a living (they charge the Jews and fellow-travellers but there ain't no checky, as your friend Zero Mostel so memorably put it in the original movie of *The Producers*) but it is an ego trip. Nothing like getting laughs, as Aeschylus used to say in the greenroom after the *Oresteia* had scarified the punters.

I find that I am able to hold an audience better now than ever, perhaps because of senile shamelessness, perhaps because it seems that no-one knows anything and therefore they can all be frightened first and amused (and relieved) afterwards, especially if you give them the answers to the toughish questions before they are humiliated beyond redemption. Afterwards I sold quite a few books, and signed a stack more, which must mean that the book-sellers suivants are not expecting to have to send them back to the publisher. I had to pay £8 to park the VW Golf (nothing flash about Fred these days) in the Royal National *sous-sol* and expect to have to go fifteen rounds with the organisers getting what the English call reimbursed. This is fame but never fortune.

Among those who lined up to have their purchases signed were several people, of different ages, who had been at the same English Public School, Charterhouse, as I had. During the course of the evening, one of my experi-ences of Jew-baiting happened to be mentioned. I don't THINK I dragged it in, like Cromwell's body on a hurdle (trust me for fancy and wished-for similes), but it played well. One of the Carthusians who later craved my signa-ture had been at the school a quarter of a century after me. He was an amiable-looking young guy, of not remarkably Semitic cut, and I asked him, expecting the answer no (such questions in Latin were preceded by '*num*', a sort of predecessor of *nu*, perhaps), whether C'house, as we called it, was still anti-Semitically endowed in his day. He was *sans complexes*, as the frogs say, but told me that he had only discovered what anti-Semitism was when he arrived at our common alma mater. It may be that all English schools are alive with the same sounds and the same music, but there seems to be something incurable, a kind of verbal malaria, which cannot be purged on that Surrey hill where – why deny it? – I also learned a good deal, though not as much as I had between the ages of eight and thirteen when sequestered in North Devon while London burned, Omaha beach turned into a death trap and, yes, millions died. I recall drawing endless doodles of the Battle of Stalingrad. My favourite figures – analyse this – were German officers, in those falsely stiffened and elevated caps.

This leads into the latest weirdness to which the Holocaust has given rise, the book called *The Kindly Ones*, in its English translation, by Jonathan Littell, a novel which – but you have seen the happy fires on the horizon – sold 600,000 copies in France and, at 900 pages, is the Sumo champion of the literature (sic, and ye shall find) which trades on the charm of the swastika and reminds us that we would all be Nazis if we had the pedigree and the tailor. I think back to little Freddie and his German officers in their open Mercedes, mit outriders even, and still won't buy the facile notion that there is a little Himmler in all of us. I should, I suppose, actually read Littell's volu-minous volume before ranting about it, but I do not think I have enough days left, even if I haven't seen a doctor for quite a while. The new penury (you can hear the cherry orchard being cut down for firewood even as we blame the bloody Americans for everything that Gordon Brown did and did again) keeps us from once prompt valetudinarianism. Poverty, of a fairly sumptuous kind, reminds me that I never expected a rose garden and that being a writer, in the prospectus I wrote for myself, was going to be a matter of getting into a boat and rowing against the current for as long as it took. I always wanted to be published, not to be successful; I lacked that final thrust of vulgar ambition that might have guided me to bestsellerdom.

In a burst of flattering excess, the brochure for Jewish Book Week said that I was 'loved' for my novels about Adam Morris and I felt a flush of, I swear it, nausea at the idea that I might have generated something as disturbing as a constituency. You talked about the 'ethos' of Chicago U and I suspect that it was – whatever the quota of Jews who subscribed to it – of somewhat Anglo-Puritanical origin. My dream of being a published writer, perhaps great but NEVER popular, was a function of something similar: success was a sign that you must have done something wrong. Now, who knows how much time, how many more books remain before the fell bracket closes? I should sorta like to become The Greatest all of a sudden, but as with those men who discover fucking late in life (fairly late, at least, as Bertrand Russell did), there is something at once understandable and a little bit yucky in being converted to loud, oh, grossness.

On the OTHER HAND (here it comes), I was vexed by a woman called Miranda Seymour who – reviewing *Fame and Fortune* – announced her disgust that a writer of my age should still be delving into the erotic mode. You know, of course, that we fictioneers are always nineteen, in some department of our shameless bag of tricks, and that there is nothing human that isn't accessible to the fingers, even when (no if) other parts do not always measure up. I recall (I do a lot of that, Mnemosyne and I being old pals) that the same Miranda, when married to a philosopher called Anthony Gottlieb, at a time when I was editing a philosophy series (now in its eleventh impression) with Ray Monk, a professor at Southampton, came up to me, somewhat kittenishly, at a literary party and asked that I be receptive, *disons*, to her (very smart) husband's new philosophical conspectus. And so I was, not for her sake, when I came to review it. Now she's dumped him in favour of some richer picking and, perhaps, remembers with shame that she put herself out, in the chastest possible sense, procuring what I should probably have granted anyway to her ex. The same lady – you may as well hear me out here – wrote a memoir called, I think, *In My Father's House* (a title as well-used as a pantaloon's slipper) in which she disclosed her sorry relationship with her charmless dad. I rather fear that my seniority has disposed her to displace her grievances onto me. Like Louis B. Mayer, I will turn the other cheek, and bide my time. It's not my sweetest habit, but it is, I fear, habitual.

Your wife sounds good. Mine too is older than me. No: WAS. Life's revolving door sometimes has a Hungarian doorman. I am a lucky man, but I don't want it to get around.

Tout à toi,
Freddie

Dear Freddie,

Have I picked up your reference to the Hungarian Doorman correctly? Does it refer to the joke that defines a Hungarian as a man who enters a revolving door behind you and, out of devious Hungarian cleverness, emerges ahead of you? I have an unending appetite for Hungarian-linked-to-Romanian jokes. One that my friend Edward Shils loved asked what was the difference between a Hungarian and a Romanian? The answer is that each will sell you his grandmother, but the Romanian won't deliver. (More available on request.) Edward's knowledge of ethnic and nationality qualities was nearly inexhaustible. "Yes," he might say, "he's quite intelligent – for a Bengali." One day he took me to lunch with François Furet, the historian (as you know) responsible for turning around the standard interpretation of the French Revolution as on balance a damn fine thing. When, afterwards, I commented on some quality of Furet's – I cannot recall which quality it was – Edward replied, "What do you expect? He's a Corsican." Since I had not before, nor have I since, met another Corsican, this came as wholly fresh news to me.

I'm pleased to learn that your show with Tom Conti went well. (From the other shore, as Alexander Herzen might put it, your relationship with Tom C. seems odd. He has never had so rich a part as the one you wrote for him in *The Glittering Prizes*, and one wonders if he is playing it still.) I feel rather differently than you about personal appearances. Whenever I am interviewed – either on a stage before an audience or for print – though it doesn't happen all that often, I feel a very great fraud. Somewhere from my boyhood comes the admonition against talking about oneself, especially against bragging about one's self. Being asked about my brilliant career, I always feel like the old songwriter Sammy Cahn, sitting at the piano, saying, "And then I wrote . . ." and breaking into a hammy, arpeggioistic rendition of "The Tender Trap." I don't mind talking about myself for money, which at least justifies the excess, but I hate, as the girls in the trade say, giving it away for nothing.

I quite agree with your notion that Great but never Popular was thought the right standard for a writer of our generation. I partially believe this still. If a book is an enormous success I tend to think that the reason for this is that a writer is telling his audience something they want to (but shouldn't really) hear, usually something false, if not positively harmful. Some enormous best-sellers, in my experience, are great mysteries. A decade or so ago, an American academic named Allan Bloom – a strange fellow who lived as if he were immensely wealthy even before he in fact became so – wrote such a bestseller called *The Closing of the American Mind,* the large center of which had to do with whether Max Weber or your namesake Freddie Nietzsche had the real lowdown on human nature. Far from a subject, this, that was on every American mind, open or closed. What's more, Allan was able to make it less than blindingly readable, yet this didn't stop hundreds of thousands of people – in France as well as in America – from setting cash on the barrelhead for the book. Lucky man, Professor Bloom.

Great without being Popular is connected, too, to the largely bogus notion of selling out. One was always in the good/bad old days in danger of selling out, whether there were buyers on the scene or not. All the people who worked for *Time* and *Newsweek* or went off to Hollywood had a little drama going in their minds that they were sell-outs. Were it not for their heavy alimony, or sick children, or high-maintenance wives, they wouldn't be in this fix, but would instead be home and at their desks writing that verse drama that would give them a purchase on immortality. Going along with this, Edmundo Wilson, the great Bunny himself, wrote that Henry Luce and Hollywood were the two great destroyers of talent in his time. My own harsh view is that the talent wasn't there in the first place. I'm told that the origin of the phrase *selling out* is in American Communism; one was always in danger, in not adhering (add herring and stir lightly) to the party line, of selling it out. Lots of other problems facing writers and artists in our day, but I don't think selling out is high among them.

My only (mild) success in the bestseller realm was my book *Snobbery.* With paperback and foreign rights and the rest I believe I made perhaps half a million dollars on it. (Cautionary note: never trust authors on royalty figures or actors on the size of their audiences.) Very pleasing when the book first came out were the calls from my editor – like most American publishing editors, now long gone, off to another firm – to inform me that they were reprinting another 10,000 copies, then another 10,000, and so on, not far enough into the night, alas, but pleasing nonetheless. I don't suspect I shall hit the bestseller gong again. (Mind, not a word of this to my publisher.)

Miranda Seymour fades for me into that blur of English biographer-women: Hilary, Hermione, Claire and the rest – One Fat Englishwoman, as I like, collectively, to think of them. I do believe I recall reading about her book about her father. As for Mme Seymour reviling you for writing about sex beyond a certain age (yours), I think we can bring her up in political-correctness court, charging her with ageism, Your Honor.

Lots of characters in my stories end up in the sack, but I have never been able to describe, with a straight face, what they do once they arrive there. Instead I bring them into the room and I later see them out. But they zip no zippers, I name no parts (unlike Henry Reed's soldiers), I allow no-one to emit any grunts (à la the current crop of women tennis players), or moan no moans (à la the people who had money with Uncle Bernie Madoff). Whatever happens goes on behind the curtain; and I let my readers become their own pornographers, mindful always, as La Rochefoucauld had it, that a dirty mind never sleeps.

Let me assure you that I have no intention of reading the Jonathan Littell novel, which has already been nicely blasted in these United States. You are incontrovertibly right, though, about Nazi tailoring: untoppable.

Well, I had better stop here lest, as Max Beerbohm once said in a letter to his dear friend Reggie Turner, "I lapse into brilliancy," even though it hasn't happened for me thus far.

Best, Joe

Dear Joe,

'Have the breasts you want and pay later', says the subscription to the space in which I write this. How sweet this call to whoever the female Narcissus is! Note that the ad does not offer her (the addressee is portrayed as feminine) the breasts HE wants, and might well, in another age, pay for in advance. No, this lady is assumed to want to please herself more than any other, however significant. I recall, many years ago (God knows, no shortage there) when we lived in southern Spain, being very surprised when an American friend, whose outspokenness was a sharp surprise, came out with the advice that I should on no account 'do anything' about my nose. Back in 1960 it was, of course, not unknown for girls with large conks (a Britishism for nasal attachments) to have them – usually very noticeably – 'corrected', but the idea that I should wish to abbreviate my nose, or that I was, so to say, 'allowed' to, was startlingly Yank. My nose was my nose and I'd live with it, as I would, and have, with other attributes. I try to keep fit, but I have never addressed myself to pectoral improvement, abs abolition or any of the other things that today's nervous Narcissi do in order to endure the sight of themselves. My French alternate, Michel Pic, has remarked, '*En vieillards, les Narcisses ne se regardent jamais à l'eau*'.

I had, of course, known a fair number of Americans before we went to live in Fuengirola, then a fishing village, still without a jetty because vindictive Franco denied it one, on account of the poor fisherfolk having burned the church before the Moors came and restored Christian order, but most of the Yanks I met had been GIs from my mother's generation, who came to our apartment with care packages from PX and 8th Air Force wings for little, but growing, Freddie. In Fuengirola we got to know Americans of our own age and I started to feel a certain nostalgia for the States which has been growing in a strange surge of silly regret in the last few years, not least because the British became so virulently anti-US that my split personality began to come apart at its seemingly seamless seams. Nothing a quick, bicephalous dialogue-exchange can't profit from, but there it certainly is.

The American thing probably held me closer than I knew all along. Looking back (is this an Orpheus complex that I see behind me?), I have never been an entirely English writer: at Cambridge I read huge amounts of off-subject stuff, not least almost all the novels of Sinclair Lewis, Faulkner (author of *As I Lay Parenthesising*), Hemingway, Dos P., J.P. Marquand (not so bad) and who all else, Dorothy Parker and the *New Yorker* short story compendia in some future volume of which I dreamed of figuring. I wrote a column in *Varsity* in which, though no-one much noticed, I intruded descants on Perelmanly themes and waxed Winchelly where I might, sniping at contemporaries in a way that I imagined to be endearing. Some still hate me for having drawn a bow at their ventures.

We all read Thurber in those days. I recall (and so, alas, does she) how I tried to seduce, well charm, Beetle by DESCRIBING Thurber's cartoons and telling her the captions – 'Perhaps this will refresh your memory', and 'Who is this Hitler and what does he want?' – in the fond expectation that she would laugh. She did too, a little bit; she has done the same to my jokes down the years. That's my girl, and then some. I still remember some of Thurber's stories, not least that bit from, surely, 'Walter Mitty', when he becomes a gangster and chides his wife with 'What a dumb moll I picked!' I didn't; nor, I know, did you. Thurber now seems a somewhat sorry figure, immortal but only just, addicted – as so many of the so few have been – to the institutional comfort, enviable as hell, of the *New Yorker*, in which I have appeared just once, as a publishing scoundrel at Kubrick's expense. The editor sent me a letter saying, sorta, that my piece was the highlight of his tenure, but he probably sends out a dozen of those a day. Cheaper than flowers.

I went up to Cambridge armed (I'll say) with that vaunted major scholarship and half a bottle of sophisticated whisky. On the train, I happened to be in a compartment with an American whose accent, I suppose, must have declared itself. Imagining that he might be as lonely as I feared I should be myself, I invited him to come and visit me in the college that I had yet to visit. Oddly enough (perhaps, for a brief time he WAS lonely), the already graduate US student DID come and knock on my 'oak' (the outer door of our rooms could be closed to visitors, the assumption being that one was too busy with Aristotle to have time for chitchat) and I unscrewed the bottle of whisky like a grown-up tough guy. I don't remember what was said, but my visitor must have had access to many smarter doors. His name, however, I DO remember: George Plimpton. He was, unknown to me, of course, one of the big fish that slipped my net before I had time to unfold it or enfold him. He went on to . . . ubiquity pretty well and the *Paris Review* in particular. I nearly knew George Plimpton, Joe, and now what am I going to do? Is there a book in it?

Tout à toi,
Freddie

Dear Freddie,

I was interviewed by the *Paris Review*, ten or so years ago, by a then-young poet named Ben Downing. He took roughly eight months to type up his tape recording, and when he returned it to me I found what I had to say so intolerably dull that I killed the interview. I've never had the least doubts about having done so. The fact is that any allure that the *Paris Review* interviews had, ended with the generation of Evelyn Waugh. Who could possibly care what such writers as William Styron, Salman Rushdie or Joyce Carol Oates and other subsequent interviewees have to say about the so-called art of writing, or even the art of talking about oneself? Ms. Oates, unlike the much better Miss Otis, has no regrets, publishes faster than rabbits fornicate, or are said to (I've never actually watched them), and my regret is that she hasn't thus far won the Nobel Prize for Literature, which I think would put the final kibosh on the damn thing. I have not won many prizes for my scribbling, and I don't expect to win many, but I do know that winning any of them would not persuade me that I am a great man, if only because, not only do I know better, but they have by now all been tarnished, not to say be-pigeonized, by having been won by third-rate people.

I never met George Plimpton, though I am told that he used to say kind things about my writing behind my back. Along with William F. Buckley, Jr. and Gore Vidal, he constituted the rather pathetic aristocratic vein of recent American scribblers. Plimpton and Buckley came from money, and Buckley married still more money, while Vidal has always insisted on being well born, if rarely well behaved. What clinched it for all three was their mid-Atlantic accents, which gave them an air of unearned superiority. No-one is more snobbish than a Democrat, and no country is more democratic than the United States. Of our three pseudo-aristocrats, Plimpton and Buckley seemed to enjoy themselves hugely through good living: party-giving and -going, lots of boozing, buying swell toys, boats and harpsichords and town houses in Buckley's case. Buckley was also secretly charitable to young writers, or so I have been told, keeping a fund to help some among them with injections of cash, which makes up in part for some of the genuinely wretched political positions he took up as a young man: he was pro-Senator Joseph McCarthy in a coarse way, and he was for states' rights, which in those days meant that he wanted to keep racial segregation nicely in place.

I have no difficulty understanding your mind floating over to the question of what your life would have been like had your parents remained in America and had you been brought up here. For one thing, my guess is, your schooling would have been very different, on both sides of the ledger. You would not have encountered the ugly upper-middle and upper-class anti-Semitism that you did in England; here most anti-Semitism has been traditionally boorish, and, though it sometimes has had the threat of violence behind it, coming as it largely did from the working classes, it wasn't such as to make one ashamed of being Jewish – quite the contrary. Having been educated in the United States, you would have more likely spent your life in a single language, and not been able to pop about as jollily as you now do in three or four (French, Latin, Modern Greek). Your gift for foreign language would, as like as not, probably not have emerged. You would in every way have been a less international character (not to say rootless cosmopolitan Hebe) than you now are. As an American, your mind would have had less to play upon, or so I believe. Your style would probably be less ironic, your wit of a very different cast. Since I happen to have derived much pleasure from you, your irony, your style, and your wit, I believe that your growing up in England was an OK, if not altogether damn fine thing, and think that you ought to believe it, too.

I tried to reread James Thurber a few years ago, but with no luck. I found so much of his humor provincial and not even smile-making. "The Secret Life of Walter Mitty" and his few splendidly oblique cartoons are, I suspect, all that remain. I've long thought of the *New Yorker* of those years as divided between the small-town writers (Thurber and E.B. White) and the big-city boys (A.J. Liebling, S.J. Perelman, and – though he was born in North Carolina – Joseph Mitchell), and I preferred the big-city boys with their urban interests and urbane manner.

Not that you ever would have seriously considered doing so, but I'm glad you never de-conked yourself. Yours, which I know only from the photographs on your books, strikes me as a fine nose, a chosen nose, and one that doesn't disappoint. My own snoz (as Jimmy Durante called it, and he was himself in fact called The Snoz) is fairly ordinary. My ears, fleshy and standing out smartly away from my head, are highly Hebraic.

I've had a fairly good week: I wrote a $5,000 piece for *Newsweek* on the poor performance of the usually haughty economists during the great meltdown, another for $1,500 for a magazine called *In Character* on the subject of the need for artists never to allow the grit required by their work to show through, and was informed that a story of mine called "Beyond the Pale" was chosen for *The Best American Short Stories 2009.* I am pleased to continue to be invited to write for magazines, and if the price is respectable usually accept the invitation. Continuing to be invited means that the fourth stage of my career has not yet quite begun. You may recall these all too inevitable stages. Stage One: Who is Joseph Epstein?; Two: This is a job for Joseph Epstein; Three: What we need here is a younger Joseph Epstein; and Four: Who is Joseph Epstein?

Keep the faith.

Best, Joe

Dear Joe,

Money is one thing, vanity another; but they share the driving, don't they, when it comes to a writer's course? In some ways, I am more exhausted and strangely guilty after indulging in a spate of vanity than when I have been at the rock face, or the shithole, doing what Proust would never have agreed to do, though Faulkner and who all else, lacking family money, proved less reluctant, and serving some recruiting sergeant, or marshal, whose summons has the lure of fat payment and the promise, however rarely kept, of worthy production and high fame. The vanity-guilt is all my own fault, of course. I've been the victim these last weeks of the elderly form of a personal tour, taking the Golden Oldie role in Glasgow and Dublin before, last night, participating in a memorial show for the producer of *The Glittering Prizes*, a man called Mark Shivas. *Festschrift*, you academics might say. In showbiz/snowbiz, these things take the form of a sequence of clips from a man's life's work (quite a plump dossier in Mark's case) each introduced by or interspersed with the podium appearances of ex-chums, potentates, actors and writers who loved him as they have rarely loved anyone.

The venue was a place in Piccadilly called BAFTA, the British Academy of – oh you know – Film and Television Arts, an association which affects to be the Britannic equivalent of the Oscarmakers. The president of the said organisation, a famous unknown called Parfitt (not yet a gentle knight, but working at it), made the opening address, affecting grief and personal knowledge, and then came a clip from a British film, written by Alan Bennett, called *A Private Function*, I think; it featured Michael Palin and Maggie Smith (THE over-actress of her time, and the time before, so long has she been making faces and noises) being upstaged by a pig with diarrhoea. The audience was somewhat more amused by this outstanding instance of British art and intelligence than I was. They savoured the nasal wrinkling which pig poo provoked in La Smith and hooted at her order to Palin to kill the pink animal with a chiropodist's tool. The specification of chiropody was a typical pawky touch by Mr Bennett, now a national treasure: primly outspoken, ex-Oxford-donnish, buy-sexual and tricky as dicky while affecting up-from-the-Styx bewilderment at metropolitan sophistication.

The pig's last close-up was my cue. Had I been an antique Jew, *de bonne souche*, I should, of course, have refused to follow a pig, but I am such a sport that I even gave it a fraternal wink as I went centre-stage. I'd been debating whether to dissipate the doleful mood with the Billy Wilder line, 'You know when you're really finished in showbusiness: they don't even ask you to be a pall-bearer any more'. Not sure whether this was too risky, I still went for it, muffed my negatives but still got the laugh; it's the way I don't tell them. I got into my stride, birdying the next coupla holes so to speak, by bold reference to the Chosen and then to 'the rest of you people' (a chance for the Brits to be chucklingly gallant) and then hit a long drive onto the last green by citing Martial's line '*Sint Maecenates non deerunt, Flacce, Marones*'. For a nasty, but typically Raphael second, I affected the belief that they could all do without the translation, which is of course, 'Let there be enough Maecenases and we shall never be short of Virgils'. The modern version, which I gave them right between the eyes, was 'Give us enough Shivases and we can have some decent television'. I'd been asked to be brief, and so I was, if not entirely sincere (who needs that?). In truth, I had helped to make the guy's career and when he became a panjandrum at the BBC (head of drama and film), he never gave me a jingle. When men climb that twisty stair to a high place, they rarely crave the presence of faces that might remind them of who else they needed to get there.

Other speakers were neither brief nor witty; the evening took on the lineaments of a High Day and Holyday, without the heights but with plenty of grey holes, not the least of them being the 'clips' which, as so often, displayed the shortness of cinematic shelf-life. All that effort and money, and throat-cutting, and the result is clunking, obvious, melodramatic, specially-effective and – even when it is only yesterday's – dated. All the speakers spoke of Mark with admiration and affection and I felt somewhat like a diplomat from outer space, who attended politely, spoke warmly but lacked the chumminess that others paraded, or had other feelings entirely. Perhaps it was that American thing kicking in, but the more warmly and flatteringly I was greeted, during the canapés and no-thank-you wine that came afterwards, the more I realised that, in Willie Maugham's phrase to me, fifty-five years ago, 'More people know Tom Fool than Tom Fool knows'.

Somehow I have become obscurely famous in a society in which I have always been a stranger. Despite my affectations of showbiz solidarity, I felt only the slightest strands of – let's say – naffinity with the people present. One did talk to me about Wittgenstein and recalled a story, which I did not know, of a couple on a ship in the Red Sea (I think the guy said) to whose table a 'tall' fellow passenger came, on the third day out, and clicked his heels and said 'Wittgenstein'. This, I was told, was when W. was considering attaching himself to the Soviet Union. Why did I hear myself say, 'It's a nice story but Wittgenstein was only five feet seven, tops'? Then I got into a discussion (all this before the non-existent curtain went metaphorically up) with a man who had been commissioned to do a series about the man (?) whom an old friend of mine used to call 'the late J. Christ Esquire'. The writer had had a committee of nine pseudo-ecumenical divines to check his doctrinal line and, of course, nothing ever came of the whole enterprise except (we have to hope) the unreturnable fee. This guy told me what I think he thought I wanted to hear: that the Jews couldn't have killed Jesus because the Sanhedrin was never an 'orthodox religious body'. Again I heard myself correcting the last speaker on several points of detail which happened to be in my quiver because I have been delving deep into old Jeru in pursuit of knowledge, a new line on the ancient world, human belief, *ta meteora*, and – last, never least – Pantheon's welcome buckaroos.

Money has become an obsession in the sinking ship and fortunes of the British who have ridden the waves of decade-long prosperity without ever ruling them. That their revenues have been derived from unchained capital-istic gambling has never been part of what was said to the People, by the nabobs of New Labour (Tony Blair's vacuous political slogan standing in the place where Keir Hardie and Aneurin Bevan and Michael Foot – all probably unknowns in your political equations – once prated of Nationalisation, the Working Class and Socialism, numbers that no-one who voted for the shell of their party ever thought they would have to think of again). Now the bankers and their 'bonus culture' (cliché of the day) are the great villains and our long slothful dependence on what could be leeched out of them by the Revenue has left the British obesely unprepared for getting down to it, whatever IT is, always assuming that it's there to be got down to (nitty-gritty is in small supply). Showbiz is always said to be counter-sicklick but no-one in the film and TV world has much confidence or moolah, since want of advertising is sapping one of the major TV stations and threatens to topple another. If the Huns and the Goths were massing on our frontiers, they might well turn their stout little ponies in another direction; forget easy, even difficult pickings are rare.

I find myself sorry for others (losing houses, their pensions shrivelled, etc.) but not for myself: I never expected to get lucky, but I did, somewhat, and now we have about enough to survive, if things don't get a LOT worse, and I am still able to do what I always thought was the only thing that REALLY mattered, write stuff that people can take (great) or leave (pity) but affords them no right to give me 'notes' on or ask for rewrites because the punters don't know zip about Maecenas or anything else too much. It's not that I think I'm that smart, it's just that I still read and annotate books like a student who just might catch up, if he works at it. I still write like a man who never wanted to do anything else much, except make love, of course, and a name, I guess; but above all, I like to write those sentences that Hemingway and Scott used to talk about that have no fat on them and will survive the long haul. Readers may yet swarm to the shelves where my works (some of them) are sandwiched, thinly, not far from Roth and Rushdie. Fat chance? I'll take it. *On continue*. But enough of the (unpaid) podium for a while.

Tout à toi,
Freddie

Dear Freddie,

Good to think of you and Mme R. back in France, or *Tsarskoye Selo*, as I believe the Tsar's summer castle was called, though you are not, I realize, the Tsar and Beetle is not Anastasia and your home in France is not for summer use only. I am not a man who allows such minor inconveniences to get in the way of an exotic phrase or zippy analogy. I don't wish to refer to your place as Castel Gandolfo, the Pope's summer palace, for you are even less like the Pope than you are like the Tsar, and where would that leave Beetle. The Pope's wife? I don't think so, as the kids nowadays say.

Ah, show business, than which, we are told, there is no similar business, and everything about which, near as I can make out, is appalling. People in the biz do enjoy celebrating one another, and they are usually able to do so in obscenely public ways: award ceremonies, televised roasts, events of the kind you describe here. The display for Mark Shivas is a nifty example. (I have not hitherto heard of Mark Shivas, but *shiva*, as you know, is the Jewish ritual of week-long grieving over the dead, carried on, generally, at the home of a relative.) Mark Shivas, sounds like, has now had his *shiva* condensed into a few boring hours.

Not being remotely part of the great Biz of Show – having written one failed (though at least paid-for) screenplay and having had a few items of mine optioned for this or that unsuccessful project – I do not get to attend such spectacles. But when I attend memorials, I always do so with my radar tuned for lies and nonsense, both of which are usually in ample supply. Some wise fellow said that one must never allow anyone who asks to speak at such memorials to do so. That person will only use the occasion to talk about himself. Experience has borne (also bored) this out. When my friend Erich Heller died, six people spoke at his memorial, fully three of whom he spoke to me of as (insert your best Teutonic accent here) "utter clowns." Something oddly indecent about stupid things being said over a person's dead body. When my father died, I asked the officiating rabbi, who didn't know my father, to speak in Hebrew only, and leave the English to me, for I didn't want him saying, in the language of the Houyhnhnms, "the things that are not." I have left instructions with my son that I am to have no memorial service, and instead an afternoon party among friends. Although I won't be around to hear it, I prefer not to have any crapola spoken about my many fine deeds.

I was taken by your remarks about Alan Bennett. Of the *Beyond the Fringe* gang, he appears to be the one acquiring the most stars in his banner. Who'd thunk? He's come up quietly on the outside and defeated the other three Fringers. He is, as you say, now fully a bloody national treasure. He strikes me as a not talentless man, but in a minor key. He is for all good things, Alan Bennett, the poor, the environment, the common people, and of course against all the bad things, war, the rich (himself excluded), and all that is insensitive and vile. All this was quite predictable, and predictably boring, mostly, as such politics generally are at bottom (no puns, please), about self-congratulation: look what a sweet fine virtuous son-of-a-bitch I am! Most of this turns up in his diaries, which I used to read in the *London Review of Books* before I canceled my subscription.

Bennett's having come out in recent years makes this more than a touch worse. I saw the movie version of *History Boys*, which I thought very well acted. Very smart, too, did I find it on the subject of education, and how it really works, which, as a teacher of thirty years in Plato's old cave, I can tell you it rarely does. And then the homosexual subject obtruded; more than obtruded, it quite took over, giving the movie its theme. I took this theme to be, so what's so wrong about allowing your teacher to give you a blowjob? Not, let us agree, a major theme, but evidently one on old Alan Bennett's mind.

Your mention of Aneurin ("Nye" to insiders, was it not?) Bevan and Michael Foot reminded me of my days – in the early 1960s – as a reader of the air edition of the *New Statesman*. When I began reading it, I believe a very smooth fellow named John Freeman was its editor. Was he replaced by, or had he replaced, Paul Johnson, I cannot recall. I dropped away during the editorship of R.H.S. ("Dick") Crossman, who was a brilliant political journalist, though not a very appealing human being. But, then, I was always a back-of-the-book man, a reader of V.S. Pritchett on Books, Wilfrid Mellers on Music, Reyner Banham on Architecture. In those days I thought of myself, nonetheless, as a Fabian Socialist, which was much more elegant than the grubby American version of socialist. All this, you understand, was the purest

American Anglophiliac snobbery, but still rather tasteful for an ignorant boy in his early twenties.

The one English journalist with whom I had something like a relationship was Sir William Haley, who, I always thought, was compiling the perfect resume, editorial division. He was, you may recall, the editor of the *Manchester Guardian* and later of *The Times*, and then director-general of the BBC, following Lord Reith, I think. Both Barbara and I worked for him (before we were married) when he took up, all too briefly, the editorship of the *Encyclopaedia Britannica* (still working on that perfect resume; only the editorship of the *Oxford English Dictionary* remained for him to complete it). Barbara was his administrative assistant, and I was his senior editor for Biography, Geography, and History. He lasted perhaps two years at *Britannica*, and then office intrigues forced him, quite properly, to fold up his tent and return to the Channel Islands.

Sir William was among the last of the great Englishmen. He never went to university, yet his learning was immense. He also had an unshakably high standard. He was reticent, quite without gossip, yet penetrating in his analysis of character. He wore what looked to be three-ply English tweed suits, and in all seasons. He and his wife used to take walks of monstrous distances across Chicago. I was never his intimate – I don't think his personality allowed for intimate friends – when he was living in Chicago. But later, in letters, he opened up to me in ways I found most touching. When I left *Britannica*, a few years after he, I recall his writing to me, "I am glad you are no longer at *Britannica*. The people in charge there worship different gods than we." Can you imagine anyone alive today who could write such a sentence, irony free as it is, as that second one? I cannot. He came to a sad end, spending his last years under the torture of shingles, dying at eighty-six.

I am finally beginning to recover from what has been fully a week-long cold, one of those knock-down jobs, that sucks away all one's energy. I am a lifelong sufferer from *schpilkes*, or needles in the pants, and a serious *schilp-koid* with no energy is a pathetic being to behold. There is no cure for *schlipkes*, as you may know, nor even a rock star who helps raise money for it, but any contribution you would like to make will be gratefully accepted.

Best, Joe

Dear Joe,

The lacuna between dispatches that has widened and become a gulf (can a *kolpos* be the next rank up from a lacuna? It is now) is now bridged, filled in,

whatever seems to allow passage. The shame of it all is that I was faced in
la France profonde (another lacuna-land) with what seemed a dead laptop, a
mechanical impotence no salve could appease nor slave correct. The black
screen faced me with the impassivity I dread and was powerless to remedy. As
a result, I had that (racially?) typical feeling that the world had turned against
me and that, despite the steady beauty of a fortnight's fine days, I was, in the
lingo of the land, *largement foutu*. I wasn't, of course, and by an effort of will
which was surprisingly successful, and even a little bit smug-making, I
decided to conceal my chagrin from Beetle, whose birthday fell in the middle
of our fortnight (you can see that the English brand has scarcely failed to mark
me), in order not to spoil our idyll and made out that I did not need a machine
in order to be a writer. I once said as much to Mr Kubrick, which planted a
banderilla between his omoplates. During the last week and a bit I proved it
by writing 20,000 words in longhand on the subject of Joseph ben Matthias
latterly known as Titus Flavius Josephus, his slave name in truth, though he
was allowed to believe that he was a Roman citizen chum of the Emperor
Vespasian and his Jerusalem-burning son Titus.

I don't know if you still compose (ba-ba-ba-boom) in manuscript at all
but I do find, and did last week, that the pen between the fingers is driven
in different directions, in different spasms and rhythms, than this sweetly
restored box can contrive. I realised – pen in hand – that Josephus's *Jewish
Antiquities* (a journalistico-historical rescript of the biblical narrative, and
beyond) was the first, but never the last, example of Our People's obsessive
re-creation in words of any number of *temps perdus* ('persuds' was a typo
which our friend Jim Joyce might have wallowed in, *mais moi j'ai pas le temps*);
bref, Josephus was the first Marcel. I didn't actually manuscript that but it is
implicit in my verbiage which, true to the spirit of Balbec, was devoted almost
entirely to the turning point/crossing point of Joseph deciding not to die with
the rest of the garrison in a crappy little siege in a place called Jotapata (sounds
like a Japanese board game) where he was forced to take command, since he
was playing general at the time, even though he would never normally have
spent a night of his Holydays in such a grim little spot. Instead, he was visited
by the Holy One with a message for Vespasian that he was going to win El
Gordo and become *el jefe de todo el* known *mundo*; the need to deliver this
cancelled any moral obligation to go down with his ship, and shipmates, in a
manner of speaking, and required your namesake (it had to come up) to go
over to, it has to be said, the goyim. With whom he became a literally resident
Jewboy, regardless of the opinion of Yigael Yadin, another general of another

epoch, who described him as 'a great historian and a bad Jew'. There's the crux, professor: which would you choose to be, which would I? And, since we do not go to synagogue, can endure non-Jews in the family, and don't believe every word Norman Podhoretz tells us we should, we know the sad answer, do we not?

I wish, in some ways, that I could approach the Josephus commission in some measure of the same facetious style of the above blurbish burble, but I don't think Pantheon would keep me a niche in their temple if I did and, anyway, it would probably drive the reader to give me the Dorothy Parker hurl. What's curious, though not central, in Josephus the Jewish historian is, as John Schlesinger used to say, 'not many laughs there!' Remembering, as many of us do, that Jesus wept but never told the one about the Siamese twins and the Chicago businessman, it has to be accepted that the famous sense of humour makes a pretty late appearance in the quasi-national character. Which was the first Jewish joke? His sons laughing at Noah's nakedness? But then was Noah really a Jew? By a captain he *was* a captain, which argues against it. Also he preceded Moses who brought the good news and the bad news down the mountain and force-fed it to the guys who turned into the Jews. Kenneth Burke has a line somewhere about unification being what people decide on when they are not united. Monotheism has a similar rallying purpose: the spiritual version of one-size-fits-all and no returns; those who really share a culture don't need to kneel to the same God. Hey, you maybe know that.

Next case, as the bridge players say. There is something comic, it's a pleasure to say, in feelings of deprivation at the interruption of a correspondence with a friend who seems remarkably close although he is some 5,500 miles away and whom I have never met. *Le style* isn't entirely *l'homme*, but I suppose it has something to do with him since by your voice, which I hear with great specificity, I recognise and smile at you, as if present. 'A man's subconscious', some smart-ass screenwriter wrote in a terrible movie, 'is a maudlin swamp'. Cambridge men spell that a 'Magdalen' swamp, which is why you never know exactly where you are with the educated British. There is, I mean, something funny and slightly magic about what feels like a close friendship of our kind. How often, I wonder, did Montaigne meet the slightly older La Boétie, than whom Micheau eventually became much older, since Étienne died in his, I think, early twenties, after composing just one masterpiece that combined elegance and nerve, his superb *Discours de la servitude volontaire*? Étienne, as we all call him around here, was a native of Sarlat, our nearest town in the Perigord, and I salute his statue (not *every* time) when I pass it in the leafy parking lot. Such is the role of great lovers of freedom in the better world with which they have graced us: they become pedestalled parking attendants.

I think your book on friendship probably has a place in, as they will say, energising my end of our good'n'badinage. I read it with a kindled spirit of emulation: what might a man have to do to be wanted as a lunch companion by that picky and choosy Epstein man? I could imagine someone being greeted in the street with a beckoning wave (presidentially displayed by Marty Sheen in *The Vest Ving*, so called in some quarters because of the heavy Semitic presence in the creative team) and being asked a civil question or two ('How's the Hegel Companion coming?', 'Where do you get your snazzy blazers?') and then, well, being told that he and J.E. (*qui est un autre*, little Rimbawd noticed) must get together sometime for a coffee and Danish, and I could imagine that guy walking away thinking, 'I'm a friend of Joe Epstein's' and I could also – there's no end to this piece of string, if string is what it's a piece of – imagine the said Epstein saying to himself something between 'Why did I bother to stop?' and 'Never again'. It wasn't Hegel, by the way, in my story about this encounter, it was Herder. And the man walking away was thinking maybe he should dump Herder and go for the bigger target; did Epstein really mean to be saying that? He must like me a LOT. Yes, that little *bouquin* got me loitering around the courts, bouncing a ball against the practice wall and wondering whether one day . . .

I still wonder, as a closet series-plotter, whether the great executive producer in the sky plans for us ever to meet and what kind of a wry twist he can put on the encounter if it ever takes place. The oddity is, we HAVE met, often, and it's obvious from the variety of our (what else?) discourse. An argument for the transcendental dimension, would you say? Nobody has to. As for the friends that one *has* met, they begin to twitch on the twig of mortality and, with increasing frequency, to fall. Some friends' deaths are truly painful; I know you felt lanced by the same shaft which felled Shils, and so did I with the death of Michael Ayrton, with whom I was never, in the precise sense that the French make so much of, an *ami intime* and also with Kenneth McLeish, with whom I did a good deal of translating from Greek and Latin and to whom I spoke every Sunday, for an hour or more. He was my Carian friend, I suppose; and we always had much to say, even though I knew there was a gulf (if never a lacuna) between us. He once told me that I was the nicest Jew he had ever met. And then rang back to apologise because, on playback, it didn't sound quite as he meant it to. Oh they do have trouble with us, don't they?

I heard on our return to the smallish pile of mail that awaited us that a man who was my neighbour in my first year in Cambridge had died. We spent a good deal of time together, since he was not only in the Footlights but also switched (from maths in his case) to philosophy; we went to 'super-visions' together and once were invited to dinner in Trinity by Charlie Broad, a shiny-headed homophile whose taste was for Nordic blondes. With puckish humour he had declared himself, in published work, to share the racial tastes of the late Führer, but if this comprised anti-Semitism (which I doubt, although he was no acolyte of Ludwig der Great) he was hampered in the exercise of his supposed prejudices by not recognising one when he invited him to dine. So Tony Becher, my neighbour and – if proximity defines these things – close friend, died last week and was buried, I think, on Monday. I am as sentimental as any sad-eyed brigadier ('La Marseillaise' alone has me wondering where the Kleenex is), but I confess that I felt no emotion at all at the news of Tony leaving us. I had not, it's true, seen, spoken or heard from him since he divorced his first wife, a woman for whom I had no appe-tite when they were together but whom he treated (we were told) so badly, by breaking his word about property, that I have reserved a soft spot for her ever since.

I realise, thinking about Tony, that I have always been an easy pick-up for friendly burrs; I am content to spend a lot of time alone, the reading mit de writing make this congenial, but a little pathetic in my gratitude for company of almost any kind. Then, rather often now that I have so many years to look back at, something nearly always happens, especially with those with whom my affinity is anything but elective (if I understand Gertie's term correctly); an abreaction sets in with virulent force and that's that. This reminds me of what I may have told you already, what Allan Jay Lerner said to Andrew Lloyd Webber when the latter asked him, 'Allan, why do you suppose so many people dislike me on sight?' Lerner said, 'Well, I guess it saves time.' *Mais quel anglais ce pauvre* Webber! Walked smack into it. Some people never lern.

Let's hear from you after this movie-length special.

Tout à toi,
Freddie

Dear Freddie

Few things, outside of bad medical news, are drearier than the breakdown of one's computer. One feels a staggering helplessness, a pre-Viagranian impotence, accompanied by extreme terror that everything on the machine is forever lost in that great dystopia called cyberspace. I have known this helplessness, this impotence, this terror, and it brings no joy, in Mudville or anywhere else.

Being myself totally in thrall to computers for my scribbling I am all the more impressed at your feat – it is nothing less than a feat, early in the twenty-first century – of writing out 20,000 words of your Josephus book in longhand. Fifteen or so years ago, I wrote everything out in first draft in pen; then I copied that, making many changes in doing so, on my dear old Royal Standard typewriter, for a second draft; and then the next day, I cleaned up by retyping what I considered a third and usually final draft. I'm not sure whether this method, or my current method of going over and over my computer tappings, made me the better writer. I do know that working on the computer, especially in the matter of revisions, makes things seem greatly easier. Sometimes, owing to computers, I feel that revising is the best part of writing. Meanwhile, apart from my daily journal entries, I've not written any formal composition other than by computer for at least a decade.

Still on the subject of methods of scribbling, for years I had a fountain-pen fetish. (Strange word, fetish, sounding as it does almost like a Jewish name: Irving Fetish, Attorney at Law.) I was in search of the perfect pen, the one from which nothing but beautiful, precise, quite perfect words would flow. I acquired Mont Blancs, Pelikans, even a Cartier pen. One night I dreamed that a man named Morris Philipson, then the director of the University of Chicago Press, and himself a considerable snob – a Bloomsbury-lover, for God's sake – showed me a well-worn old Mont Blanc he acquired that he said was originally owned by Rudyard Kipling. How, I wondered in my dream, can I inveigle this valuable pen from this less than valuable man? Or would I have to resort to straight violence to get it from him? Alas, I woke before the final solution, to coin a phrase, presented itself. (Because of their poor endings, dreams, as pure story-telling, tend to be aesthetically unsatisfactory, at least mine do.) I still own twelve or so fairly expensive pens, though I use only one regularly: a slender, mid-priced Mont Blanc, and my hunt for the perfect pen is now over. Do you, I wonder, see a possible movie script here? Indiana Epstein and the Search for the Magic Quill.

Do know that if we passed on the street, you should not get away without my dragging you into a nearby restaurant – as like as not, a Grecian spoon, as we call the Greek restaurants that preponderate in Chicago – for a three-hour (minimum) schmooze. And yet, having said this, I must go on to say that I am all right with our present arrangement of never having seen each other, or even of having never heard each other's voices. When your computer went down, and I hadn't heard from you for fully a week, I thought perhaps something else was wrong, and that I ought to call you in France to find out if all was OK. The thought of doing so made me edgy, in the old-fashioned sense of the word. What if the timing of our conversation was off kilter? What if one or the other of us – more likely, me – said something profoundly stupid? I do, of course, hope that we meet one day, but for now I am perfectly content to let things stand just as they are. I am reminded here, somehow, that Wallace Stevens, the most exotic of American poets, never visited Europe, though he wrote French quite well and used to order paintings from a French agent there. My guess is that he felt no great need to be in Europe, such was the power of his imagination, and it may well have been that the Europe of his imagining was much grander than the actual continent.

When friends go down, especially more than one at a time, Edward Shils used to say, "Be careful: the machine-gunner is out." Henry James says somewhere that, once one reaches the age of fifty, someone one knows dies every week. Certainly, in our day, this is true by seventy. I sedulously read the Irish sporting pages, as the obituary pages are called, and no week passes without my recognizing someone from my past, if not a friend then the friend of a friend, who has taken the final bullet. Just now, in the casualty list, the thing I find most distressing is the dementia suffered by a dear friend who is eighty-one; he is a man, moreover, of a once powerful intellect, an accomplished critic – so much for keeping one's mind active as a way of warding off dementia. His wife reports to me that one of the latest sadnesses in the bleak closing scenes of his life is that he has taken to nicking (I believe the English slang word is) cookies and muffins from a nearby coffee shop, where, through an arrangement between the owner and my friend's wife, he now, in effect, has a running tab. Oy, oy, and oy, as a certain ethnic people say.

Grub Street notes: More than three months ago I wrote a few paragraphs for an issue of *Standpoint*. I was sent a single contributor's copy of my little piece but no check for the 200 promised pounds. Three or four e-mails still didn't produce any check. Finally, last week the check arrived, made out to the sum of 200 pounds, which my local bank informs me will cost me a fee of $45 to translate into dollars and the money on the *Standpoint* check will take as many as four weeks to collect. I got off one of those angry little blasts that e-mail makes all too easy to execute, informing a woman at the magazine that such incompetence makes writing for *Standpoint* considerably less than enticing. I seem to remember that there used to be a standing rule that the better the magazine, the worse its business department. But my own feeling is that *Standpoint* is not yet good enough to be so incompetent on its business side. Another rule, the truth to which I can testify, is that the smaller the magazine the ruder the editors.

I have spent the past week writing an essay (which I append below) on a writer you may never have heard of named Isaac Rosenfeld, who is frequently confused with Isaac Rosenberg, the English World War One poet. Isaac Rosenfeld was a contemporary, and high-school classmate, and quondam (in speech sounds like condom) friend of Saul Bellow. Isaac R. died at 38, after leading a dreary bohemian life, with much extracurricular bonking and subscription to terrible ideas: chief among them, those of Wilhem Reich, the orgone-box man. Ford Madox Ford was wrong in *The Good Soldier* about the saddest story: the early death of the promising is the saddest story.

I've also written a short story called "What Are Friends For?," whose *donnée*, as Frank and Jesse James' brother Henry might say, is a man who looks across a restaurant to discover the wife of his oldest and dearest friend at lunch with another man who is clearly not her interior decorator, and is faced with the question of whether to report this discovery to his friend. The story is not quite in finished shape, but once it is I shall pass it along to you.

Barbara and I are off tomorrow morning to spend a week in New York. We shall inhabit there the two rooms, two bath, limited-cooking kitchen of our son Mark's time-share apartment across the street from Carnegie Hall. We'll spend the week walking about Manhattan, seeing some ballet, going to a few of our favorite museums, lunching with a few old friends. I've bought tickets (two for a mere $250) to see Angela Lansbury in *Blithe Spirit*. We both much look forward to our week in New York, a nice place, as the old cliché has it, to visit. I shall tote Barbara's laptop on this trip, and so will be able to receive and send e-mail. I hope to write to you from La Grande Pomme.

Best, Joe

PS: Here, in an attachment, is the Isaac Rosenfeld piece. Feel no need to comment on it.

Dear Joe,

There's a thing I always (no, sometimes) tell those audiences of young persons who, even now, I assume have come for the pearls of my literary intelligence and not, as they mostly have, for swinish hints on how to swim with Hollywood wolves or whatever the zoological situation requires. The thing is: just because a character asks a question doesn't mean another of your characters (his interlocutor, as our friend H.J. would call him) has to answer it right away, if at all; and sometimes, I go on, as one must when alone on the platform, it's nice and true – the desired combo for dialogue writers – if later on the aforesaid interlocutor loops back and answers the question when it seems forgotten, elided or . . . choose your own past participle. You know all this, but they don't, and that's not the point anyway. I am simply circling before loping back along your trail to the traces of Sir William Haley, whom you retrieved so nicely from the oubliette where decent, literary men filed their copy.

I never knew him, but recall that, unless I am wrong, he was the editor of *The Times* (known to you as *The London* – ergo Sulzbergerless – *Times*) who altered the front page, on which there previously figured, among births, deaths and marriages, the so-called Agony Column, in which Sherlock Holmes among others advertised in see-through cryptic form in order to flush out 'Our Man', some clever villain who could be relied on to take the paper, even though it cost – when I first saw it – all of fourpence. (What, I wonder, is the origin of the obsolete English expression 'give him a fourpenny one' which, being translated, means a punch in the nose or allied destination?) Haley, if it was he who put news on the front, previously columnar page, was reviled as a man who would soon be pulling down the pillars of the temple in other respects. The beginning of the end recurs frequently in island history, which is why we're all taking it so well – otherwise known as lying down – that we have an incompetent, conceited and dishonest government: doesn't everyone? Haley always sounded a little bit like a pseudonym, and certainly had one, which I am trying vainly to recall, when he wrote his weekly, perhaps bi-weekly, *Causerie* (can it have been what he called it?) on some literary topic or other.

Your friend (never mine) John Gross – recently stricken I am told, like Agamemnon, not once but twice, and hence no longer a subject for my barbs – would have described Haley as a 'man of letters', which was in derogatory contrast, as if I need to tell you, with real critics such as (forget 'like') Frank Leavis. How the sedentary do admire those who seem unlikely to take prisoners! My friend Peter Green, introducing me in Iowa City (a man can't be famous all over), described me as a man of letters and, shucks, I was rather pleased that such ivy should have grown up my person without my noticing it. Haley was well read and read well: he was a little bit dry but he was very informative and I made lists, some few times, of things he said I should have read, and might even have sought them out. It should be an easy trick to inspire people to read, but how many have it? Haley made you want to read, rather than rock, around the clock and that was no mean inspiration. Edmund Wilson had that effect too, for which, whatever kind of an alky pug he was, I remain in debt to him. Stanley Edgar Hyman turned me on in the mid-1950s to Bodkin and Blackmur and Burke and (can he have?) Trilling and, now I look back, which I do find myself doing, hauled me into the American orbit, a bit. The great thing about men of letters was that they didn't have agendas, or hermeneutic ambitions and seldom used phrases such as 'rhetoricised discourse' or all those other peel'n'stick terminologies which persuade us that yawning is a symptom of higher education.

Your Isaac article was, I noticed, restrained when it came to revealing how you really felt about Bellow. I suppose that Rosenfeld was in part the model for the character of the failure in *Humboldt's Gift* whom I took to be a portrait of Delmore Schwartz. (Does he have a t in his name or not? Listen, I'll cross that one when I come to it.) I don't know Delmore's stuff really, but I find Berryman's phrase about 'Delmore dying' resonates – what else? – adjacent to Yeats's 'And Agamemnon dead'. I used to read Berryman quite zealously, but seem to have given him up, as I have most verse in English (Ted Hughes's huge output leaves me unwelshed). I am due in October (yes, there I go again) to go up to Manchester for some Lit Fest for which I am being paid (pennies, pennies) to choose my desert island poems. I am already wondering what kind of impostor to play; most of my blue remembered verses date from what we used to call 'prep school', i.e. the wartime days between 8 and 13 when I, (a little) like Jesus, Josephus, Spinoza, and who all else astounded the elders with my repartee. We had to learn chunks of stuff, including Greek and Latin prose, if you please, for end-of-term examinations. If Lycidas is not dead, sunk though he be beneath the (or is it 'his'?) watery bier, it's all because I was well drilled. A man I never much liked said that he could never think well of me again after I reviewed *Humboldt* without gush. I remember saying that the book reminded me of the Jewish joke about the man who's asked to a birthday party and calls up to ask for directions. 'Turn right on our street, walk up to the third lamppost and our house is right there; you open the garden gate with your elbow, come up to the front door, ring the bell with your elbow and I'll buzz you in. You open the door with your elbows and come on up.' The imminent guest says, 'What is it about your gate and your bell and your front door that I have to use my elbow? Why my elbow?' 'Because,' the imminent host says, 'your hands'll be full of presents'. The guy who told me that must have known how to tell 'em, but it gave me a chance to say that Bellow offered so many presents that it seemed ungracious to want to fend him off with mine elbows. Even before I heard you on him, Bellow lost me. His stuff combined sincerity with bad faith in a way that almost smelled. (I've never used deodorants; should I see somebody?)

You're going to the ballet; we're going to take our granddaughter Becky, next year's young woman, if it takes that long, to see the tango show at Sadler's Wells; it'll be the first time we've been to a London theatre since we saw a production of *Macbeth*, whose director has been hailed, and not yet farewelled to my knowledge, as the new Max Reinhardt. Macbeth was updated, camouflaged and had his words largely obscured by inventive emphases that left Shakespeare sounding like a Glasgow version of *The Wire*. What can they do to the tango? *Vamos a ver.*

Un abrazo muy fuerte,
Freddie

Dear Freddie,
I have a collection of Sir William Haley's literary columns at home; he wrote them under the name Oliver Edwards. Although a working journalist, always holding a more than full-time job, he seemed to have found the time to read everything. I once showed him a piece I had written about Alexander Herzen's *My Past and Thoughts*, to which, after having read it, he popped into my office to say, with characteristic laconicism, "You have caught his jumble," and departed. Your reference to his sharing a name with Bill Haley, he who sang before a group known as The Comets, was a coincidence I always thought, in an old American slang word, "rich" (as in "ain't that rich?"). I hope that he, Sir William, was able to leave the planet without having once to hear even distant strains of "Rock Around The Clock."

Someday, when the history of our era is written, the letters BR and AR (like unto BC and AD) will have to be used to designate Before Rock and After Rock, with Before Rock, need I say, much better, a veritable fucking golden age. The advent of rock'n'roll was one of those cultural watershed moments, from which we've yet to be able to dry ourselves off. I can listen to The Beatles, even think some of their non-druggy songs amusing; I also used to like another English group called Herman and the Hermits, which had a pre-adolescent, rather cute Herman sing two memorable (to me) songs, "I'm Henery the Eighth, I Am" and "Mrs. Brown, You've Got a Lovely Daughter." Then Herman came into his growth, rose to 6'3" or so, and when he sang about Mrs. Brown's daughter he seemed positively menacing (Mrs. Brown, lock up that daughter instanter). I was never able to go for The Rolling Stones, whom Tom Wolfe, I recall, called "like The Beatles, only more lower class deformed," which seems right to me. A question that goes, as the lawyers say, to character is, "Can you take Elvis Presley seriously?" I find it hard to take seriously the person who answers that question in the affirmative, even though the poor redneck sang a few rather OK songs.

Our education is congruent in our both being indebted to Edmund Wilson for introducing us to new names of writers we ought to have read. In the end, my guess is that this will be Wilson's great contribution. He was, when still vertical, a walking Modern Library, an Everyman shaped (as he was) like a Penguin. By the time I came upon Stanley Edgar Hyman I was in my middle twenties, and already had a fairly good sense of all that I hadn't read and ought to if I were to have a chance of passing myself off as a mildly cultivated gent. I knew Stanley Edgar Hyman ("Beware, Caesar, three-named, beard-wearing Jews"), who was a nice man said to have read a book and drunk a bottle of whisky a day. Which is a good recipe for living a sedentary life and still dying before one reaches sixty. (Stanley pegged out at fifty-one.) He lived as husband with a fat writer named Shirley Jackson and a house full of children in Bennington, Vermont. She preceded him into the beyond and he remarried, though did not enjoy for long, a student with the alliterative name of Phoebe Pettingell.

Edmund Wilson was always billed as the last man of letters. When he died the musty mantle fell to V.S. Pritchett. I'm not sure whose it is now, but there must be some new last man of letters. Proust says that in art, medicine, and fashion there must always be new names. So, evidently, must there be old names. I don't think of you as a man of letters; I think of you as a superior professional writer. I have no wish to be known as a man of letters myself, though I have been called that on occasion. The only thing worse is to be a national treasure, which means that you really are a goner.

Barbara and I have been in New York since Saturday. We are occupying our son Mark's time-share apartment – a bedroom, a sitting room, two baths, microwave, kitchen sink, and small refrigerator – on 56th Street and Seventh Avenue, across the street from Carnegie Hall. (You surely know the old joke about how you get to Carnegie Hall. The answer is "practice, practice, practice.") We have been taking it very easy on ourselves, keeping cultural consumption to less than a minimum. Thus far we've visited no museums; and only tonight (Tuesday) shall we see the one play we plan to see while we are here: Angela Lansbury and Rupert Everett in *Blithe Spirit*. I have always liked Noël Coward, liked his professionalism, his grounding in, if the phrase isn't entirely oxymoronic, a certain show-business reality. ("We don't want to bore the people, do we darling?" I can hear him say. "Depression in the theatre must be earned, you know, darling, and Sophocles and Shakespeare were the last people really to earn it. Decidedly not Messrs. A. Miller, T. Williams, and E. Albee. No, no, no, certainly not those ignorant cunts, darling.")

We have, by our non-French lights, been eating well. New York seems to have six times the number of good restaurants that Chicago does. Yesterday we were taken to a favorite of ours called Cellini, on East 54th Street, by Midge Decter, a long-time, much-liked-if-not-immensely-close-because-not-often-enough-seen friend. Midge is Mrs. Norman Podhoretz, but very much her own person. She is most *haimish* (old shoe), no-nonsense, but with a good sense of humor and fine laugh. Her specialty is saying the obvious when everyone else has forgotten it, a useful thing to do. When the shrill contemporary version of man-hating feminism first came to the fore, I recall Midge saying to me: "What is this nonsense about men treating women as if they were sexual objects? I never slept with any man I didn't want to sleep with." Another time, at some conference on the Family, I heard her say: "My own family has been giving me much trouble. My aged parents are the cause of ceaseless worry. I find myself in regular disputes with my children. I'm far from pleased with the way some of my grandchildren are growing up. I've had it with the family, really. But when I see who is attacking family, I'm ready to fight for the damn thing." Midge must now be beyond eighty, but continues to look chic, laughs wonderfully, and hasn't lost an intellectual step. Barbara and I left her, as she entered the subway station to return home, feeling the world remains a rich and amusing place.

You've nailed Saul Bellow nicely, in sniffing out the fraudulence behind his literary enterprise. I did not pull out both my gun and knife on him in my Isaac Rosenfeld essay because I didn't think the essay called for me to do so. A few years ago I wrote a story – can't recall if I sent it to you – called "My Brother Eli" about a very Bellow-like character as viewed through the eyes of his philistine but admirable older brother. (Let me know if you wish to see the story, and I shall arrange to get a copy of it to you.) At the center of Bellow's fraudulence is his creating in his fiction figures clearly intended to be he who are inevitably sensitive, kindly, sweet, not to say great souled, whereas in so-called real life Bellow was touchy, unkind, nasty, and black-hearted: a prick, in other words, and a particularly malevolent one. Bellow and my dear friend Edward Shils were once close friends, but had several fallings out. When Edward lay on his deathbed, Bellow asked if he might come over to make things up. Edward told me that he didn't want him to come over, that he had no wish to make things easy for "that son of a bitch." After Edward died, Bellow put a character clearly meant to be Edward in his last novel, *Ravelstein*, claiming that he smelled (which Edward never did) and that he was homosexual (which he most distinctly wasn't). Ah, me, why is it always raining in the Republic of Letters?

Keep the faith and power to (right) people.

Best, Joe

Dear Joe,

Here's an example of something I do not like to read about: serendipity – if this is what it's an example of. We returned from an excellent dinner in Edwardes Square to find the solution to what I had forgotten, the nom de Bloom of William Haley; and there's more, but not all that much: our hosts' older son is called Oliver. If I were Arthur Koestler I'd construct a teleology out of convergent data like that. However, had I been A.K. I should also have written *Darkness At Noon* which retains some of its dazzle even though he could not bring himself, for reasons of elegance I daresay, to show Rubashov (a Jewish name, although K. does not have his 'interviewer' use that against him, as he surely would have) being tortured or being threatened with the torture of his children. Koestler has been done down in England by a biographer called Cesarani, who obtained access to his papers by something approaching a subterfuge and then, more Britannico (italics to follow), depicted A.K. less as the man who blew the whistle on Stalinism and was the first to write unequivocally about the Holocaust, in Cyril 'Man of Letters' Connolly's *Horizon*, back in 1943, than as the sexual ruffian who tried to pleasure Mrs Michael Foot, the film-director wife of a Labour politician of whom you just *might* have heard, in your Anglophiled ear, after she had invited him to pop in and see her one early *après-midi* when he could be excused for imagining that he was expected to play the faun.

She claimed later that he had bumped her head on the kitchen floor (what else can you do with that kind of a cookie?) and tried to have his naturalised Hungarian way with her. So affronted and taken aback was she that she ran into the street and took a deep breath. No screams or cries for help though. She then went back into the house where Arthur was wondering what was wrong. The charge of attempted rape came only when K. was dead and the biographer needed to bury him. Cesarani had earlier written a rather good book about how, in 1945, the Brits had admitted, without too much scrutiny (Leavis had already proved that there was too much of that), a battalion or so of Baltic SS men because they needed miners in a hurry. At the same time, the victors were (who could blame them?) refusing entry to the UK to a number of unclean persons known in the press as 'DPs' (Displaced Persons, in case you're too young to do the decyphering), otherwise Jews, who had been returned from the coast of Palestine to the camps in Germany whence, as the hanging judges used to say, they had come. I think I wrote an applauding notice of the early book, but I dumped heavily on the Koestler, not least because Cesarani had advertised that his father had long been a 'loyal' Communist, somewhat disillusioned in old age when he became a sorry-but-not-very Social Democrat. The old man had never written a book, we were told, but I suspected that when Cesarani said that his Koestler book was 'my father's all the same', he meant, in no very insoluble code, that he had done for K. what his dad would loyally have done if Comrade Stalin had sent him the ice pick.

Comedy followed. I was, in those days, in regular touch with Ray Monk, a professor of philosophy in the same (Southampton) university where Cesarani was a history prof. Ray and I edited a series of Great Philosophers, mono-graphs on ... oh you know the usual *meteora phrontistai*. The monographs were only fifty or sixty pp. and our solicitation of classy contributors asked them to concentrate on a specific aspect of Plato & co., thus showing how a particular issue was treated and might be criticised. The series did pretty well. Leading from the side, I contributed a nervous number on Karl Popper and just about got away with it, I think, thanks (again) to Roger Scruton, a right-wing, but never Right-Wing, scholar and pamphleteer, of whom you are more likely to have heard than M. Foot. Roger put a tactful boot into a clutch of infelicities and there I was, with the big boys, Bernard Williams and Al. The compendium edition – didn't you know there'd eventu-ally be one? – still sells (in its eleventh impression already), although the publishers decided, some years ago, that little books were no longer as good as *petits pains*. Ray (Wittgenstein's and Russell's biographer, and soon to be that of J. Robert Oppenheimer, who already has a few) and I edited quite aggressively – I am always 'good going forward', as the football writers say – and rarely disagreed on the quality of a manuscript.

Ray paid me a delectable compliment, towards the end of our partnership, by asking whether I would be willing to accept an honorary degree at Soton, as the *Anglais* abbreviate the place. Don't you know I was a little bit thrilled? Doctor? Moi? If you insist, as one of my now dead friends used to say in his Liverpudlian way, even when professor of classics at UC Santa Bra. An ermine collar is just my sort of secret drag. A little while later – don't guess, because I'm telling the story, OK? You're right though: a little while later Ray called in a state of embarrassment. My candidature, whose endorsement he had taken for a formality, had been blackballed by (I have little doubt) my, and your, yes, co-religionist Professor Cesarani. So there went mine oimin. And who got to wear it? A nice man called Kris Akaboose (correct spelling to follow) who had recently come third in the 400 metres, I think, in some Olympic Games. Dr Chris, I wish him well to wear the drag that was going to be mine; note the Danny Kaye's 'Candy Kisses' allusion folded in there. I once mocked Michael Ayrton for being so pleased at getting an Hon. Doctorate at Exeter ('Where do I send my buck?' said smart-ass Raphael, who likes to think he can write in an American accent.) There, in short, went the ball game.

Ray grew to hate, or despise, Russell by the end of the latter's long life and the former's two vol. also long Life. He considered that Russell had done nothing worth doing after the age of forty, although he then did so much that it needed months of sifting. Alan Ryan, a Russell admirer, denounced Ray's book with some ferocity, being an Oxford left-winger who favoured CND and the decline of the West. I remarked some time later on the unfairness of Ryan's review, but Ray had begun to think that he had been unduly harsh on Russell; whether age or experience had sponsored this recantation I should not like to say. It does suggest that some people have been unlucky to 'sit' for certain biographers at the wrong period in the latter's lives. (Does that punctuation hold up, professor?) Erminent Victorians, for instance, may have been unfortunate that Lytton wrote about them when he was still in a hurry to be their queen. Michael Holroyd, on the other hand, made Strachey his ladder to the stars among whom he now gleams with renown and self-importance. It is somewhat typical of the England that never made me that Holroyd should have made the Royal Society of Literature (no band of immortals) His Own; like an old aristocrat, he has raised his own regiment who are drilled to applaud him to the echo.

The RSL of which I was made a Fellow, no less back in 1964, used to be a somewhat exclusive place, even though it has more Fellows than exclusivity could make egregious, and I was quite honoured to be elected, thanks to my old friend Peter Green, who was on the Council. It was, in them days, a tradition that Fellows presented copies of their new books to the library, which was then housed in ample leasehold (aha!) premises in Hyde Park Gardens, a fine address shared, just down the road, by Stanley Donen in his richest days, directly after *Charade*, and just before *Two for the Road*. I subscribed to tradition by sending my latest novel *Lindmann* to join the other toffs' vols on the Society's shelves. Years later, when Holroyd had become president, the lease on Hyde Park Gardens lapsed and was, despite the usual assurances, not renewed. There was a search for new premises which were finally found at Somerset House, a vast heap adjacent to Waterloo Bridge (a celluloid vehicle in which Vivien Leigh and Robert Taylor once starred, almost movingly). The RSL's circumstances were reduced in their new lodgings and Holroyd decided that, since a library was, for the most part, superfluous to a modern literary society, he would sell off the dross. OK, you've guessed again: among the books that he was bold enough to list to the membership, the fellowship even, as having been wasted was one so rare that I did not have a copy of it myself, viz. *Lindmann*.

I wrote a rather Briddish letter in which I said, *grosso modo*, that I had always been taught that selling off people's gifts was a rather oikish thing to do. The least that the biographer of George B. Shaw (yawn) and Augustus John (let his caravan roll on, while I stand by and bark) and Lytton could have done, said I, was to offer my book back to me. In a witless word or two, fuck you, Holroyd; he went to Eton but not to university, *e si vede*. Well, he did sort of apologise and he did get a copy of *Lindmann* and send it to me. But I haven't forgotten and I haven't forgiven and when I saw, as I did recently, as a speaker in what used to be some kind of a dilettanti club, that he is not only touting his own recent book but offering to sign and sell it to his audience, I discovered what a gorge was and why and how it rose. I am thinking of asking for the concession to sell bagels at the next RSL meeting. When I don't get it, you'll know why: Philip Roth and Bellow and I have met it all through our lives. I wish I liked bagels, but just because I don't doesn't mean I like other people who don't. I am now persona non grata at the RSL, but when I've been a Fellow for fifty years (five to go), I will, as Byron (whose pen we use to sign in) would say, 'make them feel it'.

Oh listen, I was delighted with the now-it-can-be-told stuff about poor (as my father would say) Stanley Edgar Hyman and Midge D., whom I have seen (and so have you) pilloried by the Corinthian (geddit?) Gore, which certainly spoke in her favour. I not only read but actually bought (the man is mad, I fear) *Ravelstein*, which is one of the worst novels I have ever read, if not THE worst, but then I haven't read Antonia Byatt's latest, so what do I know? I had read your short story on Bellow and now I have read it again. Why not? as Izzy Diamond used to say when Billy Wilder had a good idea.

All power to the Soviets, as long as I don't have to be there.

Freddie

Dear Freddie,
Thanks for this unembarrassment of riches – I at any rate am not at all embarrassed by them.

I never met Arthur Koestler, but, like you, much admire *Darkness at Noon*. I always assumed that Rubashov was a stand-in for Bukharin, the intellectuals' favorite Bolshie after Trotsky. Like all revolutionaries, both, viewed at all up close and personal, as American television has it, are sadly disappointing. I did not know that Koestler was also the first writer to expose the Holocaust, and that he did so in *Horizon* and as early as 1942. I remember reading that Bruno Bettelheim, who wrote the book *The Informed Heart*, which is about the concentration and not yet the death camps, had a difficult time getting word published in America about what was going on in Europe. People hadn't then, I think, developed the taste and appetite for bad news that we now have; and bad news of that magnitude – genocide – especially when it was about an already despised people, must have been easiest of all to avoid.

But back to Koestler, who was apparently an energetic skirt-chaser. You will recall that he had one of those Hungarian low hairlines, of a kind that grew lower with the passing years (what else do they do?). I recall an anecdote that had a rival of Koestler's for a particular skirt tell her that Koestler slept in a hair net. He denied it vehemently, adding that, true enough, he did use a hair net while bathing. Edward Shils, who knew Koestler from *Encounter* magazine days and from the Congress for Cultural Freedom, recalled him saying that he might be neurotic about a great many things but money wasn't one of them. Early in my grub street days, I was asked by the *New Republic* to review A.K.'s (also shorthand for *alte kocker*) book *The Act of Creation*, which begins by showing how humor works and then uses this same paradigm (as in Brother, can you paradigm?) to explain the new biology. The latter proved too arcane for me to write lucidly about, and I had to toss in the towel, also the tablecloth, handkerchief, and two pairs of boxer shorts, and admit that I wasn't up to reviewing the book – the first and only time in my brilliant career I ever made such a modest concession. Perhaps the most interesting – not to say terrifying – Koestler story has to do with his exit by way of suicide. His own suicide is of less interest than his (I assume) persuading his much-younger-than-he wife to join him in suicide. If he did in fact persuade her to die alongside him, this is a powerfully gruesome act.

Your tale about not getting an honorary doctorate reminds me to inform you, if you do not already know it, that I have no advanced degrees, and am rather boisterously proud of not having any. Some of the stupidest people I know have names ending in PhD. I was a mediocre (at best) student, and a boy hugely bored by almost everything that went on in classrooms. Because I taught at a university – a job arranged for me at Northwestern by Irving Howe, a critic of some power at the time, for whose magazine I wrote a bit when in my twenties – lots of people began to call me Doctor, or Professor. When addressed as Doctor Epstein, especially over the phone, I used to respond by saying, "Read two chapters of Henry James and get into bed. I'll be right over." When addressed as Professor, I used to answer: "Professor is what they call the guy who plays the piano in the bordello, as in 'Hit it, professor.'" I do have a single honorary degree, from a joint yclept Adelphi University, whose president was an amiable Greek and a nice man who ran the place as if it were a Greek restaurant. He too handsomely rewarded himself – with salary and apartments in Manhattan festooned with artworks – in a way that his trustees found unseemly, and he was fired not long after. I accepted this honorary degree chiefly because I knew that a friend, Hilton Kramer, had a hand in arranging it for me. But I have never been much impressed by such honors, chiefly because so many creeps have won them before me and will continue to win them long after me. Somewhere or other I wrote that I would rather have a sandwich named after me, as they used to do in Jewish delicatessens after band leaders and other showbiz figures, than have honorary degrees from Oxford, Harvard, and the Sorbonne, and I quite meant it. My having done so ought, I feel, to eliminate the problem of my having to leave home to pick up further honorary degrees.

I suppose the nearest analogous group to the RLS is the American Academy of Arts and Letters, a 250-member group of scribblers, daubers, and noise-makers, which meets annually to give awards and fellowships to all the wrong people. In the 1920s, H.L. Mencken advised Theodore Dreiser not to join it, for he felt it was filled with stuffed shirts, stiffos, and what we should today call establishment figures, advice and an assessment that holds up nicely in our day. Imagine a room filled with 250 Michael Holroyds, of both sexes. Everyone knows Groucho's line about not wanting to belong to any group that would have him as a member. My own view of the American Academy of Arts and Letters is that I wouldn't want to join any group that has its current roster as members: so many dullards, so many (intellectual) cowards, so many people of perfectly predictable opinions and no interesting points of view whatsoever.

We are now two days back from our week in Manhattan, and still in recovery mode. We took it very easy on ourselves while there – I never made more than two appointments on any one day – but the mere being out of one's usual routine takes its small toll. A larger toll is collected by contemporary air travel. One begins at the airport by undressing owing to the bad intentions of our good friends the Arab terrorists. Then one sits among one's detested fellow pilgrims, as Henry James once called his fellow travelers in Europe, who are screaming into their cellphones and clicking away at their Blackberries and laptops, while in the not-far-enough-away middle distance speakerines on CNN, an all-day television news station, blare out features on young Russian tennis prospects and murdered policemen in Pittsburgh. On our return trip, we had a delay of roughly five hours, owing partly to rainy weather and even more to a co-pilot who failed to show up. I did my best to shut all this out by reading from Montesquieu's *Persian Letters* and a quite good little book by the Victorianist Gertrude Himmelfarb called *The Jewish Odyssey of George Eliot*, which is an extended essay on Eliot's astonishing sympathy for Judaism and Zionism in *Daniel Deronda*, a novel I have begun to reread. Still, by the time we returned home from our holiday I felt distinctly in need of another holiday. Such is modern life.

Whenever I am in New York, I cannot help wondering whether I should have lived my adult life there. I used regularly to be taken for a native New Yorker, which was a compliment when assumed by people who lived in New York, and perhaps something other than a compliment when assumed by people who never lived there. I lived in New York for two years or so (1962–63), in my middle twenties, working for an obscure magazine called the *New Leader*, but under great financial constraint (by the age of twenty-six, I had four children; my first wife had two children from an earlier marriage) and at work that gave me little pleasure. I had opportunities to return, but felt more at ease in Chicago, the city of my birth. Life in New York is of course much more exciting – more talkative, sexier, more neurotic, more wired generally – than in Chicago, or anywhere else in America. When I return to

New York I feel in part that I have missed out on a fair amount of excitement, yet in larger part that I would have got less work done and likely have been more beaten down by life. Whenever I return from New York, I know that I made the right choice by going for imperfection of the work over imperfection of the life, though some might say that I have achieved both.

Keep the faith and pass the ammunition.

Best, Joe

Dear Joe,
'Salutary' would be the one word to describe your last. The lure of titles and decorations is part of the ongoing comedy of British life, a fat, tasteless fruit of the egalitarianism which is the advertised ethos of a society so badged with distinctions, awards, doctorates and the rest that every other person, at least, is a closet Goering, badged with cadged advertisements of courage or intellectual excellence which, on close reading, derive more from expert agitation and the right friends than from undeniable superiority. That sentence is a pretty fancy example of Writing Beyond, which I suppose is part at least of what we can't deny we're doing, now and again, when we write to each other. *Ad captum vulgi* was Spinoza's nifty little phrase ('according to the capacity of the vulgar' is how Leo Strauss renders the phrase – rather freely, *mi parece* – but I am tempted to gloss it to include trying to get their cheap attention). I'm reading Leo, as every cold-caller would coldly call him these days, between yawns and admiration, on Maimonides and Spinoza, in the undying hope that he will synopsise for me what I ought to know already as well as giving me the key to the dark rooms of their specific great works into which I shall never penetrate in detail. I am a tourist in too many segments of the available library, but then who is not?

The last (and for all I know the first) man who claimed to have read everything in the Bodleian Library, back before the first WW, was T.E. Lawrence. Robert Graves buried him in his biography of the desert mythographer by working out that his claim could be true only if, during his time at Oxford, Lawrence had read something of the order of, oh, a thousand books a week, or was it a day? It's a long time since I read the biog, though I do have it, as they say, on my shelves. I've always had a soft spot for Graves, who disliked my old school, Charterhouse, almost as much I did myself (*eppure* I don't deny that I am a Carthusian, i.e. I just vestigially vaunt myself even on that spurious definition 'OC', even though 'OE' – Old Etonian, what else? – is the only claim worth making in the Public, i.e. Private, School department).

Graves was, whatever charges the revisionists bring, a brave soldier who actually was in the trenches and hence can be spoken of in the same breath as Siegfried Sassoon, who chucked his MC into . . . I don't know, some body of water in the north of England, I think, and guessed well ahead of its savage realisation in Germany that the fondest wish of most old soldiers who had really been there was to turn and rend the civilians who applauded their feats but knew nothing of what they, and the dead, had been through.

My newish friend the historian Michael Burleigh, who spent many years researching the Third Reich, and has somewhat returned to the subject recently, e-mailed me yesterday and mentioned that his latest studies suggest that of the 8,000,000 veterans of WW2 something under ten per cent ever saw anything that could be called combat. The rest did their recruited stuff, filled gas tanks and ammo belts and who knows what not at all, but were never in battle. I remember being under fire, in the most literal sense, only when, at the age of 11 or 12, I was walking up Putney Hill with my parents during an air raid. The fire was our own, I suppose, since the loudest bangs were probably what the Brits call ack-ack, anti-aircraft in case you vasn't dere, Charlie. The experience was more enjoyable than traumatic, because I still had those intimations of immortality which, as we get older, we can only try and tag onto the very best of our work and hope, fatuously, that we get some post-mortem cheer from the use that posterity makes of us. Almost certainly disparaging if I know anything. I never thought for a moment that the Germans might win the war or that God would not save the King, still less that anything could, as they say, happen to me. When it did happen to Sarah, everything changed entirely but not altogether, which is always (that is, sometimes), I suppose, the way.

Robert Graves is being done down at the moment by Certain People, a blogging Cambridge *professoressa* not least, called Mary Beard, because – and I expect she is right – his very best-selling book of Greek myths, with its amazingly thorough-seeming concordance of discordant variant versions, which has been in print in an enviably copious number of editions since whenever (1955, I discover), turns out (aha!) to have been largely, um, cadged from some dull more antique corpus-omnium-gatherum, available in the Bodleian no doubt, which is not acknowledged even in the tiniest font available. Well, there you go, as they used to say; if you can find an out-of-copyright scholar who said what you wished you'd said first, *vae lectis*, as the Romans didn't have to bother to say, but I like to flash around. A man must choose his enemies when he can these days, before they thrust themselves upon him (for free quotes, or drop-in meals in the Dordogne).

A *proposito*, a curiosity of the British, if they discover that you have a home away from home, their envy and presumption (joined at the hype) combine to have them wish you (a) in hell, (b) their hosts for a day or two. The number of people who think of dropping in on us is not necessarily identical with the number of those we wish to see. Furthermore, those who would not invite you for a cup of tea while you and they are in London at the same time will assume that their call upon you in rural France will be the highlight of your summer. Can happen; but not a lot, if you can Astaire them down with neat footwork and diary-conning.

Part of the fun of objective senility (some read 'maturity') is, as I tried to persuade you I really felt ('believed' bothers me, when used as if it meant some extra measure of sincerity or insight), that you don't have to do things/read things/say things you don't mean or want to do. But you do have to get your fun somewhere and, as Leo Strauss says (so tediously, God knows, that he makes George Steiner – let's hear it for the kid – seem like George Burns), affectations of one sentiment will always conceal another, if you have the legs for that stuff. So, *tandem* and not a moment sooner, I revert to what I was going to say which was about your renunciation of professorial status, even though, I assume, you did/do have that entitlement formally. Be that as it may (always a chiding-inducing inceptive phrase *chez les rosbifs*), your exemplary modesty reminds me of that of Guy Lee, a Latinist (in particular, although he was also a Hellenist) who tried to teach me as an undergraduate, in which sullen capacity I failed to go to his lectures, which I am now told were excellent, but who DID teach me, a bit, in my later yaws when he checked my belated, translated attempts to prove that the Classics were something I was glad to have studied.

Guy was never other than 'Mr Lee' and glad to be a remote don, not necessarily ineffectual, in Belloc's charmless but memorable phrase (rare for an anti-Semite to merit a Tuscan cheer, but there it is), and entirely, it seemed, without jealousy or envy. My friend Paul Cartledge, now professor of ancient history at Cambridge, sent me a bundle of old penny-plain postcards (those with pictures on the front were tuppence, or perhaps required a stamp of a higher denomination) which he had found in the being-cleared-out archives of a magazine once published by the Classical Faculty and called *Farrago*; why go further? The deck of handwritten (of course) cards is some five inches thick and consists of Guy's contributions, offered not imposed, in the form of Latin or Greek versions of obiter dicta by Dicks of various style. The one that comes first (and here my Tristram Shandying style manages to match tail to top) renders J.M. Keynes's remark 'on being wrongly called professor,' viz.: 'I cannot bear the indignity without the emoluments.' I hope that the Latin will serve *ad captum vulgi*, but it's not likely (which I also hope of course, because then they will all know how I feel when Leo Strauss doesn't add a translation to his German footnotes), and here it is: '*Piget vocari perperam professorem:/ Iniuriosum est sine salario nomen.*' That's my boy, *dans ses oeuvres*, as they say of footballers when they do something nifty, as long as it's in France.

Don't ask me what metre Guy composed that couplet in, because *nescio quid* (a modern translation of which might be, I'm not paid to know that kind of thing). I've actually had the nerve, in my ever later seventies, to propose to the Ed of the *TLS* that I do a little, oh, *recueil* (why not?) of Guy's versions as a Commentary (in the *TLS* 'middle' sense) piece. Literary climbers with the right kind of nerve and pitons do that kind of hammering on doors and access to high places when they are in their teens, thus becoming butterflies, or flying butts, before their wings drop off, but there we are: late-starters work harder, maybe. I have written eulogistically about Guy in *Ticks and Crosses* and I meant every word. He was a gentle man, though not incapable of shaking off asperities when needed, and treated me with rare patience. I shall, of course, not speak anything but well of him in public, but – the adversative had to come, of course, but in no adversarial spirit – I do remember one of those odd moments which writers of fiction, in particular, should/cannot forget when he said, in some connection I DO forget, that the thing about the Jews was that they do cling together and keep other people out . . . That a man without prejudices or evident resentments should think that a minority which has been so regularly excluded was itself exclusive seemed odd, if never wicked or malicious.

Then again, it's something that's not THAT rare *chez les anglais*; Steiner, in the days when I received his newsletters, told me of a man called Roy Strong, a curator and historian of (I think) the Tudors and allied trades and TV poisonality, who wrote an article I never saw in which he proclaimed that if his name had only been Stronkski or voids to that defect he would have been really rated as an intello. Your reminiscence of how New York Jews once did reduce the significant world to that of their little mags and feuds gives a clue, I suppose, to why some people felt excluded, though it hardly explains Guy's tiny spurt of resentment, if that's what it was. There IS the pettiness of remembering petty things; but it's never only the beauty that's to be found in the details.

Tout à toi,
Freddie

Dear Freddie,

I hope that in what are advertised as "your wildest dreams" you never fantasized about one day being made Sir Frederic Raphael. Forgive my saying so, but the title would be quite as preposterous as my being Joseph Epstein, the Ben and Bessie Nourishkeit Professor of Radio Comedy. Our public personas go too strongly against the very notion of such titles, of any titles, really. If we may be said to have positions in the world, then, I like to think, the term anti-bullshitter describes these positions. In the United States, you should know, I am sometimes described as a Conservative. But I do not in the least think of myself as in possession of anything like a coherent body of political ideas that are represented by conservatism or can be captured by any other going ism. Instead I prefer to think myself an older Jewish gentleman, standing off on the sidelines, viewing the various public escapades – political, cultural, social – and calling out, with some regularity, "Bullshit! Bullshit! Bullshit!" You not infrequently do much the same, if with a slightly different accent.

Speaking of knights – and you will recall the sad old joke that runs, "Once a knight, always a knight, but once a night is enough" – I am put in mind of that knight of knights, Sir Isaiah Berlin. Sir Isaiah was in many ways the centerpiece in American Anglophiliac snobbery. "Went to the opera last night with Isaiah," I have heard people say with too great glee. "Isaiah called yesterday. What a remarkable fellow he is!" And so forth and Charles Swann. For many years, Sir Isaiah – what's in a name: what if Isaiah's had been Sid, making him Sir Sid Berlin – was the great catch of the *New York Review of Books*. Credit where it is due, while he served as that catch, he kept that paper from being so strongly anti-Israel as it has since his death become. (Act of disclosure here: I have long been excluded from the *New York Review*, neither asked to contribute nor had any of my books reviewed therein, for, I suspect, a small *mot* of mine that held that the contributors to its pages comprised "mad dogs and Englishmen.") In a nice reversal, he, Isaiah, also lent a certain ineluctable *élan* to the *New York Review* for the English. John Gross once told me that when Robert Silvers, the paper's editor, visited London, it was as if the very viceroy of India were home on leave.

Isaiah had a remarkable run, no doubt about it. But with all his prestige, his fame within English and American academic and intellectual quarters, he was still a hesitant and frightened man. He was also rendered remarkably (shall we say) nervous during the time of the so-called "student unrest." (One of my favorite euphemisms, student unrest, implying as it does that all would have been well had the little monsters been able to get in more naps.) Surely he must have hated everything the nihilistic students stood for and did, yet not a peep of protest about their hijinx out of him. Edward Shils told me that he thought Isaiah Berlin a charming but cowardly man. What he was afraid of, according to Edward, was losing the good opinion of Maurice Bowra and Stuart Hampshire, who liked the cavorting of the unrested students. Sad stuff. What, after all, is the point of being a knight if you can't say fuck off to whomever you like, short of the Queen, of course.

A false nobleman more to my taste was Hugh Trevor-Roper, who wrote a few good essays for the *American Scholar* and who wrote to me at his death about Edward Shils, who was among the small number of dons loyal to him when he became master of Peterhouse. I much admired his prose, and liked his force when on the attack. (The gentler, though no less malicious, gossipy Trevor-Roper is on exhibition in his letters to Bernard Berenson, which I not long ago read with much pleasure.) I especially liked his title of Lord Dacre, thought it somehow fitting. Whenever he wrote one of his groin-bruising attacks on some faulty English or American historian, I used to think, Ah, another acher, courtesy of Lord Dacre.

I undignifiedly giggled at your writing that the prose of Leo Strauss makes "George Steiner seem like George Burns." I once wrote that the ultra-pompous American academic Harold Bloom resembled George Steiner but without the sense of humor, but yours is much better. Wouldn't it have been fine to introduce the two Georges, Burns and Steiner, to each other? A Leo Strauss cult in America is now in its fourth generation. The cult itself took something of a beating, since a few of its members were high up in the stratospheric circles that advised President George W. Bush to go into Iraq. I recently tried to read a famous essay of Strauss' called "Athens and Jerusalem," but without much luck. The trick of tricks, which Leo Strauss seems to have brought off, is to be considered deep without being always intelligible.

Changing the subject from Athens and Jerusalem to Rome and Jerusalem, I recently read, chiefly because of your current stake in the subject, Mireille Hadas-Lebel's book *Flavius Josephus*. She is an historian of the first century AD, an abnormally sensible *Normalien*, and withal a smart woman. She has written a good but not a great book. But it does give the ignorant reader – that would be yours truly, Señor – a sense of the fascination of its subject, and also a history of the background of the various reactions to Josephus and his histories. Her book is what I suspect a scholar would call "sound," whereas yours figures to be brilliant. Doesn't Max Beerbohm somewhere cite the need for a scholarly book (perhaps on the eighteenth century) that requires an author much less brilliant than he?

Changing the subject more radically now still, I am to do an essaylet for *Newsweek* under the provisional title (mine) of "The Slow Death of Roger Federer." I have only 1,500–2,000 words to descant upon the subject. If I could have any tennis game of any player in my lifetime, I would choose Federer's. Without being overpowering, his strokes and sense of strategy seem to me as near perfection as I am able to imagine. His physique, in the non-weight-lifters style, also seems perfect. He seems a decent young man, with a great gift of even temperament, and has helped to revive the gentlemanly aspect of tennis after it was banished by those two gringo creeps Jimmy Connors and John McEnroe, who seemed to feel they could be ugly in the name of being highly competitive. Roger Federer is the very type of the Apollonian, or of the type that those who consider themselves Apollonians (yours truly again) most admire. Rafa Nadal is of course Dionysian; or to bring things down from Olympus, he is Sparta to Federer's Athens, and just now Sparta is beating the hell out of Athens. After his six or seven years at the top, Federer, at twenty-eight, is beginning to sink: he cannot defeat Nadal, he loses to Djokovic and Andy Murray, he is occasionally knocked off by lesser-known players in early rounds of tournaments. Why must this be? My thesis is that, having attained perfection in his game, there is no place for Federer to go, and perfection, at least in the physical realm, cannot be sustained forever, make that even for long. Ah, Federer! Ah, humanity! Ah, *Newsweek*!

Best, Joe

Dear Joe,

The title thing is essentially comic. The best, however, would be to have been born the Duc de la you know where and then one could have condescended all one's life without having to be in the smallest degree pretentious or ambitious. Dr Johnson, everyone's favourite Englishman it seems, said (*más o menos*) that the great thing about hereditary aristocracy was that it ensured that pure chance governed who was the nobleman and who the poor man at his gate, hence resentment of social superiority was vacuous. I'm sure he expressed it more trenchantly than I can contrive on a Saturday morning, but that was his drift. Johnson was ugly and self-made and, I suppose, must have been enchanting in person, even though he doesn't look as if he washed a lot. Many of his *obiter dicta* are worth bumping into, although that stuff about knowing that one is to be hanged in a fortnight's time 'concentrates a man's mind' has that tincture of callousness which approximates to the nastiest kind of camp (the attachment 'concentration' loiters adjacent to this obligatory Sontag reference).

In his new book *Le lièvre de Patagonie*, which I am essay/reviewing for the *TLS*, Claude Lanzmann is generally indulgent to the *gens de sa vie* but reports that he had a nasty time with Commander Cousteau, whose green submarine activities may have reached your then very small screen, since it seemed he was tanked up, in series after series, to take us instructively into the depths. Lanzmann combined *grand reportage*, editorial duties with *Les temps modernes* and sexual same with Le Castor, plus – in his maturity – the creation of that massive masterpiece *Shoah* (which should be thrust courteously down the throat of every holocaust denier) with a-million-words-a-week journalism which aspired, at times, to the *n'importe quoi* category. A man of hidden shallows then as well as depths; but while being shallow in the latter category too, he devilled for Cousteau whose brother was a disgraced *collabo*.

Commander Cousteau had no manifest fascistic qualities, unless a penchant for commanding is one, and did not appreciate Lanzmann's endeavours on his behalf; he is belatedly cudgelled for a letter that he is said to have written in 1942 in which he tells his wife that they should have an easy time finding a nice flat in Paris since the Jews have been cleared out of so many of them. It's not a nice remark, I grant, but I can only hope that the casual callousnesses of one's own correspondence (never mind conversation) are not paraded before the final judgment seat.

Drôle de type, ce Lanzmann, full of fire and ambition, he told my friend Philippe Labro, whose latest novel *Les Gens* has sold 100,000 copies, that his purpose in life was '*te dépasser*'. I confess to no such numerical ambitions at all. Just as well, when the reprint of my 1963 novel *Lindmann* sold all of 147 copies. Since the publisher was a one-man band, he was unable to toot his flute, or tout his author, sufficiently loudly for me to be heard above the barking of London publishers with publicity and hospitality budgets to impress lit. editors, a band whom I once regarded as men and women (they mostly are now) of integrity and lit. cred. Ha! One such, the bearded lady to whom I may well have adverted before, did for my Greek book *Some Talk of Alexander* by not having a word on its subject appear in the *TLS*, whose readers just might have been appetised by it. Bitter? I'd sooner bite.

As it happens, and as you ask, I was ONCE addressed (literally, on an envelope from Scandinavia) as Professor Sir Frederic Raphael. For a brief second, I imagined that the man from Uppsala knew something I did not. He may indeed have known many things (an Archilochan fox already) but nothing of the promotional finesse of the British socio-academic nexus. I recall asking John Schlesinger why he had not yet received the knighthood which many of his contemps had (including the stage director Peter Hall et all). He said that it didn't matter now because his parents were dead, but that the reason he had been passed over (this is the weekend to mention it) was that he had not done enough for charity. I said, 'You directed plays for the National Theatre'. He said that wasn't charity. I said, 'Oh'.

Beetle and I rarely go to the theatre these days; it's a schlep and it's expensive and nothing is ever as good as its reviews. However, we met a clever young actor at a dinner party and he said he would get us house seats (if we were willing to pay for them) for the play he is in at the NT called *The Pitmen Painters*. Nice of him, so on Thursday off we went, having temporary use of the London car which we borrowed back from our son Stephen. We hate to be late, so were early, in time for a slot in the small parking lot adjacent to the South Bank complex which was built, in the brutalist style, in the 1950s and hence has the modernity of a Stalinist compound in Outer Provinsky, but set on the river and all of that. You walk from the lot under a bridge as dark and reeking as a Sicilian's armpit, along a lumpy road with a permanent pattern of puddles and climb stairs to the esplanade where, to our surprise, was disclosed a range of restaurants and shops (one selling books even) which were never there when we last came to a concert. We found the tickets waiting for us (it's always a surprise when there is no surprise) and ambled along above the mudbank.

All of a sudden I saw a small, long grey-haired little man (yes, some people are small *and* little) who looked like a disused violinist and was, in fact, the long-serving drama critic of *The Sunday Times*, a role he had filled – like an antique frankfurter, an over-zealous analogist might say – for 19 and a half years, a term which I myself might have served had I not ceded the office of drama critic to him at the last moment, after being promised emoluments and all, because I suddenly thought that the title (here we go again) was, in truth, all that appealed to me and that to go to the theatre five nights a week was no treat, no career, no dice and no place, as an old friend of mine used to say, 'for a Yiddisher boy'. I embraced the small little man with that cordiality which seeks, in one bear-hug, to get the greetings over and done with it. It also enabled me to hang my face over his left shoulder, thus avoiding his hot breath. This man is and is not, you may gather, someone I am happy to see; the excluded middle is very much my kind of lodging.

He was with a woman whose flummety person I tried to morph into some kind of thirty-years-on version of the wife in whose house we dined back then and who seemed some kind of a benign witch (she put little pointed hats on the peaks of any chairs which had protruding upright backs). But the woman was then introduced to us as someone who was my benefactress at about the same *trente ans déjà* period, when she was a/the publisher at Penguin and did my *Glittering Prizes* as a paperback, thus giving me a best-seller. She has since become a novelist and is now, under the tutelage of her attached critic, writing plays. I managed my hedgehog trick, which is to recall one detail about almost anyone I have ever met, which astonishes them with my recondite skill. In this case, I said that I remembered her first novel which was called – was I right? – *The Wife*. I was right and she was duly flattered, quite as if it proved that I followed her work (the rest of which, like the contents of the said novel, is entirely opaque to me) with admiring diligence. I recalled the novel particularly because it was said to reveal to her then husband that she had been having a long and passionate affair and he was mortally stricken by the revelation. I can imagine what Billy Wilder might have crafted (honed even) out of such a *donnée*, something along the lines of: 'What has writing a book like that done for you?' 'It wasn't meant to do for me, it was meant to do for him.'

Your words about Isaiah Bling *tombent bien* as they say where we are going in a few hours. I was just packing Michael Ignatieff's biography of the old trimmer as well as a more solemn, slimmer study of the same order. I knew Ignatieff very slightly when he was the quizmaster of a fancy TV symposium on the then purportedly highbrow Channel Four. He officiated, now I press the memory-button, over a colloquy on Lanzmann's *Shoah*, which the said channel had the honour to broadcast *in toto*. Lanzmann was there and so was George Steiner (how not?) and an Israeli historian called Bauer. I can't remember much of the chat, though I can see Lanzmann's sullen menace in the face of any kind of doubt about the cinematic primacy of his undoubted (see above) masterpiece. Ignatieff, who is, I think, a Canadian Russian *intello*, probably not of your persuasion, had something in common with Isaiah, if only that air of homogenised mannerliness which gave them both the air of being the kind of lofty butler you can rely on not to come in at the wrong moment and never to bring the folded message face up on the wrong kind of salver.

Ignatieff, like Berlin, writes on vexed issues without ever being himself vexatious. He is also almost as mutable; now here, now there, always himself unless you'd sooner he was someone else. No mercenary ever gave a clearer impression of not wanting the money. I do think Berlin had his qualities, and they were essentially of the order of *haute vulgarisation* for which I have always been grateful, especially when it comes to unpacking Kraut flossophers. He writes with the elegance of the born mimic (a badge borne by not a few of our race) and his sufferance, to keep that line going, is of a piece with his tailoring; he doesn't look or sound Jewy. His timid courage re Israel is to be saluted, but not with all five fingers perhaps. I once wrote an essay on one of his essays, looking at it with, oh, bioscopic attention, which is often the best way of assessing, anatomising, a writer (saves reading every bloody word too). I met Berlin once, when I was a guest at the Garrick Club, where the intellectual *gratin* (flash department) hang out, and in. He was wearing a carnation in his black lapel. He shook my hand but I didn't notice. So it goes *chez le gratin*, otherwise known in the UK as 'the browned-off', which they often are because enough is never enough, not when you've got too much of it.

Tout à toi,
Freddie

Dear Freddie,
You are now comfortably ensconced (not at all a comfortable-sounding word) in your French Tsarskoye Selo, Czar (speaking of titles) Freddie. America has a manufacturer of golf equipment called Titlist, and one sees golfers going about with the word Titlist on their caps. But what do these yokels know about titles? I ask you. Nothing, I tell you.

Your mention of Claude Lanzmann reminds me that, on the occasion of the presentation of my one not very honorable honorary degree, Claude Lanzmann was a fellow honorand. I didn't speak much with him, but I did ride in a car back to our hotel with him and his young and beautiful and most likeable wife. I remarked to my friend Hilton Kramer on what a dazzling woman the young Madame Lanzmann seemed. "Oh," said Hilton, who was up on all the best boudoir gossip, "Lanzmann slept with Simone de Beauvoir for nearly a decade, and deserves everything he gets." Such service to literature, a decade in the bed of de Beauvoir, I must say, makes old Procrustes look like a piker.

Authors lie about sales the way actors do about the size of audiences. You, with your boast of 147 copies sold for *Lindmann*, are an exception. I remember some years ago Alfred Appel, the Nabokov man, told me that he just received a royalty check for $16.45 from Oxford U. Press for an unreadable book of his

called *Nabokov's Dark Cinema*. I recall thinking, He's a liar. The check was
probably for $11.34. Chez Epstein I refer to my royalties as my "peasantries,"
which they mostly are. I note in a piece in this past week's *New York Times
Book Review* that seven out of ten books published in America do not earn out
(as the verbal phrase is) their advances. I'm a bit surprised that the success
ratio here isn't even lower. The trick, I suppose, is not to sell lots of books but
to hustle a large advance. The old question about publishing used to be: Is it a
gentleman's trade, or merely a business? The answer is that it is neither. It is
for people of mild cultural pretensions who know diddly about business.

You did well to turn down the job of drama critic for *The Times*. Seeing
wretched plays night after night, and attempting to separate the chaff from the
crap would drive a sensible man crazy. Or how would you like to have to write
a piece on the experience of seeing *Waiting for Godot* for the eighth time. Or
viewing *King Lear* done by an all-tattooed cast? Or a musical-comedy version
of *In Cold Blood*? Or a Liza Minelli one-woman show? Or my not-yet-written
Jewish family saga, *No Ruth for Naomi*? No, no, no, much better to have sat
home those many nights, with Beetle, and a copy of Heidegger on your lap –
or, better, vice versa.

I am at present knee-deep in the big muddy of intellectual journalism
owed. I have been reading, as they emerged volume by volume, the eight
volumes of Santayana's letters, which have given me much pleasure. I found
reading them early in the morning best; Santayana's detachment, leading onto
serenity, was somehow very comforting, a pleasing way to begin the day. They
are also full of witty observations. As a young man, on a Harvard traveling
fellowship to Germany, for example, he notes that the Germans miss the
ordinary attribute of humanity in having no capacity for boredom; if they had,
he feels they would have "long ago become extinct through self-torture."
When one thinks of much of Goethe, Hegel, Wagner, and so much more
Krautish cultural produce, one realizes that there is a lot to it. Santayana, like
Henry James, is not known ever to have had anything like a serious romantic
relationship with a woman, which naturally causes many of our deeper
thinkers to conclude that he must have been homosexual, though, as with
James, there is no evidence for this whatsoever. The real corruption of
Freudianism is not in his dopey ideas (Oedipus, schmoedipus, just so long as
a boy loves his mother) but in the belief that everything important about a
person must be hidden.

I also owe a piece on Gertrude Himmelfarb's slender book *The Jewish
Odyssey of George Eliot*, which is a study of the background and reception

to *Daniel Deronda* as well as of the novel itself, which I am rereading. Gertrude Himmelfarb is also Mrs. Bea Kristol, wife of Irving Kristol, the founding – and best – editor of *Encounter*. She is the anti-Lytton Strachey, who over a long career has tried – quite successfully, I think – to undo the damage that that *longaluxsch* (Yiddish for long noodle) Lytton S. did in de-eminencizing the Victorians. The book is reminder of what a great woman George Eliot was: how learned, how penetrating, how imaginatively sympathetic. (As a young man, Henry James, upon meeting her, writes home to describe her as "magnificently ugly – deliciously hideous" and ends by noting that "in this vast ugliness resides a most powerful beauty which, in a very few minutes steals forth and charms the mind, so that you end, as I ended, in falling in love with her.") Just about every other great English writer – Chaucer, Shakespeare, Dickens, Trollope, et alia – kept a cold place in his heart for the Jews, while George Eliot genuinely understood what Jewish separateness meant and why the creation of a Jewish state was crucial to the survival of the Jews. Immensely impressive, all this, for an English woman writing in 1876. *Daniel Deronda* seems even better than I remembered. (I am reading it in a Penguin edition, which weighs in at a mere 883 pages.) I wonder if it mayn't be the best of all nineteenth-century English novels, which is saying a great deal. Unlikely to read it yet again, I also feel a sadness knowing that this is likely to be the last time that I shall keep company with this great book.

The third book on which I am to pontificate is a winning tirade on the computer-raised generation by an unjustly neglected American novelist in his sixties named Mark Helprin. The book begins by being a defense of copyright, which is apparently much in dispute these days, but soon lashes out against people who prefer collective over individual interests, who tend to be the aforementioned young, styled by Helprin as Digital Barbarians.

A mistake, I think, for older gents to take up against the young, though I much enjoy Helprin's doing so. Even when richly deserved, it turns one too quickly into a crank. Yet, yet, yet, yet, yet . . . Yesterday I had a "pre-interview" for an interview I am to do tomorrow with a Boston National Public Radio station on the subject of my Fred Astaire book, a nearly (commercially) dead horse that I am still flogging. My pre-interviewer, a sweet enough young woman, had clearly barely heard of Astaire. She called me "Joseph" straightaway. Each of her questions was quite nicely beside the point, while fully half her sentences began with the phrase "In terms of . . .". While half listening to her, I doodled the following limerick:

I've never read William of Ockham,
I figure on second thought, fock 'im.
I find his famous razor damnably crude,
And if one day I should run into the dude,
I intend to strip him entirely nude,
And in a most tender place sock him.

Shouldn't, the pre-interview, as our people say, be a total loss.

Best, Joe

Dear Joe,

The strangest thing that Lanzmann tells readers of *Le lièvre de Patagonie* (trust an *intello* for a fancy title) about his affair with Le Castor (the masculine article is sweetly attached to the lady, who appears to have swung in several directions) is that when, for whatever reasons (do people have to have them?), he made his way – ambition, lust, curiosity and who knows what all sign-posting him to the sticking point – to Simone's *lit*, she prefaced the proceedings with the warning/boast/bait that she was already involved with six men. For an innocent monogamist such as me, that seems a lot; imagine having to write a story in which the 40-something lady tells her 25-year-old unvirginal lover that he is in the lists (sic) with a half dozen other upright young men (she didn't say anything about the ladies, whom she just may have preferred, but who's counting, apart from her?).

The French make quite a thing (you may have heard) about being unshockable, but it may be that Le Castor was having a *petit* joke at Claude's expense. He is unlikely to have seen it, since he does not seem to be much given to laughter. It is, of course, typical of letters between ageing (as some shits will say, Miranda Seymour among them) literati that they knock their betters, trade low blows and take away the number they first thought of. I have now been through Lanzmann's book, and flagged it with yellow (what else?) Post-Its, but I have yet to make my notes (I do pages of them every time I review a book, even a novel) and until I do I am not sure what I shall make of the thing in detail. But I have to say, before I start pulling it apart or together, that the stuff about the making of *Shoah* is as convincing and as, yes, humbling (because of his persistence and courage and daring) as anything you will ever read about the man who thought, for a minute or two, that he was cuckolding Poulou who – and this is the most chilling part of the whole book – repaid him, if that's what he did, by setting up Lanzmann's beautiful actress sister in a flat. As Lanzmann tells it, the writer Claude Roy, a married man with whom C.'s sister fell in love and who then dumped her, was the cause of her suicide. But the scene in which Claude sits in the theatre, with Le Castor beside him, and watches Sartre falling in lust with his sister is about as ... grown-up, let's say, in a hurry, as anything one could imagine. It is difficult to imagine anything quite so hot and quite so cold *chez les anglo-saxons*. But what do I know?

I do know I can be taken to be Anglo-Saxon because a French producer got in touch last weekend asking me to do a script of a book called *My Life in CIA* by a man called Harry Mathews whom (must he?) I bet you know, but meant nothing to me until his book, and list of works, arrived the other day. My new best friend the producer whose first name is Ivan sought me out because he was/is a *grand admirateur* (don't you love him?) of *Voyage à deux* and, in particular, of *Eyes Wide Shut* and also, even more particularly the way he schmoozed it, of the little book I wrote about working with Kubrick. It has a reputation *hors de série* in France (remember Mordecai Richler's great line about a character who was 'world famous in Canada'?), where it won the only lit prize I have been awarded since 1960, when I won something called the Lippincott Prize, 2,500 real bucks and the same spent on advertising a novel called *The Limits of Love*. Someone – my guess is Updike – dumped on it in the *New Yorker* and there went the ballgame, like forever. Am I the only London-based *prétentieux* never solicited by the *NYRB*?

Cut back to today: I am wading through Mr Mathews's shallow water, enjoying his small conceit which is – did you guess? – that he was never REALLY in the CIA at all, just had it known that he was so that he could give the girls a thrill by having them think they were behind the scenes in the world's game. Matthews says that real CIA guys never called it THE CIA, hence his title. However, an old friend of mine called Stanley Baron, who was for a long, long time my editor at Thames and Hudson, WAS in the CIA and he put the *the* in it. Imagine my contusion.

I am in a position, not all that uncomfortable ackshly, to tell you that Alfie Appel may have been telling you the truth about his royalty check/cheque and here's why: I bought a copy of his *Nabokov's Dark Cinema* and that could just about cover the difference between your estimate of $11.34 and his claim to have earned $16.45. I read the book (looked at the pictures) when I was planning to do a little study of V.N. for the aforesaid Thames and Hudson. I wound up doing Byron, unless I'd already done Byron and dumped the whole thing. I did admire V.N. quite a lot (*Pale Fire* has to be the cleverest silly work of genius in the canon, unless you have worse ideas), but was a leetle unnerved when I re-read *Lolita* somewhat recently and saw that, whatever its camp following, it really IS a defence of paedophilia (the Sicilian defence which involves the child/female really being the seducer and also, of course, not the virgin which Humhum, well, took her for).

I happen to think that Kingsley Amis was the worst influence on the English novel since the war but I do recall that he said, when reviewing *Lo*, 'what did the man think he was doing?' or Clapham omnibus words to that effect, and I have to hand it to him, even though I am sure that, knowing Kingsley (a very little), I shall never get it back. I think V.N. fell out with Appel (who, no longer being the one of V.N.'s eye, ended falling a long way from the tree), though it may have been another of his acolytes, because he discovered that Volodya had done some not necessarily consummated night-work with another woman than Véra, whose acute accent could, one suspects, do a man a lot of damage when applied between the ribs. I spent one well-documented day with V.N. when I was asked to do a script of *Ada* by a producer at Columbia who had acquired the rights by winning a competition staged by V.N. and, I betcha, Véra, which required the suppliant moolah-carriers to report to Montreux with full powers and then make sealed bids against each other.

This came very soon after the supersmash bestseller *Lolita*, so the bidding was quintuple-zeroed or forget it. What the assembled execs did not take into account was that Kubrick had already made a little bit of a mess of the movie of *Lolita* (too mush respect for the text) and that it had not taken many beans. So after Columbia had won the Big One and paid up whatever they did, someone read *Ada* and retitled it (I'm romancing) *Oh Dear* and then called for Raphael, the hope of the no hopers. Nothing came of my visit to V.N. except my visit to V.N. It's all in one of my notebooks except for the fact that the Columbia exec, who is dead and beyond the uttering of writs, had worked so hard to pander to Volodya that he had his six-year-old son along in case that was the kind of candy the old guy liked (the old guy was younger than I am now, but who's counting?). V.N. imitated an elephant to make a Kim of the kid, but went no further than that.

I still think that *Speak, Memory* was V.N.'s masterpiece but I don't think I shall ever read it again. I admire your stamina re *Daniel Deronda* which I never finished and am unlikely to begin again. Why does the Jewish thing drive nearly all non-Jewish writers crazy? It's rare, as you say, for one of them to write even halfway convincingly about a Jew or 'the Jews' and amazing that,

by dint of what accurate imagination – the essential fiction-writer's quality –
the ugly and beautiful G.E. did it. Oddly enough, D.H. Lawrence had some
sense of the mysterious quality of SOME Jews, perhaps because of his friendship with that tough (?), marginal Jew Kotelianski, of whom I know almost
nothing but who, I suspect, contributed something to that very odd character
in *Kangaroo*, called Kangaroo. He was based on a General Monash, the Aussie
top soldier in WW1 and one of your people. What's more heartening is that I
can't remember ever reading a good book in favour of anti-Semitism. All
those guys (how many women are there, apart from Unity Mitford, and she
never sprang to a book or even one of those copious letters that all the other
sisters could crank out like home-made noodles?) sound silly and cheap and
defective, mentally and personally, or else lowdown pompous crackpotty like
Mr Eliot after strange goads.

I don't think I've ever read Mark Helprin but I feel like I've read things by
people almost of his name. I'm now going back to Harry Mathews, who
sounds like a pre-War Kenyan adulterer who won Bisley in 1922, emigrated
and was later shot dead several times by a remittance man second son of an
earl. I was going to tell you about this play Beetle and I went to see, and may
do so next time around (they call those second chances *repêchages*, don't
they?). But I did want to say, re *Blithe Spirit*, that it contains one unforgettable
line that make all ideologies look like stale cake: viz. 'MADAME ARCATI:
That cuckoo is very angry.' The first and last Noël, *dans ses oeuvres*.

Tout à toi,
Freddie

Dear Freddie,
Great minds not only think but act alike. I, too, take prodigious notes on
books about which I have been asked to write. I do so lest my memory fail me,
which I can more and more count on, but in fact I have done so for many
years before such problems arose. I cannot imagine reading without a pencil
nearby. When I come upon an interesting sentence or phrase or even word –
this morning I wrote out "ill-plenished" – I scribble it down in a notebook
of index cards, of which I have more than thirty. In olden days, these
little notebooks would have been called commonplace books, though mine
have no order whatsoever, and now I have so many that it is quite impossible
for me to find anything in them. Still, I persist in beginning fresh notebooks.
Why break a useless habit? These notebooks will one day become part of
my papers.

Betcha didn't think I had any fucking papers. Such am I now privileged to call the detritus of nearly fifty years of the scribbling life, since I have turned over boxes of correspondence, old manuscripts, and other hopeless items to the University of Chicago, where they are now housed in something called, I do believe, Special Collections. My own and Barbara's view is that it is good to have all this *dreck* out of our apartment. All that I have retained in this line are another thirty or so 80-page journal notebooks, which I write in daily – doing so has become part of my intellectual hygiene – chiefly about incidents and minor events in my so-called literary life. My journal pages are not so lively as yours – nor so namey – but they do serve as a useful *aide-mémoire*, if I am using that phrase correctly. In the back of each notebook, for example, I mark down books read and movies seen, with the date alongside the titles. Both Barbara's and my memory for movies we have seen is rather weak; we have come to the stage where we can see *The Pelican Brief* as if afresh every eighteen months.

A small correction: Alfred Appel (he would be shocked and deflated to be called Alfie) never broke with V. Nabokov, whom he reveres, even long after death, Nabokov's not Appel's. I wonder if the fellow you might have been thinking of is an American long since departed to Australia named Andrew Field, who wrote the first biography of Nabokov. (You did much better, I think, to write about Byron than about Nabokov.) I admire but do not adore Nabokov. He is rather too cold-hearted for me. Like you, I think *Speak, Memory* his best book, but, again like you, I have no desire to reread it. (I also rather like *Pnin*, which does show V.N. displaying some sympathy.) I was never much taken with *Lolita*, upon which I tend to side with the judgment of Philistia: to (lack of) wit, sick stuff. He could manipulate English words, our Volodya, shaping them into the most comely sentences, no doubt about that. I am a sucker, not to say a great snob, for elegant prose style, but I continue to feel, probably against lots of evidence, that there is no substitute, even in literature, for a good and generous heart, the possession of which I'm fairly sure V.N. couldn't claim.

Nabokov's wife and son are themselves rich subjects. An American woman named Schiff – our very own Miranda Seymour – wrote a full-scale biography of Véra Nabokov that I have no plans to read. I did read somewhere, though, that in his days as a college lecturer, Nabokov would refer to Véra, who attended all his academic lectures, thus: "Ladies and gentleman, my assistant will now dim the lights," which Véra would then do. The picture that results is V.N. as the great magician, Véra as the beautiful assistant in mesh stockings.

A son, Dmitri, a failed opera singer, a very tall man with a taste for fancy automobiles, has lived for years, one gathers, off his father's royalties. He brought out an unpublished novel of V.N.'s to show that the vein of gold ore in this particular mine had not yet been exhausted, at least not while Dmitri N. is around.

If Nabokov hadn't married a Jewish woman – or Jewess, in the old phrasing – he would, I think, have been capable of creating some low-aristocrat genuinely frightening, quick-call-the-anti-Defamation-League Jewish characters of devastating grotesquerie. The reason this comes to mind is that I am in the middle of my essay on Santayana's eight volumes of letters, and have had to include a few paragraphs on his anti-Semitism. Here's a little example from a letter to his fellow Jew-contemner, Ezra (quick, put this guy in the) Pound: "As to the Jews, I too like the Greek element in Christendom better than the Jewish; yet the Jews, egotistically and fantastically, were after a kind of good – milk and honey and money." Here is George Santayana, as subtle and refined a man as lived in the last century, and he has the damn Jew Bug, and in coarsest form: Jews are Communists, pushing, money-crazed, mean-spirited, the full catastrophe. What a great failure of imagination in Santayana, a man who prided himself on being imaginative. Writing my paragraphs on Santayana's anti-Semitism, I tried to think of major non-Jewish Anglophone writers who had sufficient imaginative sympathy to leave rounded and convincing Jewish characters in their work, and could think of only two: George Eliot and Willa Cather.

A larger question arises, which is what does one do about all the great and several of the good writers, from Shakespeare on, who kept a little cold spot in their hearts for the Jews. Obviously one doesn't cease reading those writers who fail the Jew-test; if one did, it would be Good-bye, English and most of American Lit. All one can do, I think, is make a mental note of the offending writer, and somehow mix it in with his or her virtues, and keep on moving. As an occasional writer about writers – which we both are – it does seem to me sensible, however, never to let the little presence of the virus known as the Jew Bug pass without comment.

I've never read *Kangaroo*. All I've read of D.H. Lawrence is *Sons and Lovers, Women in Love, Sea and Sardinia*, the poems, a few of the stories. Nor have I ever understood why F.R. Leavis got so passionately worked up about him. The Trillings, too, were devoted to Lawrence. (Now there is a bridge game for you: the Trillings and the Leavises: "Nine hearts no trump to you, Queenie, dear," says Diana, kicking Lionel under the table.) I suspect that Lawrence rode in, for that generation, on the Freudian sex express, though there must be more to it than this. Although he is scarcely a font of good sense, I rather like Bertrand Russell's pronouncement on Lawrence (in B.R.'s autobiography): "He is a writer of a certain descriptive power whose ideas cannot be too soon forgot." That may be the best example I know of damning – of absolutely crushing – with faint praise.

Write if you find work.

Best, Joe

Dear Joe,

I have just read your essay on Santayana with great pleasure and a double-shot, as the coffee-shopper says, of piquant nausea; just the right prescription for thought provocation. I don't believe I have ever read G.S., having considered Unamuno quite enough Spanish philosophising to be going on with, though a shot of Ortega y Gasset added zest to the tragic sense of the sage of Salamanca. His (literal) stand against the man who shouted '*Viva la Muerte*' makes him some kind of a right Right-minded hero.

Thanks to you, I now know that Santayana wasn't much of a Castilian or anything close, but it's a little late: he shouldn't have spelt his name that way if he wanted to be taken for a Bostonian and then again, of course, he didn't. The British have never totally trusted people whose names ended in sounded vowels; hence a contemporary climber called Portillo never got to the top of Disraeli's greasy pole – Dizzy is the exception that points up the rule. You nail G.S. gently, and without getting cross, which is typical of your, um, feline charm, in literary essaying. His calm apprehensions are at times very Isaiah Berlinish, elegant and detached and somehow indicative of an inner turmoil which philosophising is calculated to still. Your view of academic philosophy is probably based on years of observation. I have little more than sentimentality to oppose to it, but I do think thinking is possible, and beats sermonising, when it isn't doing it. Analysis, when not analytic, can produce tolerance: 'Say it if you like, but be careful' was the wisdom of John Wisdom who was the Anglo-Saxon heir to Wittgenstein.

It is difficult now to recall with any precision what impact W. made on Cambridge when I went up in 1950. He was already dying in the house of Dr Bevan (unless it was Beavan) of the prostate cancer which is now so often treated, with life-protracting success, that were he about to be dead today, he would still be alive tomorrow. I don't know, and don't greatly care to think, what price is paid to survive from those mortal coils, but men do, lots of them. A friend of ours, the renowned photographer Lee Friedlander, was saved from an advanced case by the kind of medical science that sends Haters of the West such as Frantz Fanon and Chairman Arafat in search of last resorts among the Hebrews (much as Europe's princes used to have Jewish doctors; odd that only a gangster like Stalin ever accused them of trying to kill him). Lee, an unblinking shutterbug, said that the price you have to be willing to pay for salvation is that your penis is thenceforth 'purely decorative'.

Back to Wittgenstein. The very fact that he was spoken of only by his surname (one can now imagine your TV host shaking his hand with a cry, 'Ludwig, at last we meet, kiddo!') says something of his quasi-divine status (Freud's was quasi-divan). Where Russell was Bertie, Wittgenstein was Wittgenstein; his brevities were the soul of him, however they dragged on. Dragged is cheap: his aphorisms were the kind of piquant Continental food we couldn't get in austerity Britain (look ahead, ye Jeremiahs, and here it comes again, the sawdust bread of economic affliction). W. was Viennese-exotic like Bratwurst and Pumpernickel, two philosophers from whom he had severed himself because of their apostolic plagiarism; agreeing with a man like W. could put you in deep, deep shit.

The charm of his seriousness cannot today be measured because no-one is REALLY, REALLY serious now except Osama Bin Liner, galloping around the lower Hymnyourlayers on a white horse, as if being directed by Otto Preminger. Not to mention Robert Fisk, the inverted Cassandra, telling the kinds of tales that everyone who hates Jews likes to believe, including Jews, of course. Wait till Oliver Stone catches up with him, or Steven Soddenberger, who thinks Che ripe for a double scoop of screentime. Hate alone is serious now and your anti-Westerners, in the West, are eager to confuse it with thought and progress and radicalism and here comes good old Uncle Joe again. Mao never quite went away, did he? His story is SO vile, so self-serving, so murderous that it's not surprising that he is still said to have lessons to teach us.

Wittgenstein had SOMETHING of what you admire in Santayana. With a deep (one of his favourite terms of praise) sense of the dubiousness of office, honours, possessions, he too lived a life of minimalist detachment: he gave away £800,000 in inheritance, at a time when the pound weighed something and, disapproving of a cushioned life, thought a spartan deck-chair as near luxury as a rear end should go. I use spartan with a minuscule because, as is now generally agreed, your actual Spartans – with whom the ancient Hebrews affected an affinity – were up for any kind of luxury they could find, especially when on their travels. One of them, called Eurycles, breezed in on Herod the Great and took him for everything he could get, which was plenty. The

Spartans were renowned, even back in the 8th century BC, for their appetite for money. They had iron bars for cash when in Laconia; but offshore, hedge funds were very much their sort of thing. Nasty pieces of work are not rare in your ancient Laconia, but no-one has constructed a typology in which the Spartans are crude materialists, as well as superstitious, superficial, selfish and uncreative (after the sixth century BC). Don't you wince at that BCE notation to which we are all obliged, it seems, these CE days?

Equally – now I'm thinking about G.S. and all those pollysyllabic krauts and their parroted worship of 'the Greeks', quite a few of whose fine spirits were uprooted cosmopolitans and mendicant mystifiers of a kind which we all know in short men with long faces like what's-his-first-name Dworkin, who has a multiplicity of Chairs (and tables with Henry Moores on them, I happen to know) – your high-flying Hellenists rarely curse these paradeigmatic 'Greeks' whom they think they know so well with the characteristics of the shifty Athenians whom Thucydides describes or Plato hates or the two-faced Boeotians whom Aristophanes mocks (sell you into slavery, all of them, soon as look at you, if you weren't a pretty fellow, AND if you were and didn't sing their songs). The Greeks – Shelley fell for them like he did for young girls – have been wilfully misread into Ideal Models with the same zeal that dumps 'the Jews' into the eternal sin-bin (Byron took the contrary view, probably because it WAS contrary).

The snidenesses re Hebrews that you quote from Santayana can be matched, in lighter or darker shades, and up there on a Parnassian shelf in bigger sizes too, from a whole range of Our Betters and Their Bests. They have such fine feelings that they have to hawk and spit on the you-know-whos to keep their throats clear for the high notes. Do not search your conscience, *pauvre petit Juif*, for what WE have done. Think what they have and, yes, move on, if you can; in the fast lane when possible. None of their routine dirty talk (anti-Semitism is the locker room smut of the intellectual athlete) seems to have any deposit in practical hostility when classy Jews are present, even though the folks at Palm Beach – we are told on the box, so it must be true – wouldn't have Leonard Bernstein to dinner, after they'd been to his concert. Our mistake (yours, mine, Isaiah's, who all else's) is to try to find arguments to counter or reasons to justify this all-together-in-the-men's-room kind of baby-talk. They (our judges) are riven with doubts and drivel and it comes out like the shit of the man Catullus describes who craps only a dozen times a year and when he does it emerges in such neat pellets that you can rub them between your fingers and not smell of anything but roses, or something poetic like that. The dread of juice and Jews converges nicely in English: juiciness is fruity, squirty, over-tasty, uncontrollable, lickable ... the Freudian spillage says it all, some of it, at least. Jews come out with things and if they don't, they keep them to themselves. *Jouissance!*

Shall we talk of basic insecurity when analysing the anti-Semite? *La condition Humaine*, maybe? The sad inadequacy of EVERYBODY requires a programme of one-size-fits-almost-all contempt that will make us all buddies, THEM all buddies. The Man from St Louis and ole Ez can both feel a step up from underneath the provincial lot they got allotted by constructing a social pyramid in which they deserve what passes for exclusive lodgings just because they are NOT something that doesn't qualify for anything above the piles (did T.S.E. suffer from them? Research is called for, and will come running, if the money's right). The strangest thing about Santayana is that he could not *quite* exempt Spinoza from sharing the attributes of Itzig-off-the-pickle-boat.

What I suspect is that ALL those genteel anti-Semites have a common fear: that the Jews, whether Spinoza the Apostate or Maimonides the Lawgiver or Isaiah the Trimmer or Joe E. or Freddie R. NEVER say what they really want to say, NEVER fail somewhat to mince their words for the Gentile table, and have MUCH more that they might deliver, in the way of criticism, rage, analysis, or even comedy, than they ever quite do or will. See Leo Strauss's *Literature and Persecution*, or topics to that effect and you'll see what a *passe-montagne* of humourlessness he puts on when broaching the subject of the hidden, the muffled, the tactful. Byron had a phrase about 'he could an he would' or something like that, and does it apply to you and me and even to Mel Brooks? *Je crois.*

The dread they have of what is kept from them is the same dread (only different, of course) that began in Egypt when Joseph interpreted Pharaoh's dreams and then saved his economic bacon (this was before Moses ever got the Jews' act together and their divine articles of association from the top of Mt Sinai) and could, maybe, have done MUCH, MUCH more (like 24 Hour News) had not his alien presence shown up the locals for maybe not exactly A-streamers; as a result the next Pharaoh knew not him, and the Hebrews had to get ready to sing a chorus from *Aida*. Of course you and I know that plenty of Jews are so irremediably third-rate, boring, lacking in entrepreneurial skills and the capacity to write *Zettel* even, that the Gentiles shouldn't worry ALL THAT about what's cooking in the alchemical kosher kitchens that even the most enlightened, Spinozistic of us keep in some recess of our otherwise come-on-in houses.

I had a great-uncle who said, 'It's all worked out to beat you'. G.S. said much the same. But did he ever say what my great-uncle said when a man came up to him in Hyde Park and asked, 'Have you found Jesus?' Maurice (unless he was Morris) replied: 'Why? Have you lost him again?' They never found him, of course, and you know whose fault that is. As the Chief Rabbi MUST say sometimes, 'Fuck 'em all.'

Tout à toi, cher maître,
Freddie

Dear Freddie,
You are in fine near-tirade (tear-ahd, in the best English accent) voice, rough language and all, in your last e-missive (sounds a bit like a nocturnal e-mission). My sense is that you have had more anti-Semitism directed at you than I, who bears one of the Jewyest of all Jewish names, fore and aft, have had directed at me. But you, as I know from reading you over the years, have been the recipient of anti-Semitism at the English public school and university levels, which perhaps doesn't carry the element of fear that the American version might induce in its victims – peasants, after all, throw bricks and punches and enjoy pogroms – but, my guess is, carries a greater sting. Nobody wants to join the club of peasants, but English anti-Semitism suggests (and more than suggests) that the better clubs will always be closed to you, that you will never, in general or in particular, qualify (for what, I leave blank). America's better clubs have never been all that alluring, but the English ones, at least once upon a time, seem to have been. But enough of our good friends, the Jew haters and baiters.

Let me turn to the age of transition, as Eve called it when asked with her highly significant other to depart the Garden of Eden, in this instance the transition to the world of online scribbling. A few weeks ago, I wrote a 1,700-word piece for *Newsweek* on the slow and painful decline of the tennis fortunes of Roger Federer. (I can't recall if I sent it to you, so I attach it below.) The piece was found acceptable, and was to run in this past week's issue. Toward the end of the week my editor there, a bright fellow named Tom Watson who has treated me regally, called to say that the piece had been, in effect, bumped, but would run online, and in a fairly radically cut version. The radical cutting, which Tom Watson does very skillfully, did not so much bother me; one of the greatest disappointments of the scribbling life comes with the knowledge that everything can be cut – and that includes the Lord's

Prayer, the Gettysburg Address, and the Ten Commandments – and usually improved as a result. No, what troubled me was having my writing online without first making an appearance in actual print on paper, the order which I much prefer.

From time to time a scribble of mine is picked up by a splendid website called artsandlettersdaily.com, run by an American philosophy don living in New Zealand named Denis Dutton, whose family owned and ran a number of good bookstores in Los Angeles, all of them put out of business by the great chains and Amazon. More people probably see artsandlettersdaily.com than subscribe to most of the magazines you and I write for, and I find myself pleased to have a response to my scribbles from readers in Australia and other distant lands. Tom Watson told me that one of the pleasures of appearing online is the instant gratification of reader response, and, true enough, 48 readers quickly shot off comments (printed online) to my Federer piece. But online comments tend, I think, to be generally less thoughtful than the comments one receives in handwritten (or typed) letters. And online is so impalpable, so evanescent, I won't say ethereal, but I will say fucking demo-cratic. Anyone, online, can play, whereas old boys such as you and I had the minor status of having (presumably) commercial publishers and magazine editors give us the imprimatur of being professional writers. Impalpable – if you can't touch it, can't hold it in your hand, it doesn't seem like actual writing. Yet it seems to me fairly obvious that online is the wave – sneeze? belch? – of the future. Still, if something I write appears only online, to me it feels, and probably always will, as if I have just written something and then blithely dropped it out the window.

Now here is a golden flamin' oldie for your possible dis-delectation. *Newsweek* has asked me to travel out to Palm Springs, California, to talk with and write about Herman Wouk. (Bet you haven't heard or thought about that name in some little while.) H.W. is soon to be 94, no spring (more likely sprung) chicken, as my mother might say. In my story "The Love Song of A. Jerome Minkoff" a character named Maury Gordon is told, at 85, that he has pancreatic cancer, and he takes the news calmly, saying that he hasn't been all that eager to get to ninety. "They say," he says (if I remember my own dialogue rightly), "that sixty is the new forty, seventy is the new fifty, but I have some friends in their nineties, and, Doc, 90 is the new 112." In any case, after much pre-screening (of me) by his agent and wife, I called H.W. and discovered a strong voice and absolutely alert mind.

We met once before, H.W. and I, fifteen or so years ago, at lunch under the auspices of a good man named Sol Linowitz, a lawyer from Rochester, NY, who became one of the early chairmen of the Xerox Corporation, and was thus early taken out of all financial wars. Sol L. used to take me to lunch at a place called the F Street Club in Washington, DC, a hang-out of sorts of the old Democratic Party establishment, where one could have a room alone and be served one's lunch – one main course only up for non-selection, but always an excellent one main course – by Irish waitresses. Sol L. told me that he had been invited to join the club by Ellsworth Bunker (great American WASP name, an Old-American State Department hand), and once he became a member he noted the extreme paucity of Jews on the club roster; paucity hell, he was the only Heb in the joint. Instanter he went to the club's secretary and said that, as a Jew, he not only felt lonely but felt a bit of a "token," and wondered if something couldn't be done to relieve him of both these feelings. Lo and bloody behold, they quickly found other Jewish members.

Sol Linowitz loved Jewish jokes, subtle ones, which he told very well and received appreciatively. One of his best – here is the very shortened version – is about a Jewish man, a bachelor, familyless, who wants a Kaddish service said for his recently deceased dog Buster. After much complication – the rabbi allows that Jews don't say Kaddish over animals – the man gets the rabbi to agree to do it. At the end of the service, at which only the rabbi and the man attend, the man, in tears, thanks the rabbi, saying, "I can't tell you how grateful I am to you, rabbi. Until this afternoon, I had no idea how much Buster had done for Israel."

Back to Herman Wouk, whom I rarely read when young, for the reason that he was disqualified as being the middlebrow of all middlebrows, and I, as you may somehow have failed to notice, am a modernist, irrefragable, unfungible highbrow. (Please pass the Jimmy Joyce, and I do believe that I shall have just another dollop of that Mallarmé, if you don't mind.) Although Wouk's books sold splendidly, he was inevitably roughed up by intellectual reviewers. And one of the reasons he was is that Wouk's works (Wouk's works, easy for me to say) have lots of harsh criticisms of intellectuals that boil down to this: that intellectuals do not have a stake in things, they do not take responsibility for their ideas or positions, they are not finally to be counted upon, in foxholes or anywhere else. You may remember that at the end of the movie version of *The Caine Mutiny*, the navy lawyer, played by José Ferrer, tells off the intellectual naval officer, played by Fred MacMurray, for precisely the qualities I specified above, which result in the wrecking of two careers (those of the characters played by Humphrey Bogart and Van Johnson). In *Marjorie Morningstar*, the bad-guy intellectual is named Noel Airman, and Airman is the precise English for *luftmensch*, or ungrounded dreamer.

Are Herman Wouk's novels themselves any good? I do not know. I am reading a few of them at present. Herman Wouk was in the line of Theodore Dreiser, John Steinbeck, the early James T. Farrell, at a lower rung Irwin Shaw, and others who told straight stories in which large things seemed to be at stake. The history of the novel has turned away from these writers, or so it strikes me; it has turned, in Wouk's case, from naval warfare to navel gazing, in the cases of Philip Roth & co. Are we, is anyone, the gainer? You can infer my answer.

Herman Wouk is also serious about his Judaism; I believe he goes to synagogue daily. He reads Talmud. He travels often to Israel. He has written a credible book on the history of the Jews, which is also a polemic about the increasingly troublesome question of their survival. I don't think he has written fiction for a long while. He told me over the phone that he has recently turned in to his publisher a 40,000-word manuscript about his views on God that his publisher (Little, Brown) is to bring out next year. How good this will be, written by a man of his stately age, I have no notion. But, as a moderately pious agnostic, I should rather read Herman Wouk on God than Christopher Hitchens on the absence of God.

Don't believe I have hitherto ended a composition, letter, or e-mail to you or anyone else on the word God (which good Jews aren't supposed to spell out), and so will end here, G-damnit.

Best, Joe

Dear Joe,

I didn't know Herman Wouk was still alive. Imagine, at his age, having only a u between you and fast Thai food. God is not mocked but can He do that stuff! *The Caine Mutiny* is a middlebrow masterpiece, not a term that I use with quite the condescension of Dwight Macdonald who, as far as I know, never began to write a highbrow anything much, but knew how to appeal to the vanity of those who did 'pieces', just as he did. The twist in which the liberal lieutenant (the Fred MacMurray part) is suddenly made to realise that moral superiority is not a form of virility, that's pretty fine. Without it, the book and the play and the film would have been nothing more than the prelude to *A Few Good Men* or whatever the thing was called, but Wouk somehow suggests that Queeg stands for the rednecks and even, maybe, for the anti-Semites who may be mean bastards and all kinds of stuff but who also save the sum of things, and usually for meagre pay. So *The Caine Mutiny* deserves its place in the polytheon where good bestsellers have their niche.

Then comes *Marjorie Morningstar* and SOMETHING YOU MAY NOT KNOW, because how could you? It so happens that I was paid a higher fee than ever before or since for adapting that very long and somewhat odd novel into a screenplay in which Al Pacino, none other, was to play Noel (did you say?) Airman (you did say). I didn't quite peak or peek at the million dollars which my then-agent, not a nice man, aimed to get me, but it was not far off. The deal was sweeter than the job, because when you get into Marjorie, which – as you know – Airman never quite did, there is so unlikely a tale *là-dedans* that you have to conclude that the lady was drawn from life. The story of a star who doesn't in the end get to twinkle and is, as they now say, good with that, if that's what they say, is so artless that it seems artful. The public, I suppose, bought Marjorie literally and metaphorically, and so there must have been some Eisenhower-years truth in her and the book. But it was not a lot of fun to make a script out of, even though I did it, honourably (bad as that, right?). In the end, which came quite quickly, unlike that of *M.M.,* it was realised that Al was too old to be making a play for a teenager in a movie (what they all do in life is something else). From then on I wended my downward way to the valley of mere thousands where screenwriters now come and go talking less of Michelangelo than of the *bon vieux temps* when the lousy studios were loaded and making development deals. You were right, Marcel, it hurts to remember. And you too, Marcello.

I've been thinking just a little about Santayana and the grace with which you damned him gently. I suspect (that old cop's trick) that the epistolary mode (if you have a high horse, get up there, right?) unleashes confidences of a kind that are likely to be inhibited when you face someone in the flesh, even if he shares your distastes (they do keep people together). The intimate absence of the Other, not to mention *l'Autrui*, unblocks the mind and the drains in a strange way and on one does run, half amazed at the sump on which one can draw. Letters are not quite literature, although they can be collected voluminously, and not quite conversation, with its happy dispersal rate. It's because we have so many of his letters that Cicero is not only the best known, most accessible, of the ancients but also the most often despised. He is egotistic, vain, mistaken and too smart for his own good. *Comme nous tous,* some will say, though they will be lucky if they get through to the third round with the man from Arpino. We have made a compact, you and I, of a not very devilish kind, but we are writing in this way things we would not write in another and would not, I am pretty sure, say to each other if I happened to be stranded at O'Hare overnight and we had time to tire the sun with talking. Maybe Santayana was trying to say what his correspondent would like him to say and think, or maybe it just came out and the stamp was on the envelope and, bam!, it's on the train to ubiquity.

Forgiving Santayana for his vulgarity rather than for sneering at Jews is, of course, your proper way of rising above him and the expectations of the obvious. It occurs to me that it might be fun to concoct a catchy little bouquin entitled *The Protocols of the Elders of Anti-Semitism*. In this hitherto unknown document we would find the agreed agenda and, yes, protocols, of the conference of conceited toffs, poets, philosophers and uncertain Midwesterners who met to confirm their superiority in 20th century letters (let's say this conference took place in 1923). The compiling of a phrasebook of the higher paranoia, handsomely housed in a nut-case, would have taken them a long weekend, without ladies, in Baden-Baden in worsen-worsening light. Why are there so few female anti-Semites? Or have I missed someone who isn't Unity Mitford or her sister Lady Mostly, much beloved by the Anglais because her beauty makes her affection for Nazism into a sort of ... sport? D.H. Lawrence would, of course, have been invited to take the waters, but would quarrel in no time with all those present. He praised the Jewish genius for 'disinterested speculation'. Not a bad phrase, even if sneeringly delivered, which I am not sure it was: he had this friend Koteliansky who knew the one about Levinsky.

Tout à toi,
Freddie

Dear Freddie,

One female anti-Semite that comes to mind is Virginia Woolf, whose diaries have some fine touches of the higher anti-Semitism; she applies it lavishly, as I recall, to the grand English *Juif*, Isaiah of Berlin (actually Riga). Virginia W's having married a Jewish gentleman, which is what you call a kike if he will only leave the room, didn't seem to slow her down in this realm; and old Leonard seemed the very model of the good Jewish husband (doting, solicitous, protective), and for Bloomsbury, a warren of unpleasantness, rather a decent man. Go, as our people are wont to say, figure.

Went yesterday to the Joffrey Ballet. Was much impressed with the first performance, which was of Bronislava Nijinska's *Les Noces*, music by Stravinsky.

The music is hard-driven, the choreography highly geometrical, the content intentionally emotionless, as befits the dark subject: the subjection of Russian peasant women in marriage. I was so swept away by the ballet that this morning I read the two pages that Edwin Denby, the greatest of dance critics, wrote about it. "*Noces* is noble," he writes, "it is fierce, it is fresh, it is thrilling." He also says that the ballet is "one of the finest things one can see anywhere. And if I could think of higher praise I would write it."

In one of those breathtakingly simple observations that only great critics seem able to make, Denby called ballet "the art of balance." Of course, of course, of course, only one didn't realize it until Denby said it. Yesterday afternoon, watching the Joffrey Ballet, I thought that ballet is also the art of design, with the materials being used those of human bodies, with music and motion and color (of costumes and backdrop) added.

But the reason I bother you with all this – apart from demonstrating my own exquisite susceptibilities to the greatest art – is to tell you that watching yesterday's performance reminded me of how splendid high modernist art, of which *Les Noces* is a strong example, is at its best. By high modernist art I have in mind art of a kind that is avant-garde and tradition-minded both, serious in its intention yet joyous in its effects. (George Balanchine is the great model here, a man who could easily go both ways, before that phrase was a description of bisexuality, traditional or ultra-modern in his choreography.) I also have in mind the art of Matisse and Braque, the more playful James Joyce and the comic element in Kafka, the more daring architecture of Le Corbusier and Frank Lloyd Wright, the music of Ravel and Satie. I would naturally keep out the drearier highbrow modernism, the gloomy Isben, druggy William Burroughs, boring Ingmar Bergman. (I once asked Saul Bellow if he watched the movies of Bergman. "Nope," he said. "I like my Kierkegaard straight." A good answer, I thought, and still do.) I would also exclude most of Samuel Beckett, perhaps the most overrated of modern writers.

I probably could not subsist on a straight highbrow diet. I watch my share of crappy movies, and way too much sports, though I do not watch any American policiers or dread-filled hospital shows, or sitcoms (with the exception of reruns of the old *Seinfeld* show). My late friend (he died of leukemia at 59) Samuel Lipman started out in life as a piano prodigy and kept to a strict highbrow diet (the cultural equivalent, I suppose, of keeping kosher). I once mentioned to Sam that he never seemed to mention movies or television. "I consider movies and television dogshit," he replied, not at all quaintly. When

Sam was running out of luck with conventional cancer treatment, I suggested his looking into unconventional treatments, "for example," I said, "Steve McQueen is undergoing laetrile treatments for his cancer in Mexico." "Who," asked Sam, "is Steve McQueen?"

Watching *Les Noces* yesterday afternoon, I thought, too, of how the old distinction among highbrow, middlebrow, and lowbrow art, upon which you and I grew up, is today all but dead, and wondered a bit what has been lost by its demise. Rather a lot, I suspect. The first thing lost is serious criticism. So long as the highbrow-middlebrow-lowbrow distinction was in force, highbrow critics had things to defend; they were gatekeepers, and tough ones, too. They could kill bad books, piss magisterially (lift your robe, Your Honor, please!) on artistic pretensions, shoot down the ersatz. Today everything is a great stew, or wash, with a performance artist (the Italian whose name I have chosen not to remember) winning the Nobel Prize for Literature, third-rate movies taken for major works, every kind of junky visual art selling for vast sums while producing even more vast boredom. One of the reasons we don't have strong critics nowadays is that they, the critics, don't think they really have much to defend. People writing literary criticism today – Clive Barnes, James Wood, I cannot think of a third name – seem more or less smart, more or less right about this, or wrong about that, but none of it matters very much because nothing, really, seems to be at stake. So then, Herr Freddie, when you become Minister of Culture for England and France and I for the United States, I say we bring back happy highbrowism, with, for the voters, a copy of Proust in every pot.

I have of late been receiving offers easy to refuse. The first is to join in debate with a young journalist named Jacob Weisberg who holds that the Internet is good for literature; I am being asked as an older (not to say decrepit) fellow who is likely to be skeptical about the effects of the Big I, which of course I am. A large crowd but no fee was offered. But the fee would have had to be ample for me to accept, for I do not have much taste for debate: I don't like to be shown up or made to look foolish and I suspect that, cornered, I become too fierce and no fun at all.

I have had an offer to speak about Fred Astaire, after lunch, to a small group called the Bradley Fellows at the American Enterprise Institute in Washington, DC. Half an hour or so is all that is wanted. The fee is $500. The problem is that the half-hour talk, if you include traveling to and from Washington, will remove two days from my scribbling life. Toss in that travel itself has become a great pain in the nether parts.

A third offer comes from a nice woman I've never met named Paula Marantz Cohen, who sometimes writes, and writes well, about movies and popular culture for the *TLS*. She teaches at a place called Drexel University in Philadelphia. She would like me to pop up to Philadelphia for two days as part of her school's Honors Series, give a talk, provide a student workshop (Kingsley Amis, was it not, who said that everything that has gone wrong with the world since World War Two can be summed up in the new use of the word workshop), do a half-hour television interview, be taken to a nice dinner. "I think we would give you a good time, and it would be stimulating and fun for everyone." My expenses would of course be paid, though only a small honorarium would be offered; she doesn't mention the exact sum. I have myself always taken the word "honorarium" to be a euphemism for small fee, so perhaps Paula Marantz Cohen, usually a careful writer, is unaware that she has committed a tautology. I shall in any case beg off.

Finally, four or five months ago I received an invitation to speak for ten minutes at something called *El Cuidad de las Ideas* in Mexico City. The prospect of traveling to Mexico City was – and remains – as enticing to me as exploratory surgery. Instead of saying No emphatically and straight-off, I said that I would be willing to do so for $12,000. The man who invited me, a Mexican PhD (natch) named Andreas Romero came back with an offer of $8,000. We closed the deal at $10,000. Not long afterward Mexico City became a center for kidnapping. At the moment it is the chief source of the great Swine Flu. It has long had the world's heaviest pollution. By October (I am scheduled to give my little talk in November) no doubt there will be major pogroms. That's, as the old MGM anthology flick had it, Entertainment.

Best, Joe

Dear Joe,

I write on the day on which the French celebrate what never happened, their victory over the Germans on this day in 1945 when von Runstedt and similarly high-hatted, well-tailored krauts agreed that *assez* was *assez* and agreed to be *assis* around the table with their conquerors. It is not mentioned *ici* that when they heard that the French were to be included among the Allied officers who were going to render tat for tit and treat the Germans as the Germans had not had the courtesy to treat those whom they had bullied and murdered, the quasi-gentlemen among the kraut military sighed in disbelief. Sartre said, for a moment, that the French had lived in shame everything that the British, in particular, had endured in pride, but that was then and now it's the Brits who want medals for self-inflicted wounds.

While the French parade down the Chomps Elysées with their tanks and trucks under a sky striped *bleu blanc rouge* by their loud and expensive fighter-planes, the British are doing business as usual which, to my antique shame, seems to include the members of parliament being involved in what the crime people call, I believe, a long firm (can I be right?), which is a scam involving protracted corporate fraud and fakery, what the frogs call *fausses factures* (an unofficial national industry). In the present blaringly-publicised Britlische case, MPs have rigged their expenses to allow them to embellish their 'second homes', which they are allowed to finance from the public purse (down to TV and bathroom suites, etc.) because otherwise how could the poor dears afford both to be in Westminster and to have residences in their far-flung constituencies? I am sure that something similar operates in the US, because how else would congressmen and reverend signors be able to have their homemade cakes and eat in Washington too? But there is something sad as well as ridiculous in the British, who have for so long convinced such saps as your correspondent that there was some element of moral integrity in their – how silly can you get? – superiority, turning out to be as cheap in their daily fraudulence as your average mythical kike or – T.E. Hulme's phrase – 'any creeping Turk to the Bosphorus'.

Why is that a phrase that loiters in the memory when 'to the Bosphorus' – especially the 'to' bit – doesn't play all that prettily? His 'in finesse of fiddles found I ecstasy' is *hors de série*, however, and also – hey, smart guy, right? – fits very well into my theme, which is that even I was once (back in the 1940s and 50s) a member of the deracinated group headed up (as they do say) by H.J. and T.S.E. who felt a little sorry for the Yanks with their vulgar culture and want of style.

Somehow (old fake link) my sense of the shabbiness of today's Britain, the cheapness of its clichés, the degeneration of 'socialism', as incorporated in the Labour Party, into hickery and hackery and ad hockery in the form of blaming everything on the Tories, who haven't had a chance to do anything grossly incompetent for a dozen years, because they are the naturally Bad Party of snobs and nobs, all this hinges onto what you were saying about the Jewish appetite for high culture, especially that of the crew that would, in any kind of a rough sea, be the first to jettison them from the Good Ship. Too many free-thinking Jews, in T.S.E.'s phrase, probably means a couple such as you and me, who might be seen smirking together when old Tom curtsied to the royals or even, after a few drinks, be tempted to incite Virginia to, as they say and I NEVER have, get her tits out.

The ascription of visceral vulgarity to our people has its *locus classicus* in John Cuddihy (ex-Jesuit, I think) and his idea of the Ordeal of Civility. Have you already dismissed this sadly plausible piece of sympathetico-polemic (of which the French equivalent came from the pen of Fabre-Luce and was entitled, with less subtlety, *Pour en finir avec l'anti-Sémitisme*. Alfred Fabre-Luce was a collabo not, as they say, '*de base*', but rather a toff who swam in the Vichyssoise; failing to go down with the shit, he lived to pontificate another day. His way of finishing with anti-Semitism was to finish with the Jews by having them sign in as deutero-goyim (*bien élevés* and all that) or ship out (on a flight to the stop after Ultima Thule). *La Grande Illusion* is not, of course, of the concord of nations or that one of them is better than another or whatever that pretentious movie of rare humanity said it was, but that the Gentiles are gents and the Jews had it coming to them and never learn and what else have you got. 'You' here includes the odd strand of public flagellators of other Jews' backs and fronts; not many a Jacqueline Rose chooses to blush unseen.

The zeal with which so many of the 1920s and 30s and 40s Jewish intellos were determined to find Great Art only in what was done by Others dates back at least to the Vienna of Karl Kraus and those of his unkind kind who, such as Wittgenstein and who all else among geniuses, bought into the Wagnerian dichotomy and agreed that no Jew could be an original creative artist. Some Jews decided that only *real* Jews, unreformed Hasids (cf. hayseeds such as Will Rogers), were uncontaminated articles, *ergo* capable of an authentic culture. Buying into a leetle of this, the intellos could persuade themselves that criticism at least they could do (cf. the Romans' sighing boast about 'satire at least being entirely theirs', the cue for how many undergraduate essays saying '*oui, mais*', which brings us back to today's date). So clever Jews became thrilling and trilling critics and devised, quite often, lists of Great Masters, Minor Masters and all the rest which both dignified and humiliated the judges who could themselves never make the grades they marked.

Scholarship (the next window to highbrow journalism) of the hermeneutic style enabled clever young Jews (a category for which ancient disputants qualified in the Temple, where that young Jesus was an early whizz, as was my present Sisyphean rolling stone, Josephus ben Mattathias) to stand out while remaining within the tradition and so doing nothing too original. Jesus was (my sources promise) a living version of Walter Benjamin's unwritten masterpiece which would consist entirely of quotation: messiah as montage. He said clever things and glossed like a shoeshine boy of genius, but he didn't break the mould and he didn't – ah the irony! – upset the goyim, even though they crucified him in the end, backed by enough of the Jerusalem crowd to qualify as 'the Jews' when Christianity took over the presses. This is, I confess, before being racked, rather a superficial account, but it does indicate – render unto Caesar and all that – a certain strand in Jewish intellectual/moral activity which consists in giving *them* more deference than any of our own people.

I am convinced that Vassili Grossman's *Life and Fate* is a greater novel than *War and Peace* by that other Russian guy, but would I want to argue it at length and would your *NYRB* or your *LRB* (complete with a transplanted man called Shatz who once solicited me to write for the *Nation* and then never called again, shitz/Shatz, who's counting?) ever host such a claim? I have by my bed a copy of Grossman's dispatches from various Russian fronts, a work of instant genius, of Hemingwayesque brevities and sustained arpeggios, vivid, close-up and long-shot, brave and pitiless, everything you want from a true reporter in the process of assembling the roughage (which could not get rougher) for the masterpiece to come; *bref*, a compilation which needs no apology, in the high or low sense. Yet in it one reads how grateful he is for the praise of the vicious *apparatchik* editor of the mag he writes for, a man who rejoices in the usual demanding condescension of those adjacent to artists, but never of their number.

This man (name supplied when subscription arrives) DOES recognise Vassili Simeonovich's greatness and does, to do him summary justice, give him time off from frontline duty to write a novel (not the Big One) about an Armenian hero who disdains *Catch-22* larkiness and dies for Comrade Stalin. Grossman later realised, as do those who attend to the details in REALITY, on the ground, rather than in footnotes and variorum editions, that the official version of everything is a falsification, especially in the USSR, where Stalin's self-vindication generated a holocaust, in which there was neither Jew nor Gentile, longer and numerically more murderous than anything liebe Adolf could do. And yet . . . that *pauvre petit juif* thing hangs on.

Back to Britlit, which is no great sheiks these days. The thing I wanted to say about the MPs and their sorry little crookeries and crockeries (they can claim for tea-sets in their second homes, which can then be redefined as their first homes so that their second . . . OK, you've got it) is that the revelation of their shabbiness somehow (again!) makes me realise how keenly I bought into the respect for Our Betters which made the golf clubs that didn't take Jews seem like the places you wanted to join and made the literature of Christendom so rich in nuances that poor little schnooky boy could only envy and never emulate its refinements. The hermeneutic outsider then became the chronicler of what he could never belong to, a culture which left him as a fossil in its quarry of fine imagery and high spirituality (Judaism being, it sez 'ere, essentially materialistic and mundane).

Much I care in my not so secret self which of the two 'faiths' is a greater aberration or has spawned greater work, however incredible the backstories of both. In the 1950s, Literature seemed the sublime solution to doubt about faith and the God-given provenance of liturgical verbiage; it was the socialised version of religiosity, rarely to be smiled at, always (if possible) SERIOUS. Philosophy was for the abstract intelligence and its humourlessness was pretty well absolute, although I was reminded this week, by a clever correspondent, of Kant's quoting an ancient source on the 'ludicrous spectacle of one man milking the he-goat while another holds the sieve'. My correspondent, the long-lost son of the movie director Stanley Donen, suspects that there WAS no ancient source and that the sage of Koenigsberg (sp??) was auditioning to join a top-class soap team.

What I mean to say is that we (you and I and bring a friend, do) have programmed ourselves to like the best because we imagined (not a fully causal 'because' but . . .) that Our Betters would think well of us if we learned to like what they liked naturally, because they were not like us. I don't MEAN this, but there is something in it which makes me feel now that I have been deferential and grateful (in that regard at least we are all Grossmen) when, dammit, they were laughing at my going to the mental gym so that, if selected, I could take part in their games, if never their fun, and all along they were cheats and not a lot of fun. I STILL think Winston Churchill WAS some kind of a world-historical figure, even if he never pranced through Jena to impress unreadable Hegel, and that today's Mr Brown, a humourless, sullen son of the manse, as they keep telling us as if that were a certificate of quality, should be named Mr Beige and has probably never read ANYTHING you or I would have anywhere near our bedside table. The collapse of the English *gratin* into clichés, and half-finished ones at that, and peculation (not even spectacular) makes me think that Chicago, my toddler's town, has served you well and truly while I have been on my knees to Britannia. More fool me, finally, for trying so hard not to be, as H.J. once said of himself (and only once), base.

Tout à toi,
Freddie

Dear Freddie,

I agree that you would likely have turned out differently if Shell had not transferred your father to England and you had grown up in Chicago. Your youthful yearning for elegant brilliance would have been less, for Chicago is death on pretension: death not through adeptness at puncturing it but through not understanding and hence blithely ignoring it. Although Chicago has three first-rate cultural institutions – the University of Chicago (especially in its scientific departments), the Art Institute, and the Chicago Symphony – none of these has ever seemed central to the city but more like extraordinary appendages: a fifth limb, say, or a third testicle. In the middle 1970s, when I hung around a bit with Saul Bellow, I used to be amused to discover how little-known in the city of his upbringing our very own gloomy Nobel laureate was; people used to confuse him with a once-famous criminal lawyer named Charlie Bellows. He would walk into restaurants, look around to do a fame check – checking, that is, if anyone recognized him – and not quite be able to disguise his disappointment when, as was usually the case, nobody had.

If your youthful yearning for elegant brilliance would likely have been less as a Chicagoan, I suspect that your sophistication would have been much less, too. You would have been less worldly than you are today. Like as not, you would not have sashayed round the world, as you have done, picking up foreign languages. I'm not sure you would have made a movie connection. As a novelist, you would probably have been less on the *qui vive* for irony and ironic possibilities. You would have had to seek more fundamental questions and problems in your fiction. All this, I suppose, for better *and* worse. F.R. on either shore would have been fiercely intelligent, with the same fine anti-bullshit detector, but what form that intelligence would have taken on the shore of Lake Michigan is unknowable. The very question of the Chicago F.R. *vis-à-vis* the English F.R. suggests how little we have to say about our own fate, at least it does to me, how much we are formed by accident and happenstance over which we have no control.

A few weeks ago, apropos of Nabokov, you mentioned the name Alfred Appel, who was one of the Magician of Monteux's most ardent acolytes. Eight days ago, he, Alfred Appel (pronounced ah-pell) up and died – is this "up and died" business a locution, as I suspect, that comes from Western movies? – of a heart attack at seventy-five. He came of a very long-lived family: his mother is still alive at 97; he father died at 93; a maternal grandmother made it to the embarrassing age of 106. Alfred had had a heart attack in his early forties, and wrapped himself in cotton wool during the thirty or so years left to him. He was told to have bypass surgery, but chose not to do so; a second heart attack pegged him out in Evanston, the Saturday before last.

He was, you should pardon the expression, my colleague at Northwestern University. He wrote a book you don't want in your library called *The Annotated Lolita*, which makes normal pedantry look like wilder-than-Lenny Bruce. He also wrote books attempting to establish the connection between jazz and modern painting and James Joyce and – *va den*? – good old Volodya. He knew too much, Alfred; he was all microscope, and wrote as if the telescope, not to speak of ordinary eyesight, had not yet been invented. What he wrote, that is to say, wanted the longer view, was without perspective. Everything he wrote was clotted. He is the only person I know who it is possible to imagine might have begun a composition with a parenthesis.

He taught modern literature at Northwestern; also courses in the movies. He had almost no curiosity for anything that had happened or been written, painted, or composed before 1910, the year Leonard Woolf's Missus said human nature changed, did she not? He knew a vast amount about jazz. Like a good Nabokovian, he was a man of obsessions, a collector (not to bring John Fowles into it) of jazz records (later CDs), photographs, first-editions of second-rate books, baseball hats, toy cars, and other dreck. I think of his long-suffering wife bow-backed at the thought of how she is going to clear all of Alfred's stuff out of their house.

At his request, Alfred and I used to meet for coffee, in the late afternoon, every ten or so days. We had enemies, or, in my case, antipathies, in common, but having enemies and antipathies in common, while making for congeni-ality, is not enough to sustain a friendship. Alfred's reigning feeling was that, like the great majority, he wasn't sufficiently appreciated; like the late come-dian Rodney Dangerfield, he felt he was never getting enough respect. He went to graduate school, at Columbia, then the headquarters of Lionel Trilling and Jacques Barzun and others, when a professor was still not, like a married philosopher, a preposterous figure. He wished to be thought brilliant, suave, metropolitan, none of which he truly was. He wanted all the prizes, all the regard, and not much of either came his way, either. Envy and resentment, those tail-swallowing monsters, set to work, and swallowed up much of his personality. He courted humiliation, and frequently won her.

Alfred Appel is the only person I have ever told that I no longer wished to see him. I did this after too much forethought and with genuine trepidation. The problem was that he had PD, or Professor's Disease, in a virulent form: PD makes it impossible to speak for fewer than fifty consecutive minutes – rather like a psychoanalysand encouched – without interruption. Another strong symptom of PD is the utter absence of listening. When it was time for me to go off for one of my coffee meetings with Alfred, I not infrequently said to Barbara, "Do you mind going in my place? He'll never notice. He wants only an ear." Frequently I would stop him in mid-monologue to ask him if he had heard something I had attempted to interject. "Yeah, yeah," he would burble, and plow on. Finally, one day, like Peter Finch in the movie *Network*, I couldn't take any more, and telephoned him to announce that I wasn't getting much out of our meetings, since he did all the talking and no listening whatsoever, an announcement he greeted without much surprise, and said, with dignified resignation, "Farewell, then, Joseph."

He did love his immediate family, his wife and his two children. Alfred was the son of a successful New York lawyer (Alfred Appel, Sr.), his wife is a professor of law at Loyala University, his daughter is a lawyer, his son – who currently writes animated television sitcoms – started out in life as a lawyer. If there had been a family dog, it would now be in its second year at Fordham Law School. His wife gave his life what little ballast it had. She took up the manly roles in the household, even onto bartering with the pirates who run American car dealerships. I imagine them returning home from social events, poor Alfred's shins empurpled from kicks under the table that his wife must have had to administer to him to stop him from (yet again) making an ass of himself through forced humor, displays of egotism, philippics of resentment.

"Funny 'ting, a man's life," says a character in a John Dos Passos novel, a character who knew whereof he bloody well spoke.

I had an e-mail yesterday from my friend Dan Jacobson, whom I much like. Have you ever met Dan? I think you would like each other. He is serious but not without a good sense of humor and powers of mimicry. Assuming that you don't know him, Dan emigrated from South Africa (he was brought up in Kimberley) to England in 1954, when he was twenty-five. He was smart very young, which is a splendid time-saving ploy, and wrote brilliant and mature stories and novels right out of the gate. (His collection of stories, *The Zulu and the Zeide*, is one of my favorite titles and a book filled with fine stuff.) From things he has said and written to me, I think Dan, who is now eighty, feels much as you do about the second-ratedness of contemporary England and the country's generally low tone. I suspect that he, like you, has had moments wondering if his life wouldn't have been different in an un-English setting.

But the reason I bring up Dan just now is that, in his e-mail, he wrote about attending the funeral service of a friend, whom he did not name, but at which A. Alvarez spoke, though apparently could not finish speaking. Dan noted him leaving the building supported by what he calls a "three-wheel trolley," known hereabouts as a "walker." (I declare a tie here in the transatlantic euphemism derby; the dysphemism would, I suppose, be "one of those goddamn things to help sad old fuckers whose legs are shot.") The thought of the once slashing A. Alvarez – boringly slashing, I always felt, telling us how great a poet Robert Lowell is (he ain't) or how emblematic Slyvia Plath was (she ditto) – on a walker is a reminder that one probably oughtn't to write, as did Alvarez, Norman Mailer, and others too numerous to mention, all piss and passion, as if they would never grow old and infirm, full-fledged members in sad standing in the *alter kockers* club.

The name A. Alvarez reminds me of the most strenuous piece of editing I ever undertook, that of changing an author's name. When I was editor of the *American Scholar*, I accepted a piece from a man named (as I recall) A. James Pottle, a name that seemed to me rather silly, that A period lending a touch of W.C. Fieldsian indignity to the proceedings. When I sent him back an edited version of the piece, I changed his byline to plain James Pottle. He put the A. back in. I returned a second set of galleys with the A. once again removed. He put it back in, asking why I wanted to take it out. I recall (roughly) writing to him, "Why do you want to be A. James Pottle when with no effort at all you can be *the* James Pottle." He surrendered. Whether he subsequently returned the A., I do not know. The moral of the story, of course, is that there is no end to the handsome good deeds that editors do.

Best, Joe

Dear Joe,
All England remains, in the cant phrase that Clive James used as the title of a volume of his many TV reviews, 'glued to the box'. The reason is not terrorism (last year's) or financial meltdown (we are now assumed to be used to, enjoying even, splashing through the puddles) but, yes, the continued discovery that the present-dwellers (another antique psycho-term, I think) in the Mother of Parliaments, have been, in what we might call the literal metaphorical sense, motherfuckers indeed, because they have been taking the old lady for every debased penny she has and we, Righteous Tax-Payers unless there's something clever we can do about it, have delivered to her. I had the perfect quotation for the banking thing which was (as you know, but who else does?) Bertolt Nasty-pizza-work Brecht's line, 'What's robbing a bank compared to founding one?'

My mention of Clive James was meant to lead into saying how true and how – what? – wry, let's try, is your story of that prolonged, but tapering and finally aborted, friendship of yours with Alfred Appel (did he sport a junior possibly?). Clive, as you no doubt have heard IN THUNDER (whatever happened to that guy – Fiedler? – who said *No!* in it back in the 60s?), is an Australian who came to London, after a spell at Cambridge, on a long wave and has been around ever since, TV critic, TV star, lit. critter etc. In 1976, he alone reviewed the first episode of *The Glittering Prizes* scathingly when all the other rank Tuscans were cheering. Of course I concluded that he had to be right and that the rest of them lacked wit, but I didn't smile when I thought so. 'Lucky the man', Shelley said, didn't he? referring to Keats, 'who can be made unhappy by a review'. Here's the point, I think: if the only thing that blights your life is a bad notice, you're sitting pretty, if not petty. But isn't every writer (as Rebecca West sorta said of Harold Wilson) 'waiting to be found out'? Only the greatest and the worst are exempt from the feeling that the music will stop one day and he will no longer have a seat. So Clive was the guy who had the Indian sign on me. I was sure one minute that he was right and the next that he was a showoff bastard. He was, and is, also very smart, with a barroom/baroque flourish to his prose, a few jokes above par, and all that. Well, I got over it. I said.

Then our daughter Sarah met him, I know not how, and he became devoted to her. If it went no further than that it was because Sarah pleaded her marriage. But before she would become his friend, she demanded to know why he had dumped on me. To his credit, I think, he confessed that since he wrote for a Sunday paper and all the weaklies had drooled, he had (as John Schlesinger used to say) to come out of a different hole. John went into one too, but that's another story. I miss the latter fat bastard because he was the best fun in the world, a marvellous guest, full of funny stories and imitations, not least of a spastic whose gauche walk, in his last sad days, he was only just able to equal. When Sarah died, Clive wrote a superb piece about her in the same paper in which he had given me what-for. He loved her and he loved her work and I could not go on sulking about his ancient copy. He recently set up a website, a sort of University Clive James, in which Sarah's work is handsomely ranged (www.clivejames etc should fetch it) and in which (aha, if you must) F.R. has his modest annex. Not only that, but Clive and I have got into the habit of irregular lunches (what level of *amicitia* this entails your friendship book can calibrate) and when we meet we talk like Heraclitus and Callimachus, capping and recapping and in a kind of complicity without any purpose but mutuality. I get a similar feeling from our correspondence, yours and mine, and how!

We do not dine and we do not visit each other's places (though he has come *chez nous* to check through Sarah's slides) and, yes, for once rupture preceded rapture. Nice woik if you can . . . He's also a virulent pro-Semite, as his fat essays prove. I learnt from one of them that Hermann Goering's brother set up a fund in Schweitz for Jewish refugees. And also that Heidegger's brother thought Martin's philo was a prolonged dadaist send-up. I wish.

I gotta tell you: I read and re-read your letters. I gobble your e-says as if they were signed Haagen-Djazz and your stories . . . you know how I rate them. But? But I have NOT downloaded or whatever you have to do it your video lecturette, not because I think it will be boring or anything less than charming. I assume your shoulders will be unbowed under learning lightly worn and etc. (as some say). It's just that I am postponing that moment when the idea of Joe Epstein meets the reality. I think I would sooner that happened in person than by electronic mediation. Our son Stephen likes to Skype with me and I too like to see him in the flash, but I know what he is really like, the shape of his soul as well as his person, and the Skype prompts the gestalt which is already there. I can imagine you and me meeting and each of us thinking, '*Fin de rêve*/there goes the ball game/what else've you got?', and I can also imagine what I like to think will happen, that we get along like we always have, even though we haven't. This reminds me of the only Henry Miller story that I like (that turd in the *bidet* doesn't get a laugh from me these days – *Quiet Days in Cliché*?) which is about how he was alone in Poland sometime in the 1930s, I guess, on a bleak railway platform in a provincial town when he saw, coming up the steps, one of the men whom he had always detested and who had always detested him. They took one look (each) at each other and fell into each other's arms. I shall never do that with Some People, but then I stay away from Polish stations.

The village of Auschwitz was 80% Jewish before the war, Lanzmann says. Have you discovered that if you HINT that the Poles were/are anti-Semitic you get hate mail? In Chicago you probably get a mob of the kind Spinoza supposedly sent home by the sheer force of his dignified person. They had nice mobs in Amsterdam and adjacent areas, right? Then was then. In 1941–45, the Germans paid Dutch bounty hunters 12 florins each for Jews; double (my friend the historian Michael Burleigh tells me) for those who had 'committed crimes' (tried to make a florin or two). I always used to wince, and so did my father, when the British press featured stories in the war about

Jewish 'blackmarketeers'. I read recently that there were so many because (to some extent at least) Jews were easy marks for the sob stories of provocateurs and so bulked out the police success figures.

Tout à toi,
Freddie

Dear Freddie,
Your excellent communiqué mentions a few scribblers and a single book that the world would hobble along very well without. I learned this week that my *Fabulous Small Jews* is on a list of National Public Radio Online's hundred best works of fiction of the past hundred years. The list has some genuinely splendid books and some quite dreary ones: my book appears on the list between *Portnoy's Complaint* and *Tender is the Night*. But, thought I, wouldn't it be much more useful to compile a list of the past hundred years' most overrated works of fiction? Now there is a list it would be joyous, and oh so easy, to compose.

Back to the aforementioned scribblers: Bertolt Brecht (the other Bertie; I guess he was Bert Brecht to theater folk and others in the know) is a writer who gave the absolute minimum of pleasure. My idea of hell would be having to see two performances daily of *City of Mahagonny*, and be forced to read the collected television reviews of Clive James at intermissions. B.B. (sit down, Bernie Berenson, I'm not talking about you) was apparently a considerable creepy-crawly in person (or up close and personal, as the television speaker-ines are wont to say); all the stories about him entail viciousness to women, cowardice, insouciant insensitivity to human suffering. (I throw in that last phrase at no extra charge for those who like alliterative sibilance.) Talk about imperfection of the work and life both – grim old Comrade Brecht brought it off as handsomely as any modern false classic we have.

The other scribbler you mention, Henry Miller, seems to me gone with the wind, and rightly so. I remember the boyish excitement with which I glommed on to those plain green-covered paperback versions of *Tropic of Cancer* and *Tropic of Capricorn* that came steaming off the boats from Paris and Mexico City. Even then, a boy of nineteen, I knew that only the fancy fornication parts were worth reading; all that stupid half-digested Indian philosophy Miller served up was so much fatty pastrami. Of course now the fancy fornication is boring, too. All I remember of the Miller I then read – perhaps five books in all – is a scene in one of the *Tropics* where our Henry is bonking someone's sister standing up in a hallway when he mentions that her purse fell to the ground and that a nickel dropped out. "I made a mental note to pick it up later," Miller writes. The rest of Miller has been washed away by that excellent critic, fellow name of Time.

You make me want to look into T.E. Hulme, of whom I know so little and have read even less. I never before now knew quite where to begin; sounds as if *Speculations* is the place. I have a great weakness for aphorisms, finding even poor ones amusing (in their pretensions). One of the great things about the bookish (and scribbling) life is that you never run out of things to read. Some people may have had better luck with their formal education than others, but in the end we are all autodidacts, going at things in our own disorderly way. Some have read more widely and deeply than others, but none can truly claim to be well read. Except of course George Steiner and Harold Bloom, the Frick and Frack of Heavy Erudition's Almanac, and if they represent the rewards of being well read, then I say bring on illiteracy.

The *TLS* with your Douglas Fairbanks piece on its cover arrived here only yesterday. A solid piece, yours, vintage F. Raphael, cutting through the crap, which, on the subject of all things Hollywooden, requires a heavy-duty chainsaw, which you wield, owing in good but not only part to your firsthand experience with the pirates of California. You know whereof you speak, and so your knowing tone works. But of late I have come to distrust what I think of as writers who are too knowing. The new generation of writers at the *New Yorker* seem to specialize in this: characters by the names of Hendrik Hertzberg, Adam Gopnik, Anthony Lane, names that gentlemen of our advanced years really ought not to toss around, let alone bother about reading. Nothing you can tell these guys, even though they appear never for long to have left their desks, and seem like nothing more than moderately bright students. Clive James also, I think, suffers from the too-knowing tone, a tone that more than suggests one has the real lowdown, the true gen, hey buddy I ain't goin' to bullshit you here, I know what I'm talking about, so listen, I kid you not, Schmuckowitz. The knowing tone comes from false authority; genuine authority never has to push itself forward so aggressively. The older generation of critics – Edmund Wilson, T.S. Eliot, F.R. Leavis – never had to come on as all-knowing, chiefly because they really did know a thing or two. (Is this the place to insert that the *No! in Thunder* man was Leslie Fiedler, whose febrile career proves that if you want your name to be remembered long after your death, writing criticism may not be the best way to go about it.) The too-knowing tone is for those who don't truly know; hence the need for the tone.

The review in the *TLS* after yours is of a biography of the unfortunately-named writer Elizabeth Taylor – unfortunate, of course, because of her much inferior but much more comely (though, poor once-dazzling baby, no longer) movie actress. The novelist Elizabeth T. came by her last name through marriage; she was born in 1912, and thus could have no idea that hers would be an unfortunate name to carry around. An erstwhile friend of mine, the historian Peter Gay, came to this country from Germany named Peter Frohlich, and, thinking to Americanize himself, changed his last name to Gay (English for *frohlich*), not knowing that the homosexuals were one day to swoop down and complicate his patriotic intentions.

But every name brings with it its own complications. Yours, I should imagine, have to do with people adding the K onto Frederic and half the time mispronouncing Raphael (in Hebrew, I think, Raphael, my grandfather's first name, was pronounced Raphoil). I labor, though not very heavily, under the Epstine/Epsteen problem. I am a stine Epstein. Leonard Bernstein, I'm told, used to get wildly ticked off if anyone called him Bernsteen. When younger my name was not infrequently confused, in print, with that of Jason Epstein, who was, many moons ago, a young publishing genius (the Robespierre of the paperback revolution, he was known as in these parts). Upon meeting me, people in publishing in New York used to ask, "You aren't by any chance related to Jason Epstein?" When I would allow that I wasn't, they would almost invariably reply, "Good. I hate that prick!" As a young man, Jason Epstein apparently had to suck up to Edmund (The Bunny) Wilson, Vladimir Nabokov, and who knows how many other superior senior men. (Watch the eyes of those who bow lowest, an old Polish proverb correctly has it.) In one of his books of journals Wilson mentions throwing an ashtray at the Robespierre of the paperback revolution, whose power in those days was insufficient to send our Bunny off to the guillotine. Jason E., perhaps to make up for all his scraping before the great, evidently took things out on the less than great, and made himself disagreeable to all and sundry (especially to sundry) with less power than he. Ain't human beings delightful?

Your paragraph about Clive James reminds me to tell you that I do not despise or even dislike him, though I see that I have written negatively about him and his works twice in this letter. I merely distrust his energy and his cultural omniscience. I knew before now that you have come to think better of him because of his generous words about your daughter Sarah's paintings, which strikes me as a good enough reason. Still, somehow or other, I find myself, quite irrationally, pleased to learn that your daughter did not agree to share his doubtless shaggy (there's no denying, entendres are flying) bed. Terribly snobbish of me to say so, but the thought of waking up in bed next to this particular Australian is not one that goes down easily. Hold the jive, Clive.

Your sentences about not wanting to watch me making a jackass of myself on a video of a talk I gave in Wilmington, Delaware, a year or so ago makes good sense to me. Ours is, for better or worse, a friendship *electronique*, and for now that is how it ought to stay. I do not so much imagine our encountering each other in the flesh, as I do over the telephone, at which time everything goes all wrong. In the (dopey phrase) worst-case scenario – have you, I wonder, ever been asked to write a worst-case scenario, for Joseph Levine, for example? – you call and I instantly get a furious case of logorrhea, gassing away, cutting you off every time you wish to speak, making plain that I am socially quite hopeless, and a very great pain generally. So don't be surprised, should you ever need to telephone, announcing, "Hello, Freddie Raphael here. Is Joe there?" if a voice on the other end replies, "Joe, Joe Epstein? Oh, he died earlier today, but thanks for calling."

Best, Joe

Dear Joe,
Re your voted plaudits, *chapeau*! You Montaigne, I Étienne de La Boétie? I'd like to think so. Étienne, as we all call him these days, was older than Micheau but got younger and younger the longer M. de M. survived him. His *Discours de la servitude volontaire* is a remarkable piece of work by someone of 23 (the same age that Freddie Ayer wrote the much more derivative but hugely precocious and (more important!) successful *Language, Truth and Logic*). I've kept threatening to do a translation of the *Discours*, but suddenly I find myself wondering for whom that bell is tolling and so I keep scribbling at my own stuff.

The *Portnoy's Complaint* selection in the fiction hit parade is, I suppose, justified but of Philip's work I admired *American Pastoral* and *I Married a Communist* more. And, of course, *The Great Gatsby* is infinitely superior to the overwritten and overlong *Tender is the Night*. How sad that so many of our most successful writers are so bloody miserable about it! H. Pinter (whose initials mimic those of a famously piquant sauce, much spilled to conceal the tastelessness of most British cooking) never managed more than a lopsided sneer and was so ferociously determined to denounce everyone, Zionists *en tête*, that one has a suspicion that Jesus of Nazareth might have been more like him than contemporary reports suggest.

It is generally assumed (I don't have the figures in front of me) that Jesus was, as the Victorian hymnographer said, 'meek and mild', but he was quite a fulminator for a fine-weather man and seems to have had as many accesses of impatience, if not rage, as your average messiah. He put down his betters in a very 1960s-ish way and showed off as he did it, but he never said anything that one wished one had said oneself, did he? I have an obstinate itch to write a story about that wedding at Cana in Galilee (a spot which Joseph ben Mattathias had to include in his defensive line) in which a little man (Solly Levine if you must know his name) holds out his glass and has it filled with the wine that Jesus has just miraculously supplied. 'To tell you the troot', Solly is heard to say, 'I'd sooner have water'. Try that line on an Olympian deity and you'd be rolling a barrel uphill through all eternity, but after an Olympian chuckle at least. Jesus just wouldn't get it, I fear.

I broke off from digging in ancient Palestine at the request of John Podhoretz whom internal evidence suggests you have known since a boy, if not longer, in order to help him make the new *Commentary* look cheap and nasty by supplying a piece about the movies and my experience *là-dedans*. Which reminds me of a British (i.e. Irish) comic writer of some genius called Spike Milligan who is best known for composing the scripts for a radio show of the 1950s called *The Goon Show*, which featured Peter Sellers in the days when he was a suet-pudding-faced impressionist of mere genius. Radio is a rare medium which still gives one's imagination more liberty than any other public outlet (a word polluted, *disons*, by Kinsey *à jamais*).

Spike wrote one show a week, with no empanelled help, and periodically went off his head doing it (he was several voices in the show as well). When his bogeys left the rails others were occasionally called in to fake his work. I and a fellow Cambridge person were asked, once, to do as much, but it was too much. Can it be that if we were asked to fake an Andy Warhol we would find that he was a genius after all? Say it ain't so, Joe. Why I am reminded of Spike remains unclear but here goes: he once wrote a little book about his wartime experiences as a squaddie in the Western Desert entitled *Hitler: My Part In His Downfall*.

ANYWAY, as the sub-teenagers say (those below five years old in today's ever accelerating race to pubescence), I was asked to do this piece for youngish Podhoretz, who offered a sum that seemed generous when translated into degenerate pounds but for which you, I suspect, would not have composed a haiku. I wrote a piece somewhat longer than he asked (unprofessional, I know, I know, but all my sonnets go to eighteen-plus lines) and sent it before the deadline (another symptom of amateurism) and added that I had left some leeway so that he could cut my best jokes and eliminate all the things which, with whatever light a touch, I wished to thrust up the right nostril of one Terry Teachout and others of the *Commentary* party line who trashed an animated movie called *Waltz with Bashir*, an Israeli piece that showed people feeling bad about the Chatila massacres (all that time ago). I mentioned it not to vex the zealots but because it proved that the use of animation on human faces can isolate an expression as photography no longer does, especially with the advent (without a Christmas this one) of digital, which issues in a kind of accurate blandness and deep two-dimensionality.

Teachout (you can imagine his lessons being delivered round town in large flat boxes by bullet-headed kids on motorbikes, as we call them in jolly old) disagreed with a wanton statement of mine, in a letter to the editor, that *La Règle du jeu* was an overrated bore. It isn't apparently, so I have been taught out; because actually it is the greatest movie ever made. The bottom of the class is not low enough for me; I'm supposed to dig (which takes me back, fast, to Palestine, its rocks and its hard places). *Eppure, La Règle du jeu* still gets a Lope de Vega award (explanation infra) from me, and so does DeLillo and so do Ian McEwan and Kingsley Amis.

Well, it came to pass precisely as I forecast (colour me Cassandra): John P. read the piece so fast that I might have supplied a rift filled with awe. Then came the scissorhandedness of a deftness that spoke for clever years of knowing what Our Readers want, in whatever department of journalism might be involved, from the *Weekly Standard* through to the *Daily Post* to secular High Priesthood: every allusion to anything that the meanest subscriber would fail to recognise went into the shredder. Lots were left; kill fees were not mentioned; I have escaped the Great Terror, but . . . I began my piece by citing a line from Lope de Vega in which, told by the medico that – *lastima!* – he was on his deathbed, he came out with 'In that case, I can say it: Dante bores the shit out of me.' Attamuchacho! He joins our club; not that he would accept membership, because he was a fully paid-up Friend of the Inquisition: ringside at the *auto-da-fé* there he would be, sitting next to the ranking *amigo del rey* who wrote a learned paper – they did it then too, you know – about why male Jews menstruate and also have tails. A Marrano doctor called Cardoso was called in to attend to the same counsellor who was in agony from piles so aggravated that he had a, well, tail. That may be an example of Jesus playing for laughs *par personne interposée* as all the peasants say around here, but then again . . . Byron is still alleged to have had a tail by some mythomanes. If he didn't, why did he menstruate?

By the way, re Henry Miller, he wasn't too much of a waiting-for-the-mailman person to have a correspondence with, judging not only from his We Are Famous For Fucking exchanges with little (five feet plus what exactly?) Larry Durrell, but also from a slimissimo volume I bought in a secondhand shop just around the corner from our London apartment only because I had dawdled so long among their shelves that I felt I owed them some backsheesh. The little volume is of another correspondence between H.M. and some unknown scribes in which *de haut en bas* ain't the half of it. I don't have it with me (Josephus archives took up all my hand-lugged allowance) but if I quoted from it you'd say 'Don't bother'. Durrell at least did coin, or pass on, some memorable phrases, including one which I have to admit I have used more than 'saved the sum of things for pay' and other mercenary excuses, viz., the saying attributed to the transvestite British head of police in wartime Alex, '*C'est de la grande bogue*, old man!' They don't make cracks or crackpots like that anymore in Gran (as in granmother) Bretagna. I liked *The Alexandria Quartet* to distraction, the verbal cassata of England's glory days, until I had to read it again. Gone, *ceu fumus in auras*, as Virgil so cleverly put it when Orpheus swivelled to Eurydice with a cry of 'Still with me, darling?' She was gone in a flash and he was home free, but we must never say so. Oh god, I've gone into overtime, the word-counter says. Nuts, sez I, but not before General McAuliffe did, in brave circumstances.

Tout à toi,
Freddie

Dear Freddie,

Hope that in my pathetic vanity I didn't make too much of my *Flabby Tall Screws* being on that National Public Radio list of the 100 best novels. The list was simply a column by their online editor, a man whose name I had not known before now, and my book's being on it is far from a "distinguished thing," as Henry James called death; it's not, after all, as if I had won the Irish Sweepstakes, if they, the Irish Sweepstakes, still exist. The dreary truth is that there are no lists or prizes that can any longer, as a druggy old rock group called The Doors had it, light my fire. The prestige of all the prizes has been leached, not to say pissed away, by having been given to second- and third-rate people for a very long while. If someone tells you that you are the best (screenwriter, novelist, aphorist, journal-keeper, critic, sack-artist), ask him who is second best. The answer, I am confident, is likely to calm you down. In the case of winning a prize, ask who won it last year, and the same calming effect will kick in instanter.

All this being so, the chief points of prizes, or so it strikes me, are: preventing even dopier people from winning them, and the money that sometimes comes with them. Your having won an Oscar as early as you did – at thirty-four, no? – had to have been a great boon, for it had to have given the price of F.R. screenplays a great jolt upward. Take the money and walk, say I. But also know, as you already do, that in a world without real peers, no prize conferred upon one by these non-existent fellows (peers, that is) is finally convincing. Praise, official and unofficial, is fine, but in the end I think the better players among us know with some precision how worthy of it we are, which is not very.

Sorry to hear that you have been made to go through Podhoretzian dances. I have known John P. since he was a young boy – known him and liked him. In his early days as editor of *Commentary* he is proving to provide one of the best of all services that an editor can provide a writer: prompt response. Neal Kozodoy, John's predecessor, would often make me wait a week or more for manuscripts that I had sent him by e-mail, which was, to put it gently, tiresome. This scribbler, after all these years in the business (and still wearing a cardboard belt, mind you), remains nervous about acceptance. One would think an old Grub Streeter would develop a bit of a shell about such matters. But I seem not to have done, or at least not a very effective one.

Commentary has long been known as a serious magazine, but it has also been more than a touch dour in recent decades. The politicization of the United States has made it a more political magazine than it once was, which has not helped make things livelier. The American intellectuals of the 1930s through the early 1960s operated through a wider lens than the intellectuals of the current day do. Dwight Macdonald once said that he considered the two major American political parties as Tweedledumb and Tweedledumber. Largely ignoring American politics, it could go on to cover a larger range of topics in a rather more high-spirited – though not all that light-hearted – way. So much in the magazine in recent decades has been about punching out the enemy. Not, mind you, that the enemy doesn't deserve punching out, but at a certain point it began to result in dreary journalism. The pre-John Podhoretz *Commentary*, for a notable example, seemed to have no room for one F. Raphael. That John, who I happen to know has long admired you, is making room for this same aforementioned F. Raphael is a good thing. The hope is that John P. will enliven the magazine without divesting it of its seriousness. Remains, as they say about the effects of revolutions in small South American countries, to be seen.

Since you dropped the name Jesus (a pretty heavy drop, as I said to the Pope only this morning), I have to make the unsurprising confession that, as a historical or theological figure, the old boy has never had the least attraction for me. He was, as you say, no phrase-maker, and I think you are onto something when you connect him to the fun-loving yet always-leaving-room-for-moralizing 1960s. He was a bit of a hippie, our Jewish carpenter's son, without the weed. He was also the virtucrat *nonpareil*. The word virtucrat is my one addition to the English language, my small contribution to the fund off which, lo, these many years I have made my meager living. What the word means is someone who is propelled and thinks himself ennobled and empowered by his own wondrous virtue. The difference between you and the virtucrat, Monsieur Freddie, is that the virtucrat happens to care a lot more about the fate of the planet than do you, you insensitive dog. The difference between me and the virtucrat is that the virtucrat cares a lot more about people than I do (and he may be right). Jesus was, in Morgan's (I do not mean J.P.'s) phrase, a flat character, nothing surprising about him. The characters in our book, the Previous Testament, are wilder, more unpredictable, rounder, more of what today we should call "fun guys." But that Jesus, he could put an end to a jolly party more effectively than playing two LPs of Ludwig Earnhardt explaining the German economic miracle.

Your mention of Harold Pinter, may he rest only half in peace, reminds me of a story I heard about his pukey little poems, which apparently he used regularly to Xerox and send off to friends, awaiting their sumptuous praise by return mail. One day he committed the following poem: "I knew Len Hutton in his prime/ Another time, another time." (The English friend who told me about this explained that Len Hutton, the cricketeer, was our Joe DiMaggio.) He promptly makes forty or fifty Xerox copies of the poem, which he posts off to his adulators. Presently the praise comes rolling in: "Oh, Harold, you've caught it exactly." "Dear Harold, you've somehow managed to put into words what I have for so long thought and been unable to express." "You've caught it, Harold, exactly and miraculously." And more of the same. Except one correspondent, fellow by the name of Simon (Gray, Callow?) doesn't respond. A week, two weeks go by, and Harold, unable to bear not receiving the final droplet of hosanna, calls Simon. "Simon," he says, "sent you a little poem a few weeks ago. Just a small thing, you know. But am surprised not to have heard from you about it. Wondering if it got lost in the mail. You know how wretched the post is nowadays." "No, no," says Simon. "The poem arrived here ten days ago." "Relieved to know it," says Harold, "but tell me, what did you think of it?" "Oh," says Simon, "I haven't quite finished reading it."

What was Pinter's political anger about? His hatred of America, of Israel, of just about everything that made a career such as his possible? Pure self-righteousness, is my guess. Saul Bellow had this self-righteousness, without the anti-Americanism, and so does Philip Roth. These angry scribblers, despite the world's setting all its prizes on their tables, placing ladies in their beds, raining shekels down upon them, still don't seem much to like it here on earth. The miserable place, somehow, isn't good enough for them.

Someone told me that Philip Roth has a new novel coming out in October about an old actor whose sexual machinery isn't working as it should, or at least as he prefers it would. Bonking, he discovers, with one's bonker on the fritz, is no longer an easy roll and that ain't hay. What a fine rich theme Roth has hit upon! Move over Gogol and tell Dostoyevsky the news, the great tradition lives and breathes. We sleep tonight.

Best, Joe

Dear Joe,

I don't know if you've come across a magazine called *Areté*, edited by Craig Raine, a poet of some wit and ingenuity, if not of the lyric flight, who – having somewhat withered on the vine, like Larkin (and not on the wine, like Amis) – is now an Oxford don. Craig has been very pleasant to me and has even been reported as saying nice things about me behind my back. That's sly. He once said that I was the only man in London who put on a dinner jacket to write a review. Once is probably enough and you could make that out to be suggesting that I overdid a chore and turned it, too ostentatiously, into a form of head-waitering, which may well be so. Be that as it may, and how often it is!, he was a distant friend who became closer when Sarah died, and that is something one doesn't forget. There are also those who receded to vanishing point.

Well, that's the backstory, so here's the shit. *Areté* (which, now I come to think of it, sports a rather dinner-jacket name) has published a good deal of stuff about Harold Pinter, including a recent poem which was not all that short, merely repetitive. The word fuck alternated with love, I think, quite a lot and the thing needed a lot of performance and wishing meaning into sorry crap to amount to a Duino Elegy. The most recent *Areté* contains a piece about Harold backstage, wishing to express displeasure at a performance by the limpid question 'Where is that cunt?', and then again . . . playing bridge with Susanna Gross (daughter of your friends and not mine John und Miriam, I presume), thanks to the summons of the Lady Antonia, who taught the rough barrow boy she married to become a gentleman and, the *Tablet* recently informed its readers, almost a Catholic (he could sniff the wine but not savour the wafer?).

The determination to make a great man of Pinter does not irk me, but it is a leetle odd. The last time I saw a play of his will also be the last time I saw a play of his. His ranting about Israel and America strikes me as nothing so much as insularity on stilts, quite like Kingsley Amis's; and a form of cowardice too, actually. Ex-Jew, ex-oik, now enNobelled, that was Harold: top of the world, *mutti*. Amis was afraid of flying, abroad, anything that might lead him not to be recognised as Mr Big. Harold constructed a final role for himself in which he could play the king on every stage like the Jean Cocteau of whom Cyril Connolly (someone unknown to the readers of *Commentary*, young Podhoretz tells me) once or (if I know anything) twice said, 'In the last fifteen years of his life all he wanted was incense and burnt offerings'. Gold, he could do without? I should live so long.

I knew Harold to say hullo to, since back in 1967, when we were both on a committee to save Israel from all the Arabs by issuing a statement of support. When the war was over, while Harold was still hesitating where to add his comma, we all felt slightly cheated, like going to watch Joe Louis in his prime, glancing at the time and there was Max Baer flat on his back, if he ever was (I used to know those things). We had been assured by the man from the embassy that Israel had no territorial ambitions and we believed him. After the show was over, Harold, I recall, said to me, 'We've given the Arabs a bloody nose'. Without bruising a knuckle personally or spending a nickel, which wasn't bad.

After the Israelis decided to hang onto what they'd spilled blood to obtain, I confess that my partisanship lost some of its righteous rage, but I have never turned against Israel in public, whereas Harold became so violent an anti-Zionist that he would evict people from his dinner table if they uttered a word in demurral (I am told) when he wished Hamas well. Listen, it was his table. I wish I'd been as stroppy with Karl Miller when he was a rude and lousy guest but the crawler in me kept me quasi-polite.

My Pinter story is one that Craig would never print. Harold was in the cast of a film I wrote in 1976, at the pleading request of a producer who never again asked me to do anything, based on the one memorable work of Geoffrey Household, a very British, very decent chap, who said that he wished he had had access to my dialogue when he wrote the book. It was all about a gentleman who, in 1938/9, tries single-handed to go and assassinate Hitler and misses and is then tracked by Bad Guys all the way back to the UK. I invented a Jewish solicitor for Peter O'Toole to turn to when posher friends had ratted on him, or were likely to. Harold was enrolled to impersonate him by Clive Donner, who had directed a movie of mine, *Nothing But The Best*, some ten *jahren* earlier. We rehearsed the script in the usual way, beginning by all sitting at a long trestle table and reading it through. Peter O'Toole played the hero, Sir Robert Hunter, and all went well (i.e., without any embarrassing pauses from the cast while they tried to say what couldn't be said) and then we came to the scene where O'Toole turns up, filthy and *sans* fingernails, in the solicitor's office. Harold was supposed to look up and, it said in the script, exclaim: 'Robert, what IS the matter?' Harold did not come in on cue. He did not come in when nudged. He sat there. Then he leaned along the table and said, 'Freddie, would you mind very much if I didn't say "Robert, what is the matter?", but said, "Robert, what's the matter?"' I paused (oh yes, and then some) and then I said, 'OK, but does this mean you're going to rewrite the whole fucking script?' Even in 1976 there was a sort of gasp as well as a giggle or three.

After the read-through came the walk-through: the set was marked on the rehearsal room floor with tape and a few elementary props put in place. So we started all over and finally it was Harold's time to be seated at a table and Peter O'Toole was cued to come in, tousled, *sans* fingernails, etc. Harold looked up from his papers and said, 'Robert, what IS the matter?' This time they did all laugh. He gave me no further trouble and was always very polite when we met in foyers. Beats *simchas*.

Coda. A few years after *Rogue Male* (I just saw it's up 20% in the polls this week), H.P. wrote me a letter enclosing a contract that he had struck with Paramount. He had agreed to write a screenplay provided he received sole credit or none at all. If other writers were called in, he had the right to remove his name, but before that five Persons of Quality had to adjudicate (not the Writers Guild of America and their Zionist members) on whether he should have ALL the credit. Would I be enrolled on the bench? I said I didn't mind, if he really wanted me to, but perhaps he could have the grace to delete the 'k' which he had appended to my Frederic in his encyclical. His response was a poem that Craig would print like a shot: 'Tsk. Tsk. Tsk.' Anyone could have written that first tsk; many might have managed the second; the third puts him, I think none will dispute, in the *ipsissimus vir* class. You can't hope to live with a man like that, unless you're Antonia Fraser, the only woman I have ever seen who gave me the problem that Woody Allen had in one of his iffy but not bad movies (none was ever as bad as *Vicky Christina Barcelona*): Antonia looks blurred. If she was painted by numbers, she ran. I have nothing against her (unlike a lot of men in old London town, I never had the chance) but she did go on record as admiring *The Reader*. I have THAT against her, and anyone else who liked it: Steiner, Byatt et al.

So what else have I got? A shitty job rewriting a movie which I never wanted to do, because my son Paul is involved with people who think it's good and it isn't. I woke this beautiful morning very early feeling sick and sour and wished I was every kind of a recusant shit. So I revised a piece I've written for the *TLS* and heightened its falutin' just a notch or two and then I drudged and drudged and, nuts to it all, I shall wind up having turned chalk into cheese, the kind with holes in it maybe, but cheese. Thomas de Quincey and the friend who brought you and me together, William Hazlitt, and who all else would give me a small wink of hack complicity as I did what Harold would never do and wrote only on the condition that my name never appeared on the credits of what, I suspect, I shall not be wholly ashamed of having written. You don't need to misspell anyone's name to make a condition like that.

Time to go and swim. If only I had ever learnt how to do it properly.

Tout à toi,
Freddie

Dear Freddie,

"You knew Harold Pinter in his prime./ What a swine! What a swine!" Along with the list I proposed of 100 overrated books, we ought to compose another list of 100 contemporary Jews who deserve excommunication. Harold Pinter, had he persisted in breathing, would have been near the top of the list. The mechanics of Jewish excommunication must be cumbersome in the extreme, for the Jews certainly don't do it very efficiently. Or so I judge from their having excommunicated Baruch Spinoza, one of the best Jews going, then kept some of the worst creeps in the club.

Jews who take a strong stand against Israel are not among my favorites. The line they tend to take is that just because they are Jewish, perhaps especially *because* they are Jewish, they shouldn't take sides; better, they show themselves even grander, larger-hearted, greater-souled, more highly virtucratic, when they take the side of the enemy of their own people. And the Arabs of the Middle East, bred over at least three generations to red-hot Jew-hating, are real enemies; they shouldn't in the least mind a genocide such as the Turks brought off against the Armenians, who were, quite literally, driven into the sea.

My current morning book, read with my first cup of tea, is *Pages from the Goncourt Journals*, and, apropos of the above paragraph, in an entry for 8 June 1863, the Bros. G., who often adopt the first-person, write: ". . . I feel convinced that every political argument boils down to this: 'I am better than you are,' every literary argument to this: 'I have more taste than you,' every argument about art to this: 'I have better eyes than you,' every argument about music to this: 'I have a finer ear than you.'" Much to it, I suspect. The larger import is that it makes all political discourse and artistic criticism seem so much personal competition. Sad to concede, an awful lot of it is, methinks.

Craig Raine is a name I know but not at any depth. He had a mildly disturbing short story in the *New Yorker* a few weeks ago, a story set in a Polish background, which background he seemed to handle quite well. The un-O'Henry-like ending of the story had two brothers turning out to have been bonking the same girl, whose "genitals smelled" (God, surely, can't be in *all* the details). I also seem to recall first hearing his name in connection with Ian Hamilton and the *New Review*, to which I was an only mildly satisfied subscriber. Not a talentless man, Mr. Raine, but I don't envy him his career as a poet. One of the not-so-dirty little secrets of our time is that poetry is finished. A vast number of people teach it, study it, write it, even go to hear the louts read it, but the truth is that nobody, outside the trade, gives a rusty rat's rump about it – not really, not deeply, not truly.

Poetry in our day is in the same condition as verse drama at the beginning of the last century: an archaic practice, a dead genre, a done deal. We still have people playing the role of major poets, but only because the world seems to require a few people to play the role: "In art, in medicine, in fashion, we must have new names," wrote our little Marcel, nailing it once again. We know the names: Seamus Heaney, Derek Walcott, John Ashbery, Adrienne Rich, and a few others. In and out the room the poets come and go,/ muttering yo!,/ where's the prize and what's the dough? But if I ask a literary gent or lady to quote me a single line or phrase from any of our putative major poets, it ain't going to happen. The magazines – the *TLS*, the *New Yorker*, *Poetry*, and the rest – solemnly go on publishing the stuff, prize committees meet to issue awards and descant on the importance of poetry to civilization, but it is all finally an intramural activity. The stuff doesn't register, resonate, ring, do any of the elevating things that poetry is supposed to, and once indeed did, do.

When was the last time you bought a book of verse by a contemporary poet? My guess is around the same time that I did – the 12th of Never, if a precise date is wanted. And we are literateurs, lovers of language and its artful deployment, for crying out quietly. Auden said that if one were born later than the 1890s, one had no chance to become a major poet. (He was born in 1907, but somehow got his untidy bottom over the bar.) Philip Larkin, who may not have been major, at least created some memorable lines and phrases: "They fuck you up your Mum and Dad" and so forth.

But otherwise the poetry game is over, kaput, *fini*, time, gentlemen, time. Years ago I wrote an essay on this subject called "Who Killed Poetry?" which stirred up beehives of poets in protest. I suggested that the academicization of poetry did a lot to help kill it; I also thought that too much of it was in production, with Gresham's Law relentlessly at work, in this instance the crappy driving out the second-rate. I also concluded that so many people who drifted into the writing of poetry didn't have very interesting minds: a family member dies, they saw a tree, a little-known Matisse excited them, so they take to their machines and trivialize it in a more or less complex contraption of verbal self-absorption called a poem. But now I wonder if quite as considerable a reason for the death of poetry is that the international attention span has been much reduced by so many fresh distractions and with few people left who have the patience and intellectual curiosity to work out the rich complexity of a well-wrought poem, if anyone could actually produce one. My main point, the moral of this sermonette, is that if any of your grandchildren come to you and declare the wish to be a poet, do him or her a favor and break the kid's hands.

Sorry to learn that John Podhoretz counseled you that *Commentary*'s readers have never heard of Cyril Connolly. I'd say that this was their problem, not yours. A great mistake, in my view, for an editor to gauge his reader's knowledge, and then dumb things down accordingly. If readers don't know who Cyril Connolly, or for that matter Georgi Plekhanov, is, I say, fuck 'em; let 'em look it up. Doing so is, or used to be, called getting an education. I edited a magazine for twenty-three years, and I don't think I once thought that something was over the heads of its readers. The only courtesy I extended to my readers was clarity; after that, they were on their own.

England remains more resistant to dumbing down to pick up readers, or so it seems from here. I've just read your excellent piece on Claude Lanzmann's autobiography, written for the *TLS* (your "Maoism was his Viagra," apropos of Sartre, is worth the price of a year's subscription), and thought that there is not a magazine in the United States that would permit the use of so many French words as you avail yourself of in the course of a review of what is after all a book published in France. I note that even our allegedly highbrow

New York Review of Books translates all French passages in parentheses following them. The working assumption is that the readers don't know any other language, so let's give them a helping hand.

In your e-mail accompanying your Lanzmann review, you mention that you think the *TLS* unlikely to print the full 3,000 words of the piece. I hope they do; the piece may be long but it doesn't read long. I've read 900-word pieces that read like four-decker Victorian novels. Which reminds me that my last appearance in the *TLS* was marked by my choosing not to review a book – I don't remember which it was – at 900-word length. I said that I preferred not to write at fewer than 1,500 words. I dealt with a woman editor – whose name I also don't recall – but since that time I've not been asked to lighten their door again. I had a decent run at the *TLS* under John Gross and Ferdinand Mount; the latter asked me to review the history of the *TLS* by Derwent May, which I took as a pleasing compliment.

The uncheering note on which you end, about having to rewrite a screenplay in which you have no interest, recalls my own fantasy about screenwriting. (The traditional writer's fantasy about the movies is the one in which a writer is paid a million dollars upfront for the movie rights to his book and then the movie never gets made.) After the one not particularly good screenplay I did write – for Warner Bros, which, soon after it was completed, fired the would-be film's producer – I imagined myself setting up as a (very) part-time scenario doctor, called in for brief stints and heavy bread to fix up other people's botches. In this fantasy, I am doing this work, which I tossed off (the English slang term for masturbation, no?) with astonishing alacrity, from my villa in Tuscany. The ample checks always get through the famously poor Italian mail, and I laugh, oh how I laugh, all the way down to the *banca* in the charming little village at the bottom of the hill. Ah, sigh, in the next life perhaps.

Best, Joe

Dear Joe,

Four days of hard labour in an idyllic setting (the Perigord, never rosier or fruitier in our memory, with the pool clean and sparkling blue and silver, better than any Hockney) leave me with the back broken of the odious labour which I have undertaken in the understanding that the producers (Parisian) were going to honour their implicit promise to commission a screenplay from me and our son Stephen with the exquisite title *On Parle d'Orages*, of which we had already supplied a seductive outline. Need I go on? 'Implicit promise' tells you all you need to guess about when a promise isn't a promise. So a strange cussedness, funded, I confess (title of another bloody silly Hitchcock movie) by an honorarium that was fat enough for a lecturer, if derisive for a screenwriter of the old brigade, obliged me to render some unspeakable dialogue speakable, even if, as I suspect, no actor will ever get to say it. Doing such work, you understand something of the surgeon's bloody vanity and persistence when he operates on some slob he despises and whose problem is likely to be incurable: save the sonofabitch (who won't thank you and will be slow to pay) and the pleasure will be in proportion to your lack of wish ever to see him/her again.

But what is this compared to what is happening to the land of my father? For nearly seventy years I have lived in an England which had to be played like a course that is all wide bunkers and very tight greens and where the flag gets moved even as you putt. (I haven't played golf for over fifty years, but its imagery is sweet.) Education and emulation were one: the little American kid/ Yid embarked on a lifetime of attempting to earn the good opinions, respect, applause of his, well, hosts. He did it like any scholarship boy, obliged to Latin and Greek (oh yes, and much obliged in the end), but also to cricket, to long 'a's, to creased trousers (you call them pants, I believe), and above all the deference to what Willie Maugham made famous as 'Our Betters' (the title of a play of his).

My father was happy that I should be a sort of gentleman, even though no Jew ever really was one, apart from the Rothschilds and, I suppose, little Marcel's Swann, though the duc de Guermantes didn't quite rate him one, did he? Even when I knew that I never wanted to work with or for Englishmen or join their professions (at times my father thought I had surgeon's hands, at others an advocate's tongue) and felt as isolated as middle-class anti-Semites can make you feel, which is damnably isolated, I was drawn to their language and to those who articulated it as well as those whose 'snippets' – chunks of verse or prose (signed Macaulay, Froude, Swift, Junius, Hazlitt, and who all else) – we had to render into appropriate ancient stuff.

I thought that the classiest English people were pretty damned classy and had a kind of refinement that was grand enough to be just (British justice was the refuse-all-substitutes *vraie chose*). I did fantasise about being some kind of Disraeli, finally applauded by the ranks of Tuscany and – who knows? – ennobled among them. None of this quite perished as life took its usual unusual turns: my ambition was limited by a certain appetite for, oh, comeliness. When I was savage, it was in the style of the ironists and satirists who made English literature a certain kind of paradise. I even imagined that Cambridge was the great good place that our old friend H.J. wanted it to be: lawns were the outward and visible sign of an orderly elegance which centuries alone could engender.

The war confirmed a patriotism which never quite went away. I recall being in a huge demonstration in Whitehall during the 1956 Suez crisis (when we were all more afraid of a WWIII than worried about doing an injustice to the bloody Gyppos) and quite suddenly I felt completely detached from the loud rage that had the crowd surging down Downing Street (now gated and roadblocked like an American embassy in a friendly Muslim country) and found myself thinking, almost in so many words, 'Poor Anthony Eden! How can he get any work done with this din going on?' Recent research shows that Anthony Eden was a shit, as was his predecessor Ernest Bevin, a salt-of-the-docks anti-Semite who threatened that if the violence continued (in Palestine) it would be so much the worse for 'the whole Jewish people'.

Well, that can go on for a long time but here's the kicker, as you and I would say if I were you: the whole edifice of illusion has crumbled in the last months to the point where (as if anyone cared) I feel like . . . oh how about Simone de Beauvoir, but only when she said, at the end of one of her many memoirs, '*J'ai été flouée*'. I should strike out the last 'e' but otherwise (to insert the translation you say the *NYRB* now demands of any frenchifying) I too feel 'cheated'. The English have dwindled into a society without grace, without honour, without *fric* (it's the shortage of the last that reveals the other deficiencies, of course). As for Civility, the Ordeal of, what civility would that be? A new magazine, funded by right- (and Right-) minded persons, has told me six or seven times that the cheque is in the post for a piece they published in March and guess what: they're jewing me and they aren't even Jews. What do you call people like that?

Jews are too, of course. The *TLS* is a funny place and not a nest to foul without wondering where you're going to go next time. I was asked to do a couple of big pieces for them in the last few months, both about actors (I think you saw them), and I didn't like to say no, nor was I thrilled to say yes, though the old classical routine does still mean that one can 'compose' on any theme without (it's nice to imagine) it mattering what it is as long as it scans. Your friend Gross never asked me to write a thing during his tenure; I never did anything for the paper until Jeremy Treglown came along. So what? When I was asked to do the showbizzy bits, I had the uneasy feeling which, I am told, ladies feel (*can* feel, at least) when taken from behind: the fear, sometimes, that the guy you can't see is laughing. Byron knew that laughter did not often provide a welcome accompaniment with the sex for the kind of coit he went in for, when that was the kind. The *TLS* never reviewed my Greek book (three years' work) and they had not yet published a piece on my *Personal Terms 4* and so I thought, in my low way, fuck it: I will eyeball them. So I did; and they promised that a piece had been commissioned and would appear. That is modern English for 'We weren't going to do it, but now we will, and you'll wish we hadn't'.

So they got a piece written by a man called Eric Korn, a *bouquiniste* who doubles as a hatchet man. 'One of your people', as the Brits I sought to applease (sic) sometimes used to say. He delivered ambiguity so well that my publisher, the unstupid Michael Schmidt, thought his piece was 'wonderful', but my friend Paul Cartledge (ancient history prof at Cambridge) knew better, when I asked him (and not before). Korn (who evokes the old golf-club application form question, 'Name of father, if changed') managed to imply that I couldn't really speak French and that my Greek had to be pretty bad too, since I had mistaken 'ekaton' for 'dtheka'. I know I shouldn't'a dunnit, but I did (because he was, I assumed, a Jew? Oh God, could be!) and I wrote him a longish manuscript letter in Greek pointing out that 'eka' figures in both figures and that when said by a toothless Cretan boatman who was *isos* (perhaps) planning to deceive, it was not that stupid to be duped. I told him, by way of an envoi, that he should not reply in High German since that language was *hors de ma portée*.

And yet and yet, even in the Republic of Saló, with the noose tightening, men dreamed of being deputy minister for torturing Communists or turning in Ebrei. Here we go again with my favourite quotation from that grim bastard Genet: '*Nous ne sortirons jamais de ce bordel.*' But then again, we shall and we shall not want to go, not if there's a letter on the way to us or a solicitation from a dishonest editor. Paul Goodman said, didn't he?, that you should never break relations with anyone who had access to a printing press. Innit de troot?

Tout à toi,
Freddie

Dear Freddie,
Since you end with Paul Goodman, allow me to begin with him. He is among those figures about whom one says, or should say, "Gone but justly forgotten." A renaissance man – poet, novelist, social thinker, lay analyst – he gave the

renaissance a bad name. He was really about fucking, hetero, homo, any kind of fucking you've got on hand. In his most famous book, *Growing Up Absurd*, which was one of the essential handbooks behind the sixties' student tumult, he claimed that one of the problems of young men today is that they do not have adequate "penis models." (Penis models? Now there's a poetic phrase!) Goodman himself was a tri- or quadri-sexual. The old joke about him has one fellow at a party ask another if he has seen Paul. "I last saw him at the buffet," the other fellow replies. "Oh, my God," the first fellow says, "you mean you left him alone with the chopped liver?"

As for that magazine you mention, if I have it aright – *Standpoint*? – I just this morning learned that its editors have accepted a story of mine called "Kuperman Awaits Ecstasy." Would a fee of 750 pounds (my keyboard has no pound sign) be acceptable? I was asked. I replied by suggesting that they jump the fee up to 1,000 pounds, which they have agreed to do. This all reminds me that my father used to joke, apropos of owing me my boyhood allowance of $5, "I'd rather owe it to you than not pay you at all." From him, who through a long business life incurred no debts, the joke wasn't at all bad.

"Derisive fee" is an amusing phrase, clean and pressed from the department of contempt. Do you remember an Anglo-American character named Alistair (Ali) Forbes? (In one of his letters to Diana Cooper, or was it Nancy Mitford – on third thought, who cares? – Evelyn Waugh writes that he is planning to avoid a party because "Ali Forbes and Peter Quennell are sure to attend.") Forbes used to write lengthy, heavily parentheses-laden, gossipy pieces on contemporary royalty for the *TLS*, notable for their indiscretions. I wrote to ask him to write a piece for the *American Scholar*, which I was then editing, offering him our set fee of $500. He said he should like to do so but added, "I beseech you during this Christmas season, Mr. Epstein, from the bowels of Christ not to adopt a too-Scrooge-like attitude on the matter of fee." I thought that splendidly high-handed, though could offer him no more money, and so no indiscretions for us. Had I been a man of larger heart and heavier purse, I should have paid him $500 to publish that single sentence.

I don't think you were wrong in thinking "the classiest English people were pretty damn classy." They were, indubitably. Until a decade or so ago, I used to think of myself as unashamedly Anglophile. I came by this genealogically. My father was a Canadian, a Montrealer, and my mother's mother, the great matriarch of her family, came to Chicago by way of Leeds. I was a young boy during World War Two, whose successful outcome was owed to the English, "the stolid English," as Primo Levi called them, who "had not noticed that they had lost the game," and whose courage and endurance saved the world from Hitler. I don't think that merely the classiest English people were pretty damn classy, but most English people, or so it seemed from the other shore, weren't at all bad, either. Many moons ago I gave a lecture on all this, called "Anglophilia, American Style," at the University of London (for a derisive fee, but they also put Barbara and me up for a week in a decent hotel in Bloomsbury). When first I visited England many years before, I felt a much-too-late yearning for all that you had experienced: a good public school, Oxbridge, bright young vaguely (maybe some not so vaguely) aristocratic companions. Everything about England seemed of high quality, from its historians to its motor cars to its corduroy trousers (of which I had a pair made forty years ago on High Street in Oxford and still wear on coldest of cold Chicago winter days). And then it all began to unravel. The English lost their confidence; perhaps it went with the loss, a few decades earlier, of their empire. The high good spirits of the country were replaced by snarky irony from above, potentially violent bad temper from below. England was no longer *Chariots of Fire* England, but the England of The Rolling Stones: druggy, ugly, slightly menacing England. The loss of the truly great Great Britain is one of the genuine losses of my lifetime, and of course it must be triply so of yours.

To return to the word "trousers," which you will notice I used in the previous paragraph. True enough, Americans do say "pants." Not long ago there were shops in America called "Just Pants" and (I hope you will not believe I am not making this up) "Pants Are Us." Another word in use was "slacks"; I think it came into high vogue when women began to wear trousers during World War Two. "Slacks," though, comes uncomfortably close to the word "slacker." Chez Epstein we persist in saying "trousers." Part of the reason is that I find the word mildly amusing. A trouser (singular) sounds like nothing so much as a fresh-water fish: "trousers almondine" or "trouser au truffles" is easily imagined on the menu of a mildly pretentious restaurant. The word also has the cachet of sounding, in the United States at least, mildly out of it, a condition I have aspired to for some while now. "The fact is," Théophile Gautier is quoted as saying in the *Goncourt Journals*, "nothing interests me any more. I have a feeling that I have ceased to be a contemporary." Six months later, the not-so-old boy – he was sixty-one – died. So perhaps I ought to restrain a bit my desire to be entirely out of it.

I have sent off over the weekend a 1,800-word piece on "What Happened to the Novel?" for what I hope will be a non-derisive (to me) fee of $5,000. My larger argument is that the teller has taken over the tale; it all starts with Edgar Allen Poe, of whom the French were so enamored, and continues with Flaubert, who wrote only one good book, and that a very mean one, on that poor Madame B. It was Flaubert who said: "The story, the plot of a novel is of no interest to me. When I write a novel I aim at rendering a color, a shade. For instance in my Carthaginian novel [*Salammbô*], I want to do something purple." (An unreadable book, *Salammbô*, as I recall, whatever its color.) I posit the notion that, while science and technology work on the basis of progress, art doesn't, yet it is just possible that art, literary division, is degressing. None of this will be good news to most writers of fiction, and shouldn't please those brave but diminishing troops who continue to read lots of contemporary fiction. We all want, somehow, to think we are living in the best of times, or so I suspect. Nor am I at all sure how all this will go down in the unhallowed halls – the magazine has just moved its offices – of *Newsweek*.

Eric Korn must have been Korngold or Kornfeld. No-one of the Hebrew persuasion is named Korn; he must have had the nomenclatural version of rhinoplasty done on his name. I do not approve – though no-one, I realize, is asking for my approval – of Jews changing their last names, though I must say that there are certain Jewish names that, if one or the other was mine, I wouldn't hesitate changing. My son Mark went to Hebrew school with a boy named Kevin Footlick – Footlick has to have been a name given by a cruel Russian bureaucrat; not even the Irish Kevin before it can undo the damage. Don't think I could live so easily with the name Lipschitz, either. Mencken, in *The American Language*, cites a man named Ginsberg who changed his name to Guiness-Bourg, which is comically grand. One of the nice things about the name Epstein is that it takes all ambiguity out of the question of whether or not one is Jewish.

Best, Joe

Dear Joe
See attached . . .

Tout à toi,
Freddie

[Accompanying this email was some correspondence between F.R. and *Standpoint*.]

Dear Freddie,

Many thanks for passing along your correspondence with Daniel Johnson, editor of *Standpoint*, which is filled with good and amusing things: your correspondence, I mean. I much enjoyed its tone: is it that of high harangue, or tirade, or, simply, the mode of pure "ticked to the max"? Whichever it is, you do it splendidly. I wish I could do it as well. My own tendency when things like this happen – and they haven't happened all that often to me – is to shift into high bourgeois dudgeon (don't know if you have that gear on your console), and come away looking merely stuffy and foolishly overheated.

The one time I had seriously to chase a man for a fee – a Yugoslav, as they then were, who owed me $1,500 for a talk I gave in Denver – I felt not only a certain humor but a touch of family tradition in doing so. Rather late in his business career my father became almost obsessive about chasing down debts. He was particularly keen on collecting small debts from rich people, whose negligence seemed all the more insulting to him. He would have them subpoenaed in the lobbies of their expensive apartment buildings. He would even drag some among them into what in this country is called Small Claims Court, located right next door to the Small Beer Chancellory. For a while he did this bill-collecting so insistently that I joked that he ought to think about going to law school. (He was in his late sixties at the time.) He, in turn, told me that he wanted me to understand that it wasn't the principle of the thing; it was the money. A good fellow, my dear old father.

In your tirade-harangue-fulmination-onslaught, I particularly admired two touches. One is when, after telling Daniel Johnson that you have been thanked for your patience, you declare that you would now like it back. I love such bits, which remind one how intrinsically comic is our idiomatic language. I also much liked the bit about the reason why women did not like to be taken, as the phrase is, from the servant's entrance (because they fear being laughed at behind their backs). The notion reminded me of a scene from the movie *Swann in Love*, in which Jeremy Irons, an actor not much to my taste, though he does decadence nicely, is committing the above act on a prostitute while smoking a cigarette and not bothering to take off his hat. Now that's blasé to a very high power.

If Daniel Johnson – son of Paul Johnson, whom I would rather vaguely admire than actually read – were more on the *qui vive* he would have changed the assignment and asked you to write about Joseph Losey not as one of the world's underrated but instead overrated figures. The best thing that happened to him, or so I gather from your paragraphs about him, was to have been blacklisted. Being blacklisted, clearly, is one of the best career moves a screen-writer or director could have made; it enshrined one, and permanently. I wonder if any of the blacklisted Hollywood figures was genuinely talented. The name among them that comes up most often is Dalton Trumbo, and he, I suspect, wasn't all that much. Did you ever put yourself to the torture of watching his movie *Johnny Got His Gun*? I'd rather undergo a flaying as sit through that monstrosity again. Trumbo, and my guess is most of the other blacklisted screenwriters, fall under the ample umbrella of your observation – made in *Ticks and Crosses*, I think – that the movies are made by third-rate people trying to pass themselves off as second-rate, with truly second-rate people qualifying as *auteurs*. The wonder about the movies, really, is that with so many mediocrities at work on them, with all the commercial pressures to dumb everything down and make it even more stupid than its creators intended, a few quite good movies do get made and sent out into the world.

I sent off my 1,800 word article about the novel *de nos jours* to *Newsweek* earlier today. My argument is that the novel took a wrong turn somewhere around the time of Edgar Allen Poe, much beloved by nineteenth-century French scribblers, and, slightly later, around that of Flaubert, around whom there remains a great cult. (Julian Barnes is a great Flaubertian.) The turn was away from direct engagement with the world and toward the sensibility of the artist/novelist, so that in place of story we now have style, in place of content, consciousness. My general line is that our great contemporary novelists have abandoned the great themes in favor of declaring "Look at Me! I've just had a fucking epiphany." I don't drag out that stale intellectual bagel about the novel being dead, but I do suggest that somewhere down the road a serious wrong turn was made. I ignore entirely the question of whether anyone genuinely cares about all this.

I have just returned from lunch with a remarkable man named Matt Shanahan, who is ninety years old and has been blind for, roughly, the past twenty-five years, the result of an hereditary eye disease. He lives in a place five or so miles from where we do called Friedman Place, Home for the Jewish Blind, though he is not, as you will have gathered from his name, Jewish. I met him three years ago, when my granddaughter Annabelle, as part of her junior-year high-school program, was working at Friedman Place as a volunteer. When I was waiting around for my granddaughter, someone there enlisted me to read to some of the residents for an hour on Thursday afternoons. My readings were not a great hit; perhaps five or six people came, and not all went away smiling: I was too rigidly highbrow in my selections. But Matt Shanahan did listen, and always had intelligent comments to make. After a while, I knocked off the readings, but suggested that Matt and I continue to meet, every second Friday, for lunch, which we have been doing for the past three years.

He is a most impressive character, Matt Shanahan. Brought up working-class (hold the lace curtain) Irish, he left school at sixteen, in the middle of the Depression, for what seemed a decent job working in a grocery store. He spent the majority of his working life at the Post Office, not, I gather, rising all that high. He married (his wife died twenty or so years ago) and has three children, all of whom are good to him, and many grandchildren. He is handsome, though now bald and bent over, but with dazzling (if useless) blue eyes and a sly smile, and always well turned out. I knew he was extraordinary when one day, a few weeks after I had first met him, he asked: "Tell me, Joe, why would Hannah Arendt sleep with this creep Heidegger?" Now that, you will agree, is not a question one might expect from a man who never finished high school and spent his working life at the Post Office.

The fact is that Matt Shanahan reads – more precisely, listens to – five or six books a week, and happens to have natural good taste in literature: he knows the real thing when he encounters it, and has a lively critical spirit to go with it. All of this he arrived at without the least classroom help. He's just smart, *tout court*. He also has fine antennae for picking up – and using – irony in conversation, though his hearing is deserting him.

Our lunches usually last from ninety minutes to two hours. I pick him up, and we always go to the same restaurant. Because of his blindness, he leans in close to the table to eat his food. I describe where things are as fighter pilots in the old WWII war movies used to do – green peas at two o'clock, pasta at six o'clock, potatoes at high noon – and place his hand on the cup of black coffee that he drinks with every meal. We alternate at paying the check. We talk about books, sometimes about politics (he is an old-fashioned liberal, lover of the underdog, hater of the upper classes, though he doesn't get belligerent about it), often about life when he was a small boy in a family with ten children and with parents (his father was illiterate) who were immigrants from Ireland, not infrequently about the old days in Chicago, a city we both love. We never run out of things to say to each other. Today as we were walking into the restaurant, I asked him what he was going to eat, and he replied that he didn't all that much care, for it was the conversation to which he was looking forward. I told him that what he said reminded me of a man who was involved in an affair with a homely but brilliant woman, who claimed that he was with her not for the sex but the conversation afterwards, a story that brought out one of his sly knowing smiles.

Usually I burn a CD that I leave with him after our meetings: often classical music, but frequently traditional jazz and vocal music: Louis Armstrong, Blossom Dearie, French Café songs, etc. I turn the CD on before leaving him, telling him to call if the mood strikes him, though he rarely does. I always feel a touch of sadness when I depart, leaving him in his utter darkness. He is a heroic figure, still learning, still taking pleasure from life, so late in the game, and with such poor equipment.

I haven't told many people about Matt Shanahan, lest they think I am so fucking virtuous to meet with him. But virtue hasn't the least thing to do with it. He is a damned interesting man. Besides, if I am acting virtuously, be assured that I more than make up for any good I might do, here or elsewhere, by harboring many vile opinions.

Best, Joe

Dear Joe,

After reading about you and the blind Irishman in the Jewish home, I think I have grasped the situation: you are a good man but understandably don't want it to get around. That kind of thing can ruin a writer's reputation; only rumours of marital fidelity do a man a worse turn in the *bourse littéraire* (monitored by our trilingual friend Steiner, G.) than symptoms of unselfishness. The question Mr Shanahan raised about Hannah Arendt and her wish/willingness to sleep with Herr Professor Creepstein (although I don't have the figures in front of me, sleeping was probably not something they did a lot of, not with metaphysics to smoke after Martin had his way with her, and v.v., which we must never forget). It raises the whole dread question of What Do Women Want? Some of the answer is always, as with the rest of our monkey-businesslike species, more than an average share of classy attention. The assumption that Hannah, dark and quite beautiful, though you'd hardly guess it from her rugose state when she achieved A-number-one Punditry, was a tender maiden wickedly lured to Nookieland is part of our (male, OK my) sentimental reading of femininity and its essential, kinda, goodness. The mother in the sex? Partly, but the beauty too. One forgets the appetite, because that's what really frightens us maybe: Tiresias's hot news: they get nine times more out of it than we do. Bitches suddenly, they can ride that broomstick all night.

Maybe the maternal segment supplies a clue: Martin was not only a Great Mind that Hannah wanted to think like, he was also SAD and didn't get enough, as the English put it. Oh my God what a long face and what a silly hat, und der lederhosen mit. Perhaps (there we go using the word which pundits pull when they want to exercise their short-legged, usually closely-leashed imaginations!), perhaps the mature Hannah felt the same girlish twinge when she looked on the *nudnik* Eichmann in the glass box and had another attack of the 'Poor little thing!' syndrome: hotsy and totsy, old associates. How about she delivered to Eichmann the care package, in print form, which she never quite managed to compose for Martin, whose wife was still wearing her spiritual swastika armband when Hannah came a-calling after the war?

The truth just might be that Hannah tried all she knew not to be Jewish, at least not NECESSARILY to be Jewish, somewhat in the style of the woman she admired so much Rahel Varnhagen (sp?), in the time of one Frederick or another of Prussia: Hannah tried Zionism and she kinda tried Communism, or at least a Communist, and then she became a NY intello, which was a way of eating your kikedom and still having it: you wrote so many polemics against other Jews that you very nearly came out the other side, and ON the other side: as she did when she blamed guess-who for the Holocaust: the Judenrats who tried, often valiantly and no less often, I daresay, with self-preserving hopes, to negotiate with the well-armed murderers in whose annihilatory ambitions they could not quite believe, even when they believed them. Sitting in New York, on plumped bursaries of one kind and another, she decided that the Jews should have armed themselves, drilled themselves into SS fitness and taken the bastards on. She wishes; I wish; you wish; and when we draw moral conclusions from our wishes we turn into what she did: a thinking man's *merdeuse de grande envergure*.

I'm not a passionate admirer of Isaiah Berlin (a man who had white knuckles when canoeing in shallow, pallid waters), even though I do somewhat admire his flower-in-the-buttonhole liberalism (as a diplomatic major-domo, he buttonholed for England) and the assumption, which I share and so do you maybe, that we should not subject humanity to our affectations of solutionism. Had he been a washbasin, Isaiah would have had only one tap and it would've been tepid (same temperature as his now famous, not very prosaically gifted biographer Michael Ignatieff, a man who combs his hair very carefully on the right side). HOWEVER, Isaiah did have one hate and it was none other than darling Hannah. Having lost a number of his 'gentle'

relatives in Riga and adjacent places to the murdering bastards, he took it ill
to be told that they, scholars, merchants, whatever, were to be despised for
their failure to master kriegsmanship at a few weeks' notice and 'fight back'.
It's that number thing that made Hannah feel ashamed (poor sweetie):
6,000,000 people should have been able to form battalions and procure a *jour
de gloire* or two, even though they lived at opposite ends of the continent, etc.
Jews did, of course, fight back, in many small cases, but neither Hannah nor
anyone else too much cared to know about it until some time after the
Eichmann trial.

Bref, how about Hannah was a bit of a goer from early days and that her
ambition had two locations: in her head, full of Ideas, and in her/his bed,
whoever he might be? Her friendship with Mary McCarthy, about whom
your friend Matt might have some interesting insights, was a two-of-a-kinder:
they were a couple of pull-the-boots-on/put-the-boot-in ladies, bent on
pleasure and revenge and what's the difference when you're riding that
cowboy? I have read a good deal of Arendt's 'philosophy', of which Isaiah B.
was tartly dismissive on account of its essentialist style, and – in my days
with Homo Faber etc. – was somewhat snowed by her dictatorial assurance.
Credulity is the mark of the head-down generation which thought it
could learn almost everything from books, including how to walk away
from hook-nosed shadows. The role (*tiens!*) of the novel is always, to my
mind, somewhat in opposition to the generalisations of homo this and homo
that which philosophers, in the Continental style especially, made their
speciality.

I know that you need no added dose of scepticism about 'thinkers', having
lived in professional proximity to them, but their seductiveness, like their
severity, is part of their charm. Steiner's breathy infusion of passion into
teaching, that second-personal form of being impersonal, alerts us (even as
we flinch and turn our heads, which reminds me of the old heard-it-from-a-
Marine (I did too) story about this weird girl who wanted to be fucked in the
EAR; how did he know that was what she wanted? Because every time he went
to put it in her mouth she turned her head like . . .? That's the one) – where
was I? – oh yes, Steiner: he would have us know that the pupil and the prof in
erotic synergy is an old Socratic number; disdain and desire work together in
the double act that gave us Soc and Plato and Plato and Ari and Ari and little
Alex (later Great) and who all else, including Heloïse and Abelard, who
required his *belle* to imitate the sounds of a girl being chastised when, in truth,
chastity was being chased away. Punishment and pleasure, condescension and

going down ... the word games are never entirely playful and always better in French.

Since we CANNOT be truthful about sex and what we think about it, since verbalisation is part of perversity and what old Ziggy thought perverse a form of physical poetry, per/verse form, we might Derridise if we really have to. Whereof we cannot speak is always the best part, some say, but not Philip or John U. because the full report card is always what counts with them, not the dialogue (even John O'Hara outdoes them in that department, and the 'even' is unwarranted), that and the sales. Which doesn't mean I don't wish ... no: stop right there with the franchise (italics, please, Mr Printer, as V.N. would say): *franchise* is right.

The novel and its enemies. Poor old droop-tashed, provincial Gustave, I can't help loving him; I even read *Salammbô*, with its cross-dressed title, Salaam, bo! A certain mad, valiant attempt there to enter the civilisation of The Other; Carthage was to Rome what Islam is to – dare I include myself in a group pronoun? – Us. Poor Obama, burdened with the need to have reach-out arms ready for an embrace which will be returned as it was by Dean O'Banion, the Chicago florist gangster who got rubbed out when accepting a handshake which turned into a form of carnal handcuff. I don't want to reach out to Islam or even to the inhabitants of that orthodox borough of Jerusalem; I want to keep out of their hands, even as I admire Ottoman buildings, the beauty of many mosques, the charm of dem robes dey wear and all that stuff, because finally Islam is a parody of Judaism and so, in many forms, is Judaism. I don't WANT to live in the shadow of the Lord, whatever you choose to call Him, and I don't want to have to share a value system which requires women to be hidden from my lascivious eye; hell, I don't even like the Archbishop of Canterbury. We all know, as Oscar Wilde said of the French Revolution, what that unfortunate movement leads to. I'll go along with Isaiah Berlin, trimmer and sickophant, uncertain and undogmatic, rather than crop certainty from any ayatollah you happen to have on you. Reference, cryptic, to an old English judicial joke: young judge, nervous before passing sentence for the first time on what was then a criminal act, asks old-bencher 'What do you give them for buggery?' Old-bencher: 'Oh, eighteen pence, or anything you happen to have on you.' Eighteen pence being one of your quarters. You knew that and you also knew the story. You're a tough room to play, as they used to say when trying to get a laugh out of Hannah and Mary.

Tout à toi,
Freddie

Dear Freddie,

You've dealt some solid and much deserved blows to Hard-hearted Hannah, the vamp without a bandana. You are correct also to link her, as she linked herself, with Mary Always Contrary McCarthy, that *nafka* (with a heart of coal). As Hannah leapt into Martin Heidegger's bed, so Mary let the gross Edmundo Wilson jump on her bones. She left another critic, Philip Rahv, editor of *Partisansky Review*, as the Bunny used to call it, to take up residence with the aforementioned Bunny, and went on to wed the selfsame Bunny, with (in his own description) his "large pink prong." She probably did so for no greater reasons than snobbery and careerism; Wilson was a greater critic than Rahv and could also do more for her career. They shared – as in the new cant phrase, "thanks for sharing" – one of the truly hellish modern marriages. Fifteen or so years ago, the *New York Times* reprised the complaints each had made against the other in their divorce proceedings: lots of biting, punching, kicking, insults, plenty of humiliation to go around on both sides were described – and one felt that neither party was lying. Each was quite as hideous as the other described. You must know the old saw about the one good thing about the Thomas and Jane Carlyle marriage is that at least they made only two people unhappy. The Bunny and Mary the Contrary went on to remarry, and thus make even more people unhappy.

As for Hard-Hearted Hannah, all the New York intellectuals fell for her – or almost all. I recall Sidney Hook once telling me that she wasn't really all that smart, but that her heavy-artillery German education impressed all the boys who had gone to City College on the subway with their chopped-liver sandwiches in brown bags. W.H. Auden seems to have fallen for her, too, but then his taste in human beings was always dubious (note his choice of the odious Chester Kallman as the love of his life). Hannah A. may have been able to read Aristotle in the original, and to have seen Heidegger not plain but naked, but about almost all political events on which she wrote she was wrong – and wildly wrong. I remember hearing a story in 1964, when the conservative Barry Goldwater was running for president of the United States, that she was searching for an apartment in Switzerland, so certain was she that the Nazis were now going to take over the USA. She was, in short, no great *chochema*, or wise woman, but merely a kraut with a small talent for dramatizing ideas and a large taste for the pretentious.

Nafka, chochema, you give me Latin, you will have noticed, and I return it with kitchen Yiddish. Is this a fair exchange? I hope you don't think I come anywhere near speaking Yiddish; I probably have a 500-word Yiddish vocabulary, with no sense whatsoever of the language's grammar. I have just enough Yiddish, in other words, to fool the Gentiles into thinking I know how to speak it, but not enough to speak to the real Jews, who are, alas, now disappearing. I do, if I may say so, fairly good stage Greenhorn Yiddish, which I haul out for joke-telling. But soon no-one will be around to remember what poor Greenhorn Jews sounded like.

Getting back to Hannahbanana, yes, I, too, have seen photographs in which she seemed, when young, fairly comely, if not Rachel at the well. Mary McCarthy when young was quite beautiful. Susan Sontag was every boy of intellectual aspirations' dream of the kind of raven-haired bohemian girl he should have had in his rumpled bed. Their good looks helped all these women to make their dents in the tin-foil intellectual life of their time. Great good looks and intellect, perhaps even talent (outside of acting talent), don't go together; perhaps they shouldn't go together. I recall once hearing Edward Shils and Arnaldo Momigliano describing a too-good-looking graduate student, and predicting his failure chiefly because of his good looks. Although neither man was Freudian, their reasoning, I gathered, was based on the theory of sublimation, which, in its artistic application, Freud formulated best when he said that the artist gives up money, power, fame, and the love of beautiful women for his art, through which he hopes to win money, power, fame, and the love of beautiful women. This too-handsome graduate student, Shils and Momigliano were in other words saying, can have the love of beautiful women in part (at least) without having to spend long days in the dusty stacks, fishing around for footnote fodder, so why should he bother, and he probably won't. Whatever happened to this young man, I do not know. Wish, to round out the story nicely, I could say that he went on to become Leonardo DiCaprio. Momigliano's middle name, by the by, was Dante: Arnaldo Dante Momigliano – one more vowel-ending name and you could dance to it.

I have been reading Leslie Mitchell's quite good biography of Maurice Bowra, about whom I am to write something for the *Weekly Standard*. (I was in my fifties before I knew that in England Maurice is always pronounced Morris; many moons ago, I reviewed, for the *New York Times Book Review*, E.M. Forster's *Maurice*. Had I know that hero was called Morris, I might have viewed him differently, though either way I am quite certain I would have forgotten this rather faint character, which I now have, completely.) I never met Bowra; it occurs to me that you may have done. I have met a few of the biography's supporting cast, the so-called Bowristas: Noel Annan and John

Sparrow, and I've corresponded with Hugh Trevor-Roper. Other members included C. Day-Lewis, Kenneth Clark, A.J. Ayer, David Astor, Cyril Connolly, John Betjeman, Hugh Gaitskell, Anthony Powell, Christopher Sykes, Stephen Spender, Rex Warner, Stuart Hampshire, Henry Yorke, Osbert Lancaster, and Isaiah Berlin. None of these is a full-out great man, but there are some very impressive very high second-line names here, all disciples, by design, of Bowra, who was a disciple-making man. One could not put together a list of men and women alive today who would come close to matching it. They are the generation – allowing a generation to be, in the old-fashion accounting, thirty years – before ours, and next to whom ours seems very thin, not to say dim. They are also Englishmen of a kind that made England seem impressive to you, made you feel how much you wished to belong to the great unnamed club of which they seemed charter members, and that helped turn me, an ocean away, into a boringly earnest Anglophile.

Bowra reminds me in many ways of my friend Edward Shils. They even had something like the same build: portly muscular. Edward, unlike Bowra, wasn't interested in disciples – and, truth to tell, none of the quality Bowra found was available – and he was a deeper thinker than Bowra, whose main notions were to keep alive the Greek sense of heightened human possibility and the spirit of poetry (not Greek alone, but modern poetry also). Very high-flown, this, and not likely to come about, of course, though nonetheless worth pursuing, at least within the friendly confines of Oxford. Edward Shils' notions were deeper, more complex. Bowra stood for, was in fact the leader of, the Immoral Front, which meant against all that was staid, stuffy, establish-mentarian; by the time Edward reached his fifties, the Immoral Front had all but taken over the universities and much else in modern life, and its regime, far from being grand and free, was grubby and third-rate. Both men were not to be trifled with, and were strong put-down artists. Edward used to say of Isaiah Berlin, for example, that "he was a charming man who gave much pleasure to his friends," by which I decoded him to be saying that Berlin badly wanted intellectual courage and that his work was second-rate.

Another difference is that Maurice Bowra was homosexual, and, Leslie Mitchell reports, very edgy about word of this getting round, while Edward Shils had been twice married. Easily the most talented man among the students at Oxford that Bowra had the opportunity to cut out for his herd of disciples, W.H. Auden, was not at all to his taste. Auden was too messy, too wanting in couth, for Bowra's taste. Odd and interesting the taste of homo-sexuals for other homosexuals. Toward the end of his life I was friendly with

Erich Heller, who taught at Northwestern (where I did) and was emphatically homosexual in the Teutonic manner, and I recall once when E.M. Forster's name came up in conversation between us, Heller spoke of him with genuine revulsion: "A dirty, milquetoasty little man," he called him. I cannot resist telling you here that Edward Shils, who had connections at *Encounter* and was then a Fellow of King's, where Forster lived, had arranged for Forster to give the magazine his Egyptian diary to print; and then, lo, the diary showed up instead printed in *Harper's* magazine. "Dear me," said Edward, "do you suppose he really meant 'only collect'?" How I miss my friend Edward!

Best, Joe

Dear Joe,

I always prefer to define myself as a novelist, not because it sounds finer but because it denotes, when it does, someone who determines the form of his prosaic response to life, a free man who is not dictated to by bosses nor, if I can help it, by editorial persons. It signifies someone who, at least at the time when I first wanted to be of the company, was willing to endure a measure of poverty and of obscurity even, as the price of the ability to be his own master and to say, as exactly as he could work it, what he saw, heard, felt, judged when it came to human life (I am not a great impersonator of animals). The novel, as I always wanted to write it, ever since reading Maugham's *Of Human Bondage* (a title nicely cadged off Spinoza), would reflect the horror, the horror, but also the comedy, the comedy (not Conrad's *forte*) and the pity, the malice, the irony, and above all the *mélange* of these, the happy, horrible unpredictability of things. The novel has a tradition, of several kinds, but no necessary pedigree; it has a form, but not a formality, which means that variation and divagation are part of what one can deliver without being false to its mongrel origins. I thought it my only way to resolve the contradictions, absurdities, fears and small hopes which, when I was in my late teens, seemed to clog my spirit and make me a sorry pharisee, burdened with distinction.

I read a great deal of fiction when I was at Cambridge and found plenty to admire and emulate, but not so much, among the moderns, that I doubted my ability to be in their *galère*. The 1920s and 1930s had their examples of genius and of excellence and I gobbled them up, from Hemingway to poor Scott (as if the author of *The Great Gatsby* has any jury out on him!) to Dos Passos (another sufferer from Ernest's emulous malice), from Kafka to Koestler (*Darkness at Noon* remains the prime instance of the *roman à thèse* which transcends its purpose). Lawrence and even Aldous Huxley were inspirations of a kind, *chez les anglais*, but I never liked any of V. Woolf apart from *The Waves* which, if TV had ever been an art form, would have made a superb colour/montage/sound amalgam. My American thing never went away: I greatly admired, and learnt from, Sinclair Lewis, whose mimicry was so sweetly savage and who, surely, taught John O'Hara, whose *Appointment in Samarra* should perhaps not be kept again in a hurry, but was fine in its time (Julian English is a memorable character with no specific quality except the courage of his weakness). I liked the realism of some American writers of the second rank, even including J.P. Marquand, and certainly Frank Norris, never Dreiser, because of his clumsy prose, even though *An American Tragedy* had its dramatic moments (it had another title, didn't it? when Monty Clift, and Liz Taylor and Shelley Winters got into it: yes, it did: *A Place in the Sun!*). I never understood the supposed quality of James T. Farrell or even Thomas Wolfe (I didn't WANT to go home again). I tried to like Nathanael West as much as I pretended to, not because there was any percentage in admiring him but because I wished that neatness and irony could be enough and never quite thought so. I read our old friend H.J. like an addict while always finding him, except in the shorter work (which was never exactly abbreviated), slightly absurd in his diffuse Latinate precision. I don't think I'm going to be racing through *The Princess Casamassima* again, although he did, in that one, get to radical chic almost a century before Bob Silvers and all those people whose slightest nod might have made me into their uncritical toady (lucky the man who is never recruited to say he likes things or people whom he never would unless it was a condition of promotion).

You set a mark of 50 years for the period of accelerated decline during which you think only Isaac B. Singer is likely to be a survivor down the ages. You may be right. I can imagine how sourly Nabokov would have read your article if he had still been at the Grand Hotel, Montreux, and able to cull it from the lesbian bookshop down the street where he collected his newsprint. I do think *Pale Fire* is a three-star plate of *suprême de tosh* and I like the artificial fruit and icing of verbal sugar with which V.N. managed to dress his lifelong anguish at the loss of mama Russia. *Lolita* has gone bad, I think, but was and remains an expression of 'freedom' of the kind that I liked to imagine I found by writing fiction. V.N. announced his outsiderdom there, in a way much bolder than in *Pnin*, which people like to say they like because it is essentially about a funny foreign guy, whereas *Lolita* is not only about a certain appetite which V.N. may or may not have shared (in his head) but also about the coquettishness of the American chick, whose willingness to be taken for a sexual object has been copiously enhanced *ces dernières années* by the new prudery concerning 'harassment', when every style and posture, every moue and moo, down to the ready-when-you-are tonsured pubes, solicit the grope which Women (*ci-devant* The Girls) can consider actionable.

I recall that many years ago Norman Mailer wrote a piece entitled 'An Expensive Look at the Talent in the Room' in which he picked off various rivals whose names do not rest with me. Perhaps William Styron was one. His *Sophie's Choice* exemplifies one of the reasons why 'the novel' has lost its art and its authors their autonomy (code for the right to be poor but honest). Styron's stuff is typical of 'Novels About', where the theme dominates the matter and its selection, as a commercial prospect, puts the writer in the machine which Maxwell Perkins first activated, the shredder and dicer into which a manuscript is popped for toasting and buttering and jamming. Nothing more demeans a writer than the *need* for finishing touches from Someone Who Knows, in a world in which no-one truly does. The abandonment of fine tuning to another would be absurd in any other art, which means that those who allow their work to be shaped, refined, added to and generally got ready for the shops by editors (to whom they then append genuflectory tributes) are not artists at all, but caterers. Nothing wrong with a spot of catering, old man, is there? Yes, but otherwise not.

I have only once been commissioned to write a novel for a fee I chose not to refuse. It was based on a phrase that the commissioning editor flattered me into believing I had coined: THE ELECTRIC JEW. If I did use the phrase, it was about a man called Peter Gruber, unless it was Guber, who worked at Paramount, I think it was, under David Begelman. I could not write a word and told my agent to give back all the money. He wanted me to say that I had a stack of pages already done and I had a right to keep the first slice of moolah, but I hadn't and I didn't. It wasn't a matter of virtue, more of keeping a little patch of what I do entirely under my control.

I suppose Philip Roth and John Updike would claim that success had given them even greater freedom but it has also made them Important, and I'm not sure that is as enviable as it is prize-winning and lucrative. Miserably prolific Philip rarely offers us anything new in the way of compensation for his glum facility for making the worst of life's bad job, while doing himself extremely well. The curse he wears is that of a man who can't forget *la chose génitale* and can't make anything human out of the target for his increasingly undependable *schlong. Du côté des Anglais*, Kingsley Amis worked something of the same territory, especially in a book I never read called *Jake's Thing*, not the subtlest title I ever scanned, but because he was English he did it in a saloon-bar tone, playing for laughs and appealing to the small-mindedness which has been the mark of the British since it all went wrong at Suez; 'I blame the Americans' is the unspoken coda to the decline and fallaciousness of English political and artistic shrinkage. Kingsley's remark about 'workshop' is typical of his capacity to condense everything to what can be swallowed at a gulp. Of the creation of new universities, he said 'More will mean worse', and it has, Oscar, it has. But his own work is skimpy (always precisely measured, at about 212 pp.) and lost its felicity as its author marinated his brain in whatever sauce the barman could pull. He and Pinter both married classy bints (as the young K.A. woulda said) and got worse as they bettered themselves, although H.P. was sufficiently thrilled to be threading a Lady to become a bit of a toff himself, with a town mansion and British-style eccentricities, i.e. being rude to guests who didn't dance to his monotone.

The decline of the novel probably has more to do with the rise of the pictorial arts than with some putative penury of talent. The truth is that the big bucks are now in film, TV and allied forms of high or low harlotry. Worse, the punter no longer sees himself as a Julien Sorel or a Jay Gatsby or whoever, no longer wants to be, in his private self, the hero of a book; it's better to be a soap star or a porn star even (Philip Roth's idea of heaven). Our correspondence, dear Joe, is superbly anachronistic and also – why not? – vindicatory: we have not spoken or met, and yet we have, I suspect, a kind of intimacy which most men never enjoy in the present rush of accessibilities. Nothing sweeter, at times, than to be an anachronism *à deux*. We do it on the page and, I suspect, we also both have a similar exemption from what waxes Roth: we *do* have women we like AND love and stay with and, don't never tell, THAT's what Philip and Kingsley and who all else REALLY, REALLY dare not say they envy.

Tout à toi,
Freddie

Dear Freddie,

I should rather be called Novelist than Commissioner, Prime Minister, Mr. President, or even Your Highness. Practiced at a sufficiently high level, novelist is a higher calling than these and any other callings I can think of. I should myself like to be called, and think of myself as, a Novelist, and would but for the embarrassing fact that I seem to have neglected to write any novels. (Damn! I knew I forgot something.) Instead I am stuck with being called other things, not least "arguably America's best essayist," usually with that weasel word "arguably" prominently in place. I have seen it so often that I have thought of changing my name to Arguably Epstein.

I didn't know that Maugham ripped (as we now say) off the title *Of Human Bondage* from Spinoza. I did know that André Malraux ripped off his *La condition humaine* from Pascal. I also know that Maugham's is a superior novel to Malraux's, and probably to anything else Malraux wrote, though I'm not at all certain whether the world ("that great ninny," as Henry James sometimes called it) would agree. I have no notion of Malraux's current standing in France, but elsewhere his seems to be a reputation that has sunk lower than General Motors stock. The problem, I suspect, is that he was the proponent of the heroic model of life – revolutionaries in China, air warfare in Spain, dangerous archaeological discoveries in Asia – and that model, just now, doesn't seem among life's serious possibilities, quite apart from the fact that Malraux himself may have been more than a touch of phony in allowing people to think him the model for all his heroic figures.

On the subject of French novelists, I note that the Turk Orhan Pamuk, three or four of whose novels I've read with genuine pleasure, has a piece – originally a lecture – in the current issue of *Standpoint* about his reverence for Flaubert, and how, for him, being *dans le vrai* (he doesn't use the phrase) arrives when he feels himself in his own writing in Flaubertian mode. Fiction, as the rappers like to say, is a house of many mansions, but I wonder if chez Gustave isn't among the most ramshackle among them. The cult of Flaubert is chiefly based on his letters, in which he cocks a relentless snoot at bourgeois life and complains about the difficulties of his wrestle with words: he is the pure artist with the unflagging hatred of the middle class. As for the artist part, Flaubert wrote only one successful novel, *Madame Bovary*, and that is a very cold piece of work. *Sentimental Education* is only half or two-thirds good; the rest isn't even very readable. Matthew Arnold has a fine essay-review of the French translation of *Anna Karenina*, in which he persuasively sets out why, of these two novels, Flaubert's and Tolstoy's, about the same subject – an adulterous woman – Tolstoy's is so much greater, which it indubitably is. The reason, Arnold thought, was that Tolstoy had the better heart, while Flaubert had "petrified feeling," which sounds right to me. Not that all good writing comes out of great, or grand, feeling. Maurice Bowra says that Evelyn Waugh's best writing came out of his hatred, which also sounds right. But a large heart and sympathetic moral imagination still go a long way.

In life, as opposed to in literary criticism, one doesn't have to make these strict binary choices – Tolstoy or Flaubert, Beethoven or Mozart, Barnum or Bailey – but, even when push doesn't come to shove, I much prefer the messy Balzac to the stylistically tidy Flaubert. Balzac was ravenous to understand life in all its variety; Flaubert to destroy everyone who wasn't an artist, little realizing, or perhaps not giving a hoot, that among artists are numbered some of the great monsters (hold the *sacré*) of all, himself of course included. I fear I am getting a little nutty on the subject, but I would like to retain my suspicion of all scribblers who are too keen on Flaubert; they tend to be men and women who value the artist, with all his prerogatives (including that of being a son of a bitch in the name of art), over actual art. I also think that Flaubert perhaps more than any other major novelist set the novel off on another, less rewarding track, along which it puffs all too happily today.

Which brings me to Theodore Dreiser. (One moment here while I adjust my soapbox.) I quite understand your being put off by Dreiser's style; I, too, am put off by it. His personality would have put you off even more. No-one toted around more stupid ideas. Dreiser found lots to like in Communism and Fascism both. He held that something called "chemisms" were responsible for much human behavior. He was gross in his sexual appetites; you wouldn't want to leave him alone in a room with your great-grandmother. Yet with his wretched prose, his stupid ideas, his entirely unappealing personality, Dreiser wrote some of the most powerful American novels going: partly because he was onto great themes – the hunger of the underdog, the struggle against the loaded dice of destiny, the drama of ambition – and partly because the sources of his literary power are so mysterious.

I was interested in your mentioning Sinclair Lewis as among the novelists who excited your youthful passion for the novel. I haven't read a Lewis novel for nearly fifty years. I read him for all the wrong reasons when I was young: so that I could be contemptuous of the middle-class (the Babbitts and the Mainstreeters) and have large segments of my countrymen down upon which I could look. I do remember liking the novel *Arrowsmith*, which is about a biological scientist, because it was interesting in itself and because it made Lewis seem larger, smarter about the world, more than a mere debunker. Reading Sinclair Lewis was part of growing up in America, at least in our generation. One read Lewis, one read H.L. Mencken, one learned to despise one's own social class: Lewis's Babbitts, Mencken's "booboisie." In America, the way education works is that one spends the first twenty or so years of one's life acquiring lots of coarse ideas, which leaves the remainder of one's life to try to shed them. In England you at least got to retain some Greek and Latin declensions.

Sinclair Lewis and Mencken are a good reminder that the world needs debunkers, but not for very long. Too often what they have debunked disappears, leaving everyone to wonder what the fuss was about. (Wouldn't it be nice to have the good old boring middle class back, in place of the even more boring bohemian-hip-hep-foodie-work-out-minded middle class that has replaced it?) Then, owing to the curious twists of history, sometimes things that had been debunked begin to look good. I seem to remember reading John Marquand's *The Late George Apley* in the 1960s, and finding myself siding with poor old Apley, even though this was not at all what Marquand intended. No powerful debunkers on the scene at present – none, that is, of any genuine literary power. The last two I can name were Dwight Macdonald and Malcolm Muggeridge, both of whom gave me, in their day, much enjoyment. Macdonald is famous, at least to me, for saying "Every time I say Yes I get in trouble," by which he meant that whenever he was for something, he usually got it wrong. What he chiefly got wrong was politics; he loved the student revolution, poor dope. Muggeridge of course committed all the major sins and then near the end of his life, in a neat reversal, turned in his tail and pitchfork and became, of all things, a chirpy booster of the Lord Jesus. This from a man who once wrote a review of a book in which Beaverbrook claimed that Jesus was, in his only slightly different way, a great press lord. Muggeridge gave his review the title – a title never topped, in my estimation – of "Jesus!".

This seems to be turning into a lit crit sermonette-lecture, but I thought I should also mention that I have been reading *The Collected Stories of Francis Wyndham* as my bedtime book. Wyndham's is a name I have seen around for ages but without knowing much about what lay behind it. He was born in 1924, and is still rather quietly extant. Wyndham is, I suspect by deliberation, a minor writer. He wrote well, but was modest in his ambition, not very productive, content to give small but real pleasure to his readers – and, I assume, to himself. Nothing wrong with any of this. To give pleasure is a fine thing, *n'est-ce pas*? Some of the writers dearest to me – Max Beerbohm, Sydney Smith – are minor writers. Proust may have set out to be a minor writer but somehow slipped off the track and became almost in spite of himself, capital M Major. I wonder if I mayn't be a minor writer myself, though I may write too damn much to qualify.

Best, Joe

Dear Joe,

There is an old theatrical tale about the Lunts which applies, *mutating* the *mutanda*, to me now. They, Alfred and Lynn (as I never got to call them), were in a long run on Broadway and the prompter had the easiest job in seven states, just sitting in the corner and waiting for the final curtain. And then one night there was a silence that didn't end (the kind I sometimes wish Pinter had written for his own use) and the prompter realised, with panicky astonishment, that his services were required. He found the place and whispered the line, which was not, it seemed, audible on stage. The silence continued. The prompter (*souffleur* is a much prettier term for the job, isn't it?) said the line more loudly, whereupon Alfred ambled to the prompt corner and said, 'We know the line, we just don't know which one of us says it'. Relevance? I know that one of us owes the other a letter but I don't know which. So, because I have felt little appetite for anything (Iran, the banks, the decline of the Western) which might be happening in the world that we left behind for our ten days in Puglia, apart from the pleasure of our *viavai continuo*, as the old Italian linguaphone put it, here goes.

There is some comedy in our reciprocal but never symmetrical view of the cultures we have observed from afar, enviable smart New York (usually) intellos from over here and Maurice Bowra and chums from where you sit. I overestimate what you knew/know about and you overestimate what I scarcely do, but might have, perhaps if I had gone to Oxford. A 'friend' of mine called Julian Mitchell who wrote a lot of historical TV and one hit play, *Another Country*, somewhat Alan Bennett *avant la lettre* (she does run on, that one, but then again, look who's talking AND talking), also wrote a nice mini-*bouquin* about how he had always wanted to go to Cambridge but then somehow bumped into (aha!) Maurice Bowra and was recruited to Wadham, to which, in those distant days, the Warden (M.B.) had discretionary rights to a fast-track entry for those who took his fancy, Julian among them. Mitchell was converted to Oxonian *morgue* in short order somewhat as I was to Cambridge after always hoping to go to Oxford. Happy Chiasmus, as Bowra (an eager, not to say incurable punster) would certainly have said if he had heard about it. He had a very brave spell in the trenches in the Great War and was disposed to twit E.R. Dodds – a much more important classicist and author of the ground/mould-breaking *The Greeks and the Irrational* – who was a Conbscuebrtuak* (more commonly written as Conscientious) Objector, by asking him, 'What did you do in the war, Doddy?' I don't know if the biography that you were reading included this alleged witticism, but there it was, and more than once, I gather. The jibe just may have been Bowra's acknowledgment, in the academic style, of a *miglior fabbro*, rather than any crude comparison of his virility with Dodds's (supposed) wimpishness; or it could have been an opening he didn't want to miss.

The trouble with Bowra, for those who didn't know him, was that he may have loved Greece (and Greek love, as they still tend to call it: James Davidson does in a recent very long uncloseted volume, of the kind Maurice could never write in the dark days when buggery was a crime unless you could put a college wall, and the benefit of clergy, between yourself and what John Schlesinger – similarly apprehensive in his day – used to call 'Mavis Polizei') but – wait for it and it'll come, like a closed parenthesis in William Faulkner – what Bowra WROTE about, e.g., Ancient Greek Lyric was dull, dull, dull. He evidently had all sorts of vital qualities but he couldn't write a lively sentence.

There was a Cambridge equivalent called J.T. Sheppard (NOT the good one), the gay-as-a-bard provost of King's and a specialist on Homer, I believe; Sheppard made King's a gay enclave, in which my old friend *feu* (the first of the *feux*, but alas never the last) Simon Raven was happily at home, until chucked out for heterosexual conduct unbecoming a Kingsman (while a research fellow, he got a nice girl pregnant). Simon went to my school Charterhouse and all his life longed to be taken for an Etonian (or for Evelyn Waugh, but then so did Evelyn Waugh want to be an OE). Raven was a showy classicist, despised by my other old friend, the great Hellenist Peter Green who was/is as diligent and thorough as Simon was flash and superficial (never wholly dislikeable qualities). Peter too went to Charterhouse, but never had delusions of Etonianism; he made the crucial mistake of criticising his betters (the Cambridge classical professoriate) both all too accurately and – here's the big mistake – prematurely, by which I mean BEFORE they had elected him to be one of their number, as a result of which – in logic there are no surprises – they never did. He made a world elsewhere, much bigger than theirs, and more productive too.

Oh before I forget: that asterisk I flashed a little earlier, next to 'Conbscuebrtuak'. The C word in this case is, of course, an electronic misprint for, yes, conscientious. Why I left it was (a) laziness and (b) because it reminded me of a rule which Bowra must have taught to first-year students (though some of his knew it from their sixth-forms) which in Latin is formalised as *difficilior potius*, meaning that in textual emendation the more difficult reading is to be preferred, since copyists are (no, WERE) more likely to change an unusual word into one that they knew than the other way round, sorta. Today there is no vestige of truth in this idea, since we rarely correct e-scripts with the care once exacted from scholars, and misprints are left to stand, eventually to become variant readings, etc. So the world's great age is beginning to count against it and we are all on the raod, or indeed the road, to incoherence. A mess of pottage will soon be a pot of message and no-one will know the difference.

I notice that we have met in a public place who never met in a private one: John Podhoretz's *Commentary*: your Isaac Rosenfeld which I was privileged to read before J.P. did his neatening stuff and my movie thing which he has cosmeticised into what, I believe, is called in *soutien*-gorgeland an A-cup, small but somewhat well formed apart from one sentence which I could not understand and cannot believe that I wrote. You saw an uninhibited version which was somewhat spicy and lashed out lightly at Master Teachout (a character derived from Jonson, B., another beneficiary of benefit of clergy), which I was not suffered to do *coram publico*. HE, on the other hand, was allowed to advertise his operatic adaptation of, of all things, Willie Maugham's 'The Letter', which has been melodramatised pretty well with B. Davis and that actor who always played Willie's *alter alter*. Maestro Teachout dares to anticipate a thunderous reception, which is as good a way of getting the public to rain on your parade as I can well imagine.

I somewhat fear that Podhoretz jun., against whom I have nothing, not least because he is a prompt payer, has made a mistake at, as the bridge players say, 'trick one' by signalling his editorial arrival by redesigning the mag. He printed a letter from Indignant of Newark (or wherever) deploring his inability to leave well alone and I fear Indignant may be right: the mag you used to write for had more apparent bottom than the rejacketed version. J.P. has a difficult job, it seems, since he is in hock to a set of presumptions which cannot be changed without losing the faithful. However, he is smart enough to ask you, and me, to write for him, so good luck to him. I have watched a magazine which, in my innocence and quondam affluence, I helped to set up a decade and more ago, *Prospect*, become revamped and duller as all my investment, literal and metaphorical, drained away. I realised, much too slowly, that the editor, an Etonian with a famous name Goodhart but who is not very good and does not have a lot of heart, was intent on making sure that no contributor upstaged him by a clever turn of phrase or a bold opinion; result, he drives a dreary vehicle down the middle of the road. Editors can be judged not by their editorials but by their capacity to urge/inspire/require others to astonish them by the quality of their prose.

The fear of being outfireworked is the mark of every organising hack; the provocation of excellence is, as Cyril Connolly and Willliam Shawn (we are always told) demonstrated, what makes a born editor. I wrote a column for *Prospect* for the first two years or so of its existence and then Goodhart (to hear his voice is to recognise a natural station announcer) said to me that the trouble with my column was that some people loved it and some people hated it. I dared to say that that was the same thing, as far as inciting people to buy the mag was concerned, but he said, no, SOME people liked it but just as many hated it. What the lank grimmikin doesn't/can't understand was that both sets of people were confessing that they reacted to what I wrote. So he fired me. And kept the money. He is what we now can agree to call a Conbscuebrtuak.

Your service. New balls.

Tout à toi,
Freddie

Dear Freddie,

I spent yesterday morning, as I assume you did yesterday afternoon, sitting in my pajamas for nearly five hours watching the men's final at Wimbledon. The American television network, NBC, used to advertize the event as *Breakfast at Wimbledon*, for the finals are played when it is 8.00 a.m. here. A cup of coffee on the lamp table at my side, a copy of the Evelyn Waugh–Nancy Mitford Letters on my lap, I sat for the full match, moving only for what the US Army, in its delicacy, refers to as a "piss call." I read Waugh–Mitford letters during commercial breaks. I had bet the monumental sum of $5 on Federer – I had him against the field – but found myself rooting for Roddick. Generally my antipathies are divided, but this time my sympathies were, for both players seemed quite decent, for athletes in a thuggish age positively *honnêtes hommes*.

I watched the entire proceedings, until the interviews at the close, with the sound turned very low, so that I could just barely hear the pock of the balls being rallied but not the intrusive voices of the announcers: in America, John McEnroe and an authoritative former secondary player named Mary Carillo. Both rattle on without surcease. (You don't happen to have a surcease on you, do you?) A few weeks ago, I heard an English broadcast team covering an Arthur Ashe–Jimmy Connors Wimbledon final, and they did it with splendid reticence, allowing for long stretches of silence based on the astonishing notion that they didn't need to describe everything that we were already seeing.

I was interested to see the former Wimbledon champions in the stadium and interviewed afterward – Sampras, who looked as if he would give up two of his grand slam titles to have his hair back; Borg, who looks as if he adeptly (and probably rightly) missed every Ingmar Bergman movie and hasn't wasted much time on a heavier thought than how can I delay this orgasm; and above all Rod Laver, who is my contemporary (eighteen months younger than I, actually) and looked very pink and well on the road to decay. Are you not regularly taken aback – fuck it, I mean shocked – to realize that people a bit younger than you look so ancient? Surely, one thinks, I do not look so dim, dreary, decrepit – not me, the kid, boyo himself, Mrs. Epstein's lovely son, surely not.

Laver, Rosewall, Hoad, Emerson & co. may have been tennis as good as it ever got. Much of this was owed to Harry Hopman, I gather, who took these country- and working-class boys in hand and made great players and good men out of them. They played in an era where ego, like the most artful drop shots, was nicely disguised. An American player of their personal quality was Arthur Ashe, who combined lovely manners with a winning temperament and strong serve and was a gent – perhaps the last gent in American tennis.

What you say about the dullness of Maurice Bowra's writing is agreed upon by all hands. Different explanations are provided. One is that his first Oxford tutor, a philosophy don named H.W.B. Joseph, by all accounts a fierce dryasdust, shook Bowra's confidence in his own abilities, and caused him, for the remainder of his days, to exclude his natural ebullience from his writing. The other explanation is that Bowra thought that things Greek were too sacred to allow invasion by personality, or charm, even his own. The result is that Bowra lives by his mots: "Buggers can't be choosers"; "He is the sort of man who stabs you in the front"; "Met X [a man noted for his false geniality]. He gave me the warm shoulder." To be known as an amusing, even great talker is not to be known for very long, I suspect. Bowra must have been aware of this. He was also (insecurely) aware that his homosexuality rendered him vulnerable, as he might have said, on several fronts (also backs), though some claim he was bisexual. (Stephen Spender, one of my least favorite characters from this era, used to say, "I'm neither homosexual nor heterosexual; I'm just sexual" – with the word pronounced "sessual.") For Bowra the best defense was a good offense, and he was much of the time on the offensive, knocking down everyone, even, among friends, other friends. His disciples – and he set out to create disciples, the Bowristas, they were called – lined up after his death to declare how life-enhancing being with him was; my sense is that being with him may have been much jollier than being him.

Reading about Bowra, I cannot but think, yet again, of my dear friend Edward Shils, who resembled him in many ways. Like Bowra, Edward was one of those portly men, with a fair-size stomach (front-footage is the way I prefer to think of it), but who was nonetheless all muscle. Edward, Bowraesquely, was also, as I said earlier, a very witty put-down artist. When I once introduced him to the bounderish Henry Fairlie, Edward said, "Ah, yes, Mr. Fairlie, so good to meet you. You wrote some brilliant things in the 1950s [it was then 1978]. What has happened to you? I am told that you've become a socialist. Justify yourself please." When Fairlie, who was half in the bag with drink, said that his newfound socialism derived from hearing Michael Harrington lecture in Chicago, Edward quickly riposted, "Ah, Michael Harrington in Chicago – surely a case of worst comes to worst." Like Bowra, Edward conversationally dominated most rooms in which he found himself. He wasn't a bore, or a boor, about it; he simply knew more than anyone else in the room and could be very amusing about what he knew. Unlike Bowra, Edward wasn't a pun or reversal of clichés man, but specialized in comically extended metaphors. I vividly recall one in which he described his French as in the same condition a cabinet of crystal might be in after a night of the Blitz. He once described, in great detail, the two observations Saul Bellow would have after spending two hours seated upon the lap of the Queen of England: 1. That she had no understanding of the condition of the modern artist; and 2., That she was an anti-Semite. Edward was also a great appreciator of the wit of others. He began the English part of his life after the war at the London School of Economics, then was made a Fellow at King's, and, when he found the atmosphere there noxious, took up a fellowship at Peterhouse, where he became Hugh Trevor-Roper's main confidant in his battle with the unpleasant Fellows there. Because he spent only half the year at Cambridge – and the other at the University of Chicago – Edward's devotion to it was nowhere like so intense as Bowra's to Oxford, for without Oxford Bowra may not be said to have existed. Finally, unlike Bowra, Edward Shils had no need for disciples or to form a cult round himself. Anthony Powell is good on this aspect of the cultishness of Bowra: "Bowra himself, with all his intelligence and spoken wit, remained throughout life inexplicably unhandy at writing. He was a capable, if academic and rather uninspiring literary critic. His comic poems were comic, no more. They possessed no unique quality. Any field in which he did not excel was a distress to him, the literary one most of all; therefore I think – for young men who wanted to develop along lines of their own – it was best to know Bowra, then get away; if necessary return to him in due course to appreciate the many things he had to offer."

A Bowra-like cult currently exists in the United States behind the figure of Leo Strauss, a cult, unlike the Bowristas, that is now in its third generation. One wouldn't think there would be all that much to be cultish about in the less than lucid writings of the master, Herr Leo, but members of it apparently derive great pleasure from being in the club. None among them, it must be said, is quite first class, but then the first-classness of the great man himself is itself far from authenticated. Here I must insert that I find it impossible to imagine you – or me – as lining up to be a disciple of anyone, from Jesus on down. We are too objectionable – make that objection-filled – too contrary, ornery, difficult generally to fall in line under anyone else's own banner but that of the Jokey Jakeys, which is how I prefer to think of our own two-man leaderless, doctrine-proof cult.

Your account of your dealings with the editor of *Prospect* reinforces a theory of mine: this theory holds that the best editors are not themselves writers, or at least not primarily writers, or if primarily writers then blocked or manqué ones. Included on the list of these editors are Lord Jeffrey, William Shawn, Cyril Connolly (a failed critic and novelist both), Irving Kristol (when at *Encounter*), William Phillips and Philip Rahv of *Partisan Review*. Not being writers, they weren't in competition with contributors to their own magazines; they understood their job to consist of publishing great things by other people. Your victory as a writer was also theirs as editors, your success redounded to their glory. True writers, I should even go so far to say, are probably too selfish to be great editors. I say this after having myself edited a magazine for some twenty-three years, without for a moment ever thinking of myself as other than a writer. So put that on your cat and stroke it.

Best, Joe

Dear Joe,

I had a friend at Cambridge called Gordon Pask who, so he said, and I some-what believe, began his PhD dissertation with the words 'As I have said before'. Gordon was a little old man in his late twenties, I suppose, with the mad inventor's gleam in large, rarely blinking blue eyes, a tangle of overgrown hair and teeth which disproved the old philosophical line that one cannot feel the pain of another: you had only to look at his brown mouth to have his toothache. He lived in a louche house in a sidestreet opposite my college. 5 Jordan's Yard was the *rendezvous des Bohémiens* in 1950s Cambridge. It literally bulged with a shifting population: so flimsy were its walls, so pliable its single stairway, so uncertain its floors, that it seemed as fugitive as the pleasures it housed. Beetle and I spent weekends there, lying on a mattress on the concrete (and God knows what else impastoed on it) floor of the kitchen; bliss it was. Sometimes Gordon would come in, in the middle of the night, to sate his craving for marmalade (imagine it working into those crusted crevices in what was left of his teeth, or don't). 'Don't disturb yourselves, my dears', he would say, stepping across us with his short legs. He was once asked whether aspirin was addictive. 'Certainly not', he said, 'and I ought to know: I take fifty a day'.

He took other things too, since he regarded a twenty-four hour day as inadequate for the kind of concentrated work that he was doing, on his bedroom floor upstairs, on a new computer. He stretched his days to thirty-six hours and so managed to complete the elaborate circuits on a machine which, among other things, printed the music played to it. It also generated coloured patterns in response to music, but it did not (of course!) repeat the same patterns for the same musical phrases. Thus I learnt the key term 'negative feedback'. One gets a lot of that in the literary life, I have discovered, but not in the form of brightly coloured patterns. Gordon married a large Jewish Communist. When they had a child, just the one I think, he called it 'the gadget'. I have not seen Gordon for fifty years, but he seems more real to me than a lot of people I come across in London.

Beetle and I were lucky to be able to be together in Jordan's Yard. Had she come to my rooms and been caught there after hours, I should certainly have been sent down. In my fourth year (I had switched to philosophy and persuaded the college to let me stay; they even extended my scholarship, which was very generous indeed), a bunch of us rented a house and lived in what was called 'unlicenced digs', on account of the license it allowed us, of course. *Lucus a non lucendo*. Let's not get into it. Since I was fourth-year and the house, in Montague Road, was well out of the centre of town, no-one asked any questions. My friend Tony Becher lived there with us; he got a first in Moral Sciences when I received only a 2:1. My life was blighted for a full day or two. One of the St John's College classics dons called Guy Lee (later an enduring friend) was aware that Beetle was in Cambridge. I think she cycled past his house twice a day. One day, he said to my tutor, an ex-Olympic shot-putter, multi-blued athlete and Aristotle expert, 'Do you know about Freddie Raphael living out in Montague Road with that beautiful black-haired girl?' My tutor said, 'No'. Guy said, 'Neither do I'. *Vive l'Angleterre, parfois.*

Which brings me to the confession *du jour*: sometimes a light surprises a Christian while he sings, but that sort of thing doesn't happen to me (I was converted to Roman Catholicism for about two minutes, while on the top of a 74 bus in the Cromwell Road, when nineteen and still prepared to believe that G. Greene was a serious novelist, when not being an entertainer: never trust a writer who clears his throat before assuming his plume, he will soon plume his assumptions, but then – still on the top deck of the bus – I saw – this in 1950 – a woman in a white shirt walking along the pavement and I also saw – rarity of rarities – that she was not wearing a brassiere – a trisyllable in dem days – and one of her pretty breasts bobbed its bruise-dark nipple at me, and in an instant, I was lost to popery; and, like Orpheus, looking back). None of that is what I scheduled for my confessional spiel, but postponement is one of the great arts of life, so here's the thing: I realised on Sunday that I was/am more English ('There'll always be a Britain' doesn't play for me) than my Chicago Semite (forget the Viennese, woeful folk and don't let the waltz deceive you) boasts might mislead you to think. Why Sunday? Memories of evensong in a dappled churchyard? No, cricket. CRICKET so exciting that Beetle and I sat and watched ball by ball for two or three hours. Never mind if Federer has allowed things to go to his headerer recently. Sunday was the *fifth* day of the Test Match. They had been batting and bowling, England and Australia and then England again, morning, afternoon and evening and amassing more runs, *ici et là*, than I can be bothered to recount for all that time. The climax of the game, after four++ days, came not when one or the other had to win, but when England, faced with a deficit beyond repair, had to keep its batsmen at the wicket long enough to deny the Australians the win to which their huge run surplus ought, in any sane game, to have entitled them, but which required them to remove ALL the English batsmen but one (i.e. 10 out of 11).

Are you still there? Do you, with all your learning, know the poem by a certain Newbolt (Henry, Sir) in which there is a deathly hush in the Close tonight . . . the last man in . . . and . . . I'm too choked to go on. Well, that was where Beetle and I were: watching the penultimate pair, an old pro and a bowler who shouldn't have been able to stop the Australians rearranging his furniture (i.e. bowling him out) resisting everything that the antipodals could . . . no, not throw at them, since bowling has to be delivered with an unbent arm, but . . . spin and sling at them. Twenty-fumf minutes to go and . . . the better batsman was out, and the last man, a bearded sub-continental person who wears a black skullcap (full) and a guru's beard, had to hold out, had to. And did, and did. Gunga-din to the life, that was Monty Panesar. After five days, in which Australia had done everything but the final thing, the English HELD ON FOR A DRAW. Is there any other game in the world so protracted which can reach a climax in which NOTHING has been decided; no totting of runs so far, no adjudication, no play-off, nothing even? A draw, folks, and we're clapping and smiling and have to go and have a swim to cool orf. And I'm thinking of my father, keeping wicket for his side – the Nomads – while wearing GLASS glasses, and how he would have loved it.

There is, you may know, a thing about English-type Jews and cricket. Craig Raine's hagiographical issue of *Areté* devoted to Harold Pinter (but omitting the episode where he walked on the water and the one when he fed the 5,000) has Ronnie Harwood, a man of the utmost charm and diligence, playwright and man about letters, the kosher Michael Holroyd, but shorter textually speaking, telling how Harold captained his own XI (often the only way lit. persons can get into the team) and took it VERY seriously, to the extent – which Ronnie seems to think cricket – of deterring his men, when fielding, from applauding the incoming enemy Captain. I don't like that myself. I am a terrible loser, but I do like some comely hypocrisy. *Mild* applause is one of the ways proper Englishmen announce their condescensions.

Your memory of reading Moravia's *Boredom* (which makes him sound a little more Robbe-Grillet than he was) but not remembering anything in it planted a small pic in memory's hide and I DID remember something. I read it when we lived in Rome, so even that little crumb Eric Korn will excuse me, maybe, for mentioning that I read it in Italian; the phrase that stuck tells you little about the finesse of my sensibilities, it's no more than '*un colpo del suo sesso*', delivered by the female in the piece to the artist, I seem to remember he was, whose boredom she must have hoped to alleviate. Women actually bumping you with their ... parts, that never happened in my Pubic School. Daring of Alberto to call his book *La Noia*. My *ami* (never *intime*) Louis Malle directed a movie called *Ma nuit chez Maud*, in which a Catholic fellow spends a chaste night avec la dame of that name and, of course, some smartass critic had to headline his piece '*Ennui chez Maud*'. Which didn't stop Truffaut making *La nuit américaine*, which wasn't boring at all and, he has to mention, contained a little visual tribute to *Two for the Road*. Which didn't prevent a man from Gallimard who had just seen my review of the Lanzmann autobiog from asking the *TLS* frogman '*Qui est* Frederic Raphael?' Up your ass, *amigo*, as they say at Lord's cricket ground, where our daughter Sarah has a painting hanging, a portrait of a legendary West Indian all-rounder, Garfield Sobers. He liked her a lot; she got him right AND she made him laugh. Even that she could do. Fuck it, is right; and so is *quand même*. And that's all you get *ici bas*.

Tout à toi,
Freddie

Dear Freddie,

Please to excuse this slight gap in our correspondence, but this past Sunday my hard drive died (*olev a sholem*), which was a lot of nerve. I dragged my machine into a not-so-nearby Apple store, where a small, emaciated man with yellow teeth told me that "this baby has had it." Fortunately, I had "backed-up" the manuscripts on which I am currently working and our exchanges, but I lost lots of secondary items: a few barely begun short stories, e-mail addresses, old letters of recommendation I had written for students, bookmarks, and so forth. I bought a new computer, and had to reinstall my e-mail and other old programs in it, and then had to learn about how my new word-processing program works. All this not so easy for your hands-off older gentleman, but, somehow, I seem to have got it done, though I am still undergoing frustrating jigeroos. But, as that old American bullshitter Ralph Waldo Emerson liked to say, "Man rides machine." To which I would respond, in the spirit of my grandchildren, "Sure, Waldo, yeah, right."

You are correct when you suggest that the great, all-but-uncrossable divide between Englishmen and Americans is baseball and cricket. I have known only one man who genuinely crossed that divide, and was a knowledgable admirer of both games, a black Jamaican named Jervis Anderson, who was a friend of mine and whom I asked to write about C.L.R. James for the *American Scholar* when I was editing the magazine. Jervis was a solid writer – he worked for the *New Yorker* for most of his too-short life (he died in his fifties of a heart attack) – if not, alas, a memorable one. He was unmemorable, I think, because his writing had no fist: no anger, no attack to it; it was too well-mannered, too quiet, too wanting in point of view. He was a lovely man, which by itself perhaps is sufficient to explain why he wasn't a stronger writer. The essay, in which I wasn't in the least disappointed, was chiefly about James' cricket book *Beyond a Boundary*, though Jervis allowed that the book "will be helpful in explaining some of the personal and public values that lie behind the game; but not even he [James], I suspect, is capable of making the game itself – the techniques of this leisurely and phlegmatic English institution – intelligible to an American audience. Its practical techniques and the reticences of its inner life – its aesthetics and tactics – can only be dull and elusive to an audience reared on the swifter and more declarative energies of baseball." What I find most interesting about this last sentence is that for many Americans, especially younger Americans, baseball itself is today thought much too slow and therefore dull. Cricket to them would constitute a punishment equivalent to going on the rack. I have not myself seen a cricket match, though I like the clothes, the plock sound that the bat striking the ball makes. "Only people with cricket in their bones can make sense of how the game is played," wrote Jervis. But the crux is, I suspect, that most of us cannot come deeply to love a game that we didn't play when we were young.

I begin my day, after beleaking myself, by making my tea and settling in for an hour or so of reading and allowing my skin to unwrinkle itself. The last week or so this reading has been the second volume of the letters of Isaiah Berlin. You will by now have seen A.N. Wilson's attack on these letters in the *TLS*; none of Wilson's attack is untrue, yet it is too far from the entire truth. Berlin was of course snobbish and no doubt tiresome in lots of ways, but he was also astonishing in many others. One doesn't come upon his degree of prolixity very often; he was a true logorrheaic; and the logorrheaic will always use seven words where one will do. I once asked Berlin to write a book review for me of 1,500 words, and he returned a letter of roughly 2,000 explaining why he could not do so. So in these letters he explains to a correspondent that he must be brief, then prattles on for five pages.

He was also, I suspect, a major-league neurotic, our Shahay, as his parents and *intimes* called him. He suffers from Oblomovism and cannot stir himself. He cannot make decisions, and when he does, feels they are always the wrong ones. He finds writing painful, but less painful than reading what he has written. His only love-affairs appear to have been with other men's wives, and he finally marries one of them at the age of forty-six: a very wealthy one, let it be added. He never had children; nor could he have done, being himself the perpetual spoiled child.

All this might evoke sympathy, as neurotics sometimes do, but doesn't here because Berlin turns out to be a neurotic very much in business for himself. He angles his way into an All Souls fellowship, regularly renewing it by promising ambitious books on which he doesn't deliver. He is offered the wardenship of Nuffield College, which he pretends to agonize over, causing delay and complication all round. He reports his (false) conflict about his decision to several friends; people offer him earnest advice. Much self-dramatizing ensues. But his not taking the job was never in doubt; the college was too *arriviste* – it specialized in social science, for God's sake – for his tastes. When he finally turns Nuffield down, naturally enough everyone there is ticked off, having been made to wait so long for a decision, though he tells them that he cannot possibly say how deeply honored he has been by the offer. He is forever telling people and institutions that their letters or conduct or offers mean more to him than he can possibly convey, though he requires hundreds and hundreds of words not to convey it.

Little as he pretends to care about his writing and lecturing, no-one is touchier about criticism. He sees insults everywhere; he is described by the *Listener* as "the Paginini of lecturers" and thinks it makes him sound vulgar. He discovers bullet wounds when no shots were quite fired. He is always misunderstood, poor baby, misread, insufficiently respected. Yet no-one is more critical of other people. He will thank someone with heavy-handed sincerity for his hospitality, then report to someone else on how tedious the man can be. He reports to Maurice Bowra how crucial his influence in freeing him has been in his life, then, on any number of occasions, writes meanly to others about Bowra's flaws. At one point he writes to John Sparrow to express his extreme irritation about Bowra's dominating talk with a Russian poet named Vyacheslav Ivanov, when he, Isaiah, should have been the dominant figure, but instead "O.B. [for the Old Boy] went on in his terrible French about nothing – platitudes about Sophocles, about Russia, about Rome, about everything of a most shaming, appalling kind . . ."

Noel Annan, who loved him, he describes to another party as "having no substance." Berlin truckles to friends but always reserves the right to attack them to other friends, whom in turn he will later also get round to attacking. The truckling worked splendidly for him; it allowed everyone he wished to do so to believe that he held them in extraordinarily dear regard. This worked on figures as various as Chaim Weizmann and society hostesses. At the same time, he was able to convey his own brilliance, so that they were all delighted to have such a dazzling courtier.

Weizmann wanted him to assist him in nation-building in Israel, and give up wasting his time attempting to teach English schoolboys. He, Berlin, stood by Israel; he remained anti-Communist, and never fell for anti-anti-Communism (which held that we're just as bad as they are, probably a good bit worse). But he was without any loyalty to human beings that I can make out.

Yet brilliant he could be. The letters contain dazzling portraits of E.H. Carr, Picasso, Stuart Hampshire, Ben Gurion, Raymond Aron. He can even be funny, as when he describes a visit from Mike Todd, who wants to engage his help as "an historical adviser" for a movie he wants to make of *War and Peace*. He refers to Todd's arrival flapping "an enormous cad's camel-hair coat, with a huge, outsize cigar." The index to this book is as star-studded as any I have read since Count Harry's Kessler's Diary.

All this and I am less than two-thirds of the way through the book. Prolixity, as you will have discovered, has led to prolixity. I have used nearly the full budget of my words rattling away about the prolixity of I. Berlin. This leaves me no room to comment on Gordon Pask's teeth and much else, so I had better quit here.

Best, Joe

Dear Joe,

Your article on the biography of Bowra and your remarks on A.N. Wilson's review of the Berlin Letters, and on the letters themselves, compose a little Oxford-style bouquet of barbed blossoms. Wilson's initials are the same as those of the character who, in both cricket and football team selections, is inscribed – at the bottom of the listed – as A.N. Other, a missing player who has yet to be identified, but clearly never an early or desired selection. I have never met Wilson but suspect that I have some kind of an enemy in him since, after chapter and versifying why, I declined (for somewhat explicit reasons) to write a movie script from a novel of his in which a Tory MP, if I remember rightly, gets caught *in flagellante delicto* and laborious satirical consequences follow. It is not untypical of Wilson (who was once memorably described as a 'young fogey', a typically Oxonian/Bowra-esque less-is-less style of epigrammatic designation, but smartly pertinent in this instance) that in his satire he took care to dump, so to say, on his own doorstep. Self-advertisement and self-denigration cohabit in the Oxford psyche. In some ways, the appearance of internecine hostility, the regular news of schism and feuds, is a disarming device (even though the outbreaks of *odium academicum* are every bit as savage as their publicity) which prevents outsiders from being dangerously envious and hostile. The in-group are reportedly so vile to each other (A.J.P. Taylor and Trevor-Roper were a cardinal case) that those not in the magic circle can, if naïve enough, be grateful for exemption from the swinish flightiness of those who, in fact, are iffing and butting each other in a field of clover camouflaged to look like nettles. As for the nettles, they are all edible if you know how to cook them, or how to be nice to cook.

Oxford seems to have a history of more cruelty in professorial appointments than Cambridge; probably because more prestige used to attach to

Oxford (especially Regius) professorships than to consolation prizes in the
Fens. A.J.P. Taylor was the favourite for the Regius Professorship which Trevor-
Roper, who had published markedly less, was awarded. Taylor then became a
petulantly resentful anti-Oxonian, turned less inside-out than outside-in. Our
château-owning neighbour in the Perigord, Jonathan Sumption, an excellent
historian of the 100 Years War (three vols. so far, taking us fifteen years in) who
was for a while a fellow of Magdalen (or is it Magdalene in Oxford? A silent e
can speak volumes about a man's belongingness) before he decided to make
mucho dinero by becoming a QC specialising in company law, told me that
Alan Taylor, a left-wing columnist and celebrity on chat-shows and TV in
1960s England, deliberately and pettily broke the terms of a college lectureship
which he had been given (he altered the topic wilfully so that it fell outside the
limits of the endowment) in order, it seems, to dare the Fellows to do something about it, since he was such a celebrity. They had to suspend him, so he
departed for London where he worked for Lord Beaverbrook (then *the* major
press baron) and made a fortune as a media provocateur.

Taylor made heroes of troublemakers and himself *primus inter* their
number, not least by claiming that the causes of the second world war were
not very different from those of the ones that preceded it. Hitler was a
latter-day Bismarck with a sillier moustache and no propensity to tears when
crossed. The Holocaust gave A.J.P.T. no chance he was willing to take for
naughty heterodoxy, but David Irving had a raging case of met-a-Taylor
effrontery when he denied that anything of significance had happened when
millions of Jews were murdered, especially since they never were.

The nastiest (hence memorable) story about Taylor is of his relationship
with Lewis Namier who was his teacher and who promoted his career. For
some reason (I haven't yet got hold of a recent biography of Namier) they
had a heavy falling out. When Namier was dying, he sent word that he
would like more than anything else to be reconciled with his quondam
protégé. Grievance-adhesive Taylor wouldn't go. Some principles are worse
than having no principles at all; quite a few actually. Namier was a sort of
industrious Isaiah B. He did not turn his back on the Jews, but he did turn his
side (Bowra's 'warm shoulder' supplies an apt figure) and spent most of his
eventually illustrious, unsmiling professional life 'unpacking' (an Oxford
term, much used in philosophy, especially by Gilbert Ryle) the details of the
lives of Georgian members of parliament. Apparently for the purposes only of
accuracy and in order to elucidate the (mostly corrupt) voting patterns and
motives of those long dead Whigs and Tories, Namier devoted years to close

attention to minor figures, but also – some will say – to root himself where he was no natural radish. *Vanished Supremacies* is a title of his that today's English rabbits do not care to conjure with.

A.E. Housman (an Oxonian for export, to Cambridge, where, after failing Greats, he received a professorship) did something analogous to Namier by being assiduously attentive to the *Astronomica* of Marcus Manilius, to whom he devoted five volumes of text and *apparatus criticissimus*; it kept him busy between mid-summer gondoliers, his *amore*-that-dared-not-speak-its-*nome*. Namier was a discreet Zionist, like Isaiah Berlin, and achieved the distinction of a knighthood (he didn't get to go the whole lordly hog), though not, it seems, by the exercise of high-level social clambering. Someone told me that, in his later years, he was sitting in the Athenaeum (the rendezvous des toffs where F.E. Smith used to stop off for a pee on his way to Whitehall, until one of the staff asked him if he was a member, to which he relied 'Don't tell me this is a *club*!') and someone came up to him and said, 'Hullo, Lewis, how are you?' Namier said, 'Am I a physician?' There is the Oxonian English Jew *dans ses oeuvres*, if ever I overheard of one: the putdown, the somewhat Hebraic intonation of an elaborately chosen word ('doctor' wouldn't play, would it?) in the interrogative mode, the implied 'piss off' of the Pissed-Off, it's all there, anecdotally encapsulated.

Berlin was a bird of a different feather. He would not, I think, even in old age, when fearful of being 'ga-garr', as he pronounced it, have allowed himself to vent his asperity on someone who approached him courteously and had first-person rights. I recall in Cambridge in the 1950s, a philosopher remarking 'As I said to Isaiah . . . *Berlin*', quite as if the Berlin bit outranked the proto-Isaiah, and the deutero-. In them days, it was worth boasting having spoken to the man whom A.N.W., who also has a career to hoe, found it politic to put down. I don't think I shall read the letters, but they are, I suspect, no more oily (a v. English word indicating sheeniness) than those of *le petit* Marcel, by which – it may be – they were somewhat inspired. Proust *practised* flattery in such a way that, eventually (which came *très* late in the *jour*), when he had perfected its insincerities, it became its own antidote: so elaborately did he fawn that he became aware that all effusiveness carries its rift of irony; his appreciation of the aristocracy was thus revealed to him by himself as more ferrous than the recipients of his grovels could ever guess. Flattery and put-down coincide in the last volume of *À la recherche du temps perdu*, proof that he had not wasted his time after all. He was, at the end, free. I haven't looked at H. James's letters for a long while, but I can affect to recall that there was the irony of (good-) mannered impersonation in them too; the high style always has a basement, to which the public lift (elevator) does not descend. The liftman does though, with his cap off.

Berlin was not an artist and so, it may be, he was always possessed by his own imposture, never able to transcend it. He was the captive of the manners he aped, and lost everything which could give unity to work or personality. Retrospection is an old Jewish trope that makes memory itself an achievement. Michael Ignatieff, in his allegedly 'superb' biography (the adjective appeared in a recent *TLS*) says that 'his [Berlin's] memory is freakish, so unusually fine-grained as to seem scarcely human . . . he gives the impression of having accumulated everything and lost nothing'. Giving impressions is, in another context, what a certain kind of entertainer does when he imitates what he is not. The English call such people 'impressionists', as against Impressionists, their favourite form of painter, because no-brainers and pretty with it. Ignatieff's bio is (to put the record straight) ill composed, lacking all sense of euphony, and defers all the way. At least Wilson is a bit of a shit. Ignatieff is the smoothies' smoothy. He once sent me a novel of his about Russia with a handwritten *hommage*. Personal tribute? No, I was a possible reviewer.

Berlin's capacity for giving a good impression enabled him to 'pass', not least at St Paul's School, and so become what flatters the British hugely and always: someone who devotes himself to seeming what they are already. The elegance of his diction, like his black coat and striped trousers, promised that he would always try to be worthy of those who were less clever than he was, spoke fewer languages and never read Herder. He was *so* clever and *so* beholden, so superior and so deferential. Didn't H.J. write a story about a butler called, can it have been?, Brooksmith (sounds like an H.J.ish name)? Berlin was an intellectual Jeeves, always more correct than the spoilt young men to whom he supplied the cultural etiquette that would never come naturally to them, yet never quite of their class or number. He was immensely useful, without ever being threatening; he did not even need to be threatened (by anti-Semitism) because he deprecated himself. He knew his place so well that he could be set next to the Queen, the conspicuous non-Us person who could therefore be treated as if he were one. He reflected honour on those who patronised him, the only reason I can think of for his having been given that All Souls fellowship. Oh but then again, Namier would have researched to see whom the Board had relished disappointing by choosing a Jewboy already, ahead of him. Berlin was the Gentile idea of a Jewish joke.

Oh my God, there goes the dinner bell! Next time, promise, George Steiner *fait son entrée.*

Tout à toi,
Freddie

PS A leetle po-faced this epistle; put it down to sly mimesis.

Dear Freddie,

I've owned but not read Lewis Namier's *magnum opus*, but I have read his slenderer vols, on the Revolution of 1848 and on the Jewish question. He was not in the tradition of the brilliant-stylist historians. English wasn't his first language; he was educated in Austria. He was smart about Israel, making the case, which I happen to believe, that it offers protection – however unlikely this may seem at the moment, when it provides an excuse for anti-Semitism – to all still Diasporic Jews; and arguing further, or at least suggesting (my memory on this doesn't even qualify as imperfect), that had Israel existed as a nation by 1930 the Holocaust would have been much less cataclysmic, and might not even have happened. I also fancy an aphorism of Namier's that runs: "We study history to know how things do not happen." Sounds right to me.

In Trevor-Roper's letters to Bernard Berenson, in which the young Hugh (go not) supplies the old Jewish art-connoisseur bandido with gossip in exchange for which he gets regularly to stay at I Tatti, Trevor-Roper describes Namier as "the greatest living historian writing in English . . . He is also, without doubt, the greatest living bore. And for that distinction the competition, I'm afraid, is even hotter."

I used to read A.J.P. Taylor in the *New Statesman*, in its tissue-thin air edition, which I thought quietly grand. He was in possession of a pointillist style, which entailed his using one simple, short sentence – only rarely falling back on subordinate clauses – after another. Rat-a-tat-tat-tat, machine-gun prose it was, and I then thought it most effective. And elegant in its own way; anyone after all can indite the lengthy sentence – I recently read that alcoholism is a great stimulus to the long sentence: see William Faulkner, *passim* – but to jab out one six- or eight-word sentence after required artfulness.

You are right about Taylor's being one of nature's troublemakers, taking mischievousness to a very high power – that stupid book about Hitler in World War Two being the great egregious example. Taylor enjoyed enraging people – ticking them, as the kids used to say, to the max. I do remember that when someone accused Taylor of having extreme views, he replied, in standard economical fashion, "Extreme views weakly held." I also remember Trevor-Roper's clobbering him in the pages of *Encounter* not long after he destroyed Arnold Toynbee. He would later do a similar job on E.H. Carr. All this, at the time, seemed to me high intellectual fun, very stylishly carried out.

Yet from all this the question arises of why it is that intellectuals, scholars, literary men and women, go in so for take-downs? Why can we not leave the house without blackjacks, stilettos, lugers loaded and cocked, our little spray cannisters of malice laced with irony? My guess is that your and my fathers never thought themselves under the burden of riposte and repartee. If someone at the Shell office in London was a fool, your father noted it and moved on, or so I suppose, just as my father more or less respected his business associates based on his judgments of their honesty and acumen, and let it go at that. My father, so far as I know, was quite without grudges of any kind. Is the reason that intellectuals cannot simply move on and let it go that ours is a more fraud-laden business than those of our fathers? Is it that in our line of work too many people seem to be getting away with it, and we feel it our duty to take the knout to them?

For a notable example, an American newsreader named Walter Cronkite died last week. Tributes to him since his demise have been relentless. He was known, as we have been repeatedly told, as "the most trusted man in America." He had a face, as I have previously said in print, that only a nation could love – by which I mean a face that, if looked at closely, was self-satisfied and without subtlety, ignorant and not in the least ashamed of it. Lengthy editorials, in such july (not quite august) journals as the *New York Times*, recounted his reliability. Yet all he could be relied upon for, near as I could ever make out, was appropriate platitudes, rhythmically delivered. He got decisive things entirely wrong. In an introduction to a paperback edition of *1984*, he wrote that Orwell's subject was not just the totalitarianism of the Soviet Union but the United States as well (he intended, in other words, a plague on both their condominiums). I once heard him, at the University of Chicago in the early 1970s, instruct the professoriat that they must continue to inculcate the spirit of dissent in their students – this after the students had come close to setting fire to the joint. He was, in short, a dope, a jerk, a lucky mother-humper, trading in his utter commonplaceness for many shekels and even more fame. And so few people seemed to notice.

Why does it distress me, tick me so maximally, that other people haven't seemed to notice that Walter Cronkite wasn't even fifth-class? Envy? Do I long for his gold and fame? I don't believe I do. But I do want people to get him right. I feel that the overestimation of this schmucklheimer represents a small but serious injustice, a blot on the escutcheon of my countrymen and an outrage to common sense. When I hear old Walter Crankcase praised, I reach not for my gun but my Xanax (or would if I took Xanax).

What is this about? Why do I get so worked up about Walter Cronkite, not to mention Arthur Miller, Edward Albee, Seamus Heaney, Susan Sontag, and so many others. Our fathers, confronted with such characters, would doubtless shake their heads, noting of them all, "Lucky fellows." Mine might have gone a step further to say, "Well, you know you can't really argue with success, can you?" (Oh, Dad, dear Dad, what better to argue with than success, especially of the empty kind?) Certainly he wouldn't have in any way allowed himself to get worked up about it. Meanwhile, his goofy son goes running through the streets, crying out, "The Emperor has no scrotum! The Emperor has no scrotum!" to an unresounding chorus of people closing their windows as he runs by.

Your analysis of Isaiah Berlin strikes me as just right: he was exactly the kind of Englishman other Englishmen wanted a Jewish import to be, the Jeeves of English intellectuals. You are probably correct in your decision not to read Isaiah Berlin's letters. I am myself up to page 600 in the second volume. The year is 1957, and the 46-year-old Shaya has had a good year: been made Chichele Professor of Social and Political Thought and been knighted. He is also married to one of the heiresses of the Gunzbourg family and fortune, and now lives in a house with Tiepolos on the walls and is able to buy 35 Turgenev letters to his wife's grandfather, Baron Horace (Nafthali Herz) de Gunzburg, Russian-Jewish financier, according to the footnote, "promoter of the interests of the Russian Jews, philanthropist and patron of the arts and sciences." None of all this derails him from kissing the bottoms of the mighty. See, sometime, his letter to the widow of James de Rothschild as a model of this lips-to-buttocks application.

You are also dead-on right about Proust's letters, most of which are pure suck-up, smarmy beyond the smarmy, so that it is difficult to believe they could have persuaded anyone who received them. (The editor for Gallimard of Proust's letters, a modest and decent man named Philip Kolb, was my French teacher my first year at university; he was an American who had almost entirely Frenchified himself.) Henry James had nothing of the suck-up to him, at least in my recollection of his letters. The impression I brought away from them was of someone very smart very young. He also wrote the most precise and winning letters of condolence, which may be the true test of the great letter-writer. He did engage in a fair amount of persiflage, or what he called "pure gracious twaddle," which today, I suppose, would be called "impure ungracious twitter." But he did so with no other motive in mind than entertaining his correspondent and, quite as much, himself.

I had a two-hour or so meeting yesterday with Zachary Leader, whom you will remember as Kingsley Amis' biographer and who is currently scrambling about interviewing and reading everything he can in preparation for a biography he is working on about Saul Bellow. Early in our meeting I suggested to him that I sensed a pattern in his choice of subjects: difficult, if not downright unpleasant men who weren't entirely convincing as novelists. As with the Amis, so with the Bellow, a fat volume is planned. How little I envy him this project! Writing a biography of a not-long-dead writer is a mug's game, as T.S. Eliot neglected to say of intellectual fellatio. When I was in my early thirties I signed on to write a biography of John Dos Passos, who was still alive. He died before I was able to interview him, and the project foundered, the advance returned (the bitterest words a literary man can apply to himself). Balzac used to call books that writers dream of but never get around to writing "enchanted cigarettes." He never mentioned another category, books that writers are pleased not to have written, for which my Dos Passos biography heartily qualifies; might they be known as "enchanted prophylactics?" In any case, grubbing about in the life of a less than superior or genuinely significant human being is decidedly not my idea of a good time, and is better left to earnest academics not themselves fully in possession of the long view.

Best, Joe

Dear Joe,

I fear you are right: the literary vocation is a call to malice and envy as well as, we like to think, Higher Things; nothing like the sublime to have an Acherontic downside. I am not very ashamed of a certain kind of malice, as long as it comprises accuracy. The precision of the despised masters of my youth, Sinclair Lewis in particular, but then of Balzac too, is itself a version of satire. Getting things right often looks like caricature or worse; portraits too can be assassinations. When our daughter Sarah was asked to do a portrait of the Master of Jesus College, Cambridge, she went up to see him and was greeted, I am sure, with the condescending courtesy which is the mark of such men. She had been offered a straight commission but, during their meeting, aware that the portrait would be a presentation piece, intended to display a man of dignity and learning, she said, 'I think I should perhaps do a drawing of you first'. The Master said, 'To be sure that you can get a likeness, you mean?' Sarah said, 'So that you can see what you look like'.

She never did the portrait, but then she hated commissions. She also went up to Cambridge and did a drawing of George Steiner, who referred to her when writing to me as 'the divine Sarah', a lazy compliment, some might say. She drew him, but she didn't like the drawing in which, when I look at it in the book of her drawings that was published after her death, she seems to have caught perfectly that face which is squeezed under the weight of the brain behind and above, or by the self-conscious awareness of it.

It is slightly comic that you and I, and many others, can find Berlin and Steiner to be somewhat of a piece, foreigners who managed to enchant, gull, impress the English, but without fooling them. Yet Eliot and Pound, two Yankee arrivistes, managed by a straight-nosed form of imposture to assert themselves over the London of their day. No-one ever said that Eliot was a phoney and everyone, it seems, agrees that he is a major (key Steiner word) poet. Rumour, unless it was a biographer, has it that he composed a lot of his stuff on the typewriter, *e si vede*; there is a sense of the stuff being a little *neat*, somewhat too printer-ready, even when it was more spiritual or whatever all that Ash Wednesdaying is.

I've been asked by the, alas, pretty well penniless Maeceanas who publishes my notebooks to go to Manchester in October (God help us, it's now the month after next) and discuss (as the cant has it) the poems which have influenced my life, moved my spirit and other things that get mentioned only when being Distinguished in front of a festival audience which has recently been celebrity-whipped by Martin Amis (now a Mancunian professor, thus topping, at last, his dad) and Will Self, one of 'your people' as the British say, a writer who, having ridden to the top, or the high, is now, in the odd way of those who might once have been wearing a bag over their heads in public, above all a *moralist*, hostile – of course – to the usual iniquities such as reacting uncharitably to people who try to kill us and Zionistic stuff like that.

When I ask myself, in secret, what the hell poems I am going to parade, I realise that I used to read a good deal of the stuff (including quite a lot of modern Americans including that man whose name I now forget, Rexroth, Kenneth) but that ever since I was told Seamus Heaney was a bard, if not before that, I have eschewed more than I have bitten off. How many people ever scan the poems in the *TLS*? I don't even admire Sylvia Plath, although I do recognise and somewhat admire the shamelessness with which she groped her way to the top by groping Ted Hughes first. We were given his collected works not long ago by a flattering Christmas presenter and I tried, yes, I did, to like/admire/find readable *anything* in that massive whatever the Welsh for *oeuvre* may be. I fear that the only Welsh poem I like is D. Thomas's *Do Not Go Gentile into That. Goodnight!* (which is, of course, what Isaiah did, like a shot), I can't choose that, can I? Most of the things I like seem to be foreign, and most of them Greek or Spanish (here comes that old Sephardic bullshit again, it's in the *sangre*). Lorca and Juan Ramón Jiménez, if not Neruda. A man who writes something called 'We Are Many' seems deliberately to be excluding me.

Steiner's campaign to be the deutero-Isaiah was mounted with a good deal of Alice Aforethought (he has said, with a measure of – as he would say – *insightful veracity*, that the greatest English writing is for children). He arrived from MIT with a note from Oppenheimer. How often grandiose persons have names in the comparative mode, list available, including Jonathan Miller, world-famous in London, a moltimath (implying that he moults and is often broody) who was once asked to contribute to an A-listers' *festspiel* in which they were to describe/discuss what it was like to be good in bed. Jonathan's letter of decline is said to have said that he had asked himself whether Isaiah Berlin would have contributed to such a vol. Apparently not; so nor did Dr M. These be thy g-gods, O Israel. Steiner, I resume, on arriving in the Fens was immediately on the *piano nobile*, having been appointed a Fellow of Churchill College which was still under construction. He imagined himself (his liveliest form of fiction) to have a sponsor *de taille* in the form of Charles – later, Lord – Snow, a New Man whose links with the thermo-nuclear fraternity may have led Oppenheimer to enlist him to mark Steiner's UK card. Little did Steiner (or perhaps Snow himself) know, the laurel and the millstone were one: it *was* somewhat impressive to have Snow on his boots, but it was also disastrous, since it meant that before he had *uttered a polysyllable*, in any one of his three fluent languages or any of his *manifold but not wholly idiomatic* other dialects, Steiner was ripe to be slushed.

I am told (and always believe) that Snow was disliked in Christ's, where he was a Fellow and about which he had written with accuracy approaching malice the one novel of his, *The Masters*, which hides his linguistic poverty and remains a kind of, OK, minor masterpiece. It sports a brilliantly named anti-hero called Jago, a lacklustre Iago who never becomes the Master although *consensu omnium* etc. So persistent was the vendetta against Snow (who was the fat man signalling wildly to be let into Pamela Hansford

Johnson, the wife he had married after (?) she had had her Big One with – was it? – D. Thomas) that some of his colleagues used to clip weather reports from the press of the order of SNOW FALLS HEAVILY IN SCOTLAND and pin them on the noticeboard. *Credo quia possibile?* Works for me.

As a result of being Snow's flake, George also became an immediate target for the infinite (because *moral*) malice of Frank Leavis and his Connection (all the people who A-rated the same books as he did and berated all others) and – I hope this is all true, because I do believe it is – despite Leavis's conviction that he, the Doctor, had been malevolently ostracised by the unprincipled English school and its lazy standard-bearers, the Scrutineers managed to have Steiner yellow-starred as a cosmopolitan generaliser without any specific entitlement to faculty favours. Snow and Leavis had crossed nibs over the article, rather well-intentioned, in which Snow accused Arts people of ignoring scientific culture, etc. Shades of Heidegger and 'Science can't think', which is what Leavis thought. Like all good paranoiacs, he took an article whose author never had him in mind to be an *ad hominem* assault.

By the time Churchill College was ready for occupation, Steiner had to be offered a *college* lectureship, a comedown from the university appointment which he had been semi-promised and was sure (hold the semi-) he would get. I don't know much more about what happened, but G. then contrived to be nominated an *Extraordinary* Fellow of Churchill and lectured to large audiences in the loud voice that gives his English a certain *übermenschlich* timbre. Baulked of Cambridge professorial prospects, he became, in due time, professor at Geneva where he had a *garçonnière* to which, over a number of years, I addressed a plethora of letters. Our correspondence came about, I must declare, at my solicitation and thanks to his – let us say; no: let *him* – '*disponibilité fort aimable*'.

We had first met in 1972 at the house of Michael Ayrton, the sculptor and writer who had invited George and his wife, Zara (New York historian, said by Michael A. not to be the comeliest woman he had ever seen, and he had seen many women) to lunch with us. George tried very hard to be charming and provocatively *maieutic*. In a spasm of manual eloquence, he spilt wine on Beetle's white blouse and cured the stain (like hell) with a heap of salt (not Attic). After a certain amount of conversation, he asked me, with concerned malice, why my novels were so much less intelligent than I was in person. I loved the guy right away.

He had just been a – nay, *the* – judge in the top British fiction prize, the Booker, which he had managed to arrange would be awarded to John Berger (another shit/genius in the comparative mode) for his novel *G.*, just the kind of initial George liked, and shared with Don G/iovanni, the modernised hero of Berger's sententious, pretentious and non-enduring fiction. Berger repaid Booker bros (molasses manufacturing Maecenasses) at the ceremonial dinner by denouncing how they treated the *fellahin* on their sugar plantations in the West Indies. Biting the hand that fed him was Berger's idea of Marxism in action.

Steiner was wary of Beetle who keeps fleas for ears like his. Michael Ayrton and I corresponded for the rather brief time before he died, of a sudden heart attack, in 1975, after being misdiagnosed by the family doctor, who hadn't got as far as diabetes in his studies. Michael wrote in an elegant hand and, having left school at fifteen, liked to indulge in the exchange of recondite reference and fancy phrases. His death left me oddly bereft (the oddness being that I didn't know him all that well, didn't have *that* much – except Hellas – in common, etc.) and I wrote to Steiner to say so, since no-one else was available, and asked if I could write to him instead. And so we began to correspond; we were in the Perigord (no e-mail facilities in them 1970s) and he was where the money was. I wrote long, he replied short, mostly lists of academic invitations, distinctions, review solicitations ($5,000 a pop from the *New Yorker,* can it have been?), hon. degrees etc.

Our friendship seemed to flourish. I recall that he once said that he was '*aching*' to see me, which was rather unduly Continental, but not hurtful. I never ached to see him, not least because I was slightly ashamed of telling Beetle that I was off to see someone whom she had not warmed to on sight, and sound. But I went. On one occasion he asked me to stay to dinner, *albeit at short notice*, since Arthur Koestler was coming. I wanted to stay, but I didn't, because I had told Beetle and Sarah that I would be back for dinner. 'You are uxorious, sir', quotha. Years later, in the early 90s, I think, I published a book of Greek myths, renovated in a number of styles (including a screenplay of the Pelops myth which a professor in Belgium told me recently he uses to instruct his students) and Sarah did the illustrations. I sent George a copy, which he did not acknowledge in the fulsome way which, to choose a cliché at random, used to be *de rigueur*, i.e. with well chosen instances of where he had spotted and envied my genius. Instead, as if being intimate and honest, he said merely (in a letter) that Sarah's illustrations were '*dire*'. I never spoke to him again. Some people just can't take it, am I right?

Tout à toi,
Freddie

Dear Freddie,

Ah Bartleby! Ah humanity! Ah Steiner, who may or may not be part of humanity. In matters Steinerian, I have this immense advantage over you: I have never met the old boy, and, if my luck holds out, I never shall. I recall being much impressed when, many years ago, I came across a letter of Orwell's to Stephen Spender in which Orwell explains that for many years Spender was precisely the sort of person he most enjoyed attacking: he was a Communist sympathizer, a pansy poet (I believe Orwell used precisely that phrase, which in today's steamy climate of political correctness would have meant a stiff prison sentence), and someone wishy-washy about all the things Orwell felt required courageous positions. But now, as Orwell explains in the letter, they have met, and he found Spender a fairly agreeable character, and hence can no longer attack him with "the clean brutality" he had hitherto expended upon him. As I recall, Orwell ends by remarking that this is one of the reasons he doesn't much like to go out much. But Steiner, apparently, fails the Orwell–Spender test. To meet him is not to like him any better, or to wish to soften up on him.

As for Stephen Spender, whom I've also never met, he, too, was, to put it gently, a curious character. He used to spend a term every year teaching at Northwestern, no doubt at the highest possible salary. He was probably brought here by Richard Ellmann, the Joyce–Yeats–Wilde man, who had strong English connections and himself ended up teaching at Oxford. He, Spender, was said to be a perfectly wretched teacher, ill prepared and not notably lucid in the classroom, who reserved most of his energy for chasing boys, which he did with some efficiency. Then he would return to England to write about the low quality of American students, gum-chewers, mindless, poor wretches really, all of them. Spender was one of those lucky men whose laziness did not prevent their getting a good ride through life, though he was not so lucky in being born in the same generation as W.H. Auden, who cast a long shadow that kept the sun from shining on Spender's poetic career.

Steiner wrote a book about teaching that, quietly but insistently, makes him out to have been a great teacher. That book tells two great myths about teaching: first, that one learns so much from one's students; and, second, so joyous is the experience of teaching that one would be pleased to do it for nothing. I taught for thirty years, and though some sweet and charming and reasonably intelligent students walked into my classrooms, I cannot think of a single thing I learned from any of them. As for teaching for nothing, explain that, I say, to most of the academics I regularly encountered who were rivalrous with, which is to say envious of, anyone who was making a dime more, or teaching an hour less, than they.

Teaching is in fact a bit of a racket. For one thing, it is a six months out of the year job, for which one gets a full year's salary. (Although I taught halftime toward the end of my teaching days, I was earning the equivalent of $104,000 a year.) Much of it is balls-achingly boring, especially the grading of papers, which means the endless correcting of spelling errors, grammatical mistakes, and other ineptitudes. Reading student examinations was perhaps the most chagrining experience of all, for in these sad documents one learned, with genuine precision, how little of what one was knocking oneself out to explain got through to the troops. Then there is the dreary repetition. The best definition of a teacher I know has it that he is someone who never says anything once. The great benefit I derived from teaching has been the friendships I made, and have kept, with twenty or so students, some of whom are now in their early fifties. Which reminds me that Edward Shils one day reported to me that two of his former students had come by earlier that day to take him to lunch. "One was 75, the other 78," he said. Perfectly-timed pause. "Nice boys," he added.

Your remarks on relatively contemporary poetry play nicely into a little obsession of mine. I happen to think the writing of poetry in our time has descended to the level of stamp-collecting or acquiring antique cars – it is, in other words, not much more than a hobby in which only fellow collectors (or, in the case of poetry, fellow scribblers) are in the least interested. I read some years ago that there were 26,000 registered poets in America. (I never found out where one goes to register.) By now there may well be twice or four times that number, what with all the creative writing courses and workshops bubbling up around the country. Amateur poetry slams, as poetry readings in bars are called, are fairly common events. Some poets, I'm told, draw decentsized crowds at universities. Vast volumes of the stuff are published by smallish presses with names like Zygote Press (I invented the name of that not very far-fetched firm.) Prizes, some for serious scratch, as we say out at the racetrack, are given to poets every twenty minutes or so, also grants, furloughs, and comely female undergraduates are popped into their rumpled beds. But in the end it all means nothing, nada, zilch, because, to play upon the words of that federale in *Treasure of Sierra Madre*, no-one needs their stinking poems. Because, too, with a few notable exceptions – Larkin is the only one I can think of at the moment – no-one not in the poetry biz can cough up a single line or phrase from a poem written in the last half century.

Like you, I begin many of the poems in the *TLS* – I do the same with the poems published by the *New Yorker* – but most I am unable to finish, including sometimes the quite brief ones ("I knew Len Hutton in his prime/ Vodka with lime, vodka with lime"). My fall-out rate from longer poems is very high. I find that when I am able to get through a longish poem, the poet generally is unable to land the damnable thing in a satisfactory way. If a poem presents anything like real difficulty – as Stevens, Eliot, & co. certainly did upon first and even second and third reading – I have no will to struggle for the true meaning behind the difficulty. Almost nothing stays with me after I complete reading a poem. Tabula, Señor, rasa.

Auden somewhere calls poetry "memorable speech," which I thought rather empty when first I came upon it in my early twenties. Auden meant by it that only the exciting or moving in poetry is memorable, which is, I suppose, true enough. But I think "memorable speech" is crucial in an even blunter way. Larkin again apart, I simply don't remember any poetry written after 1950. Meanwhile I have borrowed from T.S. Eliot – that anti-Semit (as my father used to pronounce it) – for two of my book titles: *With My Trousers Rolled* and *The Love Song of A. Jerome Minkoff* – while phrases from Frost, Cummings, and Wallace Stevens play in my mind like the punchlines from superior jokes. But after this raft of poets, nothing sticks; all those miles of poetry are so much pissing in the wind – and surely you know what happens when you piss in the wind.

Something has happened to the lyric poem not unlike what must have happened to verse drama and to the epic before that. The dead genre department is soon to be its destination. How this happened, and what are its consequences, are worthy of speculation. But of the death of poetry itself, I haven't much doubt.

Circling all the way back to your opening words about the malice and envy of writers to one another, I just recalled the roughest remark I have ever heard made about a writer, though it turns out to have been made not by a fellow scribbler but by a civilian. The remark caps a story about one sophisticated woman, sometime in the early 1950s, reporting to another that she has recently heard a rumor that Max Lerner – then a liberal columnist for the *New York Post* and the author of a number of excruciatingly dull, quite unnecessary books (*American Civilization*, one of his tomes, will give you an oblique sense of old Max's want of seasoning) – that this Max Lerner was engaged to Elizabeth Taylor. Along with being boring, Lerner was far from comely, which caused the second woman to exclaim about the story's genuineness. The first woman assured her that she had the story on good authority. "Oh, well," said the second woman, "I guess I'd rather fuck him than read him." Now there is a blurb that could be put on many a book of our day, assuming of course that one didn't have to do the actual fucking.

Best, Joe

Dear Joe,

Something you once asked me in a sidebar comes back to stimulate me. How come, you wanted to know, that of all the ancients Alcibiades retains his charm, while all around are losing theirs? It occurs to me that it's because he comes across as unencumbered by guilt or moralising: he never wondered where he went wrong, he just kept going. He was the first playboy of the western world, unembarrassed by anything he did, and so enabled to revel in whatever his money, charm and intelligence could procure. A bright boy who never lost his lustre, he made all the solemnities and hypocrisies of all other Greeks, even those not of his time, seem tiresome or parochial. Diogenes with a fortune and a good tailor, he made ostentation into a form of cynicism: what impressed others as excessive was not enough to make him feel he had done anything much at all. He entered five teams for the Olympic chariot race, even though you got nothing for what race-goers (never mind obstetricians) mean by a 'show'. At Olympia winning was usually all that mattered, but Alcibiades owned almost all the pretty horses and drew attention to himself all down the start-line.

If ever there was an anti-Jew, it was Alcibiades: he had no conscience, he did not blame himself, he did not believe in anything except fun and triumphs. Money was no object because he had it already (even though it is somewhat mysterious how he had so much, since his estates in Attica were no larger than a hundred acres) and seduction was no problem, since he was such a handsome fellow. No-one was less the kind of Greek that Shelley, Bowra or Heidegger admired, although Bowra might have wished he could play the Socratic role, especially in the hay. Alcibiades almost disarms even Thucydides, who never saw the end of his story. Thucydides' contempt was reserved for Cleon, who was no gentleman. Alcibiades' polar Other was Nikias, who was not as vulgar as Cleon but a bit of a businessman (he ran a big Rent-a-Slave corporation). Thucydides may have admired Nikias's caution (which resembled his own) but his prose depicted what he never quite said Nikias was: an uncharismatic loser. It might have been better if Athens had never invaded Sicily (although it stood to be a much more profitable enterprise than the US and British invasion of Iraq), but it would unquestionably have gone better if Alcibiades had been C-in-C; he would have hit Syracuse early and hard and, since the actual attack almost succeeded, might well have done the business, in which case the Athenians would never have sought to indict him for his alleged naughtinesses before the fleet ever set sail and . . . and . . . and . . .

Alcibiades gets a much more unsympathetic press from the hindsighted than Alexander the Great, whose greatness derived from what cannot be denied: he was world champion. A recent book I reviewed also described him as 'right-minded', which may have been intended to suggest that he and Dick Cheney could've been buddies, but I don't think so. No, the thing that gives him a distant halo is that he advertised a wish to homogenise the world by which he meant to Hellenise and, in particular, Alexandrise it: monotheism as a political weapon begins with him and his earnest/cynical/spoilt boyish insistence on being a God. In the process of making the world one, he crucified large numbers of brave men whose only crime was not to have opened their gates (oh and their hearts) to him. He slaughtered like a Crusader and wrote his creed in blood and the grovellers who have followed him at a safe distance from the reek have found him Good. My friend Peter Green is one of the unsentimental disabusers of his myth, but it resurges again and again.

No-one speaks well of Alcibiades, but he was irresistible without having a phalanx or the companion cavalry at his back. He advertised no self-serving message of racial reconciliation (his ballocks were between his legs, and other people's) and he founded no cities. He played the world's game as if it were skittles and when one set of pins went down, he set up some more. Eventually he was knocked over himself, but what a time he had before he went down the same old slope as the rest of us must! There's nothing to be said for the two-faced, bisexual, treacherous charmer except . . . what a man to have been! When very youngish, Peter Green wrote a novel about him, entitled *Achilles His Armour*. I wish it had been good enough to recommend to you (so does Peter), but Al escaped his pursuer. Funny about ancient Greeks in fiction; they never seem to come to life as Romans can (Graves's Claudius and Peter's own Sulla 'work' fine). The prosiness of the Romans and the convergence of our and their language probably account for the happier fit. I never warmed to

Mary Renault's Greek stuff, but the now forgotten Naomi Mitchison, a 1930s and 40s Communist English lady, wrote some almost chaste stuff in them days which I recall finding quite . . . stimulating when, as a lonely adolescent, I first and last read them.

I've been writing a review of a book about Judas Iscariot by a 'distinguished' professoressa called Susan Gubar, who teaches at Indiana U. She covers the long sad story of the diabolisation of the Juden, coil on coil, but never quite dares say that the whole Christian thing is now a myth that, as Cicero might say, has lived: i.e. is now dead. She goes through the literature with that plodding bibliographical thoroughness that marks the good girl/lady *dans ses oeuvres*, but you know she is one of the sorority that will never cross the street against the lights. She never dares to say that Christianity began as an affair between Jews and Jews, or that Saul of Tarsus (the kind of out-of-towner who claims to be proud to come from Wichita) had that blinding flash on the Damascus Road that said, as it has to so many of, oh, our people: if you can't join 'em, start your own business. His business was selling pseudo-Judaism to the Gentiles and – special offer! – no circumcision if you're not cut out for it.

Spiritual values were just what the Roman world wanted, some say, but the story needed to be beefed up with all the mythical machinery from which a *deus* can rise again. Gubar redeems Judas the bleeder and finds him, in the twentieth century, a kind of existential hero. Chagall crucifies him as the emblematic victim of the Shoah, so displacing the displaced Jew at the centre of the picture. What Gubar doesn't dare to do, and maybe doesn't see, is that the establishment of Israel gave the Wandering Jew (Judas's doubles-partner) a place to stop and so, looking at the world as myth-historical (and how the Thinkers love doing that!), or did, as Karl Barth, shithead-in-the-clouds *par excellence*, demon/strates, put a stop to Christian time: the Messiah ain't come back yet, y'all, He ain't coming at all. A rabbi that Gubar quotes, as if he were a wit, suggested to his Christian 'friends' that they cease arguing until the Messiah *does* come, and then we can all ask him whether it's for the first or second time. It needs a Frenchman to ask why He should tell us the Truth.

I've been having some mild fun reading the congeries of letters about Céline, Isaiah Berlin and Lanzmann in recent *TLS*s. Lanzmann was the least of it, since I refrained from thumping Stanislawski against the wall in public, though I did write him an old-fashioned (stamped) letter to which he replied that he would not be drawn into *ad hominem* indignity. Since he'd accused me of lacking 'due diligence', I thought (and later said) that he had his bloody nerve, but there it was, another example of Jew v. Jew, which is also in a metastatised form what Judaeo-Christianity is, although we must never say so in public, because then it really is all your fault.

The Berlin thing was fun because of the undercurrents: A.N. Wilson, who already figures in our phantom index, had to be chosen by Our Friends to take on (as they say) Isaiah, since Wilson is an Ox/onian who was nurtured in Iris Murdoch/John Bayleywick and can be hired (and lowered) to cast pearls and aspersions with equal facility. He has managed his literary career with lightfooted expertise. Starting where others have hoped to end up, as literary editor of the *Spectator*, he has become a luminary without ever throwing an interesting light; gem-like flames he does not do, only semi-precious.

As a critic, he knocks and it is opened unto him. He plays on the prejudices which have become unfashionable and to which a mere allusion comforts the others who dare no longer speak openly about oiks or Jewboys. In accordance with the British rule which requires that anti-Semitism be principled, he restricts his overt allusions to the ghastliness of certain people by attacking . . . Israel, and all who sail in her, or to her. When he disdains Berlin's social climbing (which you and I have hardly failed to find amusing), he does not say what he is also happy to imply: that all Jews are like that. The more civilised, the more deceptive, creepy and crawly Berlin is, the more typically he wears the badge of all us climbers and dissimulators. A.N. Wilson can be added to the distinguished list of people I hope I never meet. There's another list with 'Again' appended, *mais passons outre . . .*

The Céline review and repercussions have a different bitter-sweetness, featuring Herr Oberg, another Maud Bodkin archetype: the Parisian Jew (*demi*) who finds noble excuses for an anti-Semitic nutcase who is a doctor already, and hence by definition philanthropic (Mengele, *connais pas*), and – above all – a Genius, to whom mundane rules cannot apply and whose words, however rancid, cannot be judged like those of other men. I am always relieved when someone who is not a Jew steps forward and plies the old straight left and the right cross.

Tennis time! We have our son Stephen staying with us and also his friend Toby, who played the pro circuit and once met Jimmy Connors in his prime and went down 4 and 4. Terrific guy. They treat me with very discreet gentleness and I pretend I don't notice that they have tempered the wind to the old sheep.

Tout à toi,
Freddie

Dear Freddie,

Yes, of course, only now that you have said it does it occur to me that it is the utter consciencelessness of Alcibiades that, along with the gifts bestowed upon him by nature, made his dashing career possible. The play's the thing, and screw the conscience of the king, all kings, also others' subjects and the beautiful wives of other men. You also call my man the Big A. the anti-Jew, owing to this same delightful want of conscience. A great deal to this, too, though until now I hadn't thought to formulate it so.

I not long ago gave a talk with the title "What's So Jewish?" in which I began by noting that Epicurus was the world's first shrink, since he had a four-step program to eliminate anxiety. Here is the short-course version of the four steps: 1. Don't believe in Gods or the gods; 2. Don't worry about death, for it is nothing but oblivion, eternal dreamless sleep; 3. Don't be put off by pain, which will either soon enough end, or if it intensifies sufficiently will result in death, about which, as noted earlier, one is not to be worried either; and 4. Do not seek exactious luxuries, including money to buy them as well as fame and power. Follow these four steps and, Epicurus holds, serenity is yours, baby.

I then go on to say in this talk that I have met many varieties of Jew – smart, silly, stupid, wise – but have never met a serene Jew. (If you have met such a Jew, please send me his name and e-mail address straightaway, for I ardently want to meet him, though I suspect he doesn't really exist.) And much of the remainder of the talk is devoted to attempting to account for the want of serenity in our co-religionists, even those among us without much in the way of traditional religion. Religion is in the head and heart, but culture is in the bones, and conscience, in a hyper, if not positively exaggerated, state, would appear to be a part of the culture of Jews, even though so much of the rest of the world seems content in the belief that conscience is precisely what Jews do not possess.

The complexities of Jewish family life are chiefly owing to conscience: everyone wanting to do the right goddamn thing with the result that most people in the family are left divided and feeling miserable. That so many Jews have fallen for ignorant revolutionary or humanitarian radical political schemes is also in good part owing to conscience, however wretchedly misguided conscience in this realm has often been. One could cite other areas of Jewish conscience at play, causing anxiety everywhere, but my main point is that Jews are conscience-ridden.

I know I am. A notable example is that when my first wife and I divorced after ten years of a not very good marriage – putting in ten years at so failed a venture could also, I realize, be laid at the door of Jewish conscience – I gladly accepted custody of not only my two sons but her two adolescent sons from an earlier marriage. I did so not because I am so virtuous a son of a bitch – I don't even think I was a particularly good father – but because my conscience could never bear the weight of abandoning my children, even under court order. Had I been forced to do so, I have little doubt that I would have gone *machula* (or belly up), by way of some sort of unoriginal debauchery or other. Not that I wasn't fully ready for debaucheries of various kinds, but those brought on by a deeply guilty conscience would have been no fun whatsoever.

My view is that the Jewish conscience derives from the idea, however inchoate in the minds of many non-religious Jews, that Jewishness (with Judaism staunchly behind it) is a culture (and of course religion) of tests, endless bloody tests. Not even stone-cold Jewish atheists are exempt from such tests. The first such test, of course, was set by God about the tree of knowledge, which Adam, with the aid of his new ladyfriend, notably failed. The second was God's asking Abraham to sacrifice his son Isaac, which he passed, though I'm not sure how much pleasure passing this test brought the old boy. I'm not sure either how much our own passing of tests brings each discrete (and usually indiscreet) Jew, for no sooner does one pass a test than another is set for one, and at the end of all the tests in a Jewish life of test-taking no clear prize is offered, not even acceptance at a good Oxford college.

Lovely though it would be to imagine oneself living the Alcibiadean life – no conscience, no tests imposed from without, fuck 'em and forget 'em, so to speak – the option just isn't open to many Jews. So it's pencils down for us, with proctors all around, the clock ticking, and no hiding place down here. Jolly, jolly!

I like the high kick of your animus against A.N. Wilson, who has never been a central figure in my anti-Pantheon. I read only his reviews, and it would not occur to me to read him at book length. He writes too easily, which is to say too much, and looks to be a leading candidate for the Jeffrey Meyers Award, which goes to writers who produce many books nobody needs. ("His books were all unnecessary," Santayana wrote about a Harvard English professor in the early decades of the past century named Wendell Barrett, causing one to wonder if one's own books would pass the Santayanan test.) Wilson writes books quite as unnecessary as Meyers but, if visual memory serves, a good bit thicker, and thus more otiose, than Meyers'.

To feel genuine high-spirited animus toward a contemporary writer, I suspect that he has to be one's own countryman. Such a fellow for me is – or was – a literary critic named Richard Poirier (rhymes with warrior, the *New York Times'* obituary writer was kind enough to inform the paper's readers), who pegged out the other day at 83, the result of injuries suffered in a fall in his own home. Poirier liked and wrote in praise of all the wrong writers – Walt Whitman, Emerson, Norman Mailer, Allen Ginsberg – for all the wrong reasons. The "performing self" was his great notion, holding that artistic creation, in the words of the obituarist, is "a performance, a self-aware exercise of self-expression in which artists are attempting to liberate themselves from the cultural, moral, political and psychological structures of society's expectations." This is a notion up there with Harold Bloom's anxiety of influence (or is it the other way round?). Poirier was pretty much a "lunatic of one idea," in Wallace Stevens' good phrase. He was also an academic his life long; and I am always suspicious of academics who call for more wine, higher fires, more dancing girls (in Poirier's case, more dancing boys). Don't they realize that academics are permitted to be clever, brilliant, deep if possible, but not to call for revolutions in any sphere, except perhaps that of clear thinking. To do so is unseemly, not to say contradictory and stupid on the part of one holding tenure.

I always think of Richard Poirier as the man who helped bring down *Partisan Review*, which was forced to take him on as an editor when Rutgers University, in New Jersey, where he taught, bought the magazine. His opening salvo as editor was a piece extolling The Beatles, putting their songs up there with Eliot's *Four Quartets* and *Ulysses*. He then went on to found and edit another magazine, this one called *Raritan*, which featured the writing of Edward Said, that steadfast friend of the Jews, and many boring academics and a few established but uninteresting poets, John Hollander and John Ashbery best known among them. I am on the comp list at *Raritan*, and every three months I receive and am able to read almost nothing in its thick and subsidized pages. Poirer was, as I alluded earlier, homosexual, though I don't believe he ever formally came out. The *NYT* obit ends with those saddest of all words: "no known suvivors." Well, I seem to have spoken enough ill of the recently dead for today, and so will say no more about Richard rhymes with Warrior.

For two gents of a certain age, as I mentioned earlier, we have not spoken much of our health, a great subject, the greatest perhaps next to bemoaning the life of the current day, for men in our chronological condition. I broke this charm when, early last week I mentioned to you that on an annual eye-doctor appointment, I was discovered to have had a slightly detached retina, which was treated straightaway with a surgical procedure of a kind that didn't land me in a hospital, which was fine by me, for hospitals are clearly, apart from Baghdad and certain villages in Afghanistan, among the most dangerous places in the world. People die there, not infrequently of infections that they didn't bring in. My retinal surgeon, a decent fellow in his fifties named Marc Levin, told me yesterday that my injured eye is healing well, and if things go on as they have I am unlikely to lose any vision. I am to continue taking eye drops, administered by Barbara (known during my illnesses as Sergeant) Epstein, and to sleep exclusively on my left side, and walk and read with my head bent slightly to the left. (This, a wiseguy friend remarked, is the only time in decades that Joseph Epstein could be described as left-leaning.) Meanwhile, I have developed a rash along my left shoulder creeping up to my neck. I wonder if this isn't a side effect of the drops I have been taking, or of the surgery itself. And, pray, please tell me why all side effects have to be unpleasant? Why can we not have pleasant side effects from drugs and medical procedures, such as surprisingly vigorous and perfectly timed erections, or frequent periods of dazzlingly deep insight? Alas, we were born too soon for handsome side effects, but surely future generations will live to see the day . . .

Best, Joe

Dear Joe,

Among the many soothing sayings of philosophers is one of Descartes's in which he says that the ivy cannot grow taller than the tree. I shall fail the great *viva* in the sky which George Steiner thinks/hopes will be the intellectuals' form of the Last Judgment, because I cannot tell you/Him in what connection Big René made this observation, which is – why else mention it? – manifestly false. The modern world is top-heavy with parasites who are bigger and, in their own view, better (as in better-informed, better-placed etc.) than those on whom they feed. What's this all about? My feeling of having been put in my place – or, as H.J. and I should prefer, *piazza* – by Steve Wasserman and his remarks about our (yours and my) mutual admiration and, by implication, our misguided belief that what we have said to each other could possibly be of buck-extracting interest to *quiconque* and his *petite amie*. I suspect many things, including the possibility that we have been seen by envious eyes to get along fluently and urgently without being commissioned by some editorial person. This is tantamount to a *fronde* from the world where numbers are what count.

Agents are now the rock *and* the hard place: we rely on them, I suppose, to extract the plums and we (I, at least) fear words of warning when it comes to unprofitable or unwise activities (my attacks on Ian McEwan and *The Reader*, novel and film) under the 'why make waves?' rubric. Comedy cuts in when you realise that agents are no better primed to chart the market than the financial advisers without whose help you (and certainly I) would be better off. I don't know how carefully you read the letter that Richard Davenport-Hines wrote to me and I forwarded to you, but the two characters whose presence at London tables upset him so much were both of the brand known as Top Agents. Yet I doubt if Swifty Lazar would have spared them a quicky or a listen on his red telephone. Their affectations of knowing what's what spring almost entirely from their acquaintance with who's who. Caroline Michel was a very good, better-looking publicist (and did me proudish in that role on the publication of my novel, *A Double Life*), but she was also well-connected not only at the hype with Matthew Evans of Faber mit Faber, whom T.S. Eliot has made passing rich with *Cats*, one of Lloyd-Webber's many masterpieces which wild horses would not drag me towards if I could dig deep enough heels in. Peter Straus (spelt with British economy without terminal doppfelness) I have never met, but he once ran Penguin, I think, and can, it may be, still roll an egg with his toes. The main skill of these tall parasites is to seem to be able to Make Things Happen, often – one guesses – when they have happened already. Cf. Tony Curtis in *The Sweet Smell of Success*.

I remember being careful, when I was doing one of the few really successful things I have ever done, *The Glittering Prizes*, for British TV, not to push the character of Jewboy deutero-Freddie (not as like as Sainte-Beuveans supposed) too hard for fear of, oh, special pleading, otherwise known as banging on; as if the whole of modern culture and politics . . . Yes, yes, but that was then – *quarante-quatre ans déjà* – and I was wary of boring the people, so I kept Adam Morris and his nose out of three episodes. Then we found Tom Conti and so did all the *donne* and then I found I'd been a fool and deprived them of what their dreams were made on. Furthermore, the Jews have some kind of furtive (what else?) fascination for the Great British Public. I will not harp, nor yet will I trumpet, but my guess is our double act will go down better with the punters than nervous persons believe. In the course of reading my every-other-daily dose of modern Frenchified Montaigne, I notice that, in his self-effacing way, there he is waving to the camera as often as may be. 'Can You Hear Me, Mother?' an old British comic used to have as a tag line. But, in

Michel de M.'s case, what a range of reference beyond himself the hybrid son-of-a-*marrana conversa* had at his whinger-tips!

I'm also reading a typical piece of unpublishable-in-the-UK *bellelettrisme* entitled *Maman* by a man called Michel Schneider, about Proust's relationship with his mother. You might not imagine that there is a fresh furrow to be cut in that well-ploughed field, but Schneider is a smart Gallimardian, who has also been director of Music and Dance at the Ministry of Culture. In today's London this would entail that he had tooted his own flute and stepped on enough toes, in an upward movement, to gain office, but in Paris he probably knew his stuff. His line is that little Marcel had to wait for the death of his mother before he could switch from being her baby to being the Master. An elegant version of the *post hoc/ad hoc* but maybe he is right. There is a moment when those of our persuasion, even of the cut known in the French veal trade as *quasi* (that part of the said sad beast which is not quite fillet but could be passed off as such to the well-wined diner), cease to be the creatures of their families and become versions of the creator who gets his own back.

I have a theory, well an idea, that the destruction of the Second Temple in 70 AD (my unredeemed old British-style notation) not only led to the investment of the Jews in The Book, as against sacrificial theatrical religion in the High Priestly style, as finally agreed at Yavneh (yes, I am still bloody well writing this book about Flavius Josephus), but also to the liberation of the Jewish intelligence, dismayed and therefore acute, into literary activity, of which remembrance has been the essential form. Of course this is all wild extrapolation from selective evidence, but time is short when you reach September, or its metrical equivalent. Josephus's whole apology for betrayal (and his mother, folks, was indeed in Jerusalem when it fell) becomes an act of incessant written verbosity.

When Freud tells us that men are never really free until their *fathers* are dead, might it just be that he is making a Freudian error and that the truth is that he is masking what he really wants, the death of the *mother*, who really keeps him (us) a baby? Proust hinted as much in that famous *Figaro* article in which he boasted/confessed that he had more than a mite of empathy with a man who had just been convicted of killing his *maman*. He never mentions anyone wanting to kill his father, does he? The mother, Schneider says, prevented him from being his own self by being hers, etc. Portnoy is little Marcel in Newark. The Freudian question What Do Women Want? just may have an unspeakable answer: they want to be fucked by their sons; and this only ever happens (usually) when they are dead. Hence (Oh Jesus this is a terrible train to be on!) Susan Son/*et lumière*/tag's smart-ass line about pornography 'really' being about death. Duplicity is the nature of the beast, and much of the anatomy. But we have only one heart . . .

So here we come, by a long way round, to your notion that the Jewish conscience is overdeveloped and what keeps us as we are because of the specific family orientation of Jewish life. This is borne out (on a big plate) in another book, *Le Destin des immigrés*, which I happen to be reading, written by a slightly insane, very clever man called Emmanuel Todd, who is a *sociologue* and derives the characters of people, and especially pipples, from – in determining measure – their marital and property-inheriting practices. The Jews, he says, have a tendency to favour the youngest, thus giving precociousness an inside track in life's great relay race. He seems to think that Jews stayed in the ghetto because they were so much more literate than those who locked them in there and agreed/conspired/arranged to come out only when some of the folks outside had read enough to make tolerable company for smart folks. No, of course he doesn't say anything like that in so many words (he says it in a lot lot more) but he does suggest that Jewish endogamy, including not infrequent (first) cousin marriage, created a society of ingrown and inward-looking concern and mutual surveillance. I don't actually think I'm all that conscience-riven (unless that's the same thing as not wanting to be found out and told/seen off) but that could be because I have no cousins at all and virtually no blood relations, except my mother, whose longevity has not inhibited my verbosity any more than worrying about what she thinks about my work has done anything other than encourage me to shock the bourgeoisie, nicely (aha! you may say, and I take the point).

Tout à toi,
Freddie

Dear Freddie,

Apologies for getting back to you so tardily. I had intended to do so this past weekend, but then realized that I had agreed to give a talk Sunday morning at a Jewish United Fund breakfast. I do not give talks easily; I have to prepare with some care to achieve the effect of (false) *sprezzatura* for which I am not very widely known. The synagogue turned out to be a Conservative one, the audience of roughly 150 people were far from young, the men all wearing yarmulkes. Along with its fundraising aspect, this meeting was also convened to honor a couple who had done much for the synagogue over the years. The name of the honorands is Jabo, Cy and Sally.

Now no Jew, not even a Japanese Jew, is named Jabo. Nomenclatural rhinoplasty, clearly, had been performed. When Cy Jabo arrived, I recognized him as a quite hopeless boy from the school I went to between the ages of 6 and 10; he was then fat, wearing thick-lensed glasses, without an athletic bone in his shapeless body, so far out of it as to be scarcely worth tormenting. His name in those far-off days was Cyril Jabowicz; the name fit the boy as perfectly as the Mikado would have the punishment fit the crime. Where I grew up, if a boy weren't a decent athlete, he had better be witty – and Cyril Jabowicz wasn't close to either.

The reason I bring this up is that Cy Jabo, the former Cyril Jabowicz, turns out, thanks to the work of that great sculptor Time, to be, a mere sixty or so years late, a quietly impressive human being. (He did not, by the by, recognize me, nor did I introduce myself to him.) He is no longer a fat boy, but a small man, with white hair, wearing two hearing aids, quite nicely dressed in blue blazer, blue shirt, and tasteful maroon necktie. His son gave a toast to the Jabos, testifying to what a kind, thoughtful, and generous man his father has been, and did so convincingly. (The son is married to a Filipina, and has presented the former Cyril Jabowicz with two beautiful little bi-racial girls who are being raised as Jews.) My old classmate's wife is not beautiful, but one of those women who our mothers would have said was full of pep. She had been through a long and frightening bout with cancer, which she survived, "thank God," as the new Cy was quick to add at the lectern. When Cy Jabo spoke in thanks for the honor paid him – a plaque, as in "a plaque on both your houses" – he spoke with genuine feeling about how much being a member of this synagogue has meant to him over the years.

We haven't, in our exchanges, brought up much things that touch or move us. I found myself much touched by Monsieur Jabo – touched by how this rather pathetic child has grown into a serious, gracious, and apparently honorable man. Strange and wonderful, like the man says, are the ways of the world.

On the matter of agentry, Steve Wasserman must be more direct with you than Georges Borchardt is with me. Georges B. didn't suggest that what we were doing was wretched, or marred by this or that weakness; the prevailing sense he left me with is that he didn't get it, and from this he concluded, as the logicians used to say, "by extension," neither would anyone else. Have I mentioned to you that Georges B. went to lycée with that 's'-less George, Herr

Steiner; and that when boys they planned to collaborate on a biography of Napoleon? Ah, me, here is another book for that immense library of volumes dreamt of but never written. The only library larger, of course, is that containing all the unnecessary books that, alas, did get written.

I spent a good part of last week reading and writing about a well-made biography of George Gershwin by a man named Walter Rimler, which I was asked to review for the *Wall Street Journal*. I wrote the piece in mid-week, revised it and sent it off, roughly 400 words longer than was requested. I hope cuts won't be required, though I suspect, the *WSJ* being a newspaper with limited space, that they will be. When it comes to biographies, cutting is almost never a mistake. The Gershwin book I reviewed was a pleasingly slender 173 pages, while the definitive job (which I did not read), by a man named Howard Pollack, runs to 882. The older one gets – what with the grave yawning and all that – the less one yearns for great fat books written by people named anything other than Gibbon or Proust. Such at least is my aging Jew's-eye view.

Apropos of Gershwin, I enjoy reading about that generation of American (mostly Jewish) songwriters, figures chiefly from the 1920s and '30s. They seemed to have had a good time on their visit to the planet: knock off a tune, pop in some words, collect the shekels, and hit the golf links, tennis courts, gin-rummy table, booze, broads, whatever your pastime of choice. My favorite name among them is that of the lyricist, Irving Caesar, a name that conveys a great deal about the comedy of the Jewish experience in America. (If his name were Caesar Irving, he might have turned out a producer, or a movie mogul, if you please.) What's in a name? A whole hell of a lot, I'd say.

Gershwin was alone among his generation of songwriters in aiming higher, and the highbrow composers for the most part kicked his keyster for doing so. They viewed his attempts to write serious music as interloping, unfairly crossing jurisdictional lines. When he brought out *Porgy and Bess* they lined up to say how muddled and inept it was. The opera, I was surprised to learn, was initially a great critical and commercial flop. That Gershwin was a natural genius I am sure did not help his cause. I have already mentioned a friend, who died at fifty-nine, named Sam Lipman who began life as a piano prodigy, and from the stories Sam used to tell me, the envy and malice floating around the milieu of serious music makes the literary world seem a tea party in Louisa May Alcott. The backbiting in music goes all the way down to the tailbone. They shoot, in that world, not to disable but to kill.

I have my doubts about the thesis of Michel Schneider's book on Proust and his mother. I recently read a quite good biography of this same

Maman – by a Frenchwoman named Évelyne Bloch-Dano – and she, Maman, turns out to have been a remarkable woman and our little Marcel was, I should judge, lucky to have had her. True, when our parents die we do feel, along with much else, a touch of freedom, and to go with it a touch of fear: we are next in line for the garrotte. But I also think blaming parents can be vastly overdone, unless the parents are genuine tyrants. Perhaps I am a touch unimaginative on this subject, for my own parents were so kindly and generous about allowing me to grow up without undue interference.

M. Todd's sounds a book only a Frenchman could write. Orwell, as I mentioned earlier, once remarked that "Only an intellectual could be so stupid." The occasion for his saying this, I not long ago discovered, was in response to an English socialist speculating that the only reason that the Americans had entered World War Two was to do what they could to stop socialism in England. But the French, in the right mood, can take this stupidity to a much higher plane. Do you suppose that it is the clarity – specious clarity, I suspect – that the French language permits for abstract, also abstruse, thinking that allows French thinkers to speculate so airily and so foolishly. I sometimes think that Descartes' "I think, therefore I am" should have been "I'm French, therefore I'm wrong." Now I defy you to top that for simple large-hearted prejudice.

I had meant to thank you earlier for passing along Richard Davenport-Hines' kind words about my *Snobbery* and *Envy* scribbles. Some years ago I read his biography of W.H. Auden, which I thought excellent; and, more recently, I thought he did a most intelligent job of editing the Trevor-Roper letters to Bernard Berenson. I also always read his pieces in the *TLS,* and don't recall being disappointed in them. Praise is always pleasing, but it is especially nice to have it from those who turn out good work in the same vineyard one has been working oneself. Hope this doesn't sound too smug, but I think I have the good opinion of most of the small number of living writers I admire, and the hatred of many of those whose enmity makes me proud.

Best, Joe

Dear Joe,

I've had a schizoid week. At its outset, I told *le jeune* Podhoretz why I was glad I hadn't agreed to review the new Tarantino movie for him, because it allowed me to tell him, uninhibitedly, what I thought of it. Having been in Virgilian rural France all summer, we had just been in to see *Inglourious Basterds* in our local small town, not having read anything about it in the (apparently loud) press. And then what? You've guessed: he liked my *obiter scripta* enough to ask me to do the piece after all. Should I deny that I was doing a leedle fishing when I said I wasn't going to? J.P. discouraged me from repeating my *déchaîné* speculation that the original script must have contained a scene in which the Jewish basterds – I assume you know something of this Inglourious movie – gangbang Eva Braun who, under their blanket bombardieering, gasps zat she neffer knew it could be anysink like zis. Julius vos right, in the early porning editions of *Der Stürmer*, in maintaining that the *Juden* could go *schtupping* on all night, despite being equipped with foreshortened weapons. Streicher supposedly abated his rant about Jewish sexual studiousness since it excited more Aryannes than it scandalised.

The other scene that I wanted to include, but Podhoretz wouldn't green-light, was one in which Harvey Weinstein agrees *pro bono Judaico* to be filled with helium and – a Manhattan Projectile with the prototypical Big Boy strapped to his manhood – floated over Berlin for a spot of apocalypse sooner than History has chosen to record. However, I *was* licensed to play the 'American, Chicago-born', which J.P. reminded me I was/am (I did too take the reference), and to conclude that Weinstein and Q.T. had realised that there is 'No business like *Shoah* business'. It is a line of which I am almost ashamed but, in the light of Weinstein/Q.T.'s piece of prolonged yuck and of H.W.'s preceding (possibly even less excusable) *The Reader*, I thought I would stick to them whatever it tastes like. So, by Tuesday evening I was like, Hey! Mr Front Page (but not as in the lousy remake), waiting for Ben Hecht to call me kiddo.

Then, come Wednesday, I recalled that I had promised the *TLS* a piece about my deceased friend Guy Lee, a fellow of St John's College, Cambridge, and a Latinist who tried to coax/coach me to write Ovidian verses. I preferred larky theatricals and the intellectual clever-cloggery of analytic philosophy, which required an adroit tongue, a capacity for mimicking Wittgensteinian sign-language and no great amount of reading, not least because most of the Great Philosophers, especially those beginning with H (except for Hume and Heraclitus), were deemed full of metaphysics (*la merde polysyllabique*). Guy was then an amiable young, grey-haired scholar, lacking only in the kind of demanding scorn that might have shamed me into being a proper Latin scholar, though I doubt it.

We became friends when I reverted to the Classics in the 1970s, first with a version of Catullus, in collaboration with Ken McLeish, who taught our children at Bedales, and with whom I translated Aeschylus and a bunch of other tragedies, and then, after Ken's death, when I dared to fly solo with my (recently paperbacked) *Satyrica*. I wrote about Guy and his terse notations in the introduction to *Ticks and Crosses*. All this is preambulatory to the fact that, at the beginning of the summer, Paul Cartledge, another of those generous godfathers on whom, as a perpetual probationer in the Classics, I have been lucky enough to be able to call on for help (Peter Green, the oldest, was the first man ever to accept a story of mine for publication, when he was, temporarily, a literary impresario), sent me a stack of penny-plain postcards lately disclosed in the archives of the defunct Classical Faculty magazine *Farrago*. They contained, in Lee's neat hand, a baccarat-thick deck of epigrammatic contributions, Greek and Latin, which he had sent to the editor, with sporadic diligence, during the 1970s. He expected them to be published, and doubtless they were, but there was something typically modest in their submission.

Paul had no use for them, but thought I might find one, if only as amusement. I will subjoin, as they say, what I made of them during long work/copying sessions in the second half of this week, but the schizoid thing kicked in because, of course, no-one could have been more English, more Anglo-Saxon, more correct, and more – alas – obsolete than Guy's handwritten neatnesses. In order to play the *TLS* game, and to match my strokes, as it were, to those of Guy (who would, I suspect, have played tennis, if he ever did, in slightly jaundiced white flannels, secured with a strangulated school or college tie), I had to adopt a Cambridge persona, matching my marginalia, as best I might, to Guy's. In this I tried to honour the classical tradition in which I was inducted just 70 years ago. Since the war had just broken out, I was dispatched to an English 'prep' school where, almost immediately, I began to lisp not in numbers but in cases: *amo, amas, amat* and so on for another decade, by which time my Chicago birth and Ethical Kulchur were lost on me, or in me. I am not sure that I was false to myself in the second half of the week, even though I had somewhat less fun playing the pundit than I had belabouring Quentin T. and his fat friend, but I was certainly conscious that the (now dated) British manner is a game and that the same rules never apply both sides of the ocean that the old *M.V.* (short for 'Motor Vessel') *Britannic* used to ply with little Freddie in it. (My mother has saved a spoof copy of the *New York Times*, with FREDDIE RAPHAEL VISITS WORLD'S FAIR as its main headline, souvenir of our last summer in NYC.)

I sent our son Paul (51) the piece I wrote about *Inglourious Basterds* and, being a film producer of resourceful memory, he corrected a couple of things but said how much he had enjoyed it (not a tribute he would pay to my piece for the *TLS* if, by some marooned obligation, he were ever to read it). The oddish thing is that when I said that I could never have written about Tarantino like that for any English publication, Paul – being *más o menos* unmitigatedly British – could not understand why. The reason is, of course, that no British editor would accept something from me written in what he would find a funny (odd) accent. Nor could I have written it for such an editor, because I would know that he wouldn't get it, would be uneasy at the Jewy boldness of tone etc. And so, by a roundabout way, I come to your last letter and your proper appreciation of the Man Of No Account that you were at school with and how, fulfilling a duty to Your People, you realised that he had, in a quiet way, done something fine with his unpromising self.

The Jewish thing works for you, I realise, in a way that it never has for me because, not least, you live among people, not only Jews, who may think whatever they think but do not find you . . . try *singular* (your stories are rarely about loneliness). Maybe it all comes back to the silly circumstance that plucked me out of 1938 NYC and turned me into the two people I am today. When we came to London, my parents elected not to live in a Jewish neighbourhood (north-west London, in those days, was Refugeeland) but in SW15 where they would not be 'labelled'. Of course my father, who had been to Oxford and might have played golf for the university had he not worn glasses, which became mistified when he was having a trial for the team, was denied membership of Royal Wimbledon, the SW golf course of choice. He was content to go where the 'artisans' played. The Jewishness that he never denied was stoic: it bore no social dividends and had no spiritual dimension. He played the course that he had been set to tee up on and did not complain about the depth of the bunkers or the narrowness of the fairways. But there was a kind of loneliness in him, although he kept his friendships in formal repair (hospital visits, etc.), whether with Jews or, somewhat more often, 'Christians'. He too was an only son and, although his parents had many brothers and sisters, his sense of family was dutiful and gave him, I think, little warmth.

One of his Christian friends, later a famous surgeon, had operated on him when he was a young man and lacked the expertise he affected; while doing a relatively simple operation, to remove a kidney stone, I think, this man managed to sever my father's urethra. As a result he suffered from a stricture all his life, which made urination problematic when it was not painful. He bore this with tight lips, but pain too generates apartness, and humiliation: he was a man (a lounge lizard in his youth) who . . . but you can supply the rest. We went only occasionally to *shul* (I can't even be sure I have spelt it rightly), most memorably when, in 1943, I think, he took me to the East End, where the poor Jews lived. The Great Temple had been bombed, but an open-air service took place there, as the news of the *Shoah* began to percolate into the consciousness of the lucky ones in London. He took me (not my mother) to listen to the speeches and the invocations (some, of course, in Hebrew, which I have never understood). We stood there, solid with Our People, no doubt, but without speaking to or knowing anyone, and then we went back to south-west London.

So: I have never *swum* in Jewishness, socially, vulgarly, intellectually, as you have, and I am not, I fear, nourished by it or warmed by it as you have been, to your good fortune (not least because you don't have to think about it to live it). England has made me wary, wry, somewhat tart, somewhat (?!) suspicious, always expecting ejection from even the literary equivalent of Royal Wimbledon. I tee up and I drive off *en solitaire*. It ain't that sad, and it ain't been at all terrible, but I sometimes look across the water and see myself in the same skin and another life, and maybe that double-vision is what keeps my mill turning. *Il faut y croire.*

Tout à toi,
Freddie

Dear Freddie,

What you have written about yourself – about the two-Freddies – is full of interest. It reminds me a little of my friend Edward Shils, who used to spend half the year at Cambridge and half at the University of Chicago, and who became – in accent, in dress, in manner generally – what I thought a mid-Atlantic character. But Edward brought this about deliberately; in the cant phrase, he reinvented himself. (He was in fact the son of a cigar-maker in Philadelphia, a working-class Jewish boy, with astonishingly high intelligence added.) But your case is very different, if only because the two Freddies – the slightly donnish Freddie and the dashing, slashing jokie-jakey Freddie – did not come about by the same planning that Edward put into his self-creation.

The slightly donnish Freddie is fairly easily explained. Who wouldn't, if he could manipulate Latin well enough, wish to play with the professionals in this somewhat arcane but altogether superior game? Doing so without, in effect, a license, makes your participation in the game even more charming. I envy you here, and wish I could join in the game.

As for the dashing, slashing jokey-jakey Freddie, I wonder if he hasn't come into existence in good part because of your screenwriting, that is to say showbusiness, connection. Hollywood seems to bring out the Jew in everyone. I remember when Sammy Davis, Jr. converted to Judaism (from what I have no notion), a friend of mine named Albert Goldman (he wrote biographies of Lenny Bruce, Elvis Presley, and John Lennon, for the latter of which Elton John called him "human vermin," which I thought, considering the source, a great badge of honor), anyhow Albert Goldman said that there was nothing surprising about this, for Davis was only adopting the religion of the industry in which he worked. Dealing with the many monsters you must have dealt with in your movie-making has sharpened your irony and cynicism and given you a slightly-angry-yet-still-amused-at-the-swine edge, without which your Tarantino piece or your piece on *The Reader* could not have been written.

Two of course does not exhaust the number of Freddies. There is the defender of the faith Freddie, the literary equivalent of Simon Wiesenthal, hunting down anti-Semites hiding in the culture. There is the novelist Freddie, who is deeper than the others, the paterfamilias Freddie, the *TLS* Freddie, and who knows how many others – Freddies, in short, all over the joint.

As for your not being on as easy terms as I with the Jewish part of yourself, this must come from the colder, in some ways crueler version of anti-Semitism on offer in England, which I had alluded to earlier. As for my Jewishness, I, though like you in not turning up often in *shul* (you've transliterated it correctly), I find it is a central strain in my character and even exult in it, which is rather a new phenomenon among Jewish American intellectuals and artists. Lionel Trilling – and isn't it thrilling not to be Lionel Trilling? – has a number of statements in which he exclaims that there is nothing Jewish about his writing or reasons for writing, and anyone who finds anything Jewish in it is probably doing so to use it against him. Saul Bellow used to say, with his standard note of easy irritability, that people (for which read, the *goyim*) took him, Philip Roth, and Bernard Malamud as the Hart, Schaffner, & Marx (a successful American men's clothing manufacturer) of American literature, and he wasn't having any of it. Trilling, Bellow & co. were of course of an American generation more on the *qui vive* for anti-Semitism than those who came after – and rightly so. Anti-Semitism is still out there, of course, but I think it has become rather more defensive than formerly; to be caught out at it is more disgraceful than formerly, and that, I suppose, is progress of a sort.

Enough progress for someone like me openly to recognize that, of the few Joes extant (fewer perhaps than the multitudes of Freddies floating around), one is the distinctly Jewish Joe. Of the broad items that have contributed to my being the not altogether satisfactory fellow I am today, my being Jewish has played a significant part. My being a Chicagoan is another. Both have informed my outlook, my personal style (if I may be said to have one), my sense of humor and imagination for disaster (last phrase courtesy of that mild anti-Semite Henry James). But, as a certain ethnic people are wont to say, enough already; Jew, Jew, Jew, so, tell me, what else is new?

I have been indulging myself by reading things I know nothing about. Yesterday, for example, I bought, on the basis of a persuasive review in the *New York Times Book Review*, a biography by an English science writer named Graham Farmelo of the theoretical physicist Paul Dirac, one of the chief founders of quantum mechanics, about which I know a little less than zilch. I read three chapters of it during a fit of insomnia early this morning, and found it excellent; the book doesn't bar the ignorant (that would be me) from enjoyment. Dirac was an eccentric (he rarely spoke) and apparently a genius (when someone objected to Florida State University making him an offer of a professorship late in his career, someone there countered by saying that turning him down would be equivalent to the English Department turning down Shakespeare for a professorship.) I like to read about genius, even when I don't quite know, in a specific case, what qualifies for it.

I have also been reading about the great classicists in Hugh Lloyd-Jones' various essay collections: about E.R. Dodds and Eduard Fraenkel and Wilamowitz. I read Lloyd-Jones' lecture on the state of Pindar studies. Still, the pleasure of reading about such things, even though I don't expect to remember much of what I read, is the recollection that scholars and scientists have done – and let us hope continue to do – higher things and that life isn't devoted solely to personal ambitions (my own among them) and trivial popular culture.

Do you know Hugh Lloyd-Jones? I imagine your friend Peter Green has the lowdown, the true gen, on him. I know him only enough to like him. I met him through his late-in-life-acquired wife Mary Lefkowitz, also, as you know, a classicist, a teacher at Wellesley College and a woman of some courage: she took on the Black Athena crowd at her own college and else-where in politically correct American academic life, for which she took lots of heavy flak. Mary was on the editorial board of the *American Scholar* when I was its editor and used to bring Hugh to the dinners we held after our thrice-yearly meetings. Hugh, now in his late eighties, is in many ways my notion of an old-line English don: he has about a hundred and twenty teeth, none of them straight, a blurry not easily deciphered accent, and himalayas of dandruff on the shoulders of his inevitable blue blazers. He is not a dazzling but feels to me a very solid writer on classical subjects. He was as you know Regius Professor of Greek, the job for which old Maurice Bowra pined. He is also very old-shoe, comfortable to be with. Once, when I was writing an essay on the art of the nap, I asked Hugh if he napped. "Frequently," he replied. Did he do so sitting up or prone, I asked? "Prone," he replied. Trousers on or trousers off? "Trousers off," he replied. And for how long were these naps, I asked? "Depends," he replied, "when the cats wake up." Hugh also once told me that when Mary ironed his shirts, he, to lighten the burdensomeness of the task, read to her from Proust or Henry James. Now there is a highbrow domestic scene it charms me to contemplate.

I am scribbling away at various things. I have a story going called "Widow's Pique," about a woman who is clearing out her recently-dead husband's things and having to contemplate whether her marriage was a grievous mistake. I'm also at work – at sea is more like it – on an essay for Podhoretz *fils* on the city of Chicago. I just tap in one paragraph after another with little notion of whether they fit together or not. As a writer, organization or structure (to use the architectural metaphor) isn't even my short suit. My method of composition is to attempt to write one interesting sentence after another and hope that the interest, so to say, will compound itself and the absence of a high plan will go unnoticed. I've also been asked by *Notre Dame Magazine* to write an essay on the stages of life, which I've agreed to do. The price is nice ($4,000) and so is the subject. You get the feeling that I'm like that little girl in the song who just couldn't say no? She, clearly, was what we used to call a roundheels, and so, *mutatis* and no less *mutandis* am I and so remain, your faithful correspondent,

Joe

Dear Joe,

Here's comedy. As quite often (M. Jourdain, Malvolio etc.) it follows pretentiousness or its pretence. I am a little hard on myself (would that it had an apotropaic effect!), but I do see the funny side of what I'm about to tell you, even if I can't quite join in the laughter (it's when the ranks of Tuscany cannot control their mirth that one feels truly mortified). So: as I told you, with a faint air of *O Tempora, O Mores* (the classicist's long-wilting fragrance of choice), I spent more than a few days at the sorry turn of the summer culling the best of the *obiter scripta* of a certain G.M. Lee whose stack of postcards my friend Paul Cartledge sent me to save them from the Great Incinerator which threatens to consume the archives of the defunct Cambridge University Classics faculty mag *Farrago*; a collapse, we may now gloss, of far away and long ago. The nightmare is now beside us, if not to stern, since such fancy in-group (some read 'in-grope') publications are now beyond Benny Faction and his once lavish chums.

Paul assumed, and I honoured his professorial assumption, that G.M. Lee was the dated, regular signature of my old friend Guy Lee, about whom I told you at least as much as you need to know last time. So, I arranged anothers' man flowers as prettily as I might and added terse commentary and then, prompted by the *TLS* editor, another of the vanishing friends of Greece and Rome (Grease and CD-rom have taken their places *chez les jeunes*), translated the Latin for the benefit of what some people might call the intellectual *goyim* and also, I feared, for the disparagement of the happy few who could pick holes in my versions and so wonder, as I do with Ted Hughes's rendering of Ovid's *Metamorphoses*, whether they have anything closely to do with the original. You can, I am sure, supply the blank form of A.E. Housmanic disparagement in which wounded academic sensibilities express themselves. Housman used, it is said, to amuse himself in idle moments, when not editing Manilius to within an inch of his death, by denouncing the books of colleagues who had yet to compose them. Tempting? 'Philip Roth, who has his many admirers and reaches always for more . . .' Don't, as the English say, get me started.

Well, I did that and I did it again and Peter Stothard, editor of the *TLS*, pronounced himself all set to do a two-page spread before the cock crew thrice when . . . he had an editorial moment of the kind for which I lack the vocation: he checked to make sure that G.M. Lee and the Guy Lee whose small (not negligible) genius I was so sure was expressed in the squibs which, as they say, sounded just like him, ONLY like him, as I did not quite say, were indeed one and the same. And – yes, why else would I be telling you this? – G.M. Lee turned out to be someone who wrote about early Christianity and, although learned, was not identifiable with A.G. Lee, my late friend, whose *cognomen* he shared. Thus (and you can say that again) I was spared, by Stothard's vigilance, the public hoots of the hosts of Midian who – in *Hymns Ancient and Modern*, which you were spared – prowl and prowl around, looking for a bout, but I did waste days which are becoming increasingly precious as one more bloody year lurches with what always seems increasing velocity towards Auld Lang Syne time.

Nothing is ever wasted, they say, and I'm trying to remember the tune to hum it to. I can come up only with the realisation that, as George Steiner would say unless he wouldn't, and possibly both, we are all Jews, postulants, fakes, fabrications of one kind and other. The two Lees were doubtless different in all manner of ways which a biographer, or a psychoanalytic publishing scoundrel, would prove showed that they had less in common than meets their reader's eye. *Après coup* (coup and err coming close on each other), I have come to realise that the G.M.L. gentleman – not, I suspect, more than an affiliate member of the Classics faculty – was hung up on, and glib in the rendering of, the words of the early Fathers, although he did, by the very act of (usually) Latin-versifying them, treat them with a certain irony.

Recent classical studies are heavily into analysing the subconscious of Romans, especially in the time of Nero, when a word and a blow came into close propinquity. The going phrase for the attitudes of Seneca & co. is 'rhetoricised mentality'. Sounds like the bell-jargon into which students are incited to encase themselves, doesn't it? What I learn from the confusion that I never suspected between Lee and Lee is that, even in the unthreatening social climate of Old England (now reduced to a gents' clothes shop in, I think, the Boulevard Malesherbes), the rhetoricised mentality, however understated, was ALWAYS a part of the classical tradition. It went back to the beginnings of Latin lit., in fact: the early (lower-class, imported Greco) poets were encouraged to a certain daring, but not beyond it. One who cheeked the Metelli (the Vanderbilts of the day) got a good cudgelling for his trouble.

The English gentleman, with his uniform of proprieties, his limited but rich field of allusion, his disillusioned pose when it came to politics or religious enthusiasm (what Byron called, ape that he certainly was, 'enthusymusy'), while going along with notions of patriotism, was trained to adopt the style of antique Romans which antique Romans themselves knew to be a sort of noble imposture (which is why they found that sincere phony Cicero a bit of a joke, since he took it all for reality). The dressed ape wears culture no less than boxers and, in the classical wardrobe, equipped himself to be remarked for being unremarkable. The similarity between Lee and Lee was superficial, it may be, but it was essential, I am pretty sure, to what carried them through life, not cheating, not claiming credit where it was not due, not using expressions that lacked sound grammatical provenance, not shouting the odds of their own originality (never a virtue in the composition of verses in Greek or Latin), not attributing sentiments or sentences to writers who never uttered them, and so on. The last snows of yesteryear are melted and flow together into the eternal ditch, one might overdo it by saying, which means that Lee and Lee converge in a set of texts which either might have composed, though only the one I did not know actually did.

One of the nicest moments, which I took to be 'typical' of the Guy I knew, was on a postcard on which the author had proposed to replace the word '*venduntur*', meaning 'they are sold' (a passive form from the root from which 'vendor' comes) by '*veneunt*' which means 'they are up for sale'. The latter term, which I either never knew or had long forgotten, derives from the rarish verb '*veneo*', which is 'active' but intransitive and means 'I am up for sale'. The epigrammatist had proposed to substitute the latter for the former not because the earlier word was not proper Latin but because he suspected that it might not be used poetically. The beauty of pedantry is that sometimes it becomes moral, as it did here: no-one was ever going to know (the oldest excuse in the one-night-standsman's repertoire), but it still worried him into a correction that may have been superfluous. Neither kudos nor cash was at stake; NOTHING was at stake but honour. And yet, the man cannot live with the possibility of – what? – gracelessness, in his unsolicited and unpaid squib in a magazine that almost no-one would read.

It is a sign of his times that when I called Guy's wife, Helen, at a moment when I had no doubt that what Paul Cartledge had delivered, in good faith, was indeed her husband's work, she was very pleased to give me permission to use it, even though – as it turned out – she had (of course) no idea whether he had actually done it. I am still mildly amazed when I talk to writers' wives who say that they never, or rarely, look at what their men have done. I have come more and more to rely on Beetle's wink or wince, smile or frown, when I think I have finished something. She taught me more about punctuation than I care to admit and she has a certain British scholarly disapproval of overstatement or adjectival prolixity. Helen Lee had lived with Guy for as long as Beetle with me, and was a Cambridge graduate, though I don't know in which school, but Guy clearly did not seek her imprimatur and, I daresay, did not care to bore her with his work. With Beetle, I hesitate, but not for long; unless the Classics are involved.

The strangely paradoxical thing about the classical tradition was that it was, or seems to the modern mind to have been, snobbish and exclusive. Yet the coteries of scholarship were, in some ways, more easily permeable, by merit, than those of social snobbery (or modern, opinion-dominated university faculties?). It's true that Jews were excluded from Oxbridge until some time fairly late in the 19th century, but the tradition of textual analysis, gloss, emendation, improvement, commentary was, of course, antecedent to Greece and Rome and part of Temple life long before it was formalised by (post-Golden Age) classicists and grammarians, Quintilian among the first. The Cuddihy-style idea that Jews were uncouth alien folk may have been a persistent social notion, even in exalted academe (Isaiah Berlin was the first Jew in, 192??, to be a prize fellow of All Souls), but the scholars always knew, surely, that what they did with Latin and Greek was posterior to what Jesus & co. did when they showed how smart, and inventively accurate, they were by trumping the rabbis in debate.

The great thing about their absolute, often wearisome standards is that philologists were immune, during the work itself, to the prejudices that, in a hundred ways, or a thousand, the same scholars might manifest in the Senior Common Room or wherever. Arnaldo Momigliano is only one (Moses Hadas another maybe) of those who were admitted without reserve to the field of excellence. I still find that more enviable than all the Pulitzers and Bookers and Nobels that laurel our betters. The great Mommsen (Caesar-worshipper though he was) stands out among the German academics – as against the philosophers and the historians – in his resolute dismissal of anti-Semitism: it had no relevance to the world in which he chose to live. It was, I suspect, Nietzsche's training in philology that made him unable to stomach Wagner's vulgar rant and made him, whatever his sister reupholstered him to seem, another of the good Germans for whom quality Jews were something to admire.

Tout à toi,
Freddie

Dear Freddie,

Until now I was prepared to be neutral about Peter Stothard, who as editor of the *TLS* has neither improved nor diminished the paper and whose own writing, on classical and contemporary political subjects, strikes me as of less than great intellectual interest and without distinctive style. But now that he has rescued you – pulled your chestnuts from the fire, saved your bacon, and here I run out of cliché food metaphors – makes him heroic in mine eyes, which have not, alas, seen the glory of the coming of the Lord. Innocent and understandable enough, such a mistake, were you to have been allowed to lapse into it, would no doubt have cast your intellectual hide among the small hyena minds who have sharp teeth. The error would not have been of the stature of Trevor-Roper's when he misidentified the (psuedo) Hitler diaries, from which, it has always seemed to me, his reputation never quite fully recovered. Or even if it may be said to have done so, it was always there, that mistake, for Trevor-Roper's enemies to use against him, which they were not loath to do. Pause here for a long breath of relief, mein Herr Freddie, then kneel and cross yourself for your good luck.

Your remarking that "nothing is ever wasted" reminds me of one of my favorite Jewish sayings, which is: "Shouldn't be a total loss." I first heard it as the punchline of the joke about the man who tells his friend that a prostitute approached him on the street offering inexpensive sex. When he asked her where they might go to have it, she replies right here, pointing to a nearby alley. He follows her down the alley. She tells him her fee is $10, which is reasonable enough and which he extracts from his wallet. "All right," she says, "take down your pants." When he does so, she runs off with his $10. "What did you do then?" his friend asks. "Shouldn't be a total loss," the man says, "I urinated." I should like you to know that, so much am I enamored of the phrase, I find myself using it at least once or twice a week, without of course the urinating part. I recommend it to you in the strong belief that the use of it will bring you, too, satisfaction.

That Guy Lee's wife was, to put it gently, less than *au courant* with her husband's writing is not surprising. I took a certain pleasure in the fact that my parents rarely – and my mother only once – read my writing. Barbara reads everything I write, often catching me out in repetitions or lapses in grammar or taste, though now, in the computer age, when I don't print everything out, I often send things along to editors without her having first read them.

Who reads one's scribbling and who doesn't is always an amusing, and sometimes rather a sad, matter. I not long ago gave a lecture at a wealthy synagogue, where, beforehand, the rabbi, one of those bearded plump gents – resembling one of those soft people in Turgenev – a man with the wonderfully un-Jewish name of Steve Mason, announced to me: "You've really written a lot. I looked you up on the Internet this morning, and there's a great deal about things you've written." By which I took him to mean, "Not that I've read a word of it, schmucko, nor am I soon likely to." Thank you, Rebbe. Virgil Thomson used to say that whenever he felt he was famous he had only to go out into the world to discover otherwise. As a relatively small public writer, I am rarely surprised at who hasn't read me and always pleased to discover some unlikely person who has.

On the other not yet shaky hand, when I have a new book, I try to be very careful about to whom I send copies. Arnaldo Momigliano (in America he would have been Arnie Mumzer, not at all the same thing) once said to me, in his Piedmontese-accented English, "You know, my dear Epstein, the cheapest way to acquire a book remains to buy it." After pausing to admire the placement of that "remains," I required a fair spell to grasp Arnaldo's meaning, which I believe is as follows: The nice thing about buying a book is that you don't have to read the damn thing, whereas if you are given a book or someone lends you a book you are under the obligation of reading it. I have in my own misspent life been gifted – as the crappy new verb has it – with some heart-sinkingly thick tomes written by unlively minds that I felt under the heavy obligation of reading. Not a nice gift but more a prison sentence is what it felt like.

This morning I finished a chapter of a book the composition of which I have been too long at, on the subject of *Gossip*, a chapter titled "Gay Gossip." My contention is that homosexual men have a tradition of artful and amusing gossip. The tradition derives, I contend, from the fact that being homosexual, and having until recent years to hide the fact, gay men have a natural instinct for looking for what is hidden in other people, especially their vices. Lots of relatively recent gay gossip has been – no surprise here – about who is secretly homosexual or bisexual. Yul Brynner, according to the gay (and sometime sour) grapevine, was bisexual and so, Truman Capote reports, was Steve McQueen. Leonard Bernstein was gay, it goes without saying, and so, according to the same grapevine, was Vladimir Horowitz. The homosexual men from whose gossip I quote in my chapter are Truman Capote, Gore Vidal, Tennessee Williams, and a man named Leo Lerman, a New York figure who was for a while the editorial director of the Condé Nast magazines. One of the small problems is that the recent herd-like stampede from homosexual closets has much diminished the pleasure in gay gossip, taken, so to say, the charm from it. The new homosexual is less clever than confessional. He doesn't wait for other people to gossip about whom he's been sleeping with but beats them to the punch by telling you himself, sometimes rather too graphically. I spent a part of last week reading a book called *City Boy* by a writer named Edmund White, who, though himself seventy, is among the new generation of gay men and whose book contains such extraordinary sentences as: "I've always been an apostle of promiscuity" and "Sadomasochism [in the late 1960s] still sounded perverted and ever so slightly tacky – sort of New Jersey." How can one possibly gossip about a guy who writes a book in which he describes himself as "a bottom" (the position from which he enjoys sex) and is pleased to report that a once-famous drag queen named Brandy Alexander called him "the universal ball"?

Writing about any aspect of homosexuality from the standpoint of a man outside the club entails the prospect of getting beat up in print for being a bigot and monster, not to say an absolute demon. As long ago as 1971, I wrote an essay for *Harper's* about homosexuality, and the many hypocrisies attendant upon the false tolerance of *bien pensant* heterosexuals toward it. The essay appeared just as the Gay Liberation Movement was cresting. The essay aroused a noisy response, including what in those days was called a "zapping" of *Harper's* offices by gay protesters. I remember giving an interview to a homosexual (not yet gay) magazine, in which I was asked, among other things, if I thought homosexual men should be allowed to serve in the Army. The Vietnam War was still on, please recall. I answered yes, so long as they are willing to abide by the same rules as heterosexual men in the Army: no fucking in the barracks and all that. I told this to my friend Hilton Kramer, who said that the headline of the interview was likely to read, "Sheeny Fag-baiter Urges Conscription," and he wasn't far wrong. I ended my *Harper's* essay by remarking that the origin of homosexuality remains an unsolved puzzle and that, because it has brought so much grief to so many men who have had to live with it, if I had my druthers, I would wish homosexuality off the face of the earth. Which sentiment Gore Vidal read to mean that I wished all homosexuals off the face of the earth and was therefore little better than Hitler. (The old argument *ad Hitlerum*, hope you never have it applied to you.) Ah, me, still another rainy day in the old Republic of Letters.

I've been sent a biography of Irving Thalberg to write about. As you well know, Thalberg is another of those Jewish princes – George Gershwin is most prominently the other – who quickly acquired the reputation of a genius and then, like Adonis, died young, Gershwin at 38, Thalberg at 37. Gershwin didn't know he was going to die until his brain tumor was upon him; Thalberg, a so-called blue baby, the result of not getting sufficient oxygen to the blood as an infant, was from the outset predicted not to live past 30. Knowing he had no time to waste, he was quick out of the gate, essentially running Metro-Goldwyn (not yet Mayer) by the time he was twenty. He was small and deli-cately handsome, and, as one of his colleagues put it, "pissed cold water," by which he meant that he could be tough and unemotional in his decision-making. Making decisions, vast numbers of them, is essentially what he did.

The parts of the book I've read thus far that interest me most, and will likely interest you even more, have to do with Thalberg's mixed treatment of screenwriters. He thought of them, as he thought of actors, as children, and sensed that, however good they were before, once they got out to Hollywood they were ruined. Yet, knowing he needed them, he continued to invite them out. He was probably a frustrated writer himself. Apart from his executive abilities, his real skill seemed to be understanding how stories worked, which allowed him to step in and unclog muddled screenplays, sometimes well into their shooting. The author of the biography, which isn't to be published until December, is a man named Mark Vieira. He writes decently and has vast quantities of information. Something here I thought you might want to look into, even possibly write about yourself.

Hugh Lloyd-Jones died yesterday, at 87. The great English line of classical scholars is, alas, dying out. Only Peter Green and Jasper Griffin are left, or at least so far as I know. A great line it was, and I hope I am wrong about its fading away.

Best, Joe

Dear Joe,

Not long ago, towards the end of the Tin Age (tin is a Wodehousian locution for money), someone persuaded Volvo to make a surely very expensive commercial in which a party of returning spacemen are greeted on the tarmac – after the completion of yet another mission of the kind which is supposed to excite us with the endurance and potential of the human animal and which, in senescent truth, bores me almost as much as the novels of, oh, take your pick from Antonia Byatt, Alan Hollinghurst, Sebastian Faulks and who all else among the award-winners *de nos jours* – by a fleet of sleek cars. The captain of the *Intrepid*, a Robert Ryan lookalike, frowns across at one of the attendant motors, asks its make and, when told it's a Volvo, says, 'How long have we been away?'

It seems a very long three weeks ago since I shut down my systems here in France and headed, via London, for Greece, but when we get back what's different, apart from the colour of our skin, darker again after a late dose of Aegean rays? It used to be that the mail had mounted into threatening sierras, usually with a nasty landslide of threatening letters from the British equivalent of the IRS. The evidence that I am no longer anything like loaded is that these red hot solicitations, headed FINAL DEMAND, no longer appear, but then nor does anything much except bills or what the frogs call '*pub*'. The best use of 'final' I ever heard was in Brisbane airport, where an Aussie voice called out 'First and final call' for some flight or other. Take off or piss off, matey.

How long is it since I (or you) received a handwritten letter or even a handwritten envelope? Now what mounts up is the tally of e-mails, although here again the number that cry out to be clicked upon is far smaller than the surrounding solicitations which are first cousin to puffery of one kind and, at this season, in particular, the other: Awards Time has come around again, so the movie companies are seeking the votes of Academy members, WAG members and who all else in their effort to encase their crappy product with ennobling emblems. All shall have prizes? And all shall write and make shit to deserve them.

I remain almost as impatient to open e-mails as I once was to rip envelopes and hope (Dorothy Parker's line 'the two sweetest words in the English language are "cheque enclosed"' has not lost its zip) that something delectable would be revealed. The young seem willing to leave their e-mails pending unread for longer than I could endure, or am likely to live: our son Stephen has literally hundreds of e-s which he is content to leave knocking soundlessly on the door of his consciousness. Me, I gobble the things. What do I hope for? Sir Walter Ralegh summarised his ambitions and, God help us, my enduring ones, I suppose: 'For Gold, for Praise, for Glory.' Glory fell at an early fence, when by the happiest of chances, I failed to be called to serve either Her (earlier His) Majesty or Dwight D. Eisenhower. While some people were finding glory, or some sour substitute, in Korea, I was in an austere facsimile of pre-war Cambridge.

Between 1945 and 1956, when Suez (and the aforesaid Ike's threat to pull the plug on the pound) proved that Britain was no longer king of the castle or ruler of the waves, we still had the impression that Yeats was wrong and that the centre *had* held; what's more, we were at it. The good did not lack conviction, least of all that they might not be all that good. The British contrived, in that decade of my teens and early twenties, still to have their imperial cake and cut slices of the local Dundee for the citizens who, having won the war, deserved free dentures and specs. The National Health Service, which has recently been the exemplary Awful Warning when the American Right set out to depict Medicare as likely to be staffed by the smiler with the knife, was the then smallish price the British chose to pay for having needed the services of the lower orders, previously largely unemployed, in order to win the war. The price of the NHS has since become (the word 'exponential' clamours for an innings) so mountainous that most of the national income, and some of the national outcome (*Touche Pas* head the prescription list of all parties), is connected with it. The British keep (have kept) down their unemployment figures by recruiting more and more people, of small qualification and often of less English, to keep their hospitals insanitary and their population in a state of more or less regular valetudinarianism.

Where was I? Glory. Its only real meaning has to be military: learning to be steady under fire was only one of the games we played at my Public (private)

School. The use of blank ammunition made sure that our Field Days – when we wore khaki and carried rifles and prefigured the boy soldiers of Africa and other sad tracts of land without a subway system – had something of the loud, disorganised dreariness of modern – as contrasted with today's post-modern – warfare, without the danger. This reminds me of the old story, which you may well have told me, or anthologised, of the pre-1914 Galician Jewboy conscripted into the Austrian army. You know it? Shucks, I'll tell it anyway. His mother wanted to subtilise him out of doing his duty, but he chose to do it (assimilationist creep). He went through however many weeks of basic training with remarkable. . . how about phlegm? While real bullets were fired over his head, he swung across chasms, he crawled under barbed wire that gave him only six inches of clearance, he waded through swamps with his rifle above his head, he aimed, he fired, he ran, he jumped. He did what the *goyim* did, and just as well, if not better. A *mensch*, why not? Then he was sent to the front. The moment came when he and his comrades had to charge the enemy trenches, just as they had rehearsed so often. Only this time real bullets were fired *at* him and his friends. As his best buddy was cut to ribbons, he called out, 'Hey, are you crazy? Can't you see there are *people* here?'

Did I miss glory? Did you? Should we? I think Sir Walter linked it pretty closely with both gold and praise. What we must never say about Bush and Blair (history's Sunshine Boys) is that if they had only been less moral, less restrained, less Christian even, we – you people and others – might today have Free Motoring For All and what's anyone gonna do about it, huh? I am not saying (would I ever?) that we/they *should* have established a proprietorial protectorate over a state manufactured into being by the British in such a form that it could *never* be stable, never be 'just', never have a common sense of citizenship (Israel/Palestine came off much the same production line), so that the Imperial presence would always be temporarily/permanently necessary, but all the same. . . Gold was never something you earned, in good Sir Walter's golden time, but something you *found*. If it worked for stout Cortez why not for us? Writers, *eheu!*, have to work for the stuff, and when it fails to come in for us as it does for all those guys who get stacked at airports, well, we imitate the *conquistador* only by being silent, in a pique, and where is Darien anyway?

Praise is still a sweet substitute for currency, I have to say. Among the e-mails that beamed in in my absence was an A-mail from young Podhoretz (now my Editor of the Month) in which he told me that my review of Tarantino in *Commentary* had excited more applause that anything written in any publication over which he presided. Twenty-five people already had mobbed him in the streets and demanded that I be famous for a day. The cheque is not yet in the mail, but I am the big man in my office right now; if also the only one. In addition (where is Ossa? I have Pelion ready to heap on it), I have been commissioned by the BBC radio to write a piece which I called, with catchpenny cunning, *A Thousand Kisses*; yet another take on Gaius Valerius Catullus, about whom I have been imagining writing a novel ever since I was fifteen and looked up the word *glubit* in Liddell and Scott. It's just one of the usages which embarrassed old-style scholars, since it occurs in a savage poem against Catullus's one time great love, Lesbia, in which she is said to be given, as it were, to a spot of '*glubit*' with the many lovers whom she entertains at ten cents a dance.

The dictionary tells us (reluctantly) that *glubo, glubere* means to 'deprive of its bark ... peel'. The organ on which she performed this activity was, of course, manifest but unspoken, Philistine not Jewish. It is a mark of the *pudibonderie* of some classicists, even in the 1960s, that they preferred to be puzzled by this poem, if not to (as one Fordyce did) eject it from the canon. The British did much the same with mutinous sepoys in the good old days in India, but the canon had three 'n's. Calmed things down for the best part of a century, that did.

I am looking forward to your *Gossip* book, and what's more I'm whispering about it to people. It seems to me that if you live long enough (and I am not saying that enough is yet enough, nothing like that), everything reminds you of something. You don't need to steep your madeleine in tepid tea nor trip on an irregular stone in the Place des Vosges; you just lodge the clue in your mental file and it will find itself adjacent to something you had forgotten until then. At Cambridge I knew a man called Gossip, John of that ilk. Yes, a Scot. He, like so many that were not like me (no shortage in that department, ever), had been in the army. The barrackroom had enriched his vocabulary and widened his mouth. I think he wore specs and was somewhat overweight as well as outspoken. A friend of mine, after spending what promised to be a virginity-losing day and evening with a girl called Janet was asked by Gossip whether the consummation wished for had come to ... climax (forget fruition). My friend (later a professor of education) reported that Janet had had the curse and so, alas ... 'Ah', said Gossip, 'so blood under the fingernails is all you've got to show for a day at the races!' Are you ashamed of me? Memory has no morals and, as I have said before and may again, not all its children are muses.

Tout à toi,
Freddie

Dear Freddie,

My definition of a pessimist is a man who doesn't check his mail. I check mine, relentlessly and in its different forms: e-mail, or snail-mail, or Pony Express. I may feel that Europe is finished, that western civilization has had the course, that humankind generally is on the way out, but about my mail I remain hopeful. Even as I write this, I am waiting for today's mail, which now, because of our having a new mailman who has been given a new route, arrives in mid-afternoon when it used to arrive no later than noon – a point of mild but genuine grievance for me. As for e-mail, I adore it, check my own no fewer than twenty times a day, would find life without it irksome in the extreme. Among other things, e-mail has put me in touch with many more readers, a few of them satisfied customers, no small benefit to your normal egomaniacal scribbler.

What I expect from the mail in its differing forms are surprises, chiefly, rare enough though their arrival is. I expect neither news of inheritances nor offers of ambassadorships. But I do more modestly hope for reprint fees (pennies from heaven, as I call them), offers I would be foolish to refuse, praise from unexpected quarters, word of my having won an insignificant but (to people who are not in the know) distinguished-sounding prize. None of these things, I do understand, are likely to change my life in any serious way. I am too old to expect a killing. Modest though my expectations are, expectations I nonetheless retain, but for small triumphs exclusively.

As for glory, I have had little in my life and can imagine none in the offing. The only chance I had for glory was in high-school sports, but my sport was tennis, and girls did not come out to watch tennis matches, and female adulation, in my reading of the matter, is a coefficient (if I am using that word correctly) of adolescent glory. Military glory is of course of a different, a higher order. I put in two years in the peacetime (dull-time is more like it) United States Army, which gave me the merest hint of a whisp of a ghost of a clue of what military combat might be like. I distinctly do not regret not having died for my country, especially for some essentially political war with an unresolved ending, such as those fought in Korea, Vietnam, Iraq, and – next up – Afghanistan. I am in my date of birth lucky to have danced blithely between the dark raindrops of war: too young for Korea, too old for Vietnam. What I do regret, though, is never having been tested by war; let me rephrase that: what I regret is never having been tested by war and (natch) having come through. I do not long to be able to say that I killed twenty-eight huns, nips, goons, wogs, fully half with my bare hands; it would be nice, though, to be able to say that I was shot at and by God did not cack my pants. Ah, well, perhaps in the next life I shall discover if I really have courage.

I had an acquaintance, a mad little Jew named William Lichtman, who carried a business card that read "Col. William Lichtman, Mercenary." He won the Medal of Honor in World War Two; one day he brought it to lunch, and showed it to me, its blue and white ribbon much bedraggled, over his chopped-liver sandwich. (I should have but neglected to say – *esprit* your own *escalier* – that medal ain't exactly chopped liver.) He also flew in the Israeli war of independence. I have never heard anyone speak with more violent language than he; he had Jewish paranoia to the highest power. In argument, in which I never engaged him, he held that if you hadn't killed anyone in warfare you ought to shut the fuck up, for you don't know what the hell you are talking about, no matter the subject up for discussion. He was a colossal bore, Bill Lichtman, a Johnny One-Note, who is, if still extant, in his nineties and probably by now nicely pickled by dementia.

I had an offer the other day that I could refuse. The offer was to write for the *Daily Beast,* and was made me by a smart youngish editor named Tom Watson (not the golfer) who left *Newsweek* to join Ms. Tina Brown, who invented and runs the *Daily Beast.* (You will recall that *The Beast* is the name Waugh gave to his newspaper in *Scoop.*) The sum I would be offered was not specified, but I don't think it would have mattered. I turned down the invitation chiefly because the *Beast*'s daily (almost hourly) rhythms are not mine; nor do I wish my scribblings to be tied, tin can on a mad dog's tail, to the news of the moment. Having said this, I must now go on to tell you that I do (as the kids used to say) check out the *Daily Beast* every morning, and find it not at all a bad way to keep up with the world's insanity, and with no trepidation recommend it to you, especially its brief videos.

Have you had to do with Ms. Tina Brown? I haven't, at least not personally, but I find her a figure of great interest. If I were William Hazlitt putting together my own little *Spirit of the Age*, Ms. Brown would be among my portraits of choice. She is indefatigable, indefatigably with-it, and even more indefatigably dedicated to creating a stir. Many moons ago I wrote a piece in the *TLS* about the journalist Joseph Mitchell and the *New Yorker*; it was around the time that Ms. T. Brown had taken over its editorship. Of her taking it over, I wrote something along the following lines: One can only compare Tina Brown's editorship of the magazine to having a dear, elegant, suavely well-mannered old friend who has discovered a novelty shop on the way home from work from which he has taken to purchasing plaster-of-Paris dogshit and rubber simulacra of vomit that, when visiting your home, he gleefully deposits on the carpeting.

Did Ms. Brown, having read this, as she must have done, make a note to have me one day castrated? Did she place my name, twice underlined, in her book of enemies? Did she bed down at night with her much older husband muttering, This Jew (me, not Harold Evans, the husband) must die! *Au contraire, mon frère*. Not long after I wrote this she got one of her minions to ask me to write for the *New Yorker*, which I proceeded to do for fun and profit. Now I say one has to admire such a girl. And, while allowing all that might be said against her, I do, grudgingly, laughingly, but genuinely admire her spirit, which suggests that it's all a game, silly, a goofy mad game, no need to get so worked up and personal about things.

Good to learn that your piece in *Commentary* on the odious Tarantino went down so well with the magazine's readers. Good, too, that John Podhoretz reported this to you. John does splendidly two of the three things a good editor should do: he responds speedily and decisively to a manuscript and he does not stint on praise. The third thing, his work on manuscripts, is thus far largely unknown to me. My guess is that his interest here is not great; his talent lies more in acquisition than in the mopping-up side of the operation. His predecessor, Neal Kozodoy, was a demon of *potschkying* with other people's prose, sometimes greatly improving things, sometimes making them worse. He liked to get in there up to the elbows and muck around. He was also keen on cutting. I once sent him an e-mail that read: "Dear Neal, I just wrote the first five paragraphs of my Solzhenitsyn piece for you; three of them, I think you will find, can come out easily." *Potschkying*, when it comes to manuscripts, has its limits. An editor can make a poor article or essay publishable, or perhaps make a mediocre article or essay decent, but he cannot make another person's writing terrific. Fellow named the actual author has to do that.

I have been rereading the first 55,000 words of my *Gossip* manuscript. Apart from discovering some appalling repetitions, I find what I have done thus far is not entirely nauseating, which is a relief. The subject is such a good one that I shall never forgive myself if I fail to honor the complexity of it. Honoring complexity, you should know, has become my major criterion, my motto and creed, for writing on serious subjects. Honor the complexity: easy to say; hard to do.

I have been reading, as my bathroom book, A.J.A. Symons' *The Quest for Corvo*, which I last read, my guess is, forty years ago. The book holds up nicely. I find I remember almost nothing about it, except for the general spookiness of Fr. (stands for both Frederick and Father) Rolfe. One of the few side benefits of growing older is that one sometimes comes to formerly-read books as if afresh.

Power to the people (with the people, drawn from a very carefully culled list, to be named later).

Best, Joe

Dear Joe,

I've been sent a new biography of Montaigne for review in one of those small magazines that pay you what an honest working man would throw in your face if you offered it to him for mowing the lawn, but which – it is called the *Literary Review* – still attracts very good writers and allows them to express themselves in unhomogenised prose, briefly but not tersely. As it happens (why do I hate the word serendipity *so* much?), I have been finishing Starobinksi's *Montaigne en mouvement* for some months now and also reading the new Gallimard compendium of Micheau's essays in modern French. This makes it easier to motor through them and yields such gems, in the essay on Philosophy and Death, as '. . . *lors de cette dernière scène entre la mort et nous, il n'y a plus moyen de feindre, il faut parler français . . .*' There is an implicit pun, of course: what he is saying is, presumably, that we must speak frankly, but it also is not far from saying that in the final negotiations between ourselves and – I suppose – ourselves, the language of diplomatic formality has to be French. It can hardly be English as she is spoke on either side of the – another expression I *loathe* – pond. I sit in a room not very far from Montaigne's château, on a crisp bright autumn Sunday morning, after our regular, almost ritual, visit to the market in the neighbouring village of Saint-Cyprien, where we always buy six *grosses crevettes* and two *cabécous* (or should it be *cabécoux*?), small, flat goats' cheeses for our sabbatical lunch, and I look up at the oak beams above my head and wonder what I should incise in them, if I were a motto man.

Back in 1971, I wrote a novel called *April, June and November* (a nifty one-volume trilogy) for which I chose an epigraph from Maurice Bowra's friend George Seferis: *Kirie, ochi m'aftous*. Lord, not with these people. It announced, with only-kidding aloofness, my disdain for the London literary and some-what artistic folk who were depicted in the novel, along with a well-disguised version of the American couple who had recently arrived on 'our' Greek island of Ios and had, by their eagerness to make a good impression, allowed themselves to be overcharged, with the result. . . But you know the story.

My affectations of disassociation from the London crowd (including a number of people whom I did not know and whose invitations to friendship/acquaintance, it can now be said, very quietly, I should probably have been pleased to have) were sincere, but probably, well, mutable. Timon of Athens would, I suspect, still have been checking his e-mails, twenty times a day, as you do, and I do, and who doesn't?

I am never sure precisely in which *galère* I might have felt totally, cosily at home. When Joe Losey (his instance leaps to consciousness) wrote to me, when we were living in Rome in 1965, and asked me to write some dialogue for a film he was working on, tears came to my eyes. It was, as Micheau might say, with a wince, the cinematic *comble.* Even though I was already quite high in the rankings, it was, so to say, *l'annonce faite à* Frederic. In the event, I never did work with/for Losey, although we did have what used to be called huddles. His way of huddling was to lie stretched out on a *chaise longue* in the house very like the one in *The Servant,* the success of which had probably funded its purchase. For a Communist, he was remarkably *ancien régime* (Louis XIV had a courtier whose privilege it was to wipe his behind after the king had satisfied his *grands besoins*); Joe's *auteur*-like condescensions stimulated my British-educated *hauteur* and, as the French say, the current did not pass between us. Later, he put it about that I was a 'dangerous fake', which was telling them; it sounds more and more flattering as the years pass (and do they ever?), but he stayed in touch and, some time after labelling/libelling me, asked me to script a book called *La Truite* by a French Communist (of course) author called Roger Vailland, whose *La Loi* had been a bestseller. I told Joe it was lacking in substance; he went ahead and later confessed to me that I had been right to warn him off.

Apart from *The Servant,* to which not only Pinter but also Willie Maugham's nephew Robin brought their brimming pitchers, I never liked his movies *that* much; nor do I now wish that I had been more deferential, or whatever it would have taken, when I had my audience with him. There is, however, something to be said for hanging in with life because Joe's grandson, a certain Marek Losey, who has just directed his first film (with a $75,000 budget) and had a success with it, is now set, as they say, sometimes of jellies, to direct a screenplay which my son Stephen and I have written and is pretty damn good. This depends, of course, on raising money in a now almost dry pool, but we can enjoy the irony at least. Young(ish) Marek is quite a tough character and has needed to be in order to survive the aftershocks of Joe, who himself had to endure, etc.

Lacking an ancestral *château*, I should not be sitting here in the Perigord playing the *homme de lettres* were it not for the movies, which I have milked and to which I have, from time to time, delivered my churn of butter and, occasionally, if you insist, cream. I do not, however, wish I had been a full-time movie guy, though I could wish that they had made more of my scripts (one of which, written fifteen years ago or so, is now in the process of being defrosted by someone with $$$), nor yet would I wish, for a moment, to have been among those dependent on the editors of fancy mags or even on publishers for my daily bread. You spoke well of Tina Brown, with whom I have small acquaintance but no quarrel. She was quickly out of the gate when I started working with Kubrick and, before I had got down to writing the script, was eager for my version of *Là-Bas*. I had tea with her at the Berkeley Hotel in London and, quick to be Maecenaetan, she also asked me to do a profile of Jimmy Goldsmith, which might have been fun (I was later asked to do a TV series about him, and discovered a lot of piquant stuff), but I never did. When Kubrick died, Tina dispatched her hatchet-cum-carrot gay emissary, whose name you may know, to get me to let her have what turned into *Eyes Wide Open*. I recall saying that the offer for it to appear in the *New Yorker* implied 'neither fame nor fortune', but my swollen head must have reduced, or the emoluments fattened, because my little book was published (*not* in its entirety) in Updike's house mag, the only time I ever appeared in it. By the time it came out, Tina had departed and Mr Remnick was in the chair, which, I suppose, he still occupies. He wrote me a letter (I can see your Cheshirish smile) saying that my piece supplied the apex to his tenure. Since then I have not been troubled by him.

The greatest good fortune for a writer, I am instructed to tell myself, in French when the time comes, is to be able to play both sides against the middle and to divide them down the middle in order to foray on either side. It needs trimming, but that's my kind of hedgefund: put them all under contribution, but depend on none. Your story of the rabbi who checked you out on the net but gave no indication of actually having read anything leads me to realise that I have no such constituency of cordial indifference. The Jewish community in England is either grand (Rothschilds, etc.) or suburban/parochial and I am embarrassed by my inability to hum or mutter in their choruses, whether Hebrew or not. My Josephan coat of many colours (several anyway) has worn pretty well until very recently, but the biggest patch – I cannot deny it – has been *Britannique*, which now looks tattered and banana-republican. When Herzl invited Arthur Schnitzler to imagine what it would be like to have his plays put on in Jerusalem, Arthur (as Kubrick called him) responded, 'Maybe, but in what language?' The living English may not greatly attract (or invite) me but the dead are still my favourite company; Hazlitt is a sort of Montaigne with a deadline; Junius is the satirist whose bolts today's blues deserve; Gibbon (cleverly criticised for stylistic confusion by Clive James in his new fat volume of essays) delights me with his rococo ironies and even a minor writer such as Harold Nicolson has instructive felicities, but but but . . .

On holiday on 'our' (the sentimental possessive) island, I took a novel by another current master (Ian McEwan was last year's), Sebastian Faulks. It was called *On Green Dolphin Street*, set mostly in New York and DC and composed, none need doubt, with cartographic accuracy, but so witless, so lamely written, so incompetent and so sexless, when dealing with love and lust, that I wondered who those people were who, cited on the back, had found it so fine. The charge of envy (of bestsellers) cannot be sustained when its object lacks all style. Back to the lonely study and another look at Proust. However, in my present fiction, *Final Demands*, I do have my writer 'hero' observe, when advised to cut something by his admired wife, 'If Marcel Proust had had a wife like you, *À la recherche* would have been a short story'.

So: the beam above my head remains in want of a rubric. But talking of that last encounter, I mentioned before that when Lope de Vega was told that he was dying, he asked for confirmation and then said, 'Well in that case I can say it: Dante bores the shit out of me', or *algunas palabras* to that effect. It isn't French, but it is frank. But here's the kicker: Who now reads Lope de Vega?

Tout à toi,
Freddie

Dear Freddie,

Barbara and I had tea once a long while ago with Jean Starobinski, in his and his wife's cozy apartment in Geneva just across the street from the university. The connection is that Starobinski and I both wrote for the *Hudson Review*, and the magazine's editrix, Paula Dietz, set up the meeting for us. Starobinski is very learned, with very little in the way of pretension, or so I judged, with a good laugh and a nice kindly feeling about him. The Starobinskis are one of those families of endless achievement. Mme Starobinski is an ophthalmologist; the son we met at their apartment was a surgeon, then traveling with the

Chicago Symphony Orchestra for reasons I cannot now recall. A daughter was doing something no less impressive. If the family had a black sheep, he would doubtless have been a theoretical physicist or a neuroscientist. I regret to say that I didn't interrogate him gently on his life's story: how does a man named Starobinski turn up in Geneva, writing about Montaigne, Rousseau, and other high fine French subjects? I also neglected to ask him about his colleague, Herr von Steiner, about whom I suspect Jean S., even though a man with no apparent malice, might nonetheless have had some highly entertaining things to report.

I love Montaigne, and hope to read through the *Essays* one more time before the bar finally closes *chez* Epstein. I hope I haven't told you this already, but I used to be on the board of trustees of an American think tank called the Hudson Institute, whose president, a nice man named Herb London, used to begin each meeting by introducing everyone in the room in a brief but ingratiating way. When he would come to me, he would say, "Next is Joseph Epstein, the American Montaigne." I let him do this three times, squirming each time, and the fourth time he did it I said, calmly I hope, "Herb, I am very pleased that you think of me as the American Montaigne, but whenever you do I try to think, without success, of Montaigne saying to himself, 'Yo, hey, hot damn, I believe I'm the French Joseph Epstein.' As you can see, Herb, it doesn't work, so please knock off this American Montaigne stuff forthwith."

Your Joseph Losey story, the part about his living so well, reminds me of an old story of another Communist, this one nameless, who used to lunch regularly, at great expense, at the Waldorf Astoria. When someone asked him if there wasn't a contradiction between his politics and the way he lived, he replied, "Not at all. Nothing is too good for us Reds." These Commies, grant them this, know how to take care of business. Norman Podhoretz, when the building on West End Avenue in which he and his wife had an apartment was up for sale, with all the current owners to share in the profits, claimed he was confident he would make out handsomely since the two lawyers handling the sale were obvious Stalinists. And so, I gather, they did. One of the many contradictions of capitalism is that it seems especially intent on rewarding its enemies.

I have one of those letters from David Remnick that you mention possessing. I cannot recall ever having received a more cheering and extensive invitation. In it he declared how he hoped that I would continue to write for the *New Yorker*, and on any subject that might interest me. The jam, as Noël Coward called praise, was spread thickly. Since that time I have never appeared in the magazine, even though I have offered him, David R., a few essays that he found of no interest but that when published elsewhere caused an agreeable stir. More than once I suggested to him that I should like to write about tennis for the magazine – years ago it had a fine writer on tennis and golf named Herbert Warren Wind – and this, too, was fended off by his remarking that he had someone else on the case, though no-one ever did write about the tennis subjects I suggested. My best guess is that someone told David R. that I am among the bad guys – that I am not, in other words, a standard liberal. Standard liberalism, in the full flower of its predictable boringness, is now the flag under which the magazine each week sets sail. I shall probably never cease to subscribe to the *New Yorker*, but I find myself reading less and less of it.

Doubtless there is a tendency to overrate the quality of the old *New Yorker,* the magazine of Harold Ross and then William Shawn. This would be the *New Yorker* of Thurber and E.B. White, of A.J. Liebling and Joseph Mitchell, of Edmund (the Bunny) Wilson and, later, Pauline Kael and the dance critic Arlene Croce. As I mentioned earlier, I not long ago tried to read the Library of America edition of Thurber and found it not merely tough but no sledding whatsoever. Nothing in the book seemed even faintly amusing. (He, Thurber, was probably best in his drawings.) I found E.B. White unbearably sensitive – I distrust the ultra-sensitive writers, especially those who are always telling you in subtle or blatant ways how sensitive they are – and light, or as the beer companies have it, Lite. (I once wrote an essay called "E.B. White Lite.") Liebling, who I liked more than either Thurber or White, doesn't read so well thirty years later, and lots of his writing is marred by his politics in a manner I hadn't been aware of when I was in my twenties and enamored of him. Edmund Wilson was immensely helpful to me in my literary education, and it was good to read someone who wrote about literature in so virile and unacademic a manner, but he wasn't, our bunny, very deep and was much put off by anything he couldn't explain, such as the writing of Kafka and Conrad. He doesn't pass the tough test of being good when read young and still good when read old.

Toward the end of his life, I met Joseph Mitchell, who turned out to have been an admiring reader of mine, which delighted me. He was a sweet character, and we put in a few long sessions at the Century Club, which is, *mutatis mutandis*, the American equivalent of the Athaeneum. He spoke with a slow North Carolina drawl, and I remember him telling me that he came of a generation that "can never consider sex a trivial act. You know, Joe," he said to me, "when I was a boy, if you did ugly with a girl, her brother might shoot you." I hope you like "did ugly" as much as I do.

This past Thursday I gave a talk on the subject of gossip to four hundred or so well-to-do (there's an old-fashioned phrase) ladies of a Chicago club called the Fortnightly. I agreed to do this talk some seven or eight months ago, fully confident that either the month of October would never arrive or that if it did I wouldn't be alive to greet it. The talk took me three days to prepare and rehearse for which I was given the derisory (your good word) sum of $500. One cannot very well give a talk about gossip without supplying some, and a fair amount of that I had to supply was about sex, not having much gossip about money in my arsenal. When it came to offer this gossip, I mentioned that my talk would now be given an X-rating, surely the first such talk given at the Fortnightly. I then promptly told them that the dreary Duke of Windsor claimed that Mrs. Wally Simpson was the best fellatrix in Europe. (A nice lady afterwards asked me how I spelled that word.) I also mentioned that Onassis liked to sodomize his women – "fuck them in the ass" was the phrase I bowdlerized, and which I came across in the journals of a man named Leo Lerman, a gay New York journalist who was patronized by divas of various fields – though Mrs. Kennedy wouldn't agree to it; the source of the story, I told them, was Maria Callas, who allowed it, though with the disclaimer that "it hurt and was boring." A few tense moments at the Fortnightly, or so I sensed, in which I dispensed these and a few other juicy items. I'm not sure how it all went over – did they à la Mme Callas find what I said hurt or were they bored by it? – though there was pleasing applause at the end.

I share your antipathy for the word *serendipity*, though it may not be the word so much as the people who use it that offends. I note that I own a book, unread, called *The Travels and Adventures of Serendipity* by Robert K. Merton and Elinor G. Barber. Merton, an American sociologist of literary pretensions, also wrote a book doing an historical etymology of the phrase "on the shoulders of giants." I have long had a notion about giving gifts to people whom one doesn't really like but to whom one must nevertheless give a gift: among the gifts on the list are a home sushi-maker and a copy of Julian Barnes' book on the fear of dying. *The Travels and Adventures of Serendipity*, I think, should be added to the list.

My literary journalism dance card for the autumn is now filled. I am committed to writing pieces on *The Quest for Corvo* (for the *Wall Street*

Journal), the *Letters of Isaiah Berlin* (for something called the *Claremont Review of Books*), Irving Thalberg (for the *Weekly Standard)*, and the decline of Jewish delicatessens (for *Commentary*). A man of greater genius than I possess could turn all these subjects into a single essay.

Keep the faith, friend, though in what exactly I am unsure.

Best, Joe

Dear Joe,

My mother told me the other day that she had watched a TV programme about what the planet would look like when the human race finally pulled off what so many of its finest sons have worked so hard to achieve, piecemeal, *ici* and *là*: its own complete extermination. The programme showed how quickly our finest monuments would crumble, bridges collapse, dams be damned and so on. The most enduring edifices would be those in which no steel was used, since it was sure to be corrupted by rust, just as the Goodish Book tells us (the moth would find other targets). Is it true that the twin towers in São Paolo have no metallic skellington? I don't know or care, actually, but some edifice of that kind would be the last man-made standing. One could, I suppose, compose an article (or two) along similar lines, trying to forecast (Enoch Soames was a version of this) which literary giants of our time will crumble into obscurity and which survive, if only as cased fragments, in the pitiless process of obsolescence and decomposition before the big implosion, if that's what's coming at a time when we don't give a damn whether it does or not.

Primed with silver, one could compose a pitiless anthology of what will be left of our literary giants, once time's erosions have worked on them for a few centuries. Sartre: 'Hell is other people.' Camus: '*Il faut imaginer Sisyphe heureux*.' Alberto Moravia: '*Beh, le donne*.' Philip Roth: 'I fucked the family dinner.' Hemingway: 'Grace under pressure' (the primal scene revisited?). Dos Passos (whom I and you admired once): Nix. Stein: 'A rose etc.' Bellow: Nix, but a title or two – whoever wants to look inside *Henderson the Rain King* again? Martin Amis: 'Lovely darts,' maybe. *Et praeterea* notta lot. Ozymandias is all our king.

You're smart to hitch your titular wagon to Mr Eliot, but I don't think *Fabulous Small Jews* is one of his, and I favour it to outlast *Possession*. The curtailment of the future makes all our ambitions for posthumous glory seem more comic than grand. And yet, it's furtive fun to check whether one has been anthologised or encapsulated in dictionaries of quotations (and others not). Cyril Connolly, *encore lui*, confessed to looking for himself in indices; doesn't everyone, sometimes? Deny it and be a saint or a liar.

Webster, as your favourite poetic out-source mentioned on one occasion, was much possessed by death. I don't quite feel that way. I'm conscious that the killer with the knife, the lethal bug, the infarctus (trust the French for a slightly grand name for heart-attacks), the runaway truck, or whatever his instrument of choice, is on his/her/its way to me, but ever since Sarah died, I have been conscious of the absurdity of seeing anything but chance and a kind of impersonal negligence at the heart of the world's design. Last Sunday, I went to see my old friend Brian Glanville in hospital (I've just been again). In most of London, you can park freely on the Lord's day, but not in Westminster, where Brian was. I came out of my fantasy of Samaritan virtue to find that I had to pay a £60 penalty. When providence owes you one, it pays in bruises.

To be possessed by death, as Julian Barnes boasts in that text which I shall never open, is a vanity not in my spectrum of conceits. Perhaps I am stuck with those narcissistic intimations of immortality which grey Wordsworth recalled in his young self; furtively, I retain the boyish illusion that something that I have written, or might yet write, will carry my name on for, as Catullus said, in my and McLeish's version of his work, 'an aeon or two'. But that something, even if it exists, is going to be but a chiselled chip off the great block of work which I have amassed, revised and lain awake at night wondering how to complete or improve. This morning I was asking around what colour (color) the line is that you have to wait behind at immigration at LAX. White or yellow? Lady, who cares? I care, because (like Upton Sinclair) I like to get things right or – nuance! – not be accused of getting them wrong. The consensus was that the line was yellow, the colour of madness someone said (Mondriaan, was it, team? Or Kandinsky?) and also, of course, the colour of cowardice and the house colour (a British term) for our antique *razza*, its star and, for all I know, its garter and certainly its tall hat.

I'm busy doing something bilateral, so to say until corrected: writing a novel, the third volume in my *Glittering Prizes* trilogy, entitled *Final Demands*, as a novel with one hand and with the other, so to say, but impossible to do, rendering it into a radio drama series. The interplay between what can be said (or intimated) on the BBC and what can be spelled out, if it must be, on the page is quite stimulating in both directions; overcoating the overcoat (time Gogol had it back) and so on makes for revelations of a kind. Among the sources for the characters whom I am parading and parodying is a certain Alan Clark, a very famous man on this tight little island, though you need not stay in after class if you have never heard of him. You will have heard of Warren Beatty, who had similar credentials in the These I Have Loved field, though Warren has not enumerated his, as they used to say, conquests as Clark did (using pseudonyms, with coy effrontery).

Pool players refer, I think, to 'visits' to the table, the occasions on which they step up to cue, which is probably a better term for what Warren and Clark did with ladies who seldom required a long siege, once the ram was in place. Clark achieved minor office under Mrs Thatcher (some sarcastic angel saw to it that his duties were, in particular, 'procurement' for the armed forces, the mackerel role) but did not become a totemic figure until he published his diaries, in which name-dropping and knicker-dropping alternated with seductive effect on the Great British Public, all of whom are supposed to crave equality and the elimination of deference, but almost all of whom are nostalgic for the days when forelock-tugging was a national sport and duty and a chap with the right tie and accent had a right to expect a lot of lesser chaps without aitches to 'Up, guards, and at 'em' when asked. Clark often wore a Guards tie (as did his arriviste rival, Michael Heseltine, despised among his Tory peers for having to buy his own furniture), and made his name first, in quasi-academic circles, by writing military history, but there is no evidence that, any more than you or I, he ever had to be steady as a Buff (my father's regiment, when he was commissioned, though he never had to fight, in 1918, the East Kent Regiment, was called The Buffs and steadiness was their pride).

Clark's abiding regiment was Eton College, of which Cyril Connolly has said what might as well be the best word, about its lasting mark on its pupils. These marks were, not so long ago, first inscribed across their hind parts but then went, and still go, lastingly, to their heads; Etonians, of whom the putative next Prime Minister is one, and his cabinet several others, often retain the *morgue* which the aristocracy has been obliged to renounce, at least in public. Cameron affects to have no 'side', as they used to say, but he does himself less good than he imagines by not seeming to enjoy the godlike other-ness of the unrepentant President of Pop, which Cyril would so have wished to be (he got into Pop's exclusive company, on his wit, but never presided). Clark was very rich and lived in a Kentish castle which, he made it known, was much admired by Queen Elizabeth the Queen Mother, a lady who died at the age of 102 or so and was the Most Loved Grandmother in the land. Your renowned fellatrix, Wallis Simpson, won the prize which the *ci-devant*

Miss Bowes-Lyon is said, by recent researchers, to have craved: the brainless Albert Edward, later Dook of Windsor, and as silly a Führer-admirer, almost, as Unity Mitford, whose sisters spent every other minute of their busy lives writing each other the letters which make Beetle laugh and laugh while I am having my quasi-nightly bath, and which I shall never read.

Clark's father was Kenneth, the connoisseur, who was eventually lorded for his services to art. This elevation and his moated address allowed Alan to play the toff twice over, if not more, although the family fortune (before Kenneth used his expertise to fatten it by doing with picture-purchase what master economist Keynes did with shares and currencies) derived from K.C.'s dad who, if I have it right, invented or (more likely) mass-produced the humble cottonreel. He was, in the derogatory description of his day, in 'trade', and provincial with it, but you would never have guessed it from Alan's 'came-over-with-the-Conqueror' conceits. A.C. imagined that he spoke perfect French and included in his diary a tribute from a member of the Quai d'Orsay, known as '*la Maison*', I believe, on his impeccable accent. (A French publisher, from Gallimard no less, congratulated me, not long ago, on having '*aucun accent*' when I spoke his tongue; not *necessarily* an unambiguous tribute.)

To show how showy he could be, Clark larded his diaries with a good many French phrases. When our son Stephen, whose entire *scolarité* was in the French system, all the way up to the pretty well upper-most, read the diaries he made a longish list of howlers, which I encouraged him to send to Ion Trewin, Clark's editor at Orion. Ion, a member of the MCC and, as my father might have said, *almost* the nicest man in the world, showed the list to Clark, who glanced at it and, wittily or inadvertently, said 'Galling, isn't it?' When asked, Stephen requested in return an autographed copy of Clark's *Barbarossa*, a tribute to the gallant Wehrmacht and its struggle with the Russkies. He got a copy, unsigned, paperback. *Noblesse* does not always oblige; pseudo-*Noblesse non plus*.

Why did I mention Clark in the first place? Because I once travelled with him on a car trip which I have reprised in *Final Demands*, on the way to a publisher's sales conference. We got lost in the fog and somehow found ourselves adjacent to Brooklands, if that's what it's called, a once car-race track on which, famously, the goggled Clark had raced his six-litre Bentley, with the leather-belted, buckled 'bonnet', which was painted in what was known as 'British racing green'. This, he once wrote, but did not say at the time when I was in the car with him, contrasted with 'Jewish racing yellow'. Funny? Not too; especially since some people can't take a joke. One of the reasons why I do not entirely favour the idea that Israel should rely on the 'world community' for its safety, and renounce nuclear weapons, has just a little to do with Clark and his ilk as well as with the little doubts I have about how much moolah would be needed to buy the nod from some future US or European administration to sanction an Islamic rectification of the map of the Middle East.

Now, I see, Mr Clark's editor, Trewin (whose father gave me some great reviews forty-something years ago), has written a book about the diarist, whose most renowned *mot* was, during some inquiry into governmental hanky-mit-panky, that he had been 'economical with the *actualité*', a misuse of the French word, which means 'news' not 'actuality', that passed for *hautement sophistiqué chez les Britanniques*. I doubt whether Stephen's list of *erreurs banales* will be mentioned.

Forward, the Light Brigade!

Tout à toi,
Freddie

Dear Freddie,

Ah, we scribblers and the immortality question! I'm glad you brought it up. Many years ago, during my *American Scholar* days, I had to inform my dear friend Edward Shils, who was dying (at that point slowly) of colon cancer, that I would have to delay an essay of his for three months. He replied that I was not to worry. He told me that if he were to die and go to hell, the pain there would be so excruciating that publication of his little essay could scarcely matter; if he were to go to heaven, such would be his joy that having had another essay printed in the *American Scholar* would be trivial beyond gauging. And, if, as was most likely to be the case, he would go neither to hell nor to heaven, but achieve instant oblivion, the matter would be, if possible, of even lesser import. "So, my dear Joseph," he said, "print the damn thing whenever you please."

That, I thought at the time, sounded like the last word on authorly immortality to me. And yet . . . and yet, one hopes against all Nadezhda Mandelstamian hope, that something somehow of the vast quantities one has indited will live on, Ozymandias to the fooking contrary notwithstanding. Completely stupid, but there it is.

Your paragraph on what the famous writers of recent years will be remembered for is devastating. Nice, I must say, not to be remembered for "I fucked my family's dinner." The paragraph also reminds one how thin so much of the most admired twentieth-century fiction really is. Poor Camus did not live long enough to establish what might have been his gravity and his greatness. Kingsley Amis ends up being chiefly a comic complainer. Hemingway was a stupid man, deeply prejudiced and vastly self-deceived, with a talent for lyrical description but not much else. Twenty or so years ago I tried to reread *The Sun Also Rises*, a book we all admired when we were young, and found myself unable to take it seriously. Having to read *Henderson the Kvetch King*, as you suggest, sounds a punishment. So few of our putative great writers have been able to dig out from under the debris of their own egotism to discover larger themes. The only line I can remember from Dos Passos comes from an immigrant character in *USA*, who says: "Funny 'ting, a man's life." Not profound, perhaps, but true enough.

I wrote a sentence yesterday morning, in an essay on the demise of the Jewish delicatessen in America, that I should like to live on for a bit, a few months anyhow. Here is it: "One day a year she [my mother] also marshaled the services of my father, who was as much at home in the kitchen as Sergei Diaghilev might have been on the range, to grind up fish for *gefilte* fish for Passover." As a writer, I have become like the man whose wife asks him if he had enjoyed the dinner party from which he had just returned. "If it wasn't for me," he said, "I would have been bored to death." So late in the game do I now discover that I have all along been writing for me – and a small number of editors who will pay me to do so – and for any strangers who might happen to be tuning in.

As for death – "the distinguished thing," as our Henry called it, though what can be so distinguished about this most democratic of all events (it happens, after all, to everyone) I've no notion – my own views are fairly close to yours. Along with being of course inevitable, it often seems so damn arbitrary. The death of the young, the death of the good well before their time when the vile often flourish and live on like the great bay tree – as the kids today say, what's that about? When death arrives for me I shall be greatly disappointed but not shocked or even much surprised.

But, then, I suspect that I, though a few years younger than you, have had more health problems, which may make me rather more death-minded. I've had bypass surgery, I was diagnosed with something called Crohn's Disease (though I suffered none of the symptoms), I had a bout of something called auto-immune hepatitis. Not quite like the prospect of hanging in the morning, these things do nonetheless tend to put one in mind of the fact that one does not have a round-trip ticket. My current health extravaganza features a rash that began on my chest and back that, having departed those majestic environs, has now taken up residence on my legs and arms. I have been to three dermatologists, have had six different biopsies, the last of which reveals that I have something called bullous pemphigoid (best pronounced in the accent of W.C. Fields), which is a (quite mysterious) result of a breakdown of some sort in my immune system. I itch, I take pills (a steroid called prednisone), I see physicians (the latter not a good way for a Jewish Scientist, à la Christian Science, to spend his days). I have no pain, but much discomfort, irritation division. This has been going on since August, and I have resisted mentioning it to you, lest I seem to have given way to that standard hobby of aging Jewish men, complaining about their health. But just now I am very pissed off at my body for letting me down so. The nerve, the goddamn nerve!

Pleasing to think that Alan Clark's French was faulty beyond a fault. I suppose he joins the majority here. Do you remember Max Beerbohm's little essay on the impossibility of speaking French well for foreign speakers? As I recall, he claims that in this realm the person who wins is the one who does so with the most confidence. My own spoken French, let me quickly insert, isn't even crappy. On those occasions when I have to call it into service, I half suspect that I must sound as if I am speaking with the Gallic equivalent of a strong Yiddish accent. I am told that the problem of speaking – and writing – French properly hits hardest those American and English academics in French departments where there are native speakers; one little screw-up (masculine adjective, feminine noun; ever so slightly misused subjunctive) and one's entire career is forfeit.

Alan Clark sounds a frightful prick. (You doubtless already know the distinction between a schmuck and a prick; it is that a schmuck just lies there.) Was it Pascal who says that being an aristocrat saves a man thirty years' time in coming into his full confidence? Let us hope that being a fake aristocrat, as Clark was, added another ten years onto the sentence, though it doesn't sound like it did. I read Kenneth Clark's autobiography fifteen or so years ago, and remember not a word of it, except, as you remind me, that the family fortune was in trade. Whenever I hear or read the word "connoisseur," I think of "kind of sewer."

Your mention of Alan Clark causes me to wonder who are more loathesome, contemporary American or English politicians? Probably a dead-heat, photo-finish tie. The only member of the United States Senate that I would care even to have had a cup of coffee with over the past thirty years was Daniel

Patrick Moynihan. The politician part of him was of course – or is the word here *perforce* – a fake, but he was a large enough man to retain genuine parts. He contributed to the *American Scholar* during my days there, and used occasionally to call me to talk about Émile Durkheim, Max Weber, and other names that no American president or English prime minister of the last half century had ever heard of. I gather he had the Irish problem and I once saw him, at an official dinner, fully soused, three sheets to the wind, and looking as if he were on roller-skates. But he also had the Irish charm. He was a man whom you didn't in the least mind calling you by your first name even before he'd ever laid eyes on you.

We are on a good-flick roll *chez* Epstein. A roll means that we have seen what we judge to be *two* good movies in a row, one Spanish-Argentinian made, the other Swiss. *Fred and Elsa*, about a late-life romance, is the first; *Vitus*, about a boy genius striving to pass himself off as normal, is the second. By today's heavy-expenditure movie-making standard, both seem relatively low-cost productions. Might it be that the more money spent on a movie the worse it figures to be, if only because everyone goes cautious under the scraggly banner of protecting investment? In any case, I recommend these two movies to you, with my usual only-half-your-money-back guarantee.

Last week I read Julian Symons' book on his oldest brother A.J.A. Symons, author of *The Quest for Corvo*, but nothing else of the least interest (I have a minor fascination with one-book authors, those literary one-trick ponies). Albert James Alphonse Symons wanted above all to be taken for upper class; his points of *entrée* were bibliomania and first editions, wine-bibbling and gourmand-dining, also fancy clothes. He acquired, on heavy mortgages, country houses. No-one so poor as he, he claimed, had ever lived so well. In the end, it all fizzled. He died at forty, broke and alone, an *arriviste* who never quite arrived. Only in the last pages of his quite good book does Julian Symons inform us that the family was Jewish and that this lent a bit of additional nervousness to his brother's always slippery climb. Odd touch to leave out. Ah, the English social-class racket – is it, do you suppose, still flourishing? Lord, I hope not.

Itchily but faithfully,
Joe

Dear Joe,
My general cultural impatience displays its most chronic (such a phoney superlative being in place in a culture which finds no fault in 'most unique'

or 'very ubiquitous') symptom in an almost instant allergy to the vocabulary of EVERYTHING, pretty well, that is relayed to us by the TV, on no matter what topic, though especially in news. Only a few programmes are now on our regular watchable list. One of these is called *University Challenge*, a series that has been in annual production since 'as far back as 1962'. It has had two officiating quizmeisters. The first an Etonian called Bamber Gascoyne, unless it's Gascoigne, a slim, forever smiling, tortoise-rimmed, curly-headed chap who gave an impression of not needing the money. His terse-cum-stylish amateurism managed, at the same time, to do things just as well as your base professional. This was, of course, in the great British tradition in which muddling-through improvisation would in the end turn the flank of Germanic automatism (not to mention Yankee almighty-dollarism) and prove that a chap who'd never necessarily had to roll up his sleeves could still deliver a straight left that took care of drilled loutishness.

In truth, Bamber is a nice man, with a nice wife, and no children (we met them once or twice socially, were asked to dinner, couldn't go and . . . the pier separated from the vessel and there we went and they stayed, or v.v.). To mention their childlessness seems like an accusation, and hence unworthy, but the childless do seem to me to suffer from what chance or some innate DNA inhibitor denies them, and they become – am I right? – oddly fused, their sexuality blending in an often touching and affectionate dead-endism, their aged youthfulness creased by bravely borne regrets re the unborn. Bamber went on being televisually perky and smiling and *almost* of an age with the young teams whom he invigilated and then he wearied of the whole thing and began, I think, to write Christian apologetics, in the English style: high on humane sentiment, low on resurrectional credulity. But I may be romancing. He was succeeded, probably longer ago than the short time (a decade, say) that it seems to me, by a much more modern version of The Uncommon Man, one Jeremy Paxman, whose provenance was/is very nearly as posh as Bamber's but, by that very qualification, does not supply quite so definitive a social and intellectual label.

Paxman went to *two* Public Schools, Malvern (minorish) and my own *alma* step-*mater* Charterhouse (majorish) and then to St Catharine's College, Cambridge where he read – here comes the prig latent in your cringing correspondence – the only thing anyone at that renownedly hearty college could read: English. Paxman emerged armed for garrulity and, it seems, affectations of intellectual versatility. He is quite tall, neither handsome nor plain, copiously capped with hair neither straight nor crinkly, literate but not bookish, and never at a loss for quizzical competence. He not only replaced or supplanted Bamber G. but he is also, more famously, an inquisitor of politicians and others on a programme which he has, as they say, made his own: *Newsnight*, on the BBC's second channel, on which, once upon a time, slightly less popular stuff had a chance of getting aired (hence *The Glittering Prizes* of 1976). As the synthesising Dickstein might be tempted to say, possibly several times, it may be no coincidence that Paxman *joined the BBC in 1977* (my italics, but I don't want them back). The corporation, as they call it over here, provided him with the security and the secular pulpit that the *New Yorker* afforded John Updike.

Paxman, like Mr U., could thenceforth combine brave outspokenness with a regular income; cash and cachet grew in leaping increments as his suave abrasiveness made him that figure whom the British still relish, the well-spoken tribune, not himself a pleb but with the common*ish* man (and intellectually moist lady) as his happiest audience. He too seems not to need the work, but he takes it and the money, which he then finds almost amusing that he gets so much of, thus allowing the public to take him for another old Britannic favourite, the chap who doesn't take himself too seriously and, like the successful gambler (yet another type), gives himself no airs for having struck it rich. It's all about luck, innit? He finds time, and perhaps research assistants, to write books about England, Home and whatever Beauty is left, and they sell and sell. He is, if the lack of rumour is to be trusted, neither Jew nor Gentile, straight nor bent; a modern Phlebas the Phoenician, as the man from St Louis, Missouri, mentioned in one of his best-loved hits, but with imperishable floatation.

I have, let me add here *fra parentesi*, met Jeremy (as we all dare to call him) only once, I believe, when he was guesting on yet another programme on BBC TV, in which other TV programmes were being fearlessly grilled and served with the tossed salad of flattery and sarcasm typical of them there vox plop shows. Treating me as an antique deserves, he refrained from sitting on me too heavily and affected to find me, as the antique-dealers say, 'right'. He had the glittering prize about which I, foolishly, had ironised rather than making a grab for it. Nothing personal here then, once you put where-did-I-go-rightism to one side. All this is leading, as every thriller trail does, to something which may be less interesting than the clues: a significant triviality in which Paxman figured in the last (but never the ultimate) University Challenge.

The format requires one member of one or other team to buzz as soon as he has an answer to the 'starter for ten' question. If he or she is right, access is gained to three supplementaries on a single topic. Geddit? Thought you might. Last Monday, on a programme which, in theory, tests the wit, culture, speed, etc. of our young and clever, one of these single topics was, to no-one's surprise, about the various characters in J.K. Rowling's Merlin-for-today sagas and who played the part in the interminable movies derived from them. These questions were all quickly got right. Master Paxman passed no comment on the facility with which the student princes and princesses displayed their sustained infantilism. A little later, there came a question about who had written *The Gutenberg Galaxy* (no-one could say) and later again – such is the logic of the quiz – the supplementaries that would have been attached earlier, if anyone had identified Marshall M. Among the cant phrases of which the smart kids had no faint recollection was 'the medium is the message' and, yes, 'the global village' (in which the global banking crises have, we may guess, been a talking-point around the pot-bellied stove). The failure of the young smart-asses to know anything about McL was received with a simperthetic wince by Master Paxman, who assured them that they were missing nothing in their ignorance of that now dated charlatan. There you are, you see: the Butler did it, again.

I grant you that, as an instance of *la trahison des clercs* (another book whose contents and author would, I betcha, have left the youngsters mute), Paxman's disparagement of McL should pass as a mere misdemeanour (Miss Demeanour might, indeed, be a camp-follower of this suave savager of suitable, suited persons), but it was a small, unbeautiful example of how a man who, as much as anyone in third-worldly modern Britville, is the living evidence of how medium and message converge and connive, could reclose history's dustbin on McLuhan, a figure who, however exaggeratedly, ostentatiously, etc., *did* have a Cassandran sense of what was coming and, by his very forecast, hastened what he gloatingly denounced. Paxman, like journalists of all stripes who become Names, has transcended the electoral process, climbed the ladder as well as any agile serpent, and become the judge of the workaday politicos who, after knocking on dreary doors and attending meetings of demanding tedium, have achieved the petty eminence of public office, in which they are paid probably a tenth (literally) of the tribune who, by impersonating the cleverest man in the bar, and then some (but never too much), is authorised to play the lay pontiff, saying unto some come and unto others piss off, but nicely.

Shall I knock the nail painlessly on the head? Paxman's scorn for McLuhan derives, I will guess from his adolescent reading of a small book on the Proud

Canadian by one Jonathan Miller, a medical person, now a knight of the realm, a quondam comic – in *Beyond the Fringe* – and a polymath, as it is always said, who stammers in private but has been ceaselessly verbose in public. Miller and I were at the same college, appeared in the same hit Cantab revue of 1954 (though he hit harder than I did) and have been *frères-ennemis* ever since. If you want more on that topic, it is on tap. But here's the thing: imagine what would have happened if Jeremy P. had sneered at the chaps and chicks who were so expert on J.K. Rowling and her Californian recensions and knew nothing of a man who, with all faults, see *supra*. Whatever the flaws and foolishness of the McLuhan industry, as it became, he was right about the domination of media, about the usurpation of intelligence by images, of ideas by advertising, of quality by quantity and . . . but perhaps my point is made. None of this is worth kicking against, since the pricks outnumber us and we will only damage our toes in the effort, but there it all bloody well is. Dear God, I can hear George Steiner knocking at the dour and claiming to have been *primus inter impares* to proclaim the terminal sickness of *Le Livre*. Well, I shall respond by telling the *TLS* readers that they should get the new Gallimard volume of *Les Essais* of our friend Micheau, now rendered into modern French with accessible accuracy and elegant apparatus criticus. That's sticking it to them, am I right?

Tout à toi,
Freddie

Dear Freddie,

On the matter of childlessness, it not long ago occurred to me how many true and near-geniuses left no children: Einstein, T.S. Eliot, Edith Wharton, Paul Dirac, Proust (for rather obvious reasons), Paul Valéry, Maurice Ravel, Willa Cather, *et alia*, and, consequently, what an astonishing gene pool has gone empty. I myself had children so young – my older son was born when I was twenty-three – that adult life without children is nearly unimaginable. My condition has been close to that of Zorba (not the Hebe), who in the movie says (approximately), "Am I married? Yes, wife, children, house, dog – the full catastrophe!"

Having children gives one, in the childless Henry James' phrase, "a sense of futurity," by which I think he meant a sense of and stake in the future. One spends, thinks, lives, differently when responsible for children. I suppose it embourgeoisifies (if you can devise an uglier word than that, be my guest) one, which is not a great problem for me, who, between bourgeoisie and bohemian, will vote bourgeoisie every time. Still, lots of people do better not to have children. Best that that fun family, the Woolfs, Lenny and Ginny, never had a child. My friend Hilton Kramer, who married in his early forties a woman not much younger than he, once told me that, such was the disorganization of his and his wife's domestic life – they generally dined at 11 p.m. – bringing a child into such a marriage would be an act of cruelty. He also once told me, in what I thought a genuine insight, that people who have themselves had troubled childhoods do not find it easy to bring children into the world. A richly complex subject all this, obviously.

We do not have anyone quite resembling Paxman in America. We specialize in earnest numbskulls. The most trusted man in the country for many years was – for all I know still is – Walter Cronkite, who does a thousand platitudes in one voice. We have professional good-doers, out to save the planet, the poor, the insulted and injured, who in the end, so far as one can make out, do good chiefly for themselves: a fellow named Bill Moyers, who as a young man worked for Lyndon Johnson and has long been in business for himself, qualifies handsomely for this list. We have others who specialize in non-penetration, keeping things bland and banal and well within the comfort zone of utter predictability: they are named Tom Brokaw, Charlie Gibson, Brian Miller, and Diane Sawyer. The rest are hairdos pulling in heavy bread. With only occasional lapses – the charming sit-com, the rare solid documentary, good sports coverage – television in America remains the solid intellectual slum it has long been advertised as being. *Chez* Epstein we watch it for a bit of news with our before-dinner drink and hope from time to time to find a good old movie; the laird himself (me), who is mentally *kaput* roughly at 8.00 p.m., often keeps it tuned to sports later in the evening, much of which he watches, with the sound off, while reading magazines or lightish books: and so it serves as a (barely) visual version of Musak.

Père Paxman's not being disturbed by the young never having heard of Marshall McLuhan is all too credible. What the young don't know is a long story, which I, as a former teacher, used to resist telling, because it was, so to say, shooting smoked salmon in a barrel. I myself did not know all that much when young, and one of my specialties was hiding my extensive ignorance. The important difference, though, is that I was ashamed of my ignorance in a way that I think the young today no longer are. I once gave a lecture at Denison University in Ohio, which contained, in the middle of a sentence, the following information: ". . . in the *Journals of the Brothers Goncourt*, composed by Edmond after the death of Jules in 1862 . . ." After the lecture, which turned out to have been deftly aimed roughly two kilometers over the head of its undergraduate audience, a professor came up to tell me that he was much amused by this particular reference, reporting with a chuckle that they, his students, "had never heard of 1862."

As for Harry Potter, I dislike the little fucker intensely. I'm pleased that his invention took J.K. Rowling off the welfare rolls, but I wish her book hadn't been shovel-fed to all the world's middle-class Anglophone children, and no doubt to those through the rest of Europe. When our granddaughter Annabelle was seven or eight, I would listen to Barbara read to her from the first Potter volume; the bits I heard I found charmless; good to report that so, too, did my granddaughter, who never went beyond the first vol. But all good American children lined up for all new vols as they emerged, their parents more blitheringly delighted at the kids' pleasure in such rich fantasy. I'd rather do differential equations than see any of the movies made from the books, though I gather they, too, have done a brisk business. If we were more entrepreneurial, I'd propose we go in as partners for printing up a few hundred thousand T-shirts that read, "Harry Potter Jacks Off" (English version, of course, "Tosses Off"). Sounds like a sure-fire seller to me.

For a futurist, Marshall McLuhan, as you say, hit the gong in an unusually high number of crucial places. Strangely, he had his vogue long before he did so, and now that he has been proven correct, he's been nearly forgot. Years ago I read Jonathan Miller's book on him in the Modern Master series, edited, you will remember, by Frank Kermode (now there's a name *not* to conjure with; one of the truly dull critics of our time, a man with ten fingers who cannot make one fist). I recall Jonathan Miller's book seeming, as it is only a polymath's right to seem, far from lucid. Don't you suppose that Miller's reputation for polymathy has everything to do with his having gone to medical school and not bothered afterwards to practice? (Stephen Potter, in one of his Upyoursmanship books, refers to this, rightly, as a superior ploy.) I do dimly remember J. Miller once being funny, but that seems to have been sometime in the early Pleistocene. (Does polymathy allow for laughs? I should think not.) He has now gone to his just reward, that old-age home for false geniuses, the direction of opera.

Does fame, like polymathy, inhibit wit? The name Mike Nichols, once a wildly funny man, comes to mind. He now strikes me as chiefly a wealthy creep. Does the name Garrison Keillor, I wonder, have resonance in England? He, as you may know, was also once funny, as the creator of a National Public Radio (our version of the BBC) show called *The Prairie Home Companion*, who also published a few amusing pieces in the *New Yorker*. Robert Altman made his final – and I thought rather dreary – movie based on the show. The reason I bring up Keillor is that, night before last, I dragged my itching carcass to hear the Chicago Symphony, and at the intermission, in the men's room, I saw a large (6'5", I'd say) and rather brutal-faced Garrison Keiller awaiting his turn at one of the urinals. Everything about him said, I'm not funny, so fuck off. He is a Scandahoovian, and perhaps naturally dour. But was he, do you suppose, darkened because no-one recognized him and offered him a urinal, or help with his fly? Difficult to say.

Allow me the vulgar use of narrative foreshadowing – perhaps a bit more than foreshadowing – to tell you that this is a story with a happy ending. I returned to the foyer to join Barbara and share her cup of decaf (older folks') coffee, when a man, very fit-looking in a black turtleneck, thinning gray-black hair and a well-trimmed beard of the same color, approached: "Excuse me," he said, "but are you Joseph Epstein?" This doesn't happen to me very often, and when it does I sometimes make the lame joke that I am and that I gather that my disguise didn't work. This time I refrained from doing so. "My name is Tom Scorsesse," he said. "You may have heard it. I'm a federal prosecutor in town. But the main thing is that I wanted to tell you that you are my favorite of all living American writers. My wife buys all your books for me. Your work has given me a thousand laughs, and much more. I want to thank you." I told him that I was not a hugging man, but if I were I should certainly embrace him with embarrassing enthusiasm, so pleasing were his words to me. He went on to tell me that he was originally from Bensonhurst, in Brooklyn, his father an Italian immigrant who never got past the eighth grade, and that he, owing to a good if severe education from the nuns, went to the University of Notre Dame and thence to the University of Chicago Law School. I told him that when I began university teaching my best students were almost always Catholics: they had been made to take Latin, knew English grammar, and their theology courses taught them how to argue. I added that they generally also had a grudge against their own education, the thing that was the making of them. "I used to say," Mr. Scorsesse said, "that I learned the rules of St. Thomas taught by the methods of Machiavelli." Now here, I submit, dear Freddie, is the reader for me. Garrison Keillor, eat your heart out.

Best, Joe

Dear Joe,

Your Mr Scorsesse (whose third 's' distinguishes him from the little man who has had many busy Hollywood days, and nights) is the admirer of whom we all dream, a nobody who is also a somebody, *sans* bullshit, used to a lot of lame excuses and fancy footwork who yet holds up your arm as champ. A week ago, I played bridge for the Savile Club, from which I keep telling myself that I should resign (I imagined that it was a privilege, back in 1982, to be proposed for membership by George Steiner). I rarely go there and then I have to affect a kind of British camaraderie, even though a good many of the members, not least the pontifical ones, are Jews of various hues and cries. One of our opponents, from the Hurlingham Club, which has some of the best grass courts in London, was a lady who, after we had played a few hands, said to me '*Glittering Prizes*?' She was no state prosecutor but a comely wife and mother whose tone of shy admiration did not wholly displease. I admitted the soft impeachment (a phrase culled from the fat, mostly fruitless bush of John Fowles's rapidly withering work), to which she said, 'I'm Emily Richards's sister'. This reminds me, in the one thing leading to another style that Montaigne has licensed, to recall how, at a party, after a long hesitation, a once somewhat well-known actor/hulk approached Noël Coward and, with the shyness which the Master induced in mere movie people, said, 'Mr Coward, I'm Chuck Connors'. To which, Mr C. replied, 'Of course you are, dear boy'. Emily Richards was a very pretty young actress who appeared in *The Glittering Prizes* as an actress lady who had all Cambridge at her feet, moved to London and discovered that the spotlight no longer fell on her with quite the same brightness, after which she took to the bottle and (in my novel sequel, *Fame and Fortune*) to embarrassing eccentricity – not washing a lot – and then to poetry, in which she proved remarkable. So, I hardly have a medal to pin alongside your Scorsesse Cross.

I hardly have a medal to pin alongside your Scorsesse Cross, but Stanley Donen did once say to me that I was the most talented man he had ever met. He liked to make his friends feel good; but he had met a lotta lotta people. I greatly regret that he and I no longer talk (I keep expecting to discover that he is dead, but you know the Good Lord: he may well do that with me first), but we don't. All passion spent? I would not put it that way. He was one of the most bankable director/producers in the business when he first called me in. He had not only done *Singin' In The Rain*, which he didn't care to hear too much about, even back in 1964, but had just had what he would always call 'my only hit' (he was talking boffo only) with *Charade*, recently remade by a very good director, Jonathan Demme, who must have taken leave of his census, since the idea was ancient and the plot of the original movie depended on a climactic twist which would not have been accepted in the first five minutes of *24*. Demme also did not notice, it seems, that Cary Grant and Audrey Hepburn were integral to the recipe.

I first met Stanley because he liked a movie of mine you will never have seen, *Nothing But The Best,* based on a Stanley Ellin story (the unmentioned mentor, I sometimes suspect, of world-famous Roald Dahl, war-hero and another candidate for Not Quite The Nicest Man In The World). The Ellin story was set in the US and entitled 'The Best of Everything'. The producers, Nat Cohen and Stuart Levy, who much preferred leading in racehorse winners to counting the house, decided that the new title would bring in the punters. They also – crucial mistake, business scholars – did not buy the underlying rights, but leased them for twenty-five years only. They were not young and they should worry if the movie could never be shown again, publicly, after 1989. It starred Denholm Elliot (perhaps his best performance ever) and Alan Bates and was directed by Clive Donner. Stanley said to me, 'Everyone says it's as good as it is because of the director, but I know it's because of the writer'. This did not hurt my feelings. *Two for the Road* followed. We had several projects after that, none of which came to celluloid or whatever the stuff is they use. There came a moment with Stanley, as there does with sportsmen, I suspect, when the confidence went, and the energy and the talent (as if they were all distinct things) at the same time. He had married the nubile, nubilious even, Yvette Mimieux, who was (and probably is) altogether too true to be good, when she was in her latish twenties (she said) and he was into his fifties (imagine an old man like that, doing a girl like that). He could not resist what he feared would end in his tears. When he was ninety, she would be only . . . do the math and eat your heart out.

The sad day when she left him could be postponed only by an accumulation of moolah by which, in the sweetest way imaginable, she could be greatly rejoiced and he rejuvenated. A movie entitled *Lucky Lady* (had to be!) was the one that did for his reputation and gave him an irreversible push – music by Johnny Mercer, maybe – down the slippery slope. *Facilis descensus Averni,* as Virgil (who knew something about the scribbler's trade) chose to put it, unless you want, with some scholars, to read '*Averno*', which could well be right, because wronger: down she goes is everyone's story. What was wrong with *Lucky Lady* was a caesura in the middle, at the point where Gene Hackman and Burt Lancaster decided to retire from bootlegging and put their feet up. They were lured back into one final coup by their twin appetite for – wait for it – Liza Minnelli, of whom the venomous but not always witless John Simon once (at least) said something along the lines of 'I never want to see her again unless she finds a way of wrapping her legs around her face'. Such gymnastics are not, I suspect, beyond all possibility but let that pass. Liza did have a voice, but – as I believe, from childhood experience only, they used to say in the Bronx – she was no earl painting. *Lucky Lady* was a palpable flop, even though it had its moments, mainly due to the script by 'the Huycks' (Willard and Gloria) who wrote *American Graffiti* and were well in (at 1% of the profits already) on things such as (the cant says 'like') *Star Wars* and *Indiana Jones*, to which dead executives in hell are subjected in 24-hour doses; they wind up screaming louder than St Laurent on his griddle.

The failure of *Lucky Lady* was somehow greater than most. The Huycks were so accustomed to success (*facilis ascensus* ain't Virgilian, but it does inflate heads) that Gloria was reported in the *LA Times* as saying that the movie was badly directed, Stanley had bungled their script, and all the usual *vestra culpa* stuff that cornered spoilt shits come out with. Stanley called her and begged her to tell him that she had been misreported. She confessed she had not been. In the voice of a strangled man, Stanley said, 'Oh Gloria.' It's only fair to say that the Huycks were Stanley's life-support machine when, not long afterwards, Yvette decided that she 'didn't want to be married any more'. Stanley had done his share of cutting and running wild in his younger days (his second wife, Marion, was probably his best) but, at this stage, when the phone stopped ringing – as mine has, but I console myself that no-one telephones anyone much these days; say it is so, Joe – and Stanley was no longer on anyone's B-list even, it was not the right moment to take a torpedo below the waistline. Stanley *did* claw his way back up the slippery slope but not too far. His filmography will show that there were assignments, as they used to say, after *Lucky Lady*, but the fluency, the fancy dancing, the capacity for bluff (essential in all the arts and sports) had gone.

During that long sad time when he hung on in Bel Air, I wrote an original movie to which Stanley's son managed to attach him as director. Steve Tisch, the hotel family's hobbywood movie producer, who later got lucky with *Forrest Gump* (adapted from an unwritten I.B. Singer story, set in a *shtetl*, *Go Rest, Schlump*) accepted Stanley as director and off we went to be turned down by Paramount. The script was derelict for a long time till I ripped it down and up and wrote a novel entitled *Coast to Coast*, which I then scripted for a Paramount TV subsidiary, thus avoiding basic rights disease (was it Perelman who wrote 'I have Bright's Disease and he has mine'?, marking the flippancy of those not yet on medication). Since Stanley had so admired the original, I encouraged the producer, a nice man called Gerry Leider, who no longer calls me, to ask Stanley if he would direct it.

I gave Stanley's number, of course, to Gerry. How not? as Sybille Bedford –
rated, by some, lady novelist – would say, if she could be with us here today.
And, of course, according to the Protocols of the Elders of William Morris, I
should not have done so. Gerry called Stanley 'direct', instead of going to the
agent (Stanley's son Joshua) first with a formal offer. Stanley, who had begged
Paramount to let him do a much less worked-over version of the script, took
instant, incurable offence. I was the bad guy. Since our daughter Sarah had died
only a few months earlier, it may be that I was not on top of my protocolar
form, but . . . When Stanley (who had not made a movie in years) reproached
me, I said, in a rather Briddish way, 'Rest assured, Stanley, it will not happen
again'. We have not spoken since, although written overtures have been made
(S. replied to a letter from Beetle, but not to one from me). And that's the
guy who comes closest to my Scorsesse. I am sad; I am even, as disappointed
footballers say, 'gutted', but you know what? Nuts to it, frankly.

**Tout à toi,
Freddie**

Dear Freddie,

What a fine rich stew of complication went into the demise of Stanley Donen's
and your friendship! Do you suppose that friendships between talented
people are even more difficult to maintain than those between less than
talented people? Add Yvette Mimieux to the mix and the Stanley D. story
becomes even sadder. I strain to recall her face and figure (we say "body" now,
I know), but the sobriquet "sex kitten" does flash back to mind. If still extant,
she cannot be very sexy or kittenish these days. Still, to quote yet again the
immortal Pinter, like Len Hutton in his prime, she was something in her time,
another time. Willa Cather has a character in her novel *O Pioneers!* say:
"There are women who spread ruin around them through no fault of theirs,
just by being too beautiful . . . They can't help it. People come to them as
people go to warm fires in winter." Especially, as in the case of Stanley Donen,
the winter of middle age.

Do the English read Willa Cather? Did they ever? I have been rereading
her novels for a lecture I am to give about her in the spring, and just this
moment think her the best of the last century's American novelists. Perhaps it
is owing to my advancing years, but I find it difficult to regard Hemingway
and the more talented Fitzgerald as little more than adolescent in their view
of life. I have never much admired the stunt show of William Faulkner, with
all his heavy symbolism and southern legend-mongering. Willa Cather's

range was wider and her penetration into character deeper than any of these writers or any other American novelist of her time or since. She wrote beautifully, and reads well in one's twenties and even better in one's (make that "my") seventies. She also wrote the best novel, in *The Song of the Lark*, about the development of the artistic temperament and personality that I have read. All of these, of course, provide the best of reasons for her being ignored by academics and other of our non-cognescenti.

I was pleased to learn, from your brief e-mail of a few days back, that your breakfast meeting with John Podhoretz went off well. I was not surprised to hear how deeply John loves his father Norman. My first contact with John came through a phone call he made to me when he was nineteen or twenty and a student at the University of Chicago, to thank me for writing a praising review in the *New York Times Book Review* of *Breaking Ranks*, the second of his father's three autobiographical books, which had otherwise taken a drubbing from reviewers.

John must have grown up in New York hearing unpleasant things said about his father, which could not have been so easy to bear. No-one who knows him has ever been neutral on the subject of Norman Podhoretz. Norman was born poor but intellectually privileged; he is said to have been Lionel Trilling's favorite student at Columbia and then among the favorites of F.R. Leavis at Cambridge. (Nice never again to have to read another stern paragraph of Leavis'.) In his twenties and thirties Norman was wildly brash: what was on his lung was on his tongue, in the old Yiddish saying, might have been Norman's motto. Doors opened everywhere for him as a young literary critic: *Partisan Review*, the *New Yorker*, *Commentary*, *Scrutiny*. All his contemporaries envied him. He was never out of opinions, none of them mild. He once interviewed me for a job as an associate editor of *Commentary*, and when we spoke about the *New Leader* magazine, for which I then worked, he remarked that "anything good in its pages was there by accident." I didn't – surprise! surprise! – get the job.

Later Norman shifted his interests from literary criticism to politics, which he must have felt – and who is to say wrongly – a larger arena of if not interest then certainly of controversy. His positions in this realm won him many new enemies. People took a genuine satisfaction in finding mean things to say about him. (Norman's brashness has, in my dealings with him, long since disappeared; in all of my dealing he has in fact turned out to be a positive gent, well-mannered and thoughtful.) Lots of this mean talk about his father must have flowed down to the young John, who took a pass on the conventional revolt from one's father and was always deeply loyal to him. But the price of being the son of a controversial figure isn't trivial, and is often long-lasting. Nepotism was the going word when John was made editor of *Commentary*. I'm sure lots of people straight off dislike John primarily because he is the son of Norman, in ways that our children will not come close to being disliked – despised, even – because they are the children of Frederic Raphael or Joseph Epstein.

Have you ever met John's mother, Midge Decter? Last time Barbara and I were in New York, she took us to a laugh-filled lunch at a place on 54th Street called Cellini. Midge is in her early eighties, and is much as she was when I first knew her in her forties: quick, anti-nonsense, one of those people on whom very little is lost. I have always found her immensely attractive. She is also one of those lucky writers who doesn't need to be always at it; she writes only when truly aroused. What seems most to arouse her is people forgetting the obvious. That she reminds them of it has not made her all that many new friends.

I have been reading the *Journals of Sir Walter Scott*, which he wrote during the last six years of his life: he died in 1832, having just reached 61. I've been reading alongside it John Buchan's biography of Scott. I've not read a Scott novel since I was in school. As you know, he was a money writer, Sir Walter, wildly popular in his day, and a man who ruined his life through land hunger and through more than dabbling in publishing and printing enterprises which forced him to sell off his estates and live out his days in complicated financial worry. He also had a true novelistic sensibility, and understood that nothing pleases so much in literature as the creation of solid characters and that facts always come before ideas.

The reason I bring up Sir Walter Scott is that he turns out to have been a genuinely dear man, good to his family, his company enjoyed by all who encountered him, even when his own Tory politics differed from theirs. What we are talking about here is a man who makes that shortest of all shortlists: Nice Guys in Literature. Can you think of many? The usual prize of ten guineas and a year's subscription to the 1950s *New Statesman* if you can come up with more than five.

I have been on a steroidal drug call prednisone for my not yet disappearing rash, a drug which fills one with lots of (probably) false energy, and am writing this to you at 4.00 a.m., though will probably not send it off until tomorrow. But I don't want to close without reporting to you that someone I know not long ago went to an Irish wake in Chicago, and when he asked the husband of the woman whose wake it was what she died from, received the reply: "Oh, nothing serious."

Best, Joe

Dear Joe,

To hell with whose service it is. Picking up on services, Sunday morning in England is a good time to be vicarious; this letter stands for that bouquet-clutching visit to your bedside which penury and lack of proximity preclude. It smacks of calculation to wait for a letter from you before writing to someone in your (I trust) temporary Job-ish condition. Odd that my having checked out what is afflicting you should have made me, at least, feel that things are under control; the role of language down the ages. Of course the medical profession has made its nominative competence into one more form of mystification. One of our French *médicins*, the one who comes when our friend is unavailable, once diagnosed my earache, with the style of a detective cracking a hard case, as *'une otite'*. The remnants of a classical education allowed me to inform him that since Galen's Greek for an ear was *ous/otos* (hope I'm right about the genitive), he was telling me what was manifest on superficial inspection. He gave me drops, for the ears not for the showy play of a small trump. My friend Brian Glanville, now home again after his quadruple bypass and valvular repair, always assumes that anyone he meets shares his now unmatched knowledge of soccer, its lore, personae and major (plus minor) results; in something of his spirit, though with the subtlety you would expect, my vocabulary somewhat assumes that references to the bridge table will be readily interpreted, not least by those of our persuasion, if persuaded we are.

In my last lecture (our French postman used to hand me letters and mags – of the former there are now very few – with the words *'Un peu de lecture'*), I told you about my very amiable meeting with the younger Podhoretz. I somewhat expected a boy, which he is clearly not, and wondered, for a second or three, how it could be that I am the only man in (adjacent to) intellectual circles who has never met P. Senior. Your reminiscence of Norman's ferocity as a lit. crit. recalls a whole slew of Jewish arrivistes who shone in that department, *ici* as well as *là-bas*: Al Alvarez, now prouder to be a poker player than a poetaster, and Wolf Mankowitz, a name possibly unknown to you, are the Oxford and Cambridge, respectively, instances from the late forties/early fifties. Wolf has a unique niche in the collected edition of *Scrutiny* which, in an early paroxysm of penitential regression, I bought at one specially-offered price. Wolf's Leavisite spell did not last long, but it issued in *Scrutiny* in a Frank party-lined denunciation of Dylan Thomas and his most recent emanation of poetic *hwyl* or whatever the damn stuff is the Welsh find in their hills. Mankowitz later became a very commercial screenwriter and East End sentimentaliser: he wrote a thing called *A Kid for Two Farthings* (no prizes for a Joycean parody of that title) and another *The Bespoke Overcoat*. He was above all a Londoner, although with intimations of racial (let's say) pride after the 1967 war. Alvarez played the *arbiter poetarum* for quite a time, but then took up suicide and poker, two forms of self-destruction from which, smart little guy, he became quite prosperous and alive.

Another instance of the makeover qualities afforded by lit. crit., a form of clerisy (as Frank Kermode would certainly say, probably within a moment of being introduced), is your friend, but not mine, John Gross, who is (to spare your splitting your loyalties, I will NOT dilate on this topic) a sort of Anglo-Saxonised Walter Benjamin, a thing of shreds and batches, an anthologiser *jusqu'au bout* who never says anything much of value *in propria persona* but hangs about with the *gratin* until he takes on the complexion of the tried and toasted. You get a very small, but rarely awarded medal for gallantry by going on record, the first of men maybe, as saying that Kermode is a bore. He bloody is, and not a particularly nice one either, but there again the English class thing was at work in transforming him from a gallant (I believe) wartime other-ranks sailor into an academic toff with the toffee-nosed style to prove it. I have laboured dutifully through his texts, from time to time, *The Sense of an Ending* for egregiously twee obscurity, and pretended, all alone to myself, *pauvre type que je suis*, that I was better informed, enlightened, stuff like that, *après qu'avant*.

Yes, the use of French indicates a mixture of embarrassment and the promise that I do have a world elsewhere, one where, I confess, I wish to spend more and more time as England disintegrates into a spiteful, cheap and – worst of all – bankrupt society (except for the banks, of course). France is no better, my mother would say (forever – and I use that word advisedly – afraid that my lack of gratitude to the British for not handing us over to Eichmann & co. will lead to a pogrom if I flaunt it too verbosely), but *douce France* is large and seems – I concede the fantasy involved in this – to retain in its beauty and structure something that Montaigne would still recognise, whereas London is no longer anything like the place which, in my imagination at least, fostered writers, made them feel . . . oh try consequential, even though it rarely named streets after them.

So, I did New York and a fancy studio apartment in Brooklyn where this director/painter David Salle has his pad, and pencils. If he can do the movie I have composed for him, well and good, perhaps, for the future: *à mon age*, as the peasants say, it is demeaning to need what the Biz calls 'a credit' but so it goes. It is not much of an honour to be listed in the Xmas promotion in some DVD store (they still have them in London, but not in NYC) as having written two of the Fifty Best British Films of the last fifty years (*Darling* and *Far From the Madding Crowd*), not least because they were both done in the 1960s. I begin to belong to the 'Is he still *alive*?' gang; if I had a group, I should qualify for lifetime-achievement awards already, as Helen Mirren just has; lacking her tits and her expressive hand-gestures, I blush unseen and ungarlanded. If I don't care, why am I telling you this?

Back in London then, two weeks plus ago, I happened to pick up the 11th paperback edition (entailing 5,000 in print, I suspect) of a compendium of philosophical essays which Ray Monk and I edited, and to which we both contributed back in the latish 1990s and, among the cited comments, saw that Daniel Johnson had spoken enthusiastically of our efforts. My own was on Karl Popper and was very generously and accurately annotated by Roger Scruton, who wrote a monograph on Spinoza for our series. Roger is an English neo-con, hence an archaeo-con, much abused by left-thinking folk and, despite (because of?) a nervous personal presence, highly polemic in style. He does not, for instance, think 'post-modern' (conceptual) art 'beautiful', and he does think it matters. He also rides to hounds and, although no kind of a toff *de souche*, is a sort of snob (I think he married a Lady). Anyway, as the young say, Daniel Johnson was the editor with whom I had a run-in (and out) over the failure to pay what he had promised for a contribution and for temporising like an absconding clerk – note careful choice of simile – when I put in, repeatedly, for payment. I was feeling Christian, though never as Christian as he is (practising RC, I discovered), and so invited him to a reconciling lunch at that unsmart club to which I belong but rarely visit and from which I threaten (myself) annually to resign.

With the generosity of a man who will take a meal from anyone, he came. He is just fifty, somewhat pink in complexion (his father being the prolix Paul), a little fluffy, grey in appearance and dress. We talked easily and at length, till the dining room was empty and the tables cleared of their cloths, and he said, towards the end, that he could not even remember what our *brouille* had been about (he didn't *say* 'brouille', but you know he would have liked to, if he had not been a Germanist). I said that I could, but so what? He told me, during our long and easy talk, that he had brought me copies of the latest issues of *Standpoint*, a mag of which I need not tell you more.

During lunch, I felt obliged to remind him of what he was missing by coining as many *mots* as I could jingle in my mouth, one of which was re George Steiner, about whom I was remarkably amiable before being otherwise. Johnson said at one point, 'You obviously hate him'. To which FR replied, 'Not at all. I save hatred for best'. I also took the trouble to say, of another editor of a posh monthly, that as far as I was concerned he was 'like a grey rag to a bull'. Why am I telling you all this? To prove *what* a good lunch I tried to provide. The guy even asked for another pitcher of wine, by the way, something I should *never* do in a million years at the shrinking South Pole. Can poles shrink? Is there a Euclid in the house?

We parted with protestations of affinity, but he forgot to give me the two back-numbers he had promised. Although he has my e-mail address, he did not send me three words of thanks, nor did he dispatch the mags to my address. This is a modern English gentleman, it is said. And now you wonder why I feel like Simone de Beauvoir (yes, this is something quite new, doctor), the bit of her, I mean, which said at the end of her many memoirs of life at the intellectual top, '*j'ai été flouée*'. Do the gender change and I am of the same view: I have been cheated, mainly by myself, of course, and by my unflagging overestimation of the British capacity for style and civility. Théophile Gautier had it right: '*Tout passe*'. And there it bloody well goes.

Joe, please be better soon. I know that Montaigne made sweet prose of his misfortunes, but I would sooner have you well.

Tout à toi,
Freddie

Dear Freddie,

A word explaining the hiatus (hold the hernia) in our (to me) delightful correspondence. My bloody skin disease (dear old bullous pemphigoid) has all but utterly dominated my life, among other things draining me of energy. I did over the past three or so weeks read page-proof for Houghton Mifflin Harcourt for my new book of stories (*The Love Song of A. Jerome Minkoff*) and wrote a 4,000-word essay on the something called "The Stages of Life" for a cordial editor at *Notre Dame Magazine*, but seem to have done little else, including much in the way of reading. I spent a lot of time in a comfortable chair watching the Tennis Channel with the sound off, reading Evelyn Waugh on Ronald Knox and trying to find a poorly made sentence of the old Bully

Evelyn's, but with no luck. This is an illness where one seems to go one step forward and then one or sometimes two steps back.

One of the things that made it all more gruesome was that I was put on a steroid called prednisone, the usual treatment for bullous pemphigoid, which did frightening things to my body, including bloating me up so that I could not fit into my usually quite roomy boxer underwear shorts or into my shoes. Each morning I would wake to some fresh hideous surprise: a hugely fattened face, with squinting eyes, great puffy arms, hugely thick ankles. The worst was that, for four or so days, I walked around with what felt like a twelve-pound scrotal sack (for long-schlong fans out there, my penis, during this time, seems to have gone AWOL). I was finally taken off the prednisone, which slowly took all the grotesquerie out of the disease, leaving only the day-to-day grind of it. Should anyone offer you a choice between acquiring this disease and a trip to Genoa, do remember to choose the latter. I hope you are writing this down. Also write down: Remember Fred, no Pred.

The name A. Alvarez reminds me of a title of one of his books, which was, I do believe, *Beyond All This Fiddle*, which I always found amusing in its sheer aggressiveness. I never found Alvarez (dare I call him A.?) other than a charmless writer. I believe I even tried one of his novels. He comes of the day when one wouldn't talk to someone if he had the wrong opinion on Robert Lowell – a serious time but, in retrospect, in many ways also a silly one. I've also read Alvarez on poker, and didn't find him very revelatory on that subject either. I wonder if anything he ever wrote gave any pleasure to anyone. I say "I wonder," but I think I know the answer.

I have just read a wretched book by Frank Kermode, a book made from his Clark Lectures and called *Concerning E.M. Forster*. My friend Edward Shils used to say that if Jesus gave the Sermon on the Mount in six lectures, by the sixth his audience would have been reduced to eleven people. I cannot imagine anyone who heard the first of Kermode's dullish lectures – all learning, no brains – returning to hear a second, but perhaps I underestimate English masochism.

The more I read of Kermode on Forster – the reason I am reading him is that someone has asked me to write about the book – the smaller Forster the novelist seemed to become. Kermode, with typical academic aplomb, never gets around to saying what he truly thinks of him. Lionel Trilling, who wrote a full book on Forster, seems to have done so with no notion that he was homosexual; Trilling commended Forster on his "refusal to be great." But, then, haven't we all.

I think Forster was probably a writer one needed to read when one was young – not much above twenty, perhaps. What his arid novels did for those of us who put ourselves through them was convince us that we, too, were members of his "aristocracy of the sensitive, considerate, and plucky" – members, that is, of one of the finest clubs in the world, the large- and kind-hearted. Of course, Forster himself was not very sensitive, considerate, or plucky, with his taste for Egyptian bus drivers and other working-class trade, and his very deep vanity; he thought himself in competition with Eliot as the greatest English man of letters. He was more than a bit of a creep, and another of the false gurus of our time, or so I have come to think. But what does actual human conduct have to do with anything? As for the novels, I should as lief speak at the funeral of A. Alvarez as have to reread *A Passage to India*, with that portentous cave scene, yet again.

Paul Johnson, father of Daniel, editor of *Standpoint*, is a problem. He has written some wretched things, but also some very good ones. Did you read him a few weeks ago on Hazlitt in the *TLS*, on which I thought him excellent? I've met Paul Johnson only once, and he was full of bonhomie. His politics are not so far from my own that when he writes crudely on a literary-politico subject, I feel embarrassed and feel, too, the need to reexamine my own views. I gather he is one of those men – out of the old English journalistic tradition – who can drink and write profusely without either activity getting in the way of the other. I do not so much admire as wonder at this.

John Podhoretz seems to have had the mixed gift of perpetual middle age. Owing to early baldness, he never has looked quite young. His father, a much smaller man than John, also had baldness early. But, more important, John has a youthful spirit. The other day, for example, he called me about the following project: leading off each issue of *Commentary* with a slightly philo-sophical Jewish joke, and asking readers for their exegesis of the joke in under 250 words, the best exegesis winning a year-long subscription to the magazine for a friend. (Why is it that when I tap out the word "exegesis" I see Raphaelian lips sounding out "Exit Jesus"?) I attach below samples of two such jokes and one Exit Jesus. John wanted to do this to enliven the magazine, make it less solemn than it absolutely has to be, and I salute him for this.

Your notion of possibly belonging to the Is He Still Alive? Club, reminds me of a piece Murray Kempton once wrote on the American political figure Arthur Goldberg. Goldberg was the former counsel to the AFL-CIO, the former Secretary of Labor, the former Supreme Court Justice, the former Ambassador to the United Nations. Kempton titled his piece "The Former Arthur Goldberg."

You have not yet attained this state of formerality, or formeraldihyde. As a scenarist you have created a number of characters whom people are not likely soon to forget. The three main characters in *Darling* stick in the mind; or so I found after rewatching the movie last year on Turner Classic Movies.

I am making my fourth run at finishing Wallace Stegner's novel *Angle of Repose*, which is supposed to be a great American classic novel. I am at last within eighty pages of finishing the damn thing. The subject of the novel is that of a cultivated eastern woman who marries an irrigation engineer and spends her life in the late nineteenth century out west in less than cultivated conditions. My problem with the novel, I have come to see, is that perhaps a third of it is description of landscape, for which I have neither taste nor talent, at least landscape described verbally (as opposed to painted or seen straight on). An urban boy, I must know the names of perhaps eleven trees and twelve flowers. I remember a recent poem that began, "Women know 279 colors, men know 9"; something to it, I fear. I have done a bit of weather in my scribbling, and I have described Lake Michigan, with its wide palette of changing colors, but that is about as far as I go. The only writer of landscape whom I find readable is Tolstoy, but then of course he peopled his landscapes so brilliantly. I am trying to recall the role of landscape in your fiction, and my best recollection is that it is not large. Am I wrong about this?

Keep the faith, preferably in a lightish scrotal sack.

Best, Joe

Dear Joe,

That's better. So light is your touch and so unscratchy your tone, that no-one would know that you are wearing some kind of shirt of Nessus, though not carrying the full dose of centaurian venom. I marvel at the gallant prose in which you describe the bloating symptoms induced, it seems quite clear, by what was meant to cure them. When the Messiah comes, he will, depend upon it, bring medicine from the same cruel cupboard and we shall all be dosed and scourged and obliged to call it redemption. I don't know what redemption will be, but I bet it won't come in my favourite flavours. Do I want to be saved? Abraham's bosom was a lodging that Queen Victoria disdained to solicit and you can't blame the old bat. She doted on Dizzy but she was not entirely sold on what the English still call, sometimes, 'your people'.

There is something missing in me, and I don't miss it: the yearning to develop my spiritual side, the oceanic dream, a craving for souls to commune with. I should like nothing better than to see our daughter Sarah again (and I sometimes do, in dreams in which I seem to embrace her and, even though I know it *is* a dream, find her quite solid), but I cannot think of having her alive again, redeemed or not, without wanting to know what she might be painting, creating, decorating, which includes mocking, parodying, inventing. Heaven cannot have any facilities for that kind of thing. It was, more than any other utopia, designed by Plato, merchant of the Big Idea, who handed the lease to the Christian Fathers. They badly needed pristine premises where Jews had not held the freehold and went for the great white beyond. They added a terrace with a view of the Judas race being barbecued, but logic insists that the essential vacuousness of perfection marks the mansions, however many there may be, with blank walls and empty shelves. There can be nothing creative going on up there, since this would imply that perfection could be improved. So, the downshot is: we can go only to the doctor when we wish to be saved, and now look what those people have done to you. 'What Then Is To Be Done?', the Russki said, and well he might.

For me the medical profession has done a pretty good job (as they have, in some cases, for you). I had piles (which I once believed/was told was a typically Jewish affliction), which were cured back in the sixties by a deft Welshman who later had a horrible car crash, and then, in the 80s, I had some kind of a growing growth on my jaw (oedema, is that you?) which needed skilful excision if my face was not to droop forever with the ineradicable melancholy to be observed, often, in those who have worked in Intelligence and seen it All Go Wrong; and then I had this pituitary tumour, which was winkled out by another clever Welsh surgeon, thus redeeming (aha!) my vision.

Welshing, as you may or may not know, is what bookies used (??) to be said to do when they absconded without paying up on the winning tickets, but it seems to have been good for me. The English (rarely British in the old days) managed to tar the other three partners/denominations in their United Kingdom with opprobrious epithets and reputations: the Irish were bog-Irish, of course, and had Polish-type jokes made about them; the Welsh were Taffies and Taffy was a thief; and the Scots belonged to the tribe who furnished extras for jokes along the lines of '. . . when they presented the bill, the Jew fainted and the Scot carried him out'. The Scot, exegetes will notice, played the virile role, having more under his kilt than his feminised burden. See under(neath the piles) . . . and there it always is.

The English snobs imagined they could take the malicious superiority out of their innate character by always confessing/boasting that some percentage of their blood was Irish, Scots or (slightly less favoured) Welsh. They also recruited Guards regiments of these lesser breeds, who were gallant in all sorts of places on behalf of those who, in social circumstances, despised or winced at them. There were, of course, no Birmingham Guards, because English regional accents, especially the Brummy one, were even less acceptable than Scots or Southern Irish (although Ulster was allegedly right, and ready to fight, the Belfast accent was off).

In the modern style, a lot of people until very recently were also discovering that they were a bit Jewish (the Mitfords never did, but Jessica did marry one of those people, I think; anything for a laugh, that one!). Even Michael Frayn, who never puts a foot wrong but – misplaced adversative, possibly? – fails to get anywhere very much except the Top, claimed that he was a Hebe of sorts, but that was before the posh end of the London literary world became convinced that Israel was the source of all evil and that anyone who wanted to be the kind of Jew that English Jews wanted to be (taken to Britannia's bosom) had better renounce all affection for, affiliation with that shitty little country, as a French ambassador to the UK pronounced it, some years ago, in company which, *sans doute* if I may say so, he had reason to assume was of like mind. Our daughter Sarah would have thrown her Chambolle-Musigny right in his (betcha) long-nosed froggish gob, but she was not invited. I fear I should have been more, oh, how about circumspect?

As you know, the *London Review of Books* is parasitic, in spirit, on the *NYRB*, to which you once or twice contributed, I think. I have never been fifty-fourth reserve in either team, though I do recall that Bernard Bergonzi (sounds like a dance-band leader in a cardboard Borscht belt) saw me off with a review of a 1967 novel of mine, *Orchestra and Beginners*, in which he said that I should stick to autobiography. Fucka him, as the majority of cardinals would say. Likewise, 'Lady, who cares?', the tag of a Jewish deli joke which I suspect you may have penned. The metropolitan Jews, with the pugnacious exception of Howard Jacobson, who is wholly to be distinguished from Dan of that ilk, a dan with no Judo characteristics, more Jew-don't, are all too fine to back those rough'n'tough Israelis who are always massacring people and provoking local bullies to beat them up and then – wouldn't you know it? – beating them up. Tricky. Harold Pinter, recently beatified, would throw Zionists out of his fancy house. It is said, in print, that Harold was considering converting to Roman Catholicism so that he could share celestial abode (mit pillars) with his literal Lady wife, Antonia, whose divorce was OK with the Pope apparently because she is so so sexy and mellifluously spoken and blurry in outline.

I mentioned Michael Frayn above just for the sweet mischief of it (he is SUCH a nice man, no-one says a word against him, but that's as far as it goes) and now realise that his mention leads sweetly into a confession: I have only twice in my life 'proposed friendship', in the form of a letter, written, *sealed* and never posted (you want to add italics? Add them!) to two people: Michael and Jonathan Miller. In his youth, Frayn was a member and prolific writer in the Cambridge University Footlights, a cabal/nursery of laddish (and later ladyish) comics who, since the Fifties, have supplied 'satire' first to the Quality and then to the Quantity. I was in a now quasi-mythical Footlights company, in Ike's first term; we went to London and for three weeks were a hot ticket. I made £15 a week and that was money. Frayn came later and so deep was the shadow we threw forwards, as it were, that he wrote me a fan letter which began 'Dear God Raphael'. A man who can combine academic excellence with that kind of grovel-power is always a candidate for elevation and up she went. He is said to have married the prettiest girl at Oxford (although he was at Cambridge) and they had three daughters. We invited them to a party at our then country house and they came and were very nice. M.F., in his thank-you letter, referred to the party as 'Gatsby Day', which I elected to take sportingly. He had been so nice that I penned, oh yes, that unsent letter soon afterwards. Why did I not send it? *Quissá?* Not long after that he left his comely wife and teenage girls and took up with Claire Tomalin, whose journalist husband had been killed on the Golan Heights by a heat-seeking missile. Nick, whom I knew (and abused tellingly at Cambridge for inviting Oswald Mosley to speak at the Union, of which Nick was president) had been about to leave Claire for a younger model. The editor of *The Sunday Times*, Harry Evans, who had dispatched Nick to cover the '73 war, was so covered in guilt that he made Claire literary editor of the paper. I had known her at Cambridge, employed her as a researcher and had reviewed books for her at the *New Statesman*, where she had been lit. ed. You don't need many guesses to know that she dumped me from *The Sunday Times*, even though I had been suborned by her (without emoluments) to puff Frayn's new book in the *Statesman*. You've never heard of this kind of stuff going on in the lit. world, have you? I'll save Jonathan Miller for a snowy day, of which we are to have no shortage in this coldest winter for thirty years. Where's Al Gore now? I hope he has no mittens.

Great to have you back on the show, cher maître.

Tout à toi,
Freddie

Dear Freddie,

At last the God question – does the Old Boy exist – arises between us. At the age of 73, I still haven't answered it. Like you, I have a hard time imagining heaven, especially Jewish heaven. My pathetic researches on the matter reveal the Jews to be extraordinarily vague on the matter. Near as I can make out, we shall await in our graves the coming of the Messiah – arrival date not shown on the board at O'Hare – after which all goes even blurrier. Philip Larkin says that the first clue he had that Christianity wasn't for him was that one day in church he learned that in heaven, all good Christians would return to the state of happy children, when he so longed to be adult, with lots of keys, money in his wallet, LP records, and the freedom to chase attractive women. I imagine Jewish heaven, insofar as I can imagine it at all, as crowded, noisy, filled with people arguing, a vague whiff of corned beef hovering in the background. Not, really, my idea of a good time.

Although I have not brooded on this excessively – there are advantages, as I need scarcely tell you, to having a short attention span – I find I do not want to give up on the idea of God. All the arguments against the existence of God are easy to make – almost too easy. Nor, on the other side, do I think Pascal's famous wager all that seductive a notion. But here is one (to me) compelling reason for, if not quite believing in God, then not giving up on the possibility of his existence – and this is that such coarse-minded men as Richard Dawkins, Daniel Dennett, Sam Harris, and Chistopher Hitchens are dead certain that he doesn't exist. I rather hope for their sake that He does. The certainty of such unattractive men on the subject is sufficient to cast grave doubt on the matter for me.

I am also impressed – envious, really – of people who have genuine and intelligent religious faith. Have you ever read the letters of Flannery O'Connor, the American southern writer who died at the age of thirty-nine of lupus? I do not much care for her fiction, but her letters, which show such grand courage, and no complaint whatsoever in the face of unfair early death, seem to me magnificent in demonstrating what true religious faith can do for a person, what dignity and forbearance and strength it can give.

As I grow older the less impressed I am with the powers of rationality (science, it strikes me, answers no really interesting questions, just does a lot of interesting description); philosophy (". . . if you had a brother, would he like noodles?") is even less impressive; and the older I grow the more impressed I am with the mysteries of life, which are manifold. I live my life, moreover, as I suspect you do, as if God, or a suitable alternative, exists, registering all my acts: the callous and insensitive ones along with the less frequent kindly and handsomely altruistic ones. Someone, I in my naïveté continue to believe, is keeping score, and I am never ahead. Guilt and shame have their uses, at least they always have had for me, who has found them genuine motor forces in his life. But guilt and shame before whom? Not, allow me to suggest, Christopher ("I have an answer, does anyone have a question?") Hitchens.

"Welshing" on a bet or a debt is a term I grew up with, without ever inquiring into its etymology. The origin of the term, *Brewer's Dictionary of Phrase and Fable* just now informs me, "is uncertain." The question of the English and their local colonies (Scottish, Irish, Welsh) are of almost no interest to me. When the annual Scottish issue of the *TLS* arrives *chez* Epstein, I sigh with relief because I know I need read almost nothing in it. (Only the figures of the Scottish Enlightenment interest me, especially Sydney Smith and David Hume.)

In the United States we have professional Irishmen, who are almost always eye-glazingly boring. I have a story in my new collection called "The Casualty" about such a figure; it is based on a man named Donald Torchiana (his mother was Irish), who had to live in the same English Department (at Northwestern) with Richard Ellmann, an amiable Jew who had, as you will recall, cornered the market on Irish literature, writing the important books on Joyce, Wilde, and Yeats, and leaving poor Torchiana no recourse but to fall back on anti-Semitism. To revert back to the mysteries of life, I came to like old Torchiana, who was a World War Two bomber pilot, and who, in his alcohol-addled old brain, seemed to have forgot that I was Jewish.

I don't know if you saw in *Standpoint*, an issue or so back, a review by John Gross of a couple of books by Clive James, in which John asks what a volume called *The Worst of Clive James* might look like. Leaving aside John G. and Clive J., about whom we share less than perfectly congruent feelings, I find this a highly interesting notion. *The Worst of Joseph Epstein* – of what, I ask myself, would such a volume consist? I fear it would be a thickish tome. I think it would chiefly include those things I wrote when young. The largest number of pieces in it would be those in which I examined the life of a man or woman of much greater achievement or fame than I possessed, and found them wanting because their opinions were not so generous, enlightened, or generally virtuous as mine.

I some while ago let lapse my subscription to the *London Review of Books*, in which I had published a single piece. (I am reminded here that when William Buckley would receive a letter from an irate reader asking to cancel his subscription, he would reply, "Cancel it yourself.") I found its pro-Arab and anti-American views more than I could bear, and thought it best not to contribute my $50 toward supporting the rag. The *New York Review* does not currently run very different views, though I think it was held in check on this subject when Isaiah Berlin was still alive. Berlin was cowardly about so much, but, give him this much, he was solid on Israel.

I fear that Israel–Palestine is one of those issues on which friendly disagreement isn't possible. I once gave a lecture, around the time that I was working on my book on friendship. In the lecture I made the point that we mustn't look for absolute congruence of opinion among our friends, lest we greatly limit the range of our friendships. Better, I argued, to look for something of larger importance than opinion – to look for an interesting point of view. (V.S. Naipaul, in his novel *Guerrillas*, says of a woman character he loathes, "she had a great many opinions but taken together they did not add up to a point of view," a formulation that struck me as most useful in our opinion-laden time.) After my lecture, Irving Kristol approached me to say that he thought I had a most interesting point about opinions and points of view, "Except, of course," he added, in his sly Irvingish way, "for Israel–Palestine."

I just this moment, over the phone, had an offer I had to refuse. Someone from the United States State Department called to ask if I would be willing to go to Shanghai to talk about urban fiction in early March. The fee was less than grand ($200 a day), though they would fly me business class. They would not pay Barbara's expenses. (I cannot conceive so long a trip, and to so exotic a place, without taking my dear wife along. Such is the closeness I feel to her that I dislike even the notion of my visiting a place such as Shanghai without her also seeing it; going alone would constitute a selfish act.) In any case (so stop my blubbering and wash my face), I had to say no, at least for now, owing to my skin problem. I was told that perhaps something could be arranged for the autumn.

The *New Criterion* magazine asked me to write about the Montaigne book that you wrote about for *Literary Review*. (Did you note that your piece was picked up and reprinted on artsandlettersdaily.com?) I thanked the editor there, but said that I thought I had had my say on Montaigne, which I have. I am instead reading away at various E.M. Forster items. He was a slick fellow, with all sorts of, as they used to say, "hidden agenda" behind lots that he wrote. If I can, I should like quietly to blow his boat out of the water. It looks from the middle-distance like a row-boat, but carries nuclear torpedoes.

Best, Joe

Dear Joe,

According to a key source, heaven will be a place where reach and grasp coincide: nothing will be beyond us, that's what the *haut-delà* is for. All that rises will apparently converge which is nice for some people but personally I can do without that sort of thing. I have been reading Edward Said's volume of essays *Reflections on Exile*. What has driven me to imbibe hemlock and (flattish) soda when there are so many more delectable things on the trolley? The stern daughter of the voice of God: she told me that if I am to write a comprehensive book about Flavius Josephus I ought to understand what exile does to people and how a single man, even if flatteringly tenured in a foreign land, can yearn for community, native soil and the joys of yesteryear. Said said it all, and that wasn't all: he set himself to deconstruct the whole moral and intellectual of the (often Jewish) society that received him so tolerantly in order to make his personal hard luck story stand for pretty well everything that is wrong with the modern world, i.e., the West and its manipulators, imperialists, colonialists, capitalists and Zzzzionists. Bernard Lewis alone really makes him lose his temper, which is otherwise evident only in a tantrumesque prose style that leaves no room for interjection. He has an incantatory vanity which leads him constantly to add clause to clause, linked with commas, until a great freight train of grand grievances, mean magnanimity, cloying collegiality, memories of mistreated Arabs, fills the horizon of the mind, bumpity-bumping, clunkety-clunking along in one great tendentious caravan.

Said seems to have had quite a cushy life as a ranking US academic, but of course a man of integrity cannot settle for anything as demeaning as gratitude when he knows that the Arab nation (whatever that is) has suffered something so permanently grievous, so utterly demoralising and degrading, as the amputation of a hangnail of territory. This is not the place, luckily, to rehearse the whole shouting match and the frequent shooting matches. No sane Jew denies that some Arabs were killed, dispossessed and otherwise misused; but all Arabs refuse to concede that the same is true of Israelis, some few of them, maybe, because they know their brethren will blow them away if they do. Speaking to the topos of community – I cannot see why Said depicts himself as so *personally* and irremediably wretched, desolate and what else have you got? There is something triumphalist in his refusal to be anything but dejected. Can it really have been *that* terrible for him to be uprooted? What is so great about being rooted anyway? He quotes Simone Weil, of course, who was an intellectual flake longing to be a turnip. Let them share quarters in paradise, rooted to the spot of all spots and see how they like it.

Said may have had his noble side and he may have had a talent for suffering or a need to believe that he was suffering, in order to excuse his pampered status and fat lecture fees. Byron, when he went to have his bust sculpted by Thorwaldsen, a Dane resident in Rome, who now has a piazza named after him, chatted cheerfully with the artist and was then invited to assume a suitable pose. Byron immediately went into a soulful und doleful crouch, chin on hand, a man acquainted with grief and then some. Thorwaldsen said that there was no need to do anything pouty like that; B. should just sit there looking as he usually did. 'That *is* my expression', he said.

Said interests a reader who never knew him because of the complexity of his sincere imposture, the endless resource with which he seeks to ingratiate himself into the company of original thinkers (if, for instance, that's how you see Foucault and the other usual suspect Parisian figures) without having anything original to say, while taking acres of print in which to plant his bitterness. Said interests me then (you are probably there before me) because he is a parody, a mirror-reversed image, of The Jew: argumentative, witless, perpetually rancorous, falsely forgiving, grievance-collecting etc. The small entertainment to be derived from reading him is that, in his case, the style is the man: he does not have the art to conceal himself. A true stylist is also a master of elevating falseness: Cioran is a manifest instance: he wrestles himself into something elegant, intuitive, almost sublime. Said is incapable of successful dissimulation: when he plays the cosmopolitan intellectual, with affectations of impartiality, he remains more flat-footed social climber than noble spirit. There is nothing whatever Spinozan about him; he sees nothing *sub specie aeternitatis* even though, so far as I can see, he has no grand scheme for the rectification of the here and now except the destruction of Israel (he *pretends* not quite to mean that) and the right of the Palestinians – who now constitute a nation (of men betrayed and robbed by their leaders) – to go back and change the names of villages to what they were before and then have family gatherings (and roast Jew, no doubt). He says almost nothing (nothing that I remember) about the vindictive enclosure of the mass of Palestinians (those without well-placed friends outside) by their 'fellow' Arabs. He is so candid about his feelings that he is honest about nothing. (But he is quite good on the limitations of George Orwell's vocabulary, which are – he doesn't say this though – among the main reasons why the English regard O. as a genius: he doesn't, for a moment, go above their heads.)

Next question. God. Interesting that you should mention Dawkins in that regard. Hitchens is, to me, a lazy facile journalist who, I confess, bugs me only because he is also a professor already at NYU or some such place near a good deli, which reminds me of how badly I have rigged my senescence, but Dawkins is what my friend George Walden would call 'a bad man'. How do I know? By inspection, as we Cambridge philosophers used to say, knowingly. I adduce (can happen) one small but indicative piece of evidence. I happen to have been reviewing – for fifty quid – Anthony Julius's new 800pp. book (everything you want to know about English anti-Semitism, if you really, really do) in which the Dawk figures only marginally, but . . . He is there cited as having remarked that the Jewish lobby (here we go a-bloody-gain) is obviously so successful in manipulating the policies of nations that it made him think (yes, yes) how wonderful it would be if . . . guess! Yep, if Atheists wielded that kind of power. I refrained (not to say reFrayned) from mentioning that actually, comrades, atheists *had* had that power pretty well, in quite well known places such as Nazi Germany and Stalin's USSR.

I remain irremediably naïve enough to believe that Prof Dawkins of Oxford U. *must* be a master of his speciality, just as he is irremediably naïve enough to suppose that being an accredited geneticist (if that's what he is) entails competence in *ta metaphysica* and allied trades. Atheism is not an idea, it is the absence of an idea; God may or may not exist, but to 'believe' in His non-existence, even if true, arms the Dawks with no scheme worth following; it gives them Hemingway's *nada* and I wish them well to wear it. I haven't, as you ask, read the letters of Flannery O'Connor, but I take the point, even though I cannot imagine finding consolation in the deity. If I am reconciled to death (big 'if') it is more because, with Sarah dead, I know that whatever time I have left is somehow more than I, oh, deserve. Which won't prevent me, I hope, from making the most of it. Having had 38 more years, to date, than she did, I have to count myself lucky. But I shall, I fear, still sulk when given out.

Perhaps what you say of O'Connor throws some light back on Simone Weil, who was born a Jewess (with incredibly patient and forbearing parents) and tried all her short, and somewhat silly, life to detach herself from those roots. Her yearning was, of course, to *be* someone else. Balthus, *né* Klossowski, had the *chutzpah* to reconstruct his lineage and pass himself off, to himself above all, as some kind of an aristocrat. It didn't matter much because his work, however limited and (some will say) kinked, was not itself affected (although *affected*) by his fanciful fraudulence as a paedophile châtelain: you don't need to know anything about his quirks to see, appreciate, read his stuff. The paintings are still the paintings and never mind the psychic provenance, unless you insist on doing so. But Weil wanted to be a *thinker*, as did Eddie boy and as does Dawk, and here it all goes differently; the thoughts of such people (and ours too, I guess) are so heavily salted and peppered by whatever furtive motives, hopes, fears are diced and marinated in them that their writing cannot step away, as an artist's work can, and be somewhat free-standing, almost *counter* to the pettinesses and intentions of its author. Without logic (alas), such thinking is wishful-ness in Sunday dress and has no acquired vitality. Fiction, I still think, can do this kind of abstracted thing too: the storyteller can confess, lampoon, parade, deride what he feels, cares about, wants without having to create a whole false ideological apparatus to make it seem somehow impersonal and hence universally, impersonally, valid. At least some art – especially literature – acquires that kind of validation somewhat (I almost lied and said 'precisely') when it is anything but impersonal. Dawkins gives the whole thing away when he imagines a group of know-nothings running the world on the warrant of what they deny to be true (even though it is an old logical trap to claim to have proof of a negative).

I didn't see John Gross's piece about Clive, and I will respect our differing attitudes to the two protagonists (sic – and ye shall often find), but I have to say that, so far as laughs are concerned, I should prefer to read James on Gross than Gross on James. Clive's latest volume, which Gross was, I assume, reviewing contains a couple of touching pages about our daughter which, I confess (and you would hope), reserve him in a warmish corner of my heart. It isn't a very good book otherwise (it reminds me of what T.S.E. said of philosemitic Macaulay concerning what too much journalism does to a man's style), but the volume of poems which came out at the same time contains one or two very good pieces about Clive's father (who died in a crash on the way home from a Japanese camp in which he had been for four years) and his loyal mother. I made a very bad career move when I reviewed John Gross's very dull, skimpy and smug autobiography. His quondam wife, the allegedly beautiful Miriam, who had made him the most famous cuckold in lit. London, then suborned reviewers to trash *my* autobiography, twice. There is a place in my design of hell reserved for her: in an inescapable single bed, with John.

Tout à toi,
Freddie

Dear Freddie,
This past Saturday I attained to the august age of 73. I am all but innumerate, but 73 seems to me rather a boring number, rather like 57 or 48, a

nowhere-number. 73 suggests that one is on the road to old age, or at least one can no longer kid oneself that one is boyish in appearance and other realms. (I hope you don't already know the joke about the man of 96 who tells his physician that he seems to be slowing down sexually. The physician, astonished that the man has any sex life at all, asks when he first noticed this slowing down. "Last night," the man replies, "and then again this morning." Pause here for sigh.) 73 – big deal, as they used to say in the schoolyards of my boyhood. My only observation about my birthday tends to be the reminder of how many people vastly superior to me in talent went down so much younger than I am now, and that when it comes to death the arrangements of the world seem especially unjust. It's not an observation that yields much in the way of deep thought, except to cause me to knock wood, something I find myself doing increasingly.

Mine was an impressively unceremonious family. I cannot recall my parents arranging birthday parties for me or my younger brother past the age of five or six. They themselves viewed their own birthdays as quite without significance. My father, whose given name was Moses, which he later changed to Maurice, was born on Christmas Day, a fact that did not much engage his imagination. In later years, my mother used to give me, on alternate years, seven underwear shirts and seven pairs of boxer-shorts, never gift-wrapped, but in a bag from a now defunct Chicago department store called Wieboldt's. "Here's for your birthday," she would say, putting paid to the matter of such chronological sentimentality. If pressed on the matter, I suspect she would have said, "Why make a fuss?"

My own view of the matter of birthdays is generally that of my parents. The less fuss the better. Each year on my birthday I wake to find a birthday card from Barbara and a small gift (this year it was an elegant Italian water bottle), I thank her and the day goes on. And so it did this year, until at 6 p.m. when my granddaughter Annabelle walked in with two helium-filled balloons, a small packet of Ghirardelli dark chocolates, and a birthday card to which she appended the words, "I love you very much no matter how old and crusty you get. Love always." Very satisfying that, I must say. Now on to 74 (with knuckles bloodied and fingers crossed).

Good to watch you lambasting Edward Said, or, as I always think of him, Ed Said (as in "He said" or "She said"). I remember reading years ago Oliver Wendell Holmes, Jr. writing to the English jurist Frederick Pollock about a mediocre legal scholar that "all his work will have to be done over." I earlier mentioned Santayana remarking of a pretentious Anglophile Harvard English professor named Barrett Wendell that his twenty-odd books were "unnecessary." Eddy Said's books seem not only to have been unnecessary but the cause of a fairly large number of books and articles required to refute them. (Especially his book *Orientalism*, in which he stakes the claim that all western scholarship of things middle-eastern is automatically rubbishy and rotten given their source in the colonialist spirit.) What a pain in a tender place he was, with his appeals to false conscience, living, as you note, in the fertile crescent of American academic life, and telling the rest of us rather relentlessly what insensitive scum we all are – especially those of us of the Hebrew persuasion – for not recognizing the plight of, you should pardon the expression, "his people," the gentle, rocket-launching, happily self-immolating Palestinians.

You are especially good on said Eddy's style. I have never been able to read him, or at least not for long. Even when his subjects interested me – English Empire writers, the formation of style late in an artist's life – something about his prose seemed clotted, piled on, without elegance of phrase or formulation. He had a good run, the said Eddy, the feeling of being always virtuous in his politics and handsomely rewarded for biting the hand that fed him. May he rest not entirely in peace.

Your passing mention of Bernard Lewis, who did yeoman's work in fending off Ed Said's animadversions, reminds me that he used to call here from time to time. He is one of those men, Bernard, who, over the phone, treat other men's wives as if they are secretaries, or, more like it, office temps. The only words he ever spoke to Barbara were "Bernard Lewis here. Is Joe in?" (I suspect that Beetle can furnish a few matching stories.) What Bernard chiefly called me for – our acquaintenceship was owing to his being a member of the editorial board of the *American Scholar* – was to report that he had been awarded another honorary degree, to remind me of his possession of several foreign languages, and to tell me four or five Turkish jokes, only one of which, on a good day, did I find faintly amusing. When Bernard's extra-scholarly fame took off, from the days of the Americans' entering Iraq, where he was the media's favorite expert on the subject of Middle Eastern woggery, the calls ceased. But that of course, as you know, is showbusiness.

The Evanston Public Library, which is a block away from our apartment, and which I use quite frequently, regularly puts books on sale at fifty cents a copy. As an old but struggling-to-retire bibliomaniac – a man who in the matter of book collecting is attempting to "deaccess," as the art museums say when they sell off their great paintings – I cannot resist checking these sale shelves. Two days ago I acquired from them the V. Nabokov novel *King, Queen, Knave*, which I had not hitherto read. I am now reading it very slowly, a few pages at a time, and what it chiefly reminds me of is that, for all his talent at manipulating the English (and doubtless many another) language, our Volodya was preternaturally drawn to the distasteful and grotesque. I know we are to cut the artist a large swatch in the realm of tolerance, but I myself find this aspect of Nabokov distasteful and grotesque. Of all his books, the only ones that genuinely please me are *Speak, Memory*, *Pnin*, and *The Luzhin Defense*. *Lolita* has some amusing bits, but seems to me a crueler novel than it had to have been, and without its censorious aspect at the time of its publication probably would never have caught on to become the classroom classic (always a bad sign) that it now is.

Which brings me to the new posthumously-published Nabokov novel. Have you already read it? Do you plan to do so? I've not read it and have no plans to do so. I find, in fact, all the high-level talk about whether the son Dmitri, à la the boring Max Brod, did the right thing in publishing the book against his father's wishes, so much baloney, thinly cut. My best guess is that Dmitri did it for one reason: the shekels. Alfred Appel used to talk about Dmitri's laziness. He is self-advertised as a singer, with a taste for sports cars, but when and where he has sung – apart from in the shower – remains a bit obscure. The novel itself sounds entirely repellent – fat men fucking barely pubescent girls – the worst of Nabokov and not, distinctly, this, my idea of a good time. It is amusing, though, to see third-class minds – John Sutherland's and others – knocking themselves out to find good sense in Dmitri's decision to publish the novel and finding vast significance in the work itself. Only an English professor, to wring a slight change on Orwell, could be that stupid.

I have recently had a nice offer from a man named Hunter Lewis, who has been a successful financier, head of something called Cambridge Associates and for a while president of the American School of Classical Studies at Athens and currently the owner of something called Axios Press – do Google him up – who wants to publish a book containing those of my essays that have not before now appeared in book form. Why does he want to do this? I asked him. "Because they deserve not to be lost," he answered. An amazing place, the US of A, is it not?

What do you know about an English classics scholar specializing in things Roman named R.H. Barrow? I have just acquired his *Plutarch and his Times*, which begins with what feels to this utter amateur a very solid discussion of Greece under Roman rule.

My bullous pemphigoid is improving a bit. At my last visit with my dermatologist, he asked that I cut out all alcohol. As a boozer, I am not a heavy-hitter, usually drinking no more than a glass of Reisling a night and, occasionally, a glass of Cabernet Sauvignon from my son's one-acre vineyard in Sonoma County. But for the past two weeks I have done without, leaving me to wonder if my ceasing to drink has brought on my improvement. Ah, diminishment, diminishment, thy name is 73.

Best, Joe

Dear Joe,

I have just received the proofs of my new novel, *Final Demands*. Is there any Narcissistic pleasure quite to match the delivery of another pool of words in which to contemplate one's own beautiful gambolling? The refrain 'What talent I had then!' gains another wholehearted chorus of one. I am fortunate to have, in Beetle, a cool and clear brain to pick up the literals and notice where the same speaker, in one of my riffs of dialogue, gets two inningses in succession, because – however severe I seek to be with myself – the sweet *glissando* speeds me like a skier who is having a good day, swiftly and almost drunkenly through the powder of my own gleaming verbosity. If I no longer have those great expectations which filled me when I wrote, I am pretty sure, less well but with the youthful confidence (not vanity) that my qualities would be recognised and applauded *un peu partout*, I remain pretty sure that I know a thing or two and that something in my work continues to threaten as well as amuse, if it does, those so reluctant to empantheon-ise me. The great satisfaction is to be in print, again. It says here.

A few days ago I received a request, through my publisher, to chair/ cheerlead an event at Jewish Book Week (an annual barkers' convention in London) in which Michael Scammell, a British-born US academic with whom I have, I think, had some amiable e-pistolary (my neologism, whaddya think?) contact during the compilation of his new biography of Arthur Koestler. As I mentioned in an earlier episode, not too many years back I reviewed David Cesarani's book on the same topic. Cesarani, a tenured historian, contrived to get access to the Koestler archive after promising that he was not really writing a biography but a study of some aspects etc. In the event, he rifled the archive in order to mount a very English attack on A.K., not because he was a political renegade or a bad Jew or a somewhat barmy scientifico-fantasist (who wanted coincidences to 'mean' something) but – as mentioned in an earlier e-pisode – because he 'raped' a certain Jill Craigie, the now-dead wife of Michael Foot, the English left-wing politico who led the Labour Party to a consummate defeat at the hands (and high-heeled feet, I shouldn't wonder) of Mrs Thatcher, back in the earlyish 80s. Cesarani extracted information from the then-living lady, although she had said nothing previously about A.K.'s assault in the 30 years or more between his bumping her on her own kitchen floor and the declaration of his enforced, unsolicited attentions. I knew Jill very slightly, and even slept once in her (and Michael's) bed, although not when they were there (there was a sex manual on the bedside table in 1954, very unusual for the 50s when sex, officially, didn't exist, especially when people were married). Jill's daughter was, at the time, the girlfriend of one Leslie Bricusse, a songwriter to whose importunity, while we were both at Cambridge, I owe my connection with The Show Business, as it used to be known on Old Broadway, and she had the key to the house.

There is, as experience if not practice will have taught you, no memory for grievances quite equal to a writer's. Nothing like hard gem-like flames to keep them warm for decades. So: like some rough beast playing the smoothy, I called the man called Fawcett, on tap at the British Library (already), who had offered me what the in-crowd call 'the gig'. He was not there but his auto-mated ghost promised he would get back to me. Before he did so, the tricol-oured brochure for Jewish Book Week tumbled onto our mat. The Scammell event was announced, but – of course – without a chairman. It took no advanced surge of paranoia for me to guess that someone must have let them down at the last minute and that I was being recruited as a sub, as the muddied oafs have it. So my tone with Mr Fawcett, when he called me back (during lunch, of course), was of the kind that causes my nearest mit dearest to wince and look away: Fred being Britishly sour and gripish.

Fawcett did not/could not deny that I had not been first choice, but he very much hoped . . . Who, I wanted to know, had been approached *prima di mi*? Well, to be honest, it was Julian Barnes. He had said yes and then no, because – here the thing grew complicated – his (late) wife, a buy-sexual literary agent, had had something to do with the Koestler Foundation and . . . and and and. When all the fine scruples were set aside, not to say bumped heavily on the lino, Julian had shillied and Shall-I?'d and finally found a hotter, if not cooler, ticket. Now you can make a (short?) list, I am sure, of people who you find it quite understandable should take precedence over you. I do not include Antonia Byatt or Martin Amis, but – in this case, introspection tells me – I might have allowed George Steiner to be the Right'n'Left Man for the chair. Julian Barnes, however, is not a flashing light that will ever dispose me to pull in to the kerb. Mr Skimpy Flashplot, words administered by dripper, French polish a speciality (can there be a speciousality? Hang about, as the Brits say), self-importance in a Gucci bag, Flaubert's sparrow. Oh, listen, Julian's fine, in the wincing, mincing flesh, but what has he to do with Koestler's life, times, concerns? Nix is more than I am willing to grant.

But of course, Master Barnes is *persona gratissima* with the billers and cooers. So, did I do the big-hearted thing and let Mr Fawcett run hot with gratitude? No. I am too old (look! he said it himself) to go out, unpaid, untaxied, un-top-of-the-billed, on a February evening in order to prime Professor Scammell to huff and puff. Did I tell Mr Fawcett that, although I am not among the prophets, Jewish Book Week audiences are the only ones, worldwide, who are likely (and if I don't say so myself, who will?) to come to an 'event' because I am on the programme? Big in Finchley, huge in Golders Green? Who says I'm not? NO; I said nothing immodest. I merely indicated that he could, as the Brits used to say, take a long walk off a short pier. And now I'm going to take a little look at myself in my proofs. Beautiful!

Tout à toi,
Freddie

Dear Freddie,

I had a little bout of galley proof (as it used to be called) reading myself in December, though these days in America no-one any longer speaks of galley proof but of pages. One reads pages. I read mine – the pages of my new story collection – with the nearly sickening glee that only insane vanity makes possible. Some of the stories in this collection were written as long as seven or eight years ago, and I found myself unduly pleased with how amusing I was then (we shall not speak of how dull I seem today). In one of my stories, a woman who was once married to a man with a gambling addiction, remarks, "The nice thing about alcoholics is that at least they pass out." Did I invent that line? Did I hear – and thus steal – it from someone else? (I cannot think whom.) All I know is that I am smugly pleased with it. I was given three weeks to read my pages, but finished in fewer than ten days, so fookin' pleased was I with what I had written. Appalling, the self-satisfaction I exhibited. I suppose the other side of this false coin is the scribbler whose page proofs fill him with remorse, with the sense of perfection too-soon abandoned, opportunities lost. In any case, as we used to say in the early 1960s, the whole thing is a bit "sick," not to say sick-making. I'm reminded here of a long-dead friend named Albert Goldman, who was the music critic for the *New Leader* magazine when I was one of its editors. Al was very psychoanalysandic and I recall once, when I handed him his galley proof for a piece to appear in our next issue, he said: "Ah, my galleys. Would you mind dimming the lights, putting on a Julie London record, and lending me a clean handkerchief while I read myself?"

As for honorary degrees, the leader in possession of them in America must be the comedian Bill Cosby, who, in this realm, is not merely a twofer but a threefer. 1. He is black; 2. He is rich (and thus a possible donor to the university); and 3. The graduating students and their parents get an amusing speech for nothing. Untoppable, really.

This is probably the place to inform you that I, who proudly, reverse-snobbishly, have no so-called advanced degrees (and rather wish I didn't have a plain bachelor's degree), have often, owing to my teaching at a university, been addressed as Dr. Epstein, which always gets a laugh from my wife. Calling oneself "Dr." in American universities has long been thought bush-league or vulgar, which may have come as hard news in the grave to Señor Leavis. Being addressed as Professor I found no better, and also asked to be called plain Mister. Nowadays, I do believe, students call professors by their first names, usually at the poor old pedagogues' request.

I recall when M. Cesarani's gun-jumping book on Koestler appeared, though I did not read it, as I shan't read Michael Scammell's either, and the (hereabouts) mild scandal it caused, which I know was much greater in England. Koestler has never been my bowl of ghoulash, though he did write that one great novel, which a student of my friend Edward Shils once called *Sunrise at Midnight* – close but, may we not agree, no cigar. Koestler is said to have been as neurotic as a flea. Not a wholesome fellow, let us agree, Mr. Koestler.

Many letters appear in this past week's otherwise boring-as-usual *New York Times Book Review* about a piece by a youngish woman named Katie Roiphe on the subject of the energy in writing about sex in the novels of the Updike–Roth–Mailer–(somewhat older)–Bellow generation. Ms. Roiphe much approves their hearty appetite for sweaty bonking – at least on the page – and is critical of the newer generation of writers (in their thirties and forties) who tend in their fiction to treat sex with hesitation, delicacy, a general edginess. Ms. Roiphe prefers her bonkers to go at it with gusto, though I suspect she would not be keen on Koestlerian, so to say, floor-play. What she hasn't seemed to notice is that, as you pointed out earlier this year, not one of her gusto-bonkers seems to have created a memorable female character. And why after all should they have done: women in their fiction are of bonking interest exclusively.

Katie Roiphe is the daughter of a writer named Anne Roiphe, whom I, in my self-appointed capacity as Lord High Excommunicator, would bar from Judaism at the first opportunity. She, the mother, writes embarrassing memoirs about her failed marriages to shrinks. One reads an Anne Roiphe piece – I should never read a full book by such a monster of candor – and asks, "Dear God, why couldn't she have been Irish?"

Apropos your dealings with Jewish Book Week, my question is what does Julian Barnes know from the Jews? I would add the simple observation that one should not appear on panels, give talks, or play the accordian at weddings for nothing, unless the cause be an especially grand and utterly good one. Once the word gets round that we girls are giving it away for nothing, the phone will never stop ringing – all the boys will want some. Several years ago I gave the main lecture at an Association of Independent Scholars' meeting; I gave the talk for nothing, because the subject of a fee never came up. I later learned that the people who commented on my talk, on a panel, received $1,000 each. Stupido, I thought when I learned this, striking my forehead with the palm of my hand the way Edward G. Robinson did when playing the Italian paterfamilias in a now forgot (at least the title is forgot by me) movie with Richard Conte. I am not infrequently asked to join – *pour rien* – book-discussion groups of ten or twelve putatively lively people. The other day I was asked to serve on the "cultural advisory board" of an expensive retirement complex – for the same fee: zilchikins. When I said that I wasn't interested in doing it for nothing, the public-relations woman who had extended the invitation told me that I would meet such interesting people also serving on the board; most of them turned out to be businessmen and academics and hopeless painters. No, no, no, Freddie, we mustn't give it away. We must remember, in the inelegant phrase of our day, that we are "content providers," and content, dearie, costs, or ought to.

I am reading Italo Svevo's *The Confessions of Zeno*, in a new translation – with larger type and leading than the old Vintage edition – by William Weaver retitled *Zeno's Conscience*. A wonderful, freaky little novel, Svevo's, one certain to guarantee its author's place as long as people take pleasure from fiction. (Pause here while I forego a gloomy forecast about the future of the novel, reading, and human speech.) As a probably too-prolific scribbler – "You certainly are prolific" is perhaps the most ambiguous comment a writer can receive – I have always admired that small number of writers of modest output but one book that will live forever. Meanwhile I, poor fool, write on and on, dragging my goddamn *oeuvre* behind me.

Best, Joe

Dear Joe,

Another tasteful convergence revealed: I have been a fan(atico) of Italo Svevo ever since I was given a volume of his *Complete Works* by Jo Janni, whose grandfather was a Triestine shipbuilder. It is impossible to think of any novelist – let alone in a foreign city, age and *senz'altro* language – in whose alien world one is so immediately at home, whose sentiments one so easily shares and whose fond perplexity at the randomness of life chimes so strangely, bitter-sweetly, with one's own. Janni was a movie producer of the kind (unEnglish accent, shameless appetites, silk socks) who confirmed to the 1955 snob that I was when I first met him that the cinema was a louche activity to which one had recourse strictly for the money. I met him because he was having trouble with a screenplay called – what else? – *The Big Money*, of which I remember two things only: it had a character in it called BLUEY, who was, of course, an Australian (they had lots of Blueys out and down there in those days) and its star was Ian Carmichael, a rather nice chap who regularly played the English silly ass in Pinewood films of the time.

Ian C. came to see me in the tiny subterranean flat in which we first lived, at 9, Chelsea Embankment (Turner's Reach House, no less, where G. Weidenfeld had/has an upstairs pleasuredome). Carmichael drove a green Ford Consul convertible. It probably cost all of $1,000, but it seemed to me the very warrant of swank; not that Ian was swanky; more nervously happy to be so lucky, although contractually obliged to ride in the c7ass vehicle which I was being asked to repair. Later I was summoned to Janni's flat (not far away, on the other side of the Royal Hospital, where the veterans of Britain's many foreign wars enjoyed free board and gruel) to discuss the rewrite. Less than a decade later, when I knew Jo better, he asked me whether I remembered the first thing I had ever said to him. I did not; but he did: it was, allegedly, 'What do you want to make this piece of shit for?' I was, you can tell, at once preco-cious and servile. The badge of all our race? Writers on the make, I mean.

Jo had come back into my life in 1962 (how the dates now seem to jostle each other in one's early life, yet at the time the days were long and the years bulged with slow promise!), after I had written *Nothing But The Best*, in which Denholm Elliot gave the performance of his life and Alan Bates was a lot better than I thought at the time. As a result I was recruited by Janni and John Schlesinger to write *Darling*, a project that then bore the working title of *Woman On Her Way*, which – I need hardly tell you – did not get us very far. I remember that, in the interests of research, we went to a fancy-dress New Year's Eve party in Chelsea on the hinge of 62/3, it must have been. Schlesinger came as a Cardinal, sporting a pectoral cross and a red skullcap. I cannot remember what Beetle and I wore. It was in the days before 'Swinging London' and our safari in search of debauchery found little wildlife to furnish us with material for our new (female) rake's progress. Jo seemed to me, in those days, quite an elderly person (in his forties already), bald, very white, paunchy, irretrievably foreign, thus – like my wartime comic's butt Musso the Wop – a figure of fun.

I learnt more about him as the years went by and he took me to be his friend. I say that because, although I have certainly come to miss him, it draws attention to the mildly dangerous side of the writer's character, the way in which curiosity, often a cold appetite, can seem to those on whom it is visited to be a sign of affection. It *is* a sign of affection, but it is the small-game hunter's love of his prey that keeps one so attentive. Jo liked me, I think, because Beetle and I had lived in Rome before we met him again and he knew that I understood (sometimes) what others missed in what he said. We shared a passion for, in particular, the movies of Michelangelo Antonioni, who was there in his great phase. Beetle and I saw *L'Avventura* in Paris in 1961, twice in the same day, once in Italian, once dubbed in French. Jo had been at university with Antonioni and knew all the Italian film crowd from which, for whatever reason, he had separated himself after coming to England and marrying a Welsh woman with hairy legs and seventeen houses in Swansea.

Jo's grandfather had been a shipbuilder in Trieste before the Great War. It was, as you know, the major port in the region, and contained (still contains) the biggest synagogue in Europe. Its shipyards were very busy. Marcus Samuel, the founder of Shell Oil, had been shipping oil literally in barrels (they are still counted according to that antique calibration) but had the idea that if he could ship crude oil in what he called 'empty ships', a great deal of time/money would be saved. Great Britain was then, of course, the great shipbuilding nation, but no British yard thought the Jewboy's empty ship could be built. So Samuel went to Trieste and shopped around. Jo's grandfather thought the idea feasible (it all depended, I suppose, on how to stabilise a liquid cargo in suitable compartments/tanks) and said he would build the first 'tankers'. Samuel had a problem: he did not have the cash to float the things. So a deal was made

in which Jo's grandfather received 10% of the share capital of Shell Transport
and Trading. *Figure-toi*, as the nearest frog might say. The tankers were built
and, no surprise, they floated and revolutionised oil transport. But – aha! –
riches made Jo's *nonno* imagine that it was possible to outsmart the English yet
again by creating a steamship line. He overreached himself and went bust and
all the 10% of Shell T and T went to appease his creditors. Had the old man
been idle and complacent, Jo would have inherited a chunk of Shell.

As it was ... Jo was the son of a rich man in Milan until 1938 when
Mussolini turned racist (just because he had a Jewish mistress doesn't mean
he was kosher right through). Jo's father was a sick, very rich man who was
told by his doctors that if he had an operation for whatever ailed him, he
might well die. 'In dat case,' Jo told me, he said, 'do it right away'. They did.
He died. His brother was less resigned and got Jo out of Italy with some of the
family money, thanks to Marcus Samuel, who was still alive, in London.
Samuel arranged for Shell Italia to buy some of the Janni assets and made the
money available to Jo in London. And that's how he still had a few bob, as they
say, when I met him.

E basta, for the moment re Peppino, about whom I have a repertoire of
anecdotes longer than a bailiff's arm. The Trieste connection started me off on
this. Jo too admired Svevo, about whom rather Janni-like stories are told.
Trieste itself is now somewhat reduced, though I think it's better since we were
last there, some fifteen years ago. James Joyce (who gave English lessons to
Ettore/Italo) and Richard Burton, the traveller and linguist not the Welshman,
both lived there. The story is that Burton, who made the hajj to Mecca
disguised as a Muslim pilgrim, was down on his luck, having been up the Nile,
and down again. One of his aristocratic friends was in the Foreign Office, heard
that the consulship in Trieste paid £600 a year when a pound was fifty pounds,
at least, and wrote to Burton: 'When they told me the salary and the fact that
there were no duties attached, I thought of you immediately.' Burton was,
according to reports, an avid pornographer, if not erotic panathlete (some, of
course, say that he was impotent, which may account for the reported sourness
of his wife who burnt a lot of his stuff after he died) and also, by the way and
as if it mattered (or made him singular), quite an anti-Semite, as Arabists do
tend to be, even before Israel gave them the chance for righteous unison.

Trieste is a grey city, with a wide canal that drives in at right angles to the
seafront. Svevo is everywhere and nowhere in particular; a quiet, smiling
ghostly presence that makes the city oddly enjoyable, not least, maybe,
because it never gives you a bad conscience about the many artistic treasures

you failed to visit, because there are almost none. Outside, along the road where Svevo had his fatal accident, is Miramare, the great fake *schloss* where poor Maximilian lived, as Austrian viceroy, before sailing to Mexico and his final framing by Édouard Manet.

Svevo survived his years of literary obscurity in good spirits, it seems, as the greatest writer ever to manage a (marine) paint factory. But when James Joyce read his tutor's novel, the Irish maestro recognised his merits and – unlike most of our scribbling tribesmen – advanced his fortunes by having him 'crowned' in Paris. On the last leg of Svevo's journey home, his chauffeur-driven car skipped off the road and he was fatally injured. As you know, one of his novels (*The Confessions of Zeno*, I think) concerned a man who, all the way through, swears that the next will be his last cigarette. As Svevo/Schmitz lay dying in the ditch, he asked one of those trying to help him whether he had a cigarette. '*Mi dispiace . . .*' etc. The guy was a non-smoker. Svevo said, 'Pity, that really would have been a last cigarette'. And died. Life limping after art yet again. I am sure you knew all this, or most of it, but those old stories are the best, aren't they?

Tutto bene?

Tante cose,
Federico

Dear Freddie,

I do not encounter many characters as exotic as Jo Janni. The screenwriting part of your career puts them in your path, or so I suppose. (Wasn't there a Janni-like character in *The Glittering Prizes*? Is he Bruno Laszlo in *Final Demands*?) I met George Weidenfeld – the man who inhabits the indexes of so many other people's books – only once, at a party for Norman Podhoretz's retirement as editor of *Commentary*. I was introduced to him by the quite effable Bernard Lewis. Weidenfeld's social-climber's eyes lit up briefly – did he mistakenly think me Jason Epstein, Jason the Freemason, the Robespierre of the paperback revolution in America? – but when he realized that I was a figure of no social significance, Xs appeared over his eyes that only moments before were aglow with the social equivalent of lust.

Jo Janni does, though, for some reason remind me of a local Chicago lawyer named Samuel D. Freifeld. Whenever I joke about going into litigation – and I invariably add when I do so that I am ready to settle out of court for $26,500 – I always say that I am going to turn the matter over to my lawyer, the late Samuel D. Freifeld, attorney for the damned, adding that if you hire him you are damned. Sam Freifeld grew up with Saul Bellow on Chicago's old Jewish West Side; the character Einhorn, in *Augie March*, is said to have been based on his father.

A man with lubricious lips and wavy hair with a low hairline that seemed to grow lower every year, Freifeld was one of those bulky Jews who was also a social lionhunter. Not much of an avocation in Chicago, this, where not all that many lions roam the flat prairie landscape. He claimed to be one among the dozens of attorneys who defended Lenny Bruce during his obscenity trial in Chicago; and, as I mentioned earlier, once at a New Year's Eve party Barbara and I met at Sam's apartment a very likeable Myrna Loy, who was in a roadshow production in Chicago of some play or other.

Freifeld's not very successful office handled my divorce. He opened our interview by asking if I happened to have a picture of my soon-to-be-ex-wife on me. I didn't. What I didn't realize at the time was that, if he found her to his taste, he would doubtless have called her up and attempted to bonk her. As part of his seduction procedure, Bellow once told me, he quoted T.S. Eliot and Nikolai Berdyaev. I assume that he hit upon all his even mildly attractive female clients. Occasionally I would note him in a restaurant with a much younger woman, whom I took to be a client in the vulnerable condition of undergoing a divorce. Women, alas, will do anything! Sam had a penchant for telling stories about being picked up by couples who asked him to return with them to their hotel rooms, where the husband would find gratification in watching him, the overweight Sam, biff his wife. Not an artful but sometimes an amusing dodger, the old attorney for the damned.

Did I mention that Freifeld was married? He invited Barbara and me to his and his (then) wife's apartment one Sunday morning for brunch (a silly word, I have always thought; if brunch, why not a repast between lunch and dinner called "linner" or "dunch"?). He arrived a bit late, in a lengthy leather coat and a leather Greek fisherman's cap – surely not even Greek fishermen could look good in such caps – toting a shopping bag laden with lox and bagels and cream cheese and other Jewish delicacies. I recall little of our conversation; I do recall his wife's coolness to Sam. (They would divorce not long afterward; she was either his second or third wife.) What I also recall – and shall not soon forget – is that after we departed the table, to take up chairs in his large apartment's ample living room, Sam put on a recording of a Mahler Symphony, which he began to conduct for us with great bullish sensitivity. He was wearing a black turtleneck and trousers that resembled jodphurs, if only because of the width of his hips and buttocks. (In the American south they say, or used to say, of a wide-bottomed woman, "Lordy, she must be four ax-handles across.") I should imagine Sam thought himself a slightly beefier Leonard Bernstein, without the propensity for chasing boys. He went on conducting for at least the entire first movement, maybe longer, during which painful time Barbara and I exchanged many glances. I was in my early thirties, and without the necessary combination of impatience and confidence to say to him, "Sam, this is a joke, right? So where's the punchline already?"

Sam and I broke off our relationship over a publishing deal. I had an offer from the now-defunct firm of E.P. Dutton of an advance of $20,000 for my first book, and he, Sam, thought I could do better, so he arranged a meeting with a hotshot editor of the time at Doubleday named Sandy Richardson, who took me to lunch in a French restaurant in Manhattan, where he complained about the cheese having been left in the refrigerator too long and told a not-at-all-bad story about Sir Geoffrey Keynes and the sommelier at the Athenaeum. (You probably know about the two delicate ladies who ask a New York waiter to see the sommelier, to which he replies, "Girls, if it ain't on the menu, we ain't got it.") In the end Doubleday, too, offered a $20,000 advance, and Georges Borchardt suggested I go with the smaller firm, Dutton, for whom $20,000 was a more important sum than it was for Doubleday. When Sam Freifeld called and I told him that I had decided to accept the advance from Dutton, he informed me that I owed him a fee for his contribution to the negotiations. I told him that he played no useful part in them. He said – and I love this phrase, an American shyster's phrase – "I am the injured party here, Joe. I need to be made whole" – I responded by telling him something equiv-ocal, like "Go fuck yourself," which put paid to our less than deep friendship.

Sam had troubled relations with his children, and he must have died alone. His kindly friend Saul Bellow gave him a cameo role in his novel *Humboldt's Gift* as a lawyer who, while in the hospital, flashes himself before nurses, which is sure to make poor Sam whole before posterity – whole as in asswhole.

Do you have any friends or acquaintances who, latish in life, outed them-selves by declaring themselves lesbians or homosexuals? I have a friend, though I haven't seen or heard from her in a long while, who declared herself a lesbian in her late forties or early fifties, after twenty-odd years of marriage and raising two sons. Her husband was a wealthy brute, which reinforces my theory – based on no research whatsoever – that homosexuals are born homosexual but lesbians tend to be made into lesbians by forces outside the genetic. The one man I know who declared himself homosexual did so at the end of a long marriage; his wife died of dreaded ALS, through which he saw her. He was a not-much-read novelist and the publisher of a large university press. He was also a great snob – loved Virginia Woolf and that wonderful gang that brought us Bloomsbury, never a good sign – and more than a bit of a narcissist.

My sense is that the real story about a man or woman who outs him- or herself is its effect on his or her family. I am trying to imagine my way into the subject by writing a story with the title "Dad's Gay." An arresting title, I think. Now all I need is the story to go with it.

I am supposed to be writing a piece on T.S. Eliot for *Commentary*. The excuse for my doing so is the publication of the second volume of Eliot's letters, which hasn't yet arrived *chez* Epstein. I shall mention and quickly move away from the question of Eliot's little – ahem – Jewish Problem, no Simon Wiesenthal of literary criticism am I, and move on to the matter of Eliot's dominance over the literary life of his day. That day is long over, and today – and for the past twenty or so years – there has not been a literary-critical presence to come anywhere near equaling Eliot's in the Anglophone world. Randall Jarrell called that time "The Age of Criticism," and rather looked down on it. Part of Eliot's eminence derived from the fact that he was also everywhere acknowledged a major poet, but one didn't have to be an artist to gain eminence and power as a literary critic: consider Leavis, Richards, Empson in England, Trilling, Yvor Winters, Robert Penn Warren, and a dozen or so others in the United States. The audience for such highbrow stuff was small, God knows, but it seemed at the time so very important that Eliot had changed his mind on Milton or that Leavis had lined up with D.H. Lawrence. Nothing in the realm of literature today can compare with that time for the sheer feeling of significance of literary opinion, or at least of the opinions of a number of literary critics of powerful authority. We had something approximating a literary culture in those days, and serious criticism, much of it dryasdust and let us admit not very readable today, contributed a good deal to it. We have nothing like it now, only discrete scribblers working away in their (no Robert, no Penn) warrens. No-one is on the scene large enough to say, Why should I take Philip Roth or John Updike or Norman Mailer or William Styron seriously? No, no, no, their interest in fucking is all very well (for them) but it doesn't have much to do with literature. Let us close the gates and not allow them in. Such is literary history, a realm that knows no progress, only that old two-step: one step forward, two steps back.

Best, Joe

Dear Joe,

I once had lunch with George Weidenfeld, as is now generally known by the
many few who have read my notebooks, some time back in the 1980s, I think.
Frank Harris, you may recall, was boasting on some occasion about dining
with some noble person, and Oscar Wilde said, 'Yes, Frank, you've dined in
every great house in London. Once'. We were all staying at the Carlyle, but I
can't remember on whose tab Beetle and I were there. Rather than have lunch,
she preferred to go to the Whitney (where I saw the last Jasper Johns I ever
care if I see and I didn't care then) because she will NEVER accept an unof-
fered invitation, even when it is from friends who run to secretarial help when
sending out what no U-person would ever have called an 'invite' in the days
when Ross and Mitford were compiling their snobs' glossary and which, I
suspect, is what all the nobs now call such things.

The Poseidon Adventure is the allegory of English class life: we are living
upside down, and mostly underwater, but no-one is supposed to notice.
Weidenfeld actually asked *me* to dinner at his place when my second novel
The Earlsdon Way was well noticed in the *Daily Telegraph,* in truth (that
suspect currency!) by an already old friend of mine, Peter Green, who is now,
I am somewhat glad to say, my much older one, being well into his eighties
but still – as our daughter Sarah would hate to hear me say, although I wish
she could – feisty. When thanked for his kind words, Peter said that it was 'the
least one can do for one's friends'. Every writer knows those who manage to
do a great deal less.

It must have been in the latish 1950s that Weidenfeld beckoned me to his
table. Our first pad, as they would say later, was in the same block of flats as
his, but we were in the basement, where no natural light permeated, and he
was on the first floor, I think, with a view of the Thames. The janitor, a
Welshman, once allowed me a glimpse of that ample paradise and I was
impressed to see that there was a *fountain* burbling in the antechamber.
George had it and he flaunted it. *Et comment.*

My summons to the top table came as a result, I seem to remember, of your
Mister Bellow's first visit to London. He was already masterly but not yet the
Master. I should have liked to go (which is not the same thing as saying that I
should have gone) but Beetle was not asked and, of course, would not allow
me to wangle or wheedle her a *couvert.* Although young and somewhat
convinced that I was a rare article, I was conscious, when I said 'no', that I had
probably done something unwise, perhaps slightly catastrophic (in the
turning-point sense). Smart young sonny-boys take the chance to shine early.

With me, diffidence and vanity are indistinguishable. I *do* give a shit about fame and fortune but I also think it uncomely to allow an appetite for them to dominate my life. I am a lousy schemer.

My father gave me the worst advice of my life when he told me, as I was going up to Cambridge, that I should not push myself forward, but should wait for 'them' to beat a path to my door. The weeds grew high as I waited, and waited. My father's fear was, of course, that I should seem to be one of those who gave 'our people' a bad name. Sentiment impelled me to believe that Cambridge was the quintessential version of H.J.'s Great and Good Place, where merit alone determined prestige. Nowhere, I suppose, is ever that great or that good. My fear of rejection was keen enough to inhibit me from taking the routine opportunities that required no-one to beat a path. Although I had done some acting, I was too timid even to present myself for audition at the ADC, *the* Amateur Dramatic Club, where anyone was welcome to enter at least once. I did, however, audition for the part of an American diplomat in a play which had won the Young Writers Competition. Ah those square days, how rectilinear indeed they were!

My American accent was a vestige of what, only a dozen years earlier, I had assumed to be natural. But my indoctrination in English ways was so severe that I had become the pill that I had swallowed. My audition was a throwback and surprised the judging panel of my precocious contemporaries, who knew nothing of my provenance. One of them, called Toby (no surprises there), told me afterwards that I was much the best of the actors who auditioned but that they had decided to give the part to someone 'more experienced', i.e., one of their own, who later became a bishop. I swallowed my rejection like the usual medicine, but derived some slow pleasure, decades later, when the same Toby Robertson, now a professional actor, had a smallish part in a piece of mine for radio. How very accurately I recalled his tones as he condescended to me, and fed them back to him, nicely! How lucky one is, after all, to have lived so long and to have, for the present, so lively a sense of the past!

I need scarcely advertise that my father's advice was utterly inappropriate in the Cambridge of the early 1950s (or probably at any time). After the grey and khaki period of post-war Socialism, the dogs of the uppety classes were sniffing for office and rampant with self-advancement. I should never have joined the baying hounds of peace had it not been for a certain Leslie Bricusse, a man of whom you may well not have heard, although he has won two Oscars for Best Song. The play for which I auditioned supra had been written by Hugh Thomas, a curly-haired historian who wore his swollen head as though he had put it on in a hurry. He became President of the Union, promoted by his Churchillian diction and adopted *morgue*. He later became a parliamentary candidate for Labour and is now a Tory peer, wearing the ermine as if it had come down to him from one of Edward II's ingles, although in truth it was off-the-political-peg. You may know of his ludship as the first historian of the Spanish Civil War, a then-neglected subject proposed to him by the egregious and then some Noel Annan. Hugh has since become a hispanofiling clerk of the first *orden* and has written fat books about Cuba, whether Si! or No! I do not know, since I have never opened one. The Spanish Civil War is now a much-visited topos, of course; the last account I read still had Franco winning, but was done by one Antony Beevor, whose output is such that one would expect that there were seven or eight of him. Beevor beavers to efficient effect and spells all the names right, but none of his characters seem to be in the slightest bit Spanish, just as Americans when played by English actors are heard to say all the right words in the right order but never sound or look American (Albert Finney in *Erin Brockovich* is an instance). The way you talk affects your face, not just the sounds you make, but it ain't no good saying so.

I mentioned Leslie Bricusse. In my second year at Cambridge, he had heard, from one of the judges in the Play Comp., that my play *With This Ring*, although suburban in content (Hugh Thomas's took place in a modern, independent Venice in which the Doge was still in power, a nice conceit, suitably fancy for the times), contained the best dialogue. Leslie is the Zelig of modern showbiz; he is seen everywhere, knows everyone, has amassed a fortune (he wrote the signature tune for *Goldfinger*) and no-one ever says a word against him, nor has he anything critical to say of anyone else. He has achieved all his ambitions, to write musicals (that is what he wanted me to do), to know all the famous people in the register, to have a house in LA and on the Côte d'As-you-were and another in Eaton Square, to marry a wife who causes people to wonder where he got her (and who, to her credit and that of her cosmetician, remains forever youngish and formidably and sustainedly breasted). Leslie spent the war in Canada and so had the kind of naïve ambition that the wartime Team Spirit had somewhat amputated from the all-pulling-together majority. Had it not been for him, and his lack of snobbery, I should, I suspect, never have had access to showbiz. For which, although I have scarcely spoken to him for some fifty years, I should be truly grateful. Showbiz taught me the charm of falseness and its emancipating qualities; it even, perhaps, allowed me to be nicer than I usually am. An actress has just written to me, re the work we have been doing on the 6-part radio dramatisation of my new novel, to say with what 'courtesy and tact' I delivered my 'notes'. A gentleman at last!

Tout à toi,
Freddie

Dear Freddie,

Ah, pushing – your remarks about it cause me to ask myself if I have ever been guilty of the crime. I don't think I have been. But what I am, little doubt about it, is a main-chancer, if there is such a word. Example: Georges Borchardt not long ago sent me an e-mail from Deborah Treisman, who is the fiction editor of the *New Yorker*, asking if any of the stories in my new collection of stories have not yet been previously published. They all have been, and she obviously did not know that an under-editor in her department, a man with the name of Willing Davidson, had previously and very politely rejected two of them (not Willing enough, Mr. Davidson, for me, a joke that I suspect has been made hundreds of times before). But I quickly revised an older story I had written, and straightaways sent it off to her, via the Borchardt office. More than a month has passed, and I haven't heard from Ms. Treisman, so I don't know if this is a story with a happy ending, but I think it does illustrate the MO of your main-chancer friend.

I shall be pleased if the *New Yorker* accepts the story, though the magazine is nowhere as good today as I think it was, when people with genuine style wrote for it. Still, $1.55 a word, which is what I received when last I wrote for it, is a decent payday. And the *New Yorker* does have the best audience of all American magazines. But each week I read the stories the magazine runs, and each week, somewhere in the middle of the story, I say to myself, I am going to be disappointed when I come to the end of this story. And so I am, for *New Yorker* stories are now dominated by the notion of the "epiphany," which I take to mean a pathetic insight at the close in place of a solid ending. "And so, as David gazed at the half moon hanging langorously over the Bosphorus, he sensed that life would never quite be the same again." (Tough luck, David, I say to myself, live with it.) The plane in many *New Yorker* stories is landed gently; the only problem is that we haven't really gone anywhere.

And what does this main-chancer think his efforts over the decades have yielded? Apart from a few welcome shekels, he is less than certain. I don't, for example, have anything like a clear example of my reputation. How I am regarded not in the great world, where my import registers less than negligible, but in the world inhabited by that ever-diminishing portion of the population that still reads books and serious magazines? Important? Significant? Mildly charming? Utterly superfluous? I get a fair number of e-mails – perhaps two hundred over a year's time – from people telling me that they enjoy my writing or that they have been reading me for years and can no longer put off thanking me for the pleasure my writing has given them. Very gratifying, this, but it doesn't speak to the question of reputation, even if some essay or story I have written echoes their own inchoate thoughts on the subject. But there are no critics at work today who can say "Joseph Epstein is a good writer," and make me believe it. When I am praised in the public prints – like onto the public baths – it is often by someone who thinks my political views are similar to his, or by someone who a week or two later turns up praising a writer I know is no good at all. It's no win, Flynn.

I used to tell students that there is only one sure way to judge one's success as a writer. If one's books sell in large numbers, that is nice but, to a serious writer, meaningless, when one considers the *dreck* that dominates the best-seller lists. Praise of critics doesn't help, for, though they might speak well of what you have written, they figure also to speak just as well or even more enthusiastically about writers who, in a just society, would have their hands cut off. The only way to judge one's success as a writer, I would say to these kids durying my teaching days, is if one is able to claim that one has honored the complexity of one's subject. I happen to believe this, but I now wonder if this isn't easier said than actually done. In the books I have written on single subjects – Ambition, Snobbery, Friendship, Alexis de Tocqueville, Fred Astaire – did I honor the complexity of these subjects or did I instead merely write as well as I could on them, which is not at all quite the same thing?

Which brings one back to one's – let's, for solipsism's sake, make that *my* – reputation. Am I thought OK, solid, merely reliable; or splendid, dazzling, delight-filled? In the view of many I am surely thought dreary, dullish, wretched. I really haven't a clue about what my true weight is. Nor, at this late stage in the game, do I have a clear notion of how good (or not so good) I think my own writing is. A month or so ago I was sent a CD of a man named Isaiah Sheffer reading a story of mine, at a place called Symphony Stage in Manhattan. The story, titled "Beyond the Pale," is about the world of Yiddish writers in New York. Sheffer is an excellent reader, and as I listened to the CD while driving in my car, I thought, This is a damn fine story, up there with Isaac Bashevis Singer, better than anything any of my near American contemporaries could write. But then I struggle with stories in the making and feel inept, cloddish, thick-fingered, less than mediocre.

I am confusing two things here: what other people think of my quality as a writer and what I think of it. Better, perhaps, that I, or any writer, not be able to judge either with any precision. Still, it is all rather like playing in a tennis tournament, sensing that one is seeded, but never discovering at what number. Possibly this is all for the best. Would it help much to know that one is the best at this or the third best at that?

I hope this isn't too much of a stretch, but I think something similar applies to teaching. Once you think you are good at it, you aren't, *ipso facto*. I remember a teacher at Northwestern named Gerald Graff who one day told me that something quite magical had happened to his teaching. He was finding himself in the classroom making intellectual connections and formulating dazzling ideas that always seemed to elude him at his desk. So exciting was it that he could scarcely wait to return to the classroom. That same day I ran into one of my brightest students, a young woman who was writing a longish paper on Rilke under the supervision of Erich Heller, and asked her how her term was going. "Wonderfully," she said, "except for Professor Graff's class, which is excruciatingly dull." So much for pride in, and self-knowledge about, one's own teaching.

I seem to recall reading sentences about Oxbridge teachers that ran (roughly): "X was known to bully his students, but an unusually large portion among them came away with Firsts," which implied that, prick though X was, he delivered the goods. Nothing similar is possible in American teaching, because we don't have neutral university examiners, and so many teachers today give out 'A's as if they were tipping with Monopoly money. One needs an outside standard to judge good teaching, which we don't have in the United States. And nowhere in the world is there such a standard to judge good writing, except among that small number of people who genuinely know what it looks like, and they are not always in a position to tell.

Do you remember a radio, and later television, writer named Goodman Ace (née, natch, Aiskowitz), who in the 1930s, with his wife Jane, had a successful radio show called *Easy Aces*? He was said to be the highest paid television writer of his day, earning $10,000 a week, but claimed that when you deduct $1,655 for loss of dignity, $1,925 for mollifying the networks, $22.80 for loss of integrity, and other such deductions, he was left earning around $16.40 a week. But the reason I bring up Goodman Ace is an anecdote about him that I recently came upon that I much liked and hope you will, too.

In a toney New York French restaurant, after waiting a long while for his dinner to arrive, he called out to his waiter, "*Gendarme, gendarme!*" The waiter came over to his table, and with great condescension, said, "Sir, I think you meant *garçon*, not *gendarme*." "No," said Goodman Ace, "I meant *gendarme*, for there's obviously a hold-up in the kitchen."

Best, Joe

Dear Joe,

I once had a publisher called Tom Maschler (so did a lot of classy writers) who had a clever, so he thought, way of disconcerting you, i.e. me, by asking, 'How many real friends do you think you've got?' This precipitated the kind of frantic rummaging which accompanies a search for driving licence, credit cards, keys etc. How many should I have? More important, how many do you have? Tom also specialised in telling me how well other writers were selling, how many languages they were being translated into and which prizes they were about to win. When was I going to start?

Maschler, no tab-grabber he, cannot have recruited pals by virtue of his generosity, but he did have, for several decades, control of that prestigious Jonathan Cape imprint. He was no great dispenser of advances (and once told me that he admired my new novel, *Like Men Betrayed*, so much that he proposed to pay no advance at all, which proved – didn't it? – just how great his admiration was), but he had a classy list and Kingsley Amis was lured onto it, along with sonny boy Mart, who is now turning sixty and worrying about death, like Julian Barnes, quite as if they were in the trenches and not in the chips. Tom, no doubt, took his authors for friends, just as they took him for whatever they could squeeze out of him, which was never lunch. He had an instinct for books that combined a certain literacy with popular appeal: John Fowles made him a fortune and vice versa.

I thought Fowles's books overweight and lightweight all at once; he had the bearded style that the gullible associate with art (and dentists with dubious teeth) and, like your correspondent, preened himself a little too much on his French, which was, if the printed instances are any guide, fallible. He was one of those of provincial, lower-middle-class provenance who, like Henry Williamson (author of *Tarka the Otter*) combined nature-loving with Jew-consciousness. Williamson was an out-and-out Hitlerian in the 1930s and had the grudge against the world which attacks closet *gauleiters* like mental shingles. Fowles muttered into his notebooks, lamented the shortage of Purple Emperors and collected fossils and gentians, I wouldn't wonder.

He had a long season, all the way to *The French Lieutenant's Woman*, which set the style for Victorian pastiche that Antonia Byatt has rendered OSS, if that stands for outsize and then some. Fowles' first book, *The Collector*, made his name and is, like *Lolita*, essentially so nasty that you know just how smart and calculating a cookie must have written it and made it, as they will say, 'work'. A novel about wanting to sequester and abuse young women might not seem, on the spotty face of it, to be the stuff to rally readers, but there was a kind of blandness in his obsession which catered to the British appetite for the *almost* obscene. I recall being on the pier at Ilfracombe, a coastal town in North Devon, where – at the age of ten, or so – I inserted a penny in the slot of a machine labelled THE NUDIST COLONY. The coin fell, the veil was lifted and there was a glass case full of ants, none of them in pants. Gotcha!

Now – and here we are coming to it – if you had corresponded with John Fowles, were he still with us, well, they would have welcomed your salt to his beef, and had I done as much with him or, preferably, with Philip Roth, say (which I never can, or rarely, without remembering the guy telling Groucho, 'The Dean is outside and he's waxing wrath', to which – you remember – Groucho replied, 'Well tell the Dean to wax Roth for a while'). He doesn't need to, of course, because Philip – another Maschler author – has had *nothing* except success and, understandably, is increasingly convinced that either life is not worth living or he has missed something. He also, to judge from some excerpts I have read, lost all appetite to write as well as he can, or once did. Do I wish I had had his success? And advances? Sure I do, because then I could drag you into the limelight and they wouldn't save the electricity. I wish equally, well almost, that you had had his success because then, hey, you'd be dragging me, wouldn't you?

Hélas, hélas, hélas, as General de Gaulle once said, three times, it ain't like that. By me you're a captain and, maybe, by you so am I, but the captains are hanging back, sitting on their hands, staying with the sinking ship or whatever captains do when they're captaining. So where do I stand or slump and what do I know about it? Well, first of all, let me say this: there is something very modern and a leetle bit despicable in the judgment that says that our letters can't be worth publishing because we are not Stephen King or smoked Salman or names 'like that' who will automatically set the tills ringing, regardless of content. In the days that were the days, if they ever were, it might have been the quality of the letters, and the comedy (Pooterish maybe from time to time, but I don't think so) of our mutual esteem and not a few good jokes, that would make us famous or publishable (a word that did not carry its own implicit negative back then). I don't think a man has to check his ranking on some cosmic scale before wondering whether he dares to express himself as if he were somebody. We're all bloody somebody. I have read more dull letters between putatively (yes, indeed) important persons than I have taken sleeping pills.

Yes, yes, but at your age, Raphael, are you not aware that you have bet in vain on becoming a Great Writer? I'm glad you asked that question (the politician's way of saying ouch!). The truth is, I have never considered other people's estimate of what I was doing as any kind of reason to do or not do anything. I learned the rudiments of the trade from old Willie Maugham and, I suppose, I should have liked to enjoy his sales (that logo of his was a smart move) and his social status (apart from the homo-from-home aspect) and all of that, but – next witness – I also admired D.H. Lawrence (not that I usually like those initial-styled people) and his willingness to head out of England and write, as they will say, what he really wanted and damn the consequences. I thought years ago that he never looked back, but of course he was a retro kind of a guy really as well as a fantasist with a phtisicky chest.

Reading about him and Frieda the other day, I thought that their marriage, which was being paraded as being about 'loyalty', not about fidelity or lerve, sounded like pretty good hell, for both of them. Yet Frank and Queenie thought we should all be mature like the Lawrences whose childlessness tells us something, just as D.H.L.'s attitude to Frieda's actual children was little short of repugnant. What a baby he was! But then again, some writer. A friend of mine knew the Leavises' son.

I wanted above all to be free. That's the good bit of freelance, isn't it? The bad bit is having to make money without the certainty of regular increments (oh for some of those!) and without the intermittent servility of paying attention to what has now become a major form of currency: notes. I hate notes; I do not want notes; I want applause, laughter and, if possible, emoluments. Cynicism is the naïveté that can't quite spell its name. Mainly, I want not to work with other people. I want to write sentences that sing, if they will, and if I like them, get printed. I have my file of happy-making praise and my memories of abuse or worse and I expect that neither is more valid currency than the other. I have spent fifty-five years writing stuff and that's what I always wanted to do. Almost everything I have written that I cared to make public has been published or performed. Yes, it was a sign of protracted puerility, maybe, that when Professor Epstein (even if he declines the honorific) wanted someone to write a piece about Hazlitt, I danced a little sedentary jig. And wondered, if only for a second, who had already said no? No, not for a nanosecond, if that's a small one, because I'm worth it: et ego in L'Oréal vixi.

So here's the thing, Epstein. I like you; I liked you more and more as our exchanges went on. I like hearing from and I enjoy writing to a clever man who doesn't miss much and can volley a volley and not jump too high and exultantly when he wins the point. Let them publish us or not, I wouldn't not have had the fun of this year of mutual call-it-what-you-will. If all else fails, and it may well, I should like to think of setting up some kind of public access point on the web, but I don't think we should depend unduly on friends and acquaintances, who *may* wish us well, but may also wonder why they weren't asked to the party. I have noticed that the performances of actors and actresses (if that term is still current) are least appetising the better one knows them personally. If we are both such unknowns, how come we are so regularly interrupted by Porlocksmiths who want pieces from us?

Tout à toi,
Freddie

Dear Freddie,

I met Tom Maschler once. Jonathan Cape was the English publisher of my first (and rather lugubrious) book, which was a quasi-autobiographical tome on the subject of divorce. In America the book was titled *Divorced in America: Marriage in an Age of Possibility*, and sold respectably well. In England the title was changed to *Divorce*, given an ugly dustjacket and sold, in the Bulgarian phrase, diddly. Maschler was nice enough; if he attempted any one-upmanship on me, it sailed blithely over my head. In Manhattan he stayed at the Dorchester Hotel, a quiet joint on the West Side that avoided the gaudiness of the larger New York hotels and attracted English men and women with pretensions to understated good taste.

This was in the early 1970s, an era, in publishing, of reputed genius editors, of whom in England Tom Maschler at Cape was putatively one and Charles Monteith at Faber & Faber another. In America the genius editors had such names as Robert Gottlieb, Robert Gutwillig, David Segal, and Henry Robbins. All lived off the legend of Maxwell Perkins, at Scribner's, the editor of, among others, F. Scott Fitzgerald, Hemingway, Edith Wharton, and Thomas Wolfe, whose dedication, in one of his novels, to Perkins the latter had to cut severely because of its excessive length.

I had one of the reputed genius editors, a man named Hal Scharlatt at
E.P. Dutton. He answered few calls, was almost Russianly late (by 45 minutes
or so) to meetings and lunches, and yet, somehow, was attractive. Or at least
I found him so. He would go around telling people what an astonishing book
one was writing long before one had begun to write it, and so calls would
come in from NBC and elsewhere asking if one could appear on this or that
show to talk about the subject of this splendid book you *have written*. As for
the actual editing, Hal Scharlatt deigned to touch no sentences; instead he
would say such things as, "This chapter seems to slow things down a bit; I
think maybe you ought to cut it by twenty percent." He was often right. Hal
Scharlatt died at age thirty-nine, on the tennis court, of a heart attack, after, I
was told, a sumptuous and expensive lunch at a French restaurant.

American publishing editors are today highly transient animals, who don't
tend to stick around long at any one firm. They are sometimes fired for not
making their nut, or sometimes they leave for what they take to be more
promising premises. I don't believe I have had the same editor twice for the
twenty-odd books I've published. My experience at my current publishing
house – Houghton Mifflin (and now) Harcourt – is not unusual. I signed a
three-book contract with Houghton Mifflin with a young man who, soon after
the contract was signed, left the firm. He was replaced by a quietly smart
woman named Pat Straughan, whom I much liked though never met; she had
previously worked for William Shawn at the *New Yorker* and then for the firm
of Farrar Straus (not yet Giroux), which had all the fashionable scribblers of
the day (Susan Sontag, Joseph Brodsky, Tom Wolfe, Robert Lowell and his
extensively long-suffering wife Elizabeth Hardwick); one felt that she, Pat S.,
had genuine literary instincts, but these were obviously not sufficient, and she
was soon enough let go. A younger editor, a man named Eric Chinski, advertised as brilliant, was next, but he soon left for Farrar Straus (and now) Giroux.
Chinski was followed, not at all as night follows day, by a cordial young editor
named Webster Younce, who offered a most useful suggestion for my book on
Friendship; the suggestion was that my third chapter should really be my first
chapter. He was right. But this didn't prevent him from being fired – like Miss
Straughan, I assume, for not bringing in enough money through acquiring
widely-selling books. Houghton Mifflin then bought – or was bought by, I'm
not sure which – Harcourt Brace, and my new and current editor is another
bright woman, this one the firm's editor-in-chief, named Andrea Schulz. As
they did in Soviet medicine during the war, women may take over publishing,
at least as long as the thing called publishing, as we know it, continues to exist.

What does one want from an editor? High on my list is promptitude. I
dislike the torture of waiting weeks and weeks for decisions or responses to
things I send out. Good news or bad, let it be dispatched quickly. The *New
Yorker*, I learned a few moments ago, has rejected a story of mine that Georges
Borchardt sent them seven weeks ago. The fiction editor there, a Ms. Deborah
Treisman, said she "enjoyed reading" the story but concluded that it "wasn't
ultimately, the story for us." (That "ultimately" helps a lot.) But why, especially
if they weren't going to kiss me, did they keep me on tiptoe so long? Another
real editorial service is for an editor to find and squelch errors and stupidities
in one's work, from the grammatical and orthographical to the factual and
historical. An editor who finds something in one's writing that doesn't work
and is able to convince one of why it doesn't is also a valuable player. An editor
who can grasp a work in its wholeness, in a way that might be lost on that
poor tree surgeon the author, is also helpful.

I have of late been reading the second volume of the letters of T. S. Eliot,
which, in the book's first few hundred pages, have chiefly to do with his
editing of the recently (1922) begun *Criterion*. Eliot went after the biggest
and best names then available, explaining to them that he was editing an
intellectual quarterly that "does not aim at a very large circulation, but aims
solely at publishing the highest class of work." He then tells them that what he
offers them is that their work published in the *Criterion* "probably receives
more intelligent attention [from readers] than a contribution to any other
review and the audience is not limited to Great Britain." He mentions that the
rate he can pay (£10 for 5000 words) is "very modest," but that it is the best he
can do for now. He doesn't tell him that he has roughly 1,000 subscribers.
Apart from informing the scientists he wishes to write for him – A.S.
Eddington, G. Elliot Smith, and others – that he is not looking for articles
resembling "popular science writing" from them, but instead articles "on
some subject within your own field which educated and intelligent persons of
only the ordinary mathematical training could understand," he seems to leave
his contributors alone and for the most part sends straight to the printer what
they send him. This is made all the easier, of course, by the fact that Eliot
invited only authentically distinguished literary artists, critics, and scientists
to write for his magazine.

In some ways this mirrors my own experience as an editor of an intellectual
magazine. When I began editing the *American Scholar* I would sometimes
almost completely rewrite the work of some contributors. But what I discovered was that the effort wasn't worth it. An editor can make something

poorly-written publishable, but, however good he is at rewriting, he cannot make it extraordinary. The extraordinary element has to come from the author; it cannot be supplied by the editor. The solution, I found, was to ask better writers to contribute to the magazine. The less editing one needs to do, I found, the better the magazine is likely to be.

Still on the subject of magazines, I'm a touch disappointed by the reaction – or lack of reaction – to my Kermode–Forster piece, which ran in last week's *Weekly Standard*. Four or five people I know sent me e-mails telling me that they enjoyed it and never understood why E.M. Forster was so highly regarded. But what I expected was a bit of anger at my attempt to topple a (granted, small) god. Thus far no-one has written to me, or so far as I know to the magazine, to attack me and defend Forster. True, the *Weekly Standard* is primarily a political magazine, neoconservative in its general outlook, still yet but and however one would like to think there are some sensitive, considerate, plucky mother-grabbers out there ready to come to the defense of Morgan's organ, which I did my best to lop off. Some possibility of the piece running on artsandlettersdaily.com, where your piece on Inglorious Cockseekers (was it?) ran, and from that popular website attracting some dissenting views. Or might it just be that no-one really any longer gives a rusty rat's rump about the just reputation of putatively great writers? I fear that no-one – or at least not many ones – does. If so, not such a good thing, methinks.

Best, Joe

PS. You were, please be assured, my first choice for the Hazlitt essay.

Dear Joe,

I don't think I've ever taken publishers as seriously as they take themselves. It's partly the English thing. I was never more anglicised than when I went up to Cambridge in 1950, although I did have a pair of American pants, with a zip, and a couple of button-down collared shirts, which I bought when I went to the US with my mother in 1948. I fell easily in love with a girl I had played with in Central Park when I was a little boy and was amazed and delighted by the eagerness with which she responded to my kisses, and initiated more, but England had a commanding culture and I was, or thought I was, among its elite apprentices. The years from 1945 onwards had been dominated by the desire, and need, to obtain scholarships: junior and senior at Charterhouse School and the Big One at Oxford or, as it turned out, Cambridge. 'Hup, Debby, hup Debby!' Gloria Grahame said in *The Big Heat* (wasn't it?) and 'Hup, Freddie, hup, Raphael!' was my unsexy rescript. Being eligible for publication, I am trying to say, was the next exam I had to take after Cambridge.

I was mortified not to get a first-class degree in Moral Sciences, but if my vanity was dented, my ambition was confirmed: I wanted to be a writer both to shine and to stick it to them. Not getting a First embargoed me, in effect, from the academic career that I never seriously craved. In fact, John Wisdom, the professor of philosophy whose style was so deliciously idiosyncratic (Wittgenstein *à l'anglaise*), had himself got a Lower Second, so we were told (I never checked). Moral Sciences undergraduates were few and we had been warned that Firsts were rarely if ever allotted. In my year, however, two were; one to my industrious friend Tony Becher, who went on, rather miserably, to become a professor of education, and the other to Andor Gomme, son of a great, now superseded (by Simon Hornblower) Thucydidean scholar, who also, I think, became a professor of the Leavisite persuasion. It was said that his name was given to him before his birth, in the days, of course, when the sex of the child was unforeseeable, hence And/or.

I was consoled in my disappointment (which I had done little, except by being clever with buzzwords in seminars, not to deserve) by being given (awarded even) a Travel Studentship for Creative Writing worth £350, which was a fat sum in those days. The 'student' part of the ship was a little galling, since it had an unsmart connotation: in my day, Cambridge 'students' called themselves 'undergraduates'. 'Student' also recalled adolescent days as a Yid at Charterhouse when, in one of his odd spasms of regressive allegiance, my father enrolled me in the Liberal Jewish Synagogue's Judaism-By-Correspondence class. Their envelopes, which I dreaded my anti-Semitic schoolfellows ever seeing, were franked on the outside STUDENT'S EXERCISE.

So anyway, as the young still say, I was given this Travel Studentship which was reserved for graduates who wanted to be creative writers. It was open, in theory, to all members of the university but it was administered by my college. I had an interview with Hugh Sykes Davies, an eccentric, much-married don (one of whose wives had been Kathleen Raine, with whom he had not remained friends), at which he treated the whole matter with impatient geniality: if I wanted the thing, I might as well have it. Whether or not the award was a fix, it gave me a silly sense of election. The previous tenant had been Thom Gunn, the son of a Fleet Street editor, of the *Daily Mail*, whose poetry was published by Karl Miller and other pundits in the magazines that they controlled and in which I was not welcome. A man called Mark Boxer, who became the cartoonist Marc, was my only admirer in fancy circles and did publish a story of mine, but otherwise I expressed myself, with weekly virulence, only in the student newspaper, *Varsity*. It was in its pages that I made my first bad career move.

One of the few Americans in Cambridge was called Robert Gottlieb. He was a graduate student and also married, to a not noticeably comely woman (later dumped). My column had to be filled and derision is a reliably quick write. I was a smart ass, in the British style, even though Perelman's *Crazy Like a Fox* sometimes infected my prose with jazzy riffs. My father had warned me against being 'pushy'; Gottlieb's had not. He rushed in where Freddie had feared to tread; and he did it to some effect. From a standing start, he became a director at the Amateur Dramatic Club, where Peter Hall was the presiding potentate. It was the age of The Method and Gottlieb seemed to have brought the kit with him. How much he knew about acting or texts, I cannot say, but he knew how to play Lee-Strasberg-for-export.

Gottlieb sometimes wore glasses and sometimes did not; his wife also. My old, old friend Joe Bain, to whom I spoke yesterday (he lives in Wales), had the fancy that they owned only one pair of specs between them and, like those antique hags the Graies in Greek myth, passed them from one to the other. It was a nice piece of whimsy, but my use of it, or something like it, in my column smacked of something uglier, which (I swear) I did not recognise at the time. In truth, I fear, Gottlieb was manifestly and even proudly what I no longer was: an American, New York (?) Jew who *had no shame*. The Nabokovian/René Girardesque motif – what else? – of the *Doppelgänger* surges to the head of the corner. Bob's presence (I don't think I ever actually spoke to him) reminded me of what I might have been and could not, now, ever contrive. He was pushy and Jewy and he had got what I wanted (I have always been a director manqué). So I let him have it. I let quite a lot of people have it and was a little surprised when they were seriously upset and wanted to give it back. Another target was another graduate American, James Ferman, who had been in the USAAF (not in the war, though) and drove a little MG convertible. He later became a close friend of a kind, the kind that isn't close, but that's another story, and a cracker, if there is ever time for it.

Gottlieb came and Gottlieb went and that, I imagined, was that. I went on my sponsored travels and had a rather solitary time of it. I had already known Beetle for several years, but she pretended that she thought it was better, for my creative burgeoning, that I travel alone. Perhaps it was; it certainly confirmed my wish to be with her, forever if possible. I made notes.

I looked at pictures. I wondered about other women. I read Shakespeare in the Gardens of the Alhambra. I started my first novel. That's all another story, ripe for telling maybe, if I ever have the time. After three months, I met Beetle in Paris and soon married her, in London. We went back to Paris and lived in a tiny apartment, where I finished my novel, *Obbligato*, on a borrowed typewriter. When my Cambridge money ran out, we returned to London.

Victor Gollancz, for whom Beetle had worked, turned *Obbligato* down (V.G.'s nephew, who was by then decisive, had fancied Beetle), but the next place to which it was sent, Macmillan, took it enthusiastically. My then agent, George Greenfield M.C., had recently lost his five-year-old son, Georgie. When my novel was accepted, he had the gallantry to say, 'This good news has quite made my day'. I never imagined his pain. Macmillan were the posh end of the publishing line (Harold, later prime minister, was a partner). They had panelled premises behind the National Gallery. One of their readers was Jack Squire, a now forgotten writer of light verse and prose. He advised them to grapple me to them, since I was likely to be the author of a score of books just as funny as my first. My editor was Alan Maclean, whose brother had recently absconded with the much flashier, fleshier Guy Burgess, to Joe Stalin's bosom. Alan had been dumped from the Foreign Office, although not suspected of any malfeasance, and had fallen into a convenient Establishment net, the kind sustained at each corner by an Old Boy. Alan was chummy and chortly and a Chelsea Football Club supporter.

My second novel was not funny at all. *The Earlsdon Way* was a satire in, I suppose, the Sinclair Lewis style, on English suburbia. It was, in a way, a tiny step back towards the Americanism which I had dropped when I sought to assimilate myself *chez les rosbifs*. I learned a lot from Lewis's use of dialogue; accuracy as sympathetic malice. Tell me, as they say, about it. Alan Maclean and 'Auntie Marge', his *adjointe*, were keen to see my MS. I told him that there was only one copy (taking carbons hampered the flight of fancy, I had discovered) and that I had better first make another. 'No, no,' Alan said, 'I'll take good care of it'. Need I go on? I gave it to him. Two days later, he called and told Beetle (I suspect that I was at the bridge club) that, oh dear, his briefcase had been stolen and my (unread) MS with it. The Macmillan offices were left open at lunchtime and . . . someone must've wanted a nice leather briefcase. I went into Hebrew lamentations of a deplorable order. Beetle endured and advised: I had a third of the text in handwriting, so . . . 'Moisten the lips and start afresh', was one of my father's mantras. Inconsolable, I got in the car (a Ford Anglia) with Beetle and we drove and drove, as far as Bath; and then back. My tether went no further. I rewrote the novel, with carbons, and sent a copy to Alan.

He and Auntie Marge took me out to lunch to tell me that, alas, the book was not for them. Must I write in such an aggressive style? I would make no friends that way. I said that I had not become a writer in order to make friends. I would sooner live in Taos, New Mexico, though not with Mabel Dodge Luhan. They did not take the reference. Macmillan gave me £50 for the trouble that they had caused me and I went shopping for another publisher.

Oh whaddya know, this is turning into a serial. Next time, if we live: the kicker on the Gottlieb story and other excitements.

Tout à toi,
Freddie

Dear Freddie,

Bob Gottlieb, no doubt availing himself of the *modus operandi* (Moe do's operate, Andy) you describe, has had one of the jeweled careers in America, though the jewel, looked at more closely, may turn out to be zircon. He was for many years the main editor at Alfred A. Knopf, perhaps the most solid of American publishing firms, and seemed to have mastered the knack of bringing out quality books alongside commercially successful ones. He left Knopf to take over the editorship of the *New Yorker*, much to the consternation of many of its staff writers, who did not at all like the fact that he did so after William Shawn, revered by so many of them, was forced out of the job owing to his age. Gottlieb didn't do much to change the magazine, except to allow the words *cunt*, *shit*, and *fuck* in its pages; he also permitted stories with sex in them to appear. (Shawn, a great, if also greatly idiosyncratic, editor, refused to pass on either dirty words or sexy stories.) After a decent interval, Gottlieb left the *New Yorker* to return to the firm of Knopf, in rather a retired field marshal sort of way. He began to write more under his own name, chiefly about showbusiness and ballet, and usually in the *New York Review of Books*. Years ago he brought out a book, with a collaborator, on plastic purses. That and his balletomania led me at the time to say that he was trying to pass for gay (a brilliant move, not at all by the way). But credit where credit isn't needed, he did write what I thought an excellent small book, in the same series as my small book on Tocqueville, on Balanchine. He has, then, come away with what I assume is a lot of money, a reputation as a cultural eminence greasy, a doyen but of no known subject or field, and an exemplar of the old saying – which I am about to make up – that when push comes to push, the pushy will out.

The English university Firsts and Seconds is for the most part unknown in American education. Scarcely anyone in the United States – prospective employers or future wives – asks how well you did at university. What is chiefly of interest is which of the joints one attended – and of interest mainly for its snob value. They used to say that the difference between Harvard and the University of Chicago was that Harvard was more difficult to get into and Chicago more difficult to get out of. Harvard also opens more doors into moneyed and socially valued places.

After thirty years of university teaching, I have come to have less and less respect for so-called higher education, the hard sciences and strict vocational education (engineering, accounting, etc.) excepted. First, I don't see what is so damned high about it, and I am far from sure it purveys much in the way of serious learning. So often students who perform well are perfect idiots outside the classroom (many of these find a way to stay in the classroom – a womb with no view – by acquiring PhDs and taking up careers in teaching). Then there is the pleasing fact (to me, at least, who was never more than a mediocre student) that so many brilliant people didn't perform well in the classroom: Henry James, Paul Valéry, Proust, and many others. One's ability to take an examination well surely shouldn't, though it too often does, determine one's fate. In *Aspects of the Novel*, our pal Morgan Forster notes that "as long as learning is connected with earning, as long as certain jobs can only be reached through exams, as long must we take the examination system seriously. If another ladder to employment were contrived, much so-called education would disappear and no-one would be a penny stupider." Sounds right to me, who over the years has found himself less and less impressed with the type of the good student. Being a good student, I discovered, meant little more than one knowing how to play the school game; like a well-trained dog, one can fetch the bone and drop it, in the form of a 1,000-word essay, at the master's feet.

I spent much of yesterday working on amendments to Barbara's and my will. No intimations of immortality *chez* Epstein. The amendments had mostly to do with how our money will be dispensed to our son Mark, who is very smart about money and a much more powerful money-maker than his father, and our granddaughter, an artist, who has and figures to remain ignorant about the intricacies and secrets of money, though I do think she respects it and has a strong sense of its usefulness. I cannot fault her for her ignorance, since I share it and have myself never been able to concentrate for long – nor, come to think of it, for short – on money. I like to have it; I sometimes worry about not having a sufficiency of it, though I have never, in a lucky life, been up against the wall with debt. But I still cannot concentrate on such matters as the stock market, about which I have remained pristinely stupid, and other forms of investment. What kind of a Jew, I ask you, Herr Freddie, is so foolish about money? A great blow to anti-Semitism, my inability to think about money, but there you have it.

Barbara and I scarcely ever go to the theater. When we do, we are generally disappointed. I rather like, though do not love, the plays of Tom Stoppard; and David Mamet knows how to arouse one's interest but not finally how to satisfy it; I am far from certain that his pretenses to seriousness aren't more than pretenses merely. Most theater is depressing, and depressing in a manner that does not earn its way; it neither instructeth, as said Sir Philip Sidney (God, I miss that guy), nor delighteth; so I say screweth-it-eth. I feel no need to spend $250 for two tickets – throw in another $35 for parking and $100 or so more for dinner before – to see a play about two gay policemen who, in the cant phrase, just can't seem to get it together; yet another revival of a Beckett play (Beckett, my view is, ought to be high on the list of the world's most overrated writers); or the bulky Brian Dennehy playing the Lee J. Cobb part in that most boring of all plays *Death of a Salesman*. Hope I haven't already told you the joke about the two salesmen whose wives drag them to see *Death of a Salesman*. After the play, walking up the aisle, one salesman says to the other: "That guy Miller really nailed it." "You think so?" asks the other salesman. "Absolutely," says the first salesman, "that New England territory was never any fuckin' good."

All this is by way of a prelude to telling you that Barbara and I went this past Saturday afternoon to a matinee performance of Noël Coward's *Private Lives*, and thought it pretty damn fine. This is partly because it was superbly well-acted and partly because the play makes so few pretenses to seriousness. In fact, its message, if it may be said to have one, is that for most people attempting seriousness is a great mistake; they do better to stay on the level of superficiality, living in the moment; don't, it is strongly implied, believe a word of a thick-fingered cluck like Arthur Miller and his ilk – ilk, spilk, the main thing is a boy should love his Oedipus – but instead enjoy life as it comes and in as uncomplicated a way as you can manage.

I admire Noël Coward. I cannot think of another person who got more out of his talent, both as a writer and as a performer. He seemed to have no complaint to him. He made patriotism – I'm not sure I can recall the title of his WWII movie about the English navy, *In Which We Serve*, was it? – seem honorable again. His songs don't date, at least not much. He appears to have been as witty in life as on the page or on the stage. Unlike other homosexual writers – Maugham, Auden – his life wasn't spoiled by some creepy, envious lover whose bills he paid in return for which his jealousy was stirred and life made immensely more miserable. Noël Coward seemed to have things nicely in control in all departments. His money and fame – and he had lots of both – gave him great pleasure. All this made for a grand run, I should say.

Since you are the one whose idea for these exchanges it originally was, I think I ought to give you the last word on our electronic correspondence – the last word, that is, for this book we are planning, for I hope we shall never cease to trade e-mails remarking on each other's scribblings, the goofy state of the world, the amusing things that we encounter amid the reigning madness. It's quite amazing, really, that we have been able to achieve such easy candor with each other over this past year or so, given that we have never met or even spoken over the phone and have only the vaguest (book-jacket) notion of what the other looks like. If I had to find a word for my feelings toward you, the word would be brotherly. You are an only child, and I an older brother, yet I wonder if I mightn't be the brother you never had and you the admirable (slightly) older brother I should have liked to help explain the world to me? It's been a great kick, bro', this weekly exchange of e-mail, and I want to thank you for all the laughter and stimulation your well-placed words have given me.

Affectionately, Joe

Dear Joe,
The undergraduate shows which distracted me from the lofty drudgery of construing Kant and his ilk, as well as from having chapter mit verse ready for citations from the wholly fragmentary writ of Ludwig W., always ended with 'the final chorus' in which we smart young things grew sentimental about the end of our 9-carat gilded youth and lines such as 'See you in the City in September/ Look me up: remember …' were sung with smarting eyes and tight throats. The way ahead sloped slightly downwards after our season in precocious paradise; the prospect of wives, careers, offices, narrowed the yellow brick road even as we liked to imagine it was widening. Now I have the unhappy awareness that our little dance, yours and mine, has reached its

last waltz and that it has all gone too fast and leaves much (luckily, tactfully, sadly) unsaid.

For me, the strangest thing about this distant intimacy is the coincidence, in many cases, of our literary taste. What you say about Beckett I have always felt; all that stuff about being born astride the grave excites merely 'Yep, and so what?' So step away for a while. I hate that dustbin cheeriness, the Oirish egotism that takes cheerlessness for a kind of profundity. All I recall from *Waiting for Godot* is the line in Lucky's monologue, '. . . tennis and all kinds of tennis'. As for *Molloy* and that, when and where were sparseness, exultant despair and whiskey verbosity more convergent? I have the unworthy feeling that an awful lot of artistic fame, access to the puff machine, I mean, came of bedroom mountaineering between Peggy Guggenheim's don't-look-down legs. There is a certain lady who is now the dowager queen of London literature of whom I have said, very quietly, that she is a mistress of sexual condescension: all her lovers are required to pass through the tradesman's entrance of her cunt. We have refrained from *gros mots* during our decorous exchanges but I cannot gloss this one. Take it or delete it.

If we were ever to take ourselves seriously enough to look closely at each other's opinions, I should not, I think, disagree violently or much at all with any of your specific judgments, including that on Noël Coward. I have always (which gets to be too often) said that Willie Maugham lent me the key to writing novels and short stories, not least in the notebooks that were typically terse and generous at once. But you remind me that before I got into *Of Human Bondage*, I read and reread two volumes of plays which were under my parents' bay-windowsill: Laurence Housman's *Victoria Regina* (to which I have never returned, but which illustrates beautifully how to turn a pageant into a page-turner) and Noël Coward's *Play Parade*. In the steps of the Master, I wrote a play when I was 19 entitled *With This Ring*. I did it in three days (as he supposedly did *Hay Fever*) and it wasn't bad at all. My amateur production of it got a very good review in *The Stage* (the trade mag of British thespianism) and, by chance, led me to the biz via the Footlights (as discussed in earlier episodes). In addition, while we are being Cowardly, Beetle and I first met when we played brother and sister, Simon and Sorel, in – yes – *Hay Fever*. Dare I confess that in our amateur production I rewrote the verses which begin the play after she says 'Listen to this, Simon!'? I did. Beetle called me Simon for our first years together, and can be pressed to reprise occasionally, but it lapsed and I became Fred because that was what the children decided to call me. I wrote a play in the late 1950s which I thought was going to get to the shortlist of a big national competition, supervised by Ken Tynan, but I fell at the second fence from home. My entry was put on in a small theatre but never came to anything, and nor, dear reader, did I, in the theatre.

I suspect that the only area where you and I might disagree seriously, if it ever came to that, is about the merits of 'higher education'. Since you have prolonged experience of what it means in practice and I have only a sentimental sense of what it *should* mean, there is comedy in my insolence. No doubt, and especially in the field of media and English and all that, there is an inverted pyramid party in the Humanities, all of the massive structure being balanced on a sixpenny packet of World's Classics or whatever. But the European in me comes out when I say that civilisation cannot do without some people who can attack ideologies and religious dogmas with a set of weapons – clarity of argument, lack of cant, capacity for honest criticism, a taste for liberty even – that cannot be acquired in laboratories or engineering shops.

The Germans, if we are to get nasty, had the best engineers in Europe from the last part of the 19th century onwards; and scientists, no doubt. But they were also dangerous monkeys with mad geopolitical fantasies and they had to be opposed not only by force of arms (which were, I grant, essential) but also by some idea of the world that might be which was not a function of scientific logic (eugenics and allied trades being easily annexed by men in white coats). The reduction – for which you do not, I know, argue seriously – of culture to science'n'engineering on the one hand and entertainment on the other doesn't appeal to me: I can't share the view that men are essentially constructive and wish only to be amused. Since they are also shits, something apart from success and technological advances has to count as worth living for. Oh dear, I seem to hear that that was Heidegger's view too.

My dear Joe, what pain it is to let the curtain fall! I have no appetite for goodbyes. Perhaps that is one reason why conjugal life suits me; I prefer repeated hellos. Our correspondence has an unusual intimacy of a kind of which, in the realm of the spirit, I also have no wish to let go. What's this all about then? Simply that I was more delighted, for a clutch of reasons, than you may have guessed when you asked me to write that essay for your compendium about literary genius. It is evidence of a blithely spirited elegance on your part, an instinct for what affinities deserve election, that you asked me to write about William Hazlitt. An obvious-minded editor would have offered me Byron, I suspect, but Hazlitt . . . The Nonesuch edition of his essays was one of the first books I ever bought. It still bears the stick-on label with which

I tabulated my first 'library', all three shelves. Hazlitt was recommended to me, and maybe to you, as a stylist, by our mutual friend Willie Maugham, a man put down so often that his resurrection has primed a dozen biographers to do him over and up again. Willie, with all his faults, had something of Micheau's candour, rejection of cant, love of the ordinary and the capacity to render it extraordinary; and so, by God, do you: your essays and stories are part of a mosaic that makes the big picture without striving for big effects.

One of the pleasures of being approached by strangers is that there is someone new to dazzle. I wrote that Hazlitt piece with more care than, it may be, I have displayed to you recently, but not all that much. Because here is the rare quality you have: you are a man who, while striking no fancy attitudes, provokes excellence. I am sure you did that when you were editor of the *American Scholar* and you have certainly worked the trick with me. You do nothing to excite pretentiousness or arcane allusion (well, almost nothing), and yet . . . look at what we have said to each other over a year and some days and you will find, *they* will find, the joy that literacy can excite, the quick of civilities that are civilised, rose and barb on a single stem sometimes. Is that vanity? Scarcely. I relish the rare pleasure of a friendship which has no dividends beyond its unlikely existence. Only after I had written the Hazlitt piece did I discover that Joseph Epstein's first book, *Divorce*, was already on my shelves. However, I didn't truly know what kind of a writer you were until you sent me *Fabulous Small Jews*. I recall (we are all little Marcels as time goes by) that after Kingsley Amis fell in love with Elizabeth Jane Howard, he went and checked on whether he could abide her novels, and found, to his relief, that he could; a triumph of lust over taste, I sometimes think. Enjoyment trumped relief with me: your stories were excellent and had an extra vitamin for me, that accurate, taken-for-granted knowledge of Chicago, our natal city.

However odd our couple, we have become friends almost . . . oh, let's say it, epiphenomenally; we have talked with such ease and such growing assumptions of intimacy that there was never a decided, formal moment when we passed from acquaintanceship to friendship, intimacy even, of a kind. And yet we have been all this time some five thousand miles apart and, should we by chance be on the same street at the same time, we might well walk past each other, willing to swear that we did not know a soul in the vicinity. Might it be that carnal contact is/can be as much an impediment to intimacy as an incentive, among men, at least? I think of that terrible literary man, known to both of us, who responded to a letter of mine, coldly denying merit to a screenplay he had written of a classic 1930s novel, by thanking me as if for a compliment and ending 'I press your hand', a phrase of such repugnant affability that I attached it to my fictional *frère-ennemi* Samuel Marcus Cohen. I have never pressed your hand, nor you mine, and given the deviousness of fate, we may never do so. I am reconciled to never meeting you in person even as I think what a silly shame it would be never to have that nervous meal together, the four of us, in which the golden bowl is healed or broken, or remains humanely cracked. I say 'the four of us' because one of the things that seems almost irrelevant to our friendship is, I am sure, capital: we both like women, our women in particular.

I have never written with such regular enthusiasm to anyone. I used to speak on the telephone to my friend and fellow-translator, Kenneth McLeish, every Sunday, often for an hour or more, but I did sometimes find it a duty to dial his number and he was never fully in focus for me, even though I loved him well enough and admired his scholarzip (he was as quick as I am, or you are, but not quite on the same wavelength, no, not quite). There is a certain reticence between you and me, which comes of age and a kind of discretion which has something to do with personal style, but there is little shame. Are we somewhat pleased with ourselves? Someone has to be. I am writing a letter that affects to be a conclusive summation, but I have no intention of concluding our correspondence and its summary is, I like to think, almost as extensive as its corpus. I would not have missed the fun of it for all the kudos-bearing, moolah-procuring commissions in the world. Not that I don't wait for that unwelcome telephone call that heralds the mogul from Porlock.

Dear Joe, it truly has been a pleasure, and then some.

Tout à toi,
Freddie

Index